ADOLESCENT PORTRAITS

SIXTH EDITION

ADOLESCENT PORTRAITS

Identity, Relationships, and Challenges

ANDREW GARROD

Dartmouth College

LISA SMULYAN

Swarthmore College

SALLY I. POWERS

University of Massachusetts, Amherst

ROBERT KILKENNY

Simmons College

Boston   New York   San Francisco
Mexico City   Montreal   Toronto   London   Madrid   Munich   Paris
Hong Kong   Singapore   Tokyo   Cape Town   Sydney

Senior Series Editor: *Stephen Frail*
Series Editorial Assistant: *Allison Rowland*
Executive Marketing Manager: *Pamela Laskey*
Production Editor: *Claudine Bellanton*
Editorial Production Service: *Publishers' Design and Production Services, Inc.*
Composition Buyer: *Linda Cox*
Manufacturing Buyer: *JoAnne Sweeney*
Electronic Composition: *Publishers' Design and Production Services, Inc.*
Cover Administrator: *Elena Sidorova*

For related titles and support materials, visit our online catalog at www.ablongman.com.

Between the time website information is gathered and then published, it is not unusual for some sites to have closed. Also, the transcription of URLs can result in typographical errors. The publisher would appreciate notification where these errors occur so that they may be corrected in subsequent editions.

ISBN-10: 0-205-50204-0
ISBN-13: 978-0-205-50204-2

Library of Congress Cataloging-in-Publication Data
Adolescent portraits : identity, relationships, and challenges / Andrew Garrod . . . [et al.]. — 6th ed.
      p. cm.
   Includes bibliographical references.
      ISBN 0-205-50204-0   (alk. paper)
   1. Adolescence—Case studies. 2. Adolescent psychology—United States—Case studies. I. Garrod, Andrew.

   HQ796.A3343 2008
   305.235—dc22   2006102120

Printed in the United States of America

10 9 8 7 6 5 4 3 2 1   RRD-VA   11 10 09 08 07

CONTENTS

CASES CATEGORIZED BY THEME

Theme	Case Number, Title
Child Abuse	1. Someday My Elders Will Be Proud 6. What If I Don't Want to Whistle? 16. Bad 17. The Simple Beauty of a Conversation 20. Seeking the Best of Both Worlds
Drugs/Alcohol	1. Someday My Elders Will Be Proud 13. Beyond the Euphoric Buzz 14. Holding My Breath 16. Bad
Eating Disorder	11. Falling from My Pedestal
Ethnicity/Race	1. Someday My Elders Will Be Proud 4. The Hatred Within 5. Una Muchacha Decente 6. What If I Don't Want to Whistle? 7. In Search of My Voice 12. They Said I Was Beautiful 15. Color-Blind 20. Seeking the Best of Both Worlds
Family Relationships	1. Someday My Elders Will be Proud 4. The Hatred Within 5. Una Muchacha Decente 6. What If I Don't Want to Whistle? 7. In Search of My Voice 8. The Girl in Me 10. The Family I Have 11. Falling from My Pedestal 12. They Said I Was Beautiful 14. Holding My Breath 15. Color-Blind 16. Bad 18. Forever an Awkward Adolescent 20. Seeking the Best of Both Worlds

PREFACE

The sixth edition of *Adolescent Portraits* includes six new cases and one new reflection by an earlier contributor on his life since writing his story. In choosing new cases and removing others, we have considered feedback from faculty and students using the book and our own understanding of the important issues facing adolescents in the first decade of this century. We welcome further comments on the usefulness of particular cases and the varied ways in which you may use them in your courses. We particularly value suggestions about critical adolescent themes that are not yet addressed in our text.

This sixth edition is accompanied by an online Instructor's Manual, which includes further suggestions for teaching strategies and assignments to be used with the cases. An expanded review of films also appears in the Instructor's Manual, along with a sampling of cases from the first four editions, which we thought were important to keep available to instructors: "Working through My Adolescence," "Running Hurdles," "To Be the Best," "Guilt Was Everywhere around Me," "No 'Boring Little Friends,' " and "Love Me for Who I Am." In addition, we have included the following five cases from the fifth edition: "A Step in the Only Direction" (and follow-up), "Courting Danger" (and follow-up), "At Least We Got One Right" (and follow-up), "Loving Women," and "Pa Jam Decourajer." The Instructor's Manual can be accessed at www.ablongman.com by clicking on the Instructor Resource Center (IRC) link. Access to the IRC is password protected and for instructors only. Instructors may contact their Allyn & Bacon representative for help with accessing the Instructor's Manual.

ACKNOWLEDGMENTS

The cases in this book are the words of college students who have taken our courses, individuals who were willing to share their life experiences with many outsiders. Although we cannot thank them by name, we wish to acknowledge their personal strength as well as the time and energy they invested in this project. In addition, we want to recognize the many students who worked with us on cases that have not been included in the book; they, too, gave tremendously of themselves as we worked to shape the final manuscript. We are grateful for the support of Amy Miner, University of Massachusetts, Amherst, in the preparation of the revised Instructor's Manual that accompanies the sixth edition of *Adolescent Portraits*. We would also like to thank the following reviewers for their comments and suggestions for this edition: Richard Brody, The College of St. Rose; Julie M. Hupp, Ohio State University, Newark; Charles P. Resavy, Wilkes University; and Wendy J. Steinberg, Eastern University.

OVERVIEW

■ ■ ■ ■ ■ ▬▬▬▬▬▬▬▬▬▬▬▬▬▬▬▬▬▬▬▬▬▬▬▬▬▬▬▬▬▬

THE STUDY OF ADOLESCENCE

The way in which we view adolescence depends, to a large extent, on our perceptions of human nature and the relationship of the individual to society. Current researchers draw on past perceptions but also bring a new set of lenses to the field. Many have begun to realize the diversity that characterizes their individual subjects and the difficulty in generating a theory that captures the experiences of all adolescents. Using the lenses of class, ethnicity, race, gender, and sexual orientation, researchers work to describe and explain the complexity seen in adolescent thought, behavior, and relationships.

Twentieth-century understanding of adolescent development has some of its roots in earlier studies of human development (see Elder, 1980; Lesko, 2001; Moran, 2000; Sisson, Hersen, & Van Hasselt, 1987 for additional information on historical trends in the study of adolescence). The first consideration of adolescence as a separate stage of life is often attributed to Plato (1921) and Aristotle (1941), both of whom described the adolescent as unstable and impressionable. They advocated schooling for girls and boys that would shield them from society and help them develop the self-control and reason that characterize a mature individual. In the Middle Ages, the prevalence of Christian views of human depravity and of knowledge as external to the individual led to a less developmental perspective. Children and adolescents were seen as miniature adults who needed to be socialized into acceptance of adult roles, values, and beliefs (Muuss, 1996).

John Locke and Jean-Jacques Rousseau helped to restore society's belief in the qualitative difference between children and adults. Rousseau, in particular, emphasized a process of development during which innate knowledge and character unfold throughout childhood and youth. In *Emile*, Rousseau presented his view of this process and the role of society in nurturing and schooling young people as they develop into responsible citizens. Rousseau attributed different natural characteristics and social roles to males and females and suggested that, while the process of development is similar for both, schooling toward the end product should differ as a result of their divergent natures and responsibilities (Martin, 1981).

In the nineteenth century, several social and intellectual movements influenced perceptions of human nature and adolescence. Charles Darwin's *The Origin of Species* included humans as part of the natural world, providing a more biological and evolutionary view of human development and growth. The industrial revolution led to a gradual de-emphasis on the family's role in socialization for work and relationships and a growing discontinuity in an individual's experience of home and work. Accompanying movements such as child labor laws and compulsory schooling contributed to society's perception of a phase of development between childhood and the assumption of an adult role in society, a phase which G. Stanley Hall named *adolescence* in 1904 (Moran, 2000).

Hall (1904) described adolescence as a key stage of life in the evolution of the mature individual. Drawing on Darwin's work, he postulated a scientific theory of recapitulation in which the individual develops through stages that parallel those of human civilization. Like Rousseau, he saw development as a natural, largely innate process that could be guided and supported by society. Hall characterized preadolescence as the "savage" stage in the life of the individual. Adolescence followed, a transitional period to adulthood filled with contradictory emotions and behaviors: selfishness and altruism, sensitivity and cruelty, radicalism and conservatism. Through the struggle of adolescence, the individual is reborn and a new self is created, ready to assume a role in modern society.

Hall's work influenced the study of adolescence through the twentieth century, but it has also been modified and challenged over the years. While Freud and those whose ideas developed from his work (e.g., Blos, 1962; Erikson, 1968; A. Freud, 1946) continued to focus on biological imperatives and their influence on the individual's psyche in the process of development, others began to take a more sociological perspective on adolescence. The work of Margaret Mead (1958) and Ruth Benedict (1950) suggested that society determines the behaviors, roles, and values of its adolescents. Others focused on the effects of social disorganization, social class, and social institutions on the life of the adolescent, documenting the role of environment in the shaping of experience (e.g., Havighurst, Bosman, Liddle, Matthews, & Pierce, 1962; Hollingshead, 1949). In the 1950s, studies of adolescence tended to emphasize the role of the peer group and the uniqueness of the adolescent experience; adolescence was seen as discontinuous with both childhood and adulthood. Adolescents had their own culture, comprised of a unique language, patterns of interaction, and beliefs.

While the events of the 1960s contributed to this perception of an adolescent subculture, they also led those who study adolescence to focus on the intersection between the life course of the individual, the age cohort, and the historical context within which the individuals act (Elder, 1980). Some researchers and theorists, following Mead's emphasis on cultural influences on adolescence, focused on the social-historical context of adolescent development. They challenged Hall's view of adolescence as necessarily stressful by examining continuity and change in adolescent behavior over time (e.g., Modell & Goodman, 1990). Others began to reexamine the period of adolescence within the context of an individual's lifespan (Arnett, 2004). Research in child and adult development and in ego, cognitive, and moral development led to an understanding of adolescence as one of a sequence of life stages during which the individual addresses key issues such as identity, autonomy, attachment, and relationship. The emphasis in this work has been on phases or stages of development that cut across social, historical, and cultural boundaries (e.g., Erikson, 1968; Kohlberg & Gilligan, 1972; Piaget, 1972).

Some of the most recent work in the study of adolescence has challenged approaches that emphasize either sociocultural determinism or universal developmental theory, suggesting that understanding adolescence involves a consideration of how social categories such as race, ethnicity, class, sexuality, and gender interact with processes of individual development (e.g., Gonzales & Cauce, 1995; Leadbeater & Way, 1996; Martin, 1996; Savin-Williams, 2005; Way & Chu, 2004). The historical and cultural context is important in understanding adolescent experience, but it may not be sufficient to explain an individual's behaviors, beliefs, and sense of self. Stage and phase theories of development tend to overgeneralize from small, nonrepresentative samples and often ignore key variables such as race, class, gender, and sexual orientation that have a profound impact on an individual's experience and identity. The study of adolescence, then, has become more inclusive in terms of who is studied, what questions are asked, and how experience is analyzed. It has also become more complex, as we take a range of variables and contexts into consideration when examining individual development.

Research in the past thirty years has also refuted the "storm and stress" model of adolescent development that grew out of Hall's work. This approach sees adolescence as a time of severe turbulence, during which relationships disintegrate as the individual rebels against internal and external value systems (e.g., Blos, 1962; A. Freud, 1946, 1958). In contrast, more current work in the field emphasizes continuity and renegotiation as processes that characterize adolescence. "Normal" adolescent development encompasses a wide range of experiences, including a variety of family structures, sexual experimentation and orientation, and ethnicity and racial exploration. Although some adolescents may experience more environmental stresses than others, these challenges occur within a meaningful personal and social context for that individual. Researchers have come to accept many variations within their definitions of normality in adolescence.

Even as researchers and teachers try to understand the multiple aspects of each individual's identity, the context within which American adolescents develop continues to change, further complicating the picture. Adolescents in the late twentieth and early twenty-first centuries are growing up in a society that takes technology and global communication as givens. On a large scale, this adolescent cohort's historical and cultural context is one in which international shifts and conflicts mean changing relationships between the United States and other countries. Increased international communication continues to change our knowledge of relationships with others around the world. Closer to home, these adolescents experience a society that is working toward greater acceptance of diversity—one in which women and minorities strive to defend and work toward their goals while simultaneously trying to change society. Although they are growing up in decades of change and progress, today's adolescents also face persistent political and social problems: educational systems struggling with declining enrollments and shrinking resources; urban, suburban, and rural communities focusing on teenage drug use, school violence, and the spread of AIDS; and continuing racial and ethnic questioning and occasional conflict. The social questions and issues that surround them demonstrate to today's adolescents that society does not have all of the answers and that it often seems to lack the direction and commitment needed to find them.

THE CASE STUDY APPROACH

Those of us who teach courses in adolescent development continue to search for materials that address our students' lives and illuminate emerging approaches in the study of adolescence. Such materials help students learn what past and present theorists and current research have to say about the adolescent experience and engage students in asking questions about those theories and approaches as well as their own lives. We want our students to be thoughtful and critical participants in the study of adolescence, contributors to our growing understanding of how this phase of life relates to the larger life cycle.

The authors of this book found this kind of material in a book called *Experiencing Youth*, first published in 1970 by George W. Goethals and Dennis S. Klos. We all used this book in our own study of adolescence and initially incorporated it into the courses we taught. *Experiencing Youth* (1976) is a set of first-person accounts written by undergraduate and graduate students (the latter appear primarily in the second edition) that highlight key issues in adolescent development: autonomy, identity, and intimacy. These cases demonstrate how powerful narrative can be as a way of examining individual lives within a framework of theory and research on adolescence.

By listening to the voices of individual adolescents, students and teachers of adolescent development can gain a greater understanding of the issues facing some of today's adolescents. Case studies illustrate the complexity of the individual experience and the interactions among an individual's needs, ideas, relationships, and context. Each case, taken alone, helps us begin to know one more adolescent and his or her experience; taken together, the cases provide a rich overview of the field of adolescence. Through them, we come to a greater understanding of key theories and current research findings in the field of adolescence as we examine patterns in their lives and the lives of others. We are indebted to Goethals and Klos for helping us and our students learn the value of the case study.

In this book, we build on the model provided by Goethals and Klos, bringing together the voices of students in our own classes and some key theories and approaches used in the study of adolescence. Each case in this book was written and revised by an undergraduate or very recent graduate, most of whom have taken a course in adolescent development.

Although it is never possible to be completely representative, we chose students and cases with the goal of achieving a cross-section of ethnicities, class backgrounds, and experiences. The twenty case writers include adolescents who are white, African American, Native American, Latino, Asian American, and several who are biracial. The writers include men and women who are gay and straight, and those who are questioning their sexuality. Case writers come from around the United States as well as the Caribbean, India, and Vietnam; from urban, suburban, and rural environments; from more and less privileged backgrounds; from single- and two-parent homes; from situations that have stimulated reflection and those that have allowed the writer to develop without thinking deeply about the implications and meanings of his or her actions and ideas. Although we have included each case under a major topic (as listed in the Contents), each case addresses a number of issues. The chart at the front of the book provides a guide to the themes present in each case, as do the abstracts at the beginning of each case. See the Instructor's Manual (available for download at: **www.ablongman.com** for further suggestions for using the cases in this book in a variety of classroom settings.

PART I

IDENTITY

THEORETICAL OVERVIEW

The nine cases in the Identity section of this book show a pattern of a struggle for meaning and a quest for wholeness. Within the categories of values and ideology, the self in social context, and sexuality, the adolescent writers wrestle with important choices—who they want to be, how to relate to others, what values should guide them, and what their place is in various spheres of their lives. Though the content of the autobiographies may differ from case to case, the reader will see that the writers share common explorations and preoccupations with the self: the self in relation to others and the self in relation to the broader society. We offer here a framework for approaching the cases in this section.

Erik Erikson (1968), who has helped shape our understanding of identity, proposed a detailed and widely applied psychosocial theory of identity development. Convinced that the study of identity is as crucial to our time as the study of childhood sexuality was to Freud's, Erikson forged a radical rethinking among psychoanalytic theorists about ego structure and the role of culture and environment in personality development. His writings have, over the last decades, been expanded (e.g., Marcia, 1967) and debated (e.g., Gilligan, 1982) by a succession of theorists, some of whom have significantly broadened and challenged his theory's applicability.

When asked to describe his adolescence, one of our students recently wrote: "I don't know where it started and have no more idea if it's ended. Something inside of me tells me I'm in transition between something and something else, but I don't know what." In transition between two "somethings," this young man is not at all sure where he has come from and even less sure of his destination; he is Kurt Lewin's (1939) "marginal man," uncertain of his position and group belongingness. As an adolescent, he is in a stage of his life in which pressures, both internal and external, to define himself become simultaneously impossible to ignore and impossible to satisfy. He is working to establish a self-concept while at the same time realizing that this concept is changing as rapidly as he can pinpoint it. Like Lewis Carroll's Alice, he may well reply to the question: "Who are you?" posed by the Caterpillar, by saying "I, I hardly know Sir, just at present—at least I know who

I was when I got up this morning, but I must have changed several times since then." In Erikson's terms, the adolescent has entered a psychological moratorium—a hiatus between childhood security and adult independence.

Adolescence is a critical stage in the individual's development. Adolescents are intensely aware of how they are seen by others—aware, as V. S. Pritchett (1971) observes, that "other egos with their own court of adherents invade one's privacy with theirs." It is a time in which the values and perspectives of others become clearer to the developing mind. The adolescent must first attempt to evaluate his or her different options—different ethical positions or religious beliefs, acceptance or rejection of societal norms, attitudes toward sexuality, ideological stance in relation to family, friends and community—before he or she can choose among them. In this sense, the search for identity is not only the process of molding an image of oneself—it is also the attempt to understand the fundamental components of the clay that will be used.

The identities of childhood, strengthened by identifications with significant others and by growing mastery of the tasks of school and family life, may no longer hold; the challenge for the adolescent is a creative synthesis of past identifications, current skills and abilities, and future hopes—all within the context of the opportunities the society offers. This challenge is made immeasurably harder because of the technological society we live in, in which multiple roles and careers tantalize us with choice. Mead (1958) suggests it might be easier to live in a society in which roles are inherited through birth or decided by gender! Yet the critical task of the developing adolescent is to balance the imposition of identities provided by his or her position in the social structure, the family, and the community with an agentic sense of who one is, what one stands for, and how one relates to the world.

Theories of identity development focus on themes of separation and individuation of the emerging individual *and* themes of connection or relationship between the adolescent and significant others in the process of renegotiating the childhood self or selves. Theories of separation stem from work of Freud (1953) and Erikson (1968) and focus on how the individual rejects prior identifications in the search for a separate, unique, and unified sense of self. Theories of connection (Gilligan, 1982; Miller, 1991; Stern, 1989) explore how individuals come to know themselves through relationship; adolescent identity development is a process of refiguring one's relationships to account for new psychological and social needs and expectations. More recently, studies of adolescent identity have focused on how adolescents draw on aspects of both separation and connection in negotiating the multiple identities they construct and perform in this stage of life and into adulthood.

Erikson's theory of ego identity formation focuses on the concepts of ego identity, the identity stage, and the identity crisis. He defines identity as "the capacity to see oneself as having continuity and sameness and to act accordingly. It is the consistent organization of experience." Erikson held to the epigenetic principle of development in which "anything that grows has a ground plan, and that out of this ground plan the parts arise, each part having its time of special ascendancy until all parts have risen to form a functional whole" (Erikson, 1968, p. 92). The stages are not merely passed through but instead add cumulatively to the whole personality; Erikson saw the quest for identity and the crises that it often produces as the defining characteristics of adolescence. His psychosocial stage theory is founded on the belief that life is composed of a series of conflicts that must be partially resolved before the developing individual can move to the next stage. He proposes eight general stages of conflict: trust versus mistrust, autonomy versus shame, initiative versus guilt, industry versus inferiority, identity versus identity confusion, intimacy versus isolation, generativity versus stagnation, and integrity versus despair (Erikson, 1968). Following psychoanalytic theory, these stages appear in sequential order but are never completely resolved. Erikson saw the quest for identity and the crises that it often produces as the defining characteristic of adolescence. The formation of ego identity does not take place only in the identity stage, however; the degree to which one satisfactorily resolves the identity crisis is heavily dependent on the resolutions to the challenges of the first four stages in Erikson's eight-stage life cycle theory. Each item exists "in some form," Erikson tells us, before its decisive and critical time normally arrives (Erikson, 1968, pp. 93, 95). That is, there are identity elements in all preceding stages just as there are in the succeeding stages, and if the conflicts in these earlier stages are concluded satisfactorily, the healthy development of the ego is more probable. If the conflicts are resolved unsatisfactorily, negative qualities are crystallized in the personality structure and may impede further development.

The psychosocial moratorium—a time of deferred choice—is the period in an adolescent or young adult's life for resolving the identity crisis. It is a time when role experimentation is encouraged and where there is little expectation that the individual will commit to permanent responsibilities or roles. The identity crisis "is precipitated both by the individual's readiness and by society's pressure" to separate from childhood identifications and find a coherent individuated identity (Erikson, 1980, p. 130). The age at which the identity crisis occurs may vary "according to such social structure factors as class, subculture, ethnic background, and gender" (Côté & Levine, 1987) or socialization factors such as child-rearing practices and identification with parents (Jordan, 1971). The moratorium must end, with the experience of role experimentation complete and the achievement of a resynthesis of positive identifications. These achievements enable the individual to find "a niche in some section of society, a niche which is firmly defined yet seems to be uniquely made for him" (Erikson, 1968, p. 156). The niche is dependent on the adolescent's feeling that commitment in the areas of values, vocation, religious beliefs, political ideology, sex, gender role, and family lifestyle are accepted, settled, and expressions of personal choice. Other more critical theorists, Jackson, McCullough, and Gurin (1981) for example, have suggested that the option of having a moratorium and being in a position to choose in the area of commitment are limited by social, political, and economic structures and dominant ideologies.

Allied with Erikson's faith in ego identity is his understanding of the difficulty involved for adolescents in creating and maintaining this identity. Identity confusion, and the resulting identity crisis, results from the individual's inability to understand the "mutual fit of himself and the environment—that is, of his capacity to relate to an ever-expanding life space of people and institutions on the one hand, and, on the other, the readiness of these people and institution to make him a part of an ongoing cultural concern" (Erikson, 1975, p. 102). Feeling pressured by society and his or her own maturation to choose between possible roles even as personal perspectives are rapidly changing, the identity-confused adolescent experiences a confusion that challenges his or her ability to form a stable identity.

Erikson believes that the success with which the adolescent resolves these crises is extremely important for the eventual achievement of intimacy with others. It is only through the commitment to sexual direction, vocational direction, and a system of values that "intimacy of sexual and affectionate love, deep friendship and personal abandon without fear of loss of ego identity can take place" (Muuss, 1996, p. 54). Identity achievement, as opposed to identity confusion, allows the individual to move smoothly from preoccupation with the inner core of identity to exploration of the potential roles this self will play in intimate relationships with others.

Erikson's construct of identity versus identity confusion has been expanded by James Marcia (1966, 1980). Marcia, whose work on the ego and identity development began with his dissertation "Development and Validation of Ego—Identity Status" (1966), establishes two concepts already mentioned by Erikson—crisis and commitment—as the determining variables in identity achievement. "Crisis refers to times during adolescence when the individual seems to be actively involved in choosing among alternative occupations and beliefs. Commitment refers to the degree of personal investment the individual expresses in an occupation or belief" (Marcia, 1967, p. 119). Using these variables as the determining standards, Marcia breaks Erikson's fifth stage down into four substages: identity diffusion, identify foreclosure, moratorium, and identity achievement.

The identity-diffused individual is characterized by having neither an active involvement in the search for identity roles nor a commitment to any of these roles. He or she is not questioning alternatives. At this point, the adolescent is like James Joyce's Stephen Daedalus, "drifting amid life like the barren shell of the moon." Identity foreclosure is characterized by commitment without crisis; that is, the individual has chosen a set of values or ideological stance, most often that of his or her parents or valued others, without examining this value or searching out alternatives. In moratorium, on the other hand, the individual is in the midst of a crisis, actively questioning and searching among alternatives, without any commitment to one option. In achievement, the individual has experienced the crises of moratorium, and has successfully made a commitment. Identity achievement is most often attained in the college years, with moratorium and diffusion characteristic of earlier adolescence (Santrock, 1990). It should be pointed out that differences exist between societies and between groups and individuals within societies in the length of the sanctioned intermediary period, the psychosocial moratorium (Manaster, 1989). Also, those not afforded the time or opportunity to engage in identity seeking may well not undergo an identity crisis in adolescence or young adulthood.

Some theorists, among them Miller (1991) and Surrey (1984), have suggested that adolescent identity development (like childhood development that precedes it and adult development that follows) is more a story of connection and relationship than one of separation and autonomy. Early theorists in this field argued that adolescent boys seem concerned with separation and individuation while adolescent girls create identity more in connection to peers and members of their families. Carol Gilligan (1982) writes of her reservations about Erikson's theory in *In a Different Voice*. Gilligan points out that Erikson recognized sex differences in identity development and discussed how for men identity precedes intimacy and generativity in the optimal cycle of human separation and attachment, but for women these tasks instead seem to be fused—the woman comes to know herself through relationships with others. Erikson nevertheless retained the sequence of identity preceding intimacy. The sequencing of Erikson's second, third, fourth, and fifth stages, Gilligan suggests, little prepares the individual for the intimacy of the first adult stage. "Development itself comes to be identified with separation, and attachments appear to be developmental impediments, as is repeatedly the case in the assessment of women" (Gilligan, 1982, pp. 12–13).

In contrast, more recent theorists explore how the challenges of adolescence—brought on by puberty, a more active role in the social structure, and changing cognitive abilities—are negotiated within and through relationships by all adolescents. Both adolescent girls and boys explore who they are through interaction with families (Hill, 1987; Taylor, 1996; Ward, 1996); with peers (Chu, 2004; Savin-Williams & Berndt, 1990); and through the other social groups and networks that are important in their lives (McLaughlin & Heath, 1993). While finding a separate, unique identity is important, that process occurs within and through negotiating the self in relation to other individuals and social groups. This relational perspective also allows us to examine how adolescents form multiple identities that differ to some extent by context and need. The adolescent in school, experiencing certain demands and opportunities, may differ from the adolescent at home, where alternate relationships and expectations influence actions and values (Ferguson, 2000; Flores-Gonzáles 2002). The adolescent must learn to balance the search for a coherent, separate identity with the multiple identities, negotiated through relationship, that characterize his or her sense of self.

The process of adolescent identity formation may also vary in accordance with the ethnic and racial background of the individual. A number of theorists have presented stage theories of ethnic or racial identity development (e.g., Cross, 1991; Kim, in Ponterotto & Pederson, 1993). These frameworks of analysis suggest that nonwhite adolescents tend to begin the process in a stage in which they either identify with the white majority or are unaware of the role of race or ethnicity in their experience. They move, often as the result of a series of events or encounters in which their race or ethnicity becomes salient, into a stage of awareness. In this stage, individuals become more conscious of their position in the society and begin to question who they are in relation to their own racial or ethnic group and in relation to the dominant culture. In a third general stage, adolescents identify with their racial or ethnic group and often immerse themselves in an exploration of that group's historical, cultural, political, and social position in the society. The final stage in most of these theories is a stage of integration and internalization, in which the individual incorporates his or her identification with a racial or ethnic group into a more comprehensive identity. This more inclusive identity may allow individuals to identify with their group and interact successfully in the dominant (white) culture. Ponterotto and Pederson (1993) provide a similar framework for examining white racial identity development. The stages they posit parallel those previously described and include preexposure, conflict, prominority/antiracism, retreat into white culture, and redefinition and integration. Stage theories of racial and ethnic identity development have their limitations, however. They tend to assume that all members of a particular group experience the process of identity development in the same way and that the process itself is both linear and progressive. More recent examinations of the impact of race and ethnicity on adolescent identity development focus on the various ways that individuals and groups engage in explorations of who they are in relation to racial and ethnic groups and to the dominant culture. Mary Waters (1996), for example, examines a number of ways in which Caribbean American teens respond to others' expectations of who they are and their own sense of self. Stacy Lee (1996) explores the multiple identities taken on by Asian American students in an academically demanding high school. And Nilda Flores-Gonzáles (2002) describes how Latino students from the same neighborhood develop different identities based on their relationship to school and their community.

In her examination of black identity formation, Fordham (1988) considers the phenomenon of "racelessness." She explores the relationship between group (black) identity and academic success, and concludes that black adolescents follow one of two paths. Some respect an "individualistic ethos," disregarding their mandatory membership in the black group—a path that may lead to academic success. Others consider this to be "selling out" and espouse the "collectivistic ethos" of their minority group in order to avoid becoming "nonblack," although they sacrifice academic success in the process. More recent research challenges Fordham's conclusions and demonstrates, again, the multiple ways in which African American students integrate their racial, gender, and academic identities. Mickelson and Velasco (2006), Annette Hemmings (2006) and Prudence Carter (2006) provide case studies of groups of African American students who negotiate school, gender, and racial identities in a range of ways. Ward (1989) examines identity formation in academically successful black female adolescents and discovers that racial identity formation is compatible with academic accomplishment. Considering not only the factors of beliefs, values, attitudes, and patterns of family socialization, but also "the girls' own subjective understanding of the role that race plays in their lives" (p. 217), she concludes that racial identity must be considered in order to gain a complete understanding of identity formation. Cases in this edition that focus in particular on adolescents' experiences of ethnic and racial identity are 1, 4, 5, 6, 7, 12, 15, and 20.

Other recent areas of exploration in identity development are gender and sexuality. Gender is an aspect of identity that is socially constructed, or performed, within available discourses and institutional structures (Connell, 2000; Walkerdine, Lucey, & Melody, 2001). Adolescents explore their gender identities, often within a binary framework of stereotypical masculinity and femininity (Kimmel, 1994; Martin, 1996). They make choices within these frameworks, sometimes challenging the norms and sometimes functioning, consciously or unconsciously, within them. Adolescents also begin to explore their sexuality and sexual identities. While Freud (1953) sees this as a natural part of the developmental process, Mead (1958) suggests that cultures impose a heightened sense of sexuality on adolescents. While past theorists have, again, posited developmental stages of sexuality development (e.g., Troiden, 1998), more recent researchers focus again on the role of relationships and interactions with others in a variety of contexts in their examination of adolescents' active construction of a sexual identity (Martin, 1996; Savin-Williams, 2005). While many cases in this book include adolescents exploring aspects of gender and sexual identity, Cases 3, 8, 9, 13, and 14 in particular allow us to examine these issues.

Other authors have explored the interactions among the multiple identities adolescents actually contend with during the process of identity formation. James Sears (1996), for example, has examined the experiences of adolescents who are both gay and African American, and Alex Wilson (1996) probes the lives of those who are gay and Native American. In Leadbeater and Way's book, *Urban Girls* (1996), researchers report on studies that investigate the experiences of male and female adolescents juggling issues of gender, race, ethnicity, and class as they figure out who they are. Maria Root (1999), Theresa Williams (1996), and others have contributed to our understanding of the complexity of racial and ethnic identity development in their studies of multiracial individuals. Their work suggests that the process of racial and ethnic identity is multifaceted and complex and an inherent part of identity development for all adolescents.

Alternative perspectives on the process of identity development in adolescence, then, focus on the examination of the individual in context. Development is seen as a process of renegotiating relationships, redefining oneself in relation to individuals and social groups (family, racial or ethnic group, class, and gender) of which one is a part. In the Identity section of this book, we include cases that address several aspects of identity development—values and ideology, the self in social context, and sexuality. In most cases, the writers are, themselves, engaged in exploring multiple identities. We encourage the reader to examine these autobiographies through a consideration of the following questions. What roles do issues of trust, autonomy, initiative, competence, and identity play in each person's case? Within what contexts does the author define himself or herself? What relationships and connections contribute to his or her sense of self, and how are they changing?

Whatever theoretical perspective one adopts, and we suggest an eclectic approach, the essential components are a simultaneous discovery and creation of self leading to a deepening self-understanding. We believe the cases in this section capture that process in both tone and substance. In each case there is a greater sense of understanding and acceptance of oneself at the end than at the beginning. Each author makes clear that the process continues, but they seem here to have reached a plateau from which they can look back and survey their progress. Readers may do well to suspend somewhat their theoretical assumptions while reading a case, lest they miss the sheer spectacle of lives unfolding. Though different identity theorists provide a useful framework for interpretation of these cases, the best of them are but a scaffolding for understanding. We should try to listen first to each author in his or her own terms, to see the authors' evolution through their own eyes. In the unique and intimate details of their individual lives we can discern the outline of a universal struggle to identify our true selves. Your readings here should influence your understanding of theory at least as much as theory influences your reading.

SOMEDAY MY ELDERS WILL BE PROUD

This Native American woman recounts her experience of living in two worlds. Jean describes how her mother raised her and her three brothers after her father abandoned the family when she was quite young. These circumstances, along with abuse at the hands of her uncle, leave lasting emotional wounds she will not address until much later. While firmly rooted in and proud of her Native American culture, Jean becomes a scholarship student at an elite secondary school. Her family's relative poverty and the condescending attitudes of her classmates further feelings of self-doubt, low self-esteem, and ethnic inferiority. Her transition to college does not succeed; she turns to heavy drinking, fails academically, and returns home. She gets a job working with troubled Native American adolescents, and through helping the self she sees in them, she finds a purpose in returning to college.

I grew up in Bismarck, North Dakota. My parents met through a relocation program. Relocation attempted to assimilate Native Americans into urban life from their reservation or tribal communities. The goal of the program was for an individual to gain economic self-sufficiency by means of a vocation or technical school education. My parents were in just such a program in Denver, Colorado, where they met and married. That is where my three brothers and I were born. My mother, a Cheyenne, was 22, and my father, a Blackfoot, was 21 when they had me. I am the oldest.

My father ran back to his reservation in Montana before my youngest brother was born. I must have been almost 4 years old. I have no concrete memories of him. My mom says that he taught her how to take care of me, because she didn't know that much about babies. He began drinking when I was born, and he was a womanizer. Soon his drinking got out of control. Despite her problems with our dad, Mom would always tell us how he loved my brothers and me and that he was a good father to us. Whenever he came home we would run and crawl all over him. We never saw him again after he left Mom and us behind. Dad died on the reservation when I was 7 years old, from alcoholism. He was only 28. I don't remember exactly when Mom told us, but it held no meaning. It seemed that he had already died when he left.

By the time I was 6, my mother had moved to Bismarck, where many of her relatives and immediate family lived. We did this because family was important to her tribe and they would help us as much as they could. Initially we lived off welfare and the help that our relatives could give us. My mother decided she didn't want us to live like that forever. She wanted to be a good example for the four of us, so she worked during the day and went to school at night to get her bachelor's degree in social work at the state university. We grew up in a single-parent family with the benefits of an extended family.

Mom worked through temporary services at factories and we got some monetary help from our father's social security benefits after he died, food stamps, and AFDC. We were very poor. We went to garage sales, Salvation Armies, and Goodwills for most of our clothes, furniture, and toys.

During those years when my mother pushed herself, my brothers and I were watched by one of my mom's younger brothers. She had no choice; he needed a place to live, and we needed a baby-sitter. I think he was in his twenties. He stayed with us from the time I was in first grade until I was in the sixth grade. He was always there after school when we came home. He taught us good things, like to stick up for each other when we used to get chased home from school by the white kids and not to be afraid of fighting for ourselves.

However, our uncle was an alcoholic and had a violent streak in him. We became convenient scapegoats for him when he was sober or drunk. Even though my mom forbade him to drink in her home, he still did. There are lots of stories about how we couldn't wear shorts because the belt or switch marks were too vivid. He never hit us when Mom was home. When he did whip us, he'd say to us after he was finished, "You'd better keep your mouths shut and not tell your mother." And we stayed silent.

It was for stupid reasons that we got whipped. Who moved his magazine, who messed up the kitchen, who lost his sock and where was it? Who did it? Guilt, innocence, truth, right, wrong, what did any of that matter? It meant nothing. We could have been perfect children but that wouldn't have changed anything. We learned to clean the house as soon as we got home, and maybe it was good enough, maybe it wasn't. We learned to hide in our rooms until Mom got home. We used to be mean to our dogs and sometimes to each other. He made everything seem our fault.

Why didn't we say anything? I don't know. I remember one time how our uncle picked up my brother Lance by the hair and Lance was screaming. I never felt so helpless. I was mad, but I was afraid too. I knew it was all wrong, but I was glad in a way too, because it wasn't me. Mom kicked him out finally when I was in the sixth grade. All that mattered to us then was that he was gone. I still remember the relief I felt.

Why so long to get him out? Mom had to know. All I can think of is how her tribe is strongly patriarchal; men rule the home, and women must listen to and abide by what their brothers say. You never tell them that they're wrong; it would be disrespectful. In the traditional way, uncles are a second father to their nieces and nephews. Alcoholism ran through her side of the family and our dad's. I know that our two uncles had a violent father and uncle too. Those behaviors were probably passed on, and were allowed to continue because men have so much power to do what they want. Mom hadn't quite broken out of that mind-set when our uncle was living with us, and she tried so hard to make our lives better at a cost to hers. I couldn't really be angry at her because I remember how she tried to make us happy.

When I first started actively remembering everything that our uncle did to us, I hated him. I was glad that he couldn't hold a job, that he had a rotten marriage, that his own kids were uncontrollable and spoiled, that his drinking gave him critical liver and heart problems. But I tell you, it's strange. He loves us. I'm not going to live fueled by hate, and so I tried to understand what there was in him and his life that let him beat four little kids. He never had it easy himself, and he is the one who has to live with what he's done. He doesn't need another person who hates him or another part of his life to make him more bitter.

Many of our relatives on my mother's side lived in Omaha. Lots of these relatives were members of the newer religion, Native American Church. NAC integrates Christianity, adapting to urban life by getting an education or keeping a job, and being aware of what's good and beautiful in life, in other people, and in yourself. At least that's what it means to me.

An NAC meeting lasts throughout a night; you pray for whoever the meeting is for, including your family. You get no sleep, people sing "hymns" that are in the native language, and you eat a bitter-tasting cactus called peyote. The old school relates the Bible to life, and others talk about what their elders told them about being good people. People talk about how to cope with problems, talk about why things are the way they are, how you can look at your misfortunes, and how we must appreciate and recognize the good that we have. They talk about humbleness and realizing that so much of what we deal with will pass in time. It was there that I felt awe for wisdom and reasoning.

We drove back to Nebraska frequently for NAC meetings and for traditional religious ceremonies, where we prayed and made offerings to the gods and spirits, holding feasts and dances to honor what was being done for the people. We used to travel around the surrounding states for powwows—intertribal gatherings where dancers and singers from different tribes got together to dance and visit with one another. We also stayed with close relatives with whom my mother's generation had grown up. They told us stories from long ago and they fed us and took us along with them in their areas. The four of us liked going out of town; our world was not defined by the city.

When I finished sixth grade at the public school, Mom had me tested for a private school that an uncle's wife highly recommended. They wanted me to go to a school better than the public junior high. I was accepted and given a scholarship, and when seventh grade came around I went there. At the time, I didn't want to go. I wanted to go on with my friends to the public junior high.

I remember feeling that I didn't fit in and being apprehensive. It was an affluent Episcopalian college preparatory school, grades K–12. It wasn't race that made me an outsider, though there were undercurrents of it. If anything, it seemed to be worse in grade school, where my brothers and I had come home crying, until they told us to fight and stick up for each other. I'd say that poverty made me an outsider.

The first day an English teacher had us write essays on the furthest place in the world we had been. After we finished, we placed them up on the bulletin board. I wrote about Nebraska, and when I looked at the other essays, I saw people saying, "I've been around the world on a cruise ship." A larger majority than I could have imagined said countries in Europe, California, all over. Showing off seemed to occupy a great deal of time at school.

Kids were mean there, not physically, but with their words. "*Who* does your shopping for you? You've *never* been to the Calhoun Club? *Where* do you get your clothes from? You mean you *haven't* been out of the U.S.? You *rent* your home? You mean you don't get an *allowance?*" I couldn't have what they had or really understand the importance of it all, and I felt it acutely. There were the times when I would be talking with someone and instead of listening to whatever it was I was saying, they'd be staring at my clothes.

It wasn't anything that my family or relatives understood. We all knew that it was a good thing for me to go to school there. They wanted us younger kids to be able to work at the jobs we wanted and not struggle like they had. Being poor was awful, the bills were too many and too much. I knew all of that in a vague sense way down and I suppose that's why I stuck it out. But still, it didn't help me in dealing with the daily questionings or scornful looks from my peers. When they did that, I just looked away or down, shoulders slumped, because I felt self-conscious.

Learning the stuff from the books wasn't ever really hard; it was just memorizing most of the time. So I'd memorize and forget everything later. Mom made sure that I did homework when I was home. She always used to say to us how important school was, because if we had it, life wouldn't be as hard for us as it was for her generation. If anything, the material was boring. I noticed that the kids were highly conscientious about doing their work. Grades mattered to them in a way I never really understood. Mom never said to me, "Jean, I want you to get As," and she never acted disappointed when I didn't get an A. All Mom ever said was, "Did you try?" and that was enough. The other kids did their work because they wanted a good grade. For me, it was a way out.

The only way I could figure out to make things better was to bug Mom incessantly about clothes. She tried her best, but it wasn't good enough in my eyes to catch up to the other kids. So I started stealing from stores and from unlocked lockers at school. And then it happened; I got caught. I felt hunted, and I knew the other kids would really talk. "Can you believe what she did?" Most of all, I knew that I would hurt Mom. That's what mattered the most to me. I got suspended for a couple of days. When my mom and I came in to talk to the middle school director and I was asked "how come?" I ended up crying and talking about how people called me names, looked at me funny, and that I couldn't take feeling bad about myself anymore. I hadn't realized that those things preyed on my mind, that they hurt, and that's why I was stealing.

So Mom and I went home and she talked with me. She said that it was wrong to steal, and that it reflected on me and the kind of upbringing I had. She said how it was easy to steal, it was cheating, and that it was hard to tell the truth and live by it. She said that we all make mistakes and that it was all right. "Just learn something good from this." And then she talked to me about the things that I had been called. "They're wrong and cruel and do not know you or your strengths. They're just a bunch of kids." I knew what I had done and felt ashamed about myself, but she made me believe in her love and in myself. From Mom, I learned to be compassionate.

I think I learned that I couldn't be myself at that school. I had to be like the other students to be happy there; I had to be rich and snobby. Because of my family's poverty and our tribal gatherings, I couldn't be like them. Not really anyway. Most of the time I was bored, or distracted by home. So what if the football team lost? So what if you're pissed off because you can't talk on the phone past 8:00? What kind of problems are those?

I felt that I had to put on airs, or have a dramatic life that people would be interested in, otherwise I was a lonely person. I needed to find a niche somehow, somewhere. So for about two years, somewhere between eighth and ninth grade, I became a liar. I made up the death of a relative, talked about things like drinking, or weed. I told people that I was part Greek. I quit when someone asked about my Greek grandmother. I knew what a lie it was, and I thought to myself, what about your real grandmother? Why can't you be proud of her and everything back home? It was like I had erased her life, said it was nothing by making up another woman who never even existed. I knew something was really wrong with me then. I cringe at the pitiful person I was. I see why I did what I did, but still . . . I decided that never again would I lie like that because it takes away from the truth of my life. It's "cheating." Parts of my life were ugly, and not understood, but it was mine. My life was no less important than my schoolmates'. Life can't be for everyone what it is to the affluent or sheltered, and none of that makes them better than those less fortunate or different.

By this time I realized how hard it was for my mom to support the four of us on her own. I know the bills and our teenage wants that got more and more expensive were getting to her. She would lash out at us about "never being satisfied" or about not helping enough around the house. She used to point out our faults to us, not in a nice way, during those times. For myself, I cowered during those times when she lost her temper. I couldn't help it. But it wasn't anything like those times with our uncle when we were kids—I understood why she was frustrated and yelling. Even so, Mom always came through for the four of us. She would tell us how smart we were, and how strong we could be. If we did something wrong, she would understand what drove us, but always tell us to learn from it all.

There were other times when we went to an NAC meeting, powwow, lodge feast, or a meal with the relatives. I loved all those things. I didn't think about why I felt that way, all I did was feel good. I remember being back at school in the ninth grade after one weekend when we'd been to a powwow. I was in math class, looking around and listening, but my attention kept fading. I kept staring out the window, remembering. We had been to Canada, and the powwow was by a huge network of lakes. During one of the breaks, my brother and I had gone out onto the lake on a motorboat. He killed the engine in the middle of the lake and we were drifting; we could see the powwow ground, all the campers, smell the fires, hear the singing, see dancers walking around in bright colors, shawls and bustles, people laughing.

We tried to start the engine, but it wouldn't, and we had forgotten to bring oars along. We were drifting farther and farther away to the opposite shore, and right before we got tangled in the reeds by the shore, we tried one last time to start the engine. It started, and we were laughing, and the wind whipped our hair back as he gunned the engine. We sped around for awhile like that, and when we got back, we had a good story to tell.

People were always teasing each other about something. That's what I liked, laughter. At night you could see all the stars; coffee tasted the best when it got chilly after the sun went down. The smell of a wood fire was always around too, and you were up late and probably tired, but you were having a good time, so it didn't matter. Out of the four of us, I liked to dance the most. When I was small, I used to dance until I had blisters and they would make me rest for a while.

No one at school, though, would know what in the world I felt good about, or why. I felt caged. What did I care about a logarithm? I was disgusted when I kept hearing three girls across the aisle talking about the teacher, how nerdy she looked, and wasn't John hot, he just broke up with his girlfriend.

Reconciling school, our trips, and home life was hard. Keeping up with us and the bills was hard on Mom, and she was alone. Even though she finished up at college and got her degree, $18,000 a year didn't go far enough for the five of us. Mom was always stressed, and then there were the four of us being adolescents going through all of our stages. Sometimes I wasn't the nicest person, and got mad or upset when I couldn't do something because we didn't have the money. I would act like it was all Mom's fault. My brothers Rick and Lance were starting to hang out with the crowd at school that smoked weed, skipped school, and acted tough. Lance tried to run away one time when our uncle who used to live with us threatened to beat him up if he kept on smoking cigarettes.

My youngest brother, Bill, went to school with me. My other two brothers went to the public high school. They also tested for our school when they finished sixth grade, but there weren't any scholarships for them. By the time they were offered one, Mom couldn't swing it. As it was, the school was always hounding her to pay up. If she had paid on time, we would have gone without food, and probably heat and electricity too. Most of me wishes that my other two brothers could have gone to school with us, but part of me feels so glad they didn't. Basically, I didn't want them to feel bad about themselves. I know life would have been "easier" for them, but do years of ridicule have to go along with it?

By the middle of the ninth grade I developed some friendships. I found it easier to talk to other new students. For the first time in two years, I had friends. Most of the time our talks revolved around classes, boys, how hard track practice was. I liked it.

I think that high school for Bill and me was a time where we numbed ourselves to being poor and to forgetting the Cheyenne and Blackfoot ways. It was easier that way. It seemed that we had to learn to be one way at school, and another at home; but it was hard, how are kids supposed to do that? I went unwillingly to family functions. My family didn't see that much of me the last two years of high school. I was involved in sports, stayed over at friends', or talked with them on the phone incessantly. I didn't want to hear about how far we were behind in bills anymore. School was easier because it was shallow. I could handle talking about classes, but I couldn't do anything to help Mom or not make us poor.

By the time I was a junior, my brother Bill was in the upper school, too. Only thing is, I didn't like him that much because I saw things about myself from his behavior. He looked down on our family for being poor; he was ashamed. School and the people in it were the most important to him. I saw it in him when he brushed my mom aside. She was trying to tell him something, and he answered in a condescending voice to her. I was angry at him for not respecting everything she had done for us. He paid more attention to his friends than family. He said derogatory things to my other two brothers like, "Oh, what do you know?" and after a while they'd say things about our "rich private school." He looked down on them, and I thought, my God, it was only luck that got Bill and me in; it wasn't Lance's or Rick's fault they had to go to public school.

By the time it came around to applying for schools I had a sneaking suspicion that I had neglected something really essential by ignoring as best I could home and the tribes for so long. I applied to colleges because it was what everyone else did. I did fairly well on the entrance tests, had a good grade average, and got recommendations from teachers who liked me. When I applied to school, I applied to out-of-state schools because I wanted to see what it was like elsewhere. The whole process was funny, because I had all these Ivy League schools interested in me. I didn't really care about going to a top school, but most of the other kids did, and a lot of them did double takes when one of my friends teased me loudly about Harvard calling for me. I liked the school I'm at now the most because it had a Native American Society. I knew that I would need some connection to my background to help me out in school without my family or relatives.

Again, my relatives and mother were encouraging. I'll amend that. Everyone but the traditionals were glad for me. As a young woman, I should have been starting a family, not running across the country for four years. They never actually said anything, but when Grandma told them, they'd look away, or talk about something else. In my eyes, going to college wasn't going to make me less Indian, or forget where I came from. If anything it would enhance it.

It used to bug me sometimes when Grandma would say where I was going, because the way she said it would make other people jealous of me. Lots of people she told this to had kids in state schools or community colleges, and I felt bad because they were just as good as me. I didn't want people to be envious, or think that I was snotty. There were a lot of relatives like that, who were proud of me, but I hated it when they would announce where I was going; they didn't always mention that Sue was doing something really good for herself by going into the Marines, or that Bob was a supervisor in a plastics factory. They weren't any less than I was; in fact, the things they did demanded so much more.

Graduation was boring, and I wasn't crying like most of the other students were. I just remember being glad that school was finally all over with. I wouldn't yearn for my years in high school, and I wouldn't miss most of the people there.

My family brought me to the airport. Mom, Grandma, Grandpa, two uncles, two cousins, and my brothers were there. They took all kinds of pictures of me and my brothers, me and my cousins, me and Mom. I said goodbye to my brothers, and Mom was crying. She tried not to, but I knew she would miss me. And all of a sudden, I knew that I would miss her, too. It startled me. I had tears in my eyes and was biting my lips, and Grandma said, "You're going away to do a good thing. Nothing bad has happened. We don't have to cry." They called my name as I boarded, and I turned as they snapped a picture. I sat in my seat and looked out the window, crying. This man tried to make small talk with me, until he saw me crying, then he let me alone. The plane started to go towards the runway, and I looked at the terminal, and there they all were, standing and waving. I could still see Mom crying. Love. I was leaving love.

I was excited about going to school, partly to be on my own, but I thought because it was college, people would be wise and mature, that there wouldn't be the cliques like in high school. I was wrong. It was freshman week, and most of the people were *just like* my high school peers. I was horrified. I couldn't get into the class spirit, I didn't like my roommate, I didn't like most of the bubbleheads I met. I didn't really feel my purpose in being there—except possibly to meet all the self-important people and party as much as I could. It was a time when I had to stand on my own and rely on my strengths. The only thing was, I didn't know what my strengths were. It didn't feel like I had any.

I was sitting alone one night that first week looking at the stars, like I used to at powwows or in Nebraska. All of a sudden I had a tight feeling in my chest, and I said aloud, "Why am I here?" I felt like walking into the woods and crying, because I didn't want to go through a repeat of being new, like when I started private school.

This is what I did my first term at school: I went to math class for the first week, I went to English for the first half of the term, and to my third class maybe once a week. I drank whenever I could. I remember being three or four papers behind in my English class. I read the books I had to; I just couldn't sit down and say something about the topic questions. I sat in front of a computer, and for the life of me, couldn't think of a damned thing to say about Conrad's imagery in *Heart of Darkness* and its effect on the reader. I went to math for the first three classes and it was all review, from like the eighth grade. The thing is, I always hated math. It was my earliest class, and I didn't feel a compelling need to wake up and go to it.

When I drank too much, I would end up crying and babbling. One time I was at a fraternity, looking at the mob of people dancing, watching people weave in and out through the tightly packed basement to get a beer, and I saw people jumping up and down and crowing with triumph about a beer pong game when a cup got knocked over. I was supposed to be having a good time. I ran out and stood under a pine tree, fists bunched up, crying for my relatives. I was always embarrassed about crying or babbling like that, and would act like I had never done it the next day. I was homesick, more than I had thought possible, but I didn't know it. I felt empty and knew something was wrong with me because I should have been having the time of my life. After all, I was young and at college.

People tried to help me. Friends would ask if I'd gone to class, if I'd caught up in math and English. I'd say no, and they'd say, "Jean, you've got to or you're going to be in trouble." I'd laugh, or say nothing. I got called in by my freshmen dean, and he asked how come I was having trouble. I said I didn't know. I was nervous and afraid of what he'd say to me. He said, "You went to a private school, you did well there, you are more than capable of doing well here. You're messing up. Why aren't you doing well?" I didn't say anything. He asked if I was homesick, and almost sobbing, I said yes. He told me that I had to go to classes, and that I could do it. I walked out of there, and composed myself. Crying, what good did it do anyway?

I used to talk with my mom about once every week. She always asked about the people who I was meeting. So I'd tell her about the people I hung out with, what we did or talked about—except the drinking parts. Mom hated to see any of us ending up alcoholic. She asked about classes, and I'd say that they weren't going so well. She'd ask about how I was doing, and I'd say, "I don't know, Mom, not so good." She always said "You can come home if you want to, Jean. You know that. We want you to be happy."

Somehow I imagined that if I had a boyfriend, everything would be okay. I had met this Native American guy my freshman week. I went looking outside of myself for what I lacked. I liked it that he still had close ties to his tribe, that that was where he drew his strength from. I had spent the night with him a couple of times after parties during the weekend. Platonically, I mean. We spent most of our days together. People were always wondering if we were ever going to get together. I wondered too.

John came up and said he wanted to talk. I had had a knot of anxiety and yearning in me, and it loosened up. He said something about wanting to wake me up with a kiss when I had slept in his room, taking it slow, how he had fun when we were together, and that he respected me. But it was almost like he was dictating a letter to me or something. Maybe I should have gotten up and gone to him when he finished talking. Instead, I said that I needed to go to the bathroom, because I really did.

When I came out, he had gone downstairs, and I felt disappointed. He ended up drinking until he passed out, and then I knew that we didn't have anything. I felt immensely alone, and sad. The next day we studied together, and that was it. He wasn't very talkative. We went back to his room, and he said I would probably hate him, because he had decided to get back together with an old girlfriend, and that he didn't want to date someone who wasn't Navajo. I told him I hoped it worked out for him, and felt surprised that I meant it. But that was the last straw for me, and I set myself on the path of self-destruction. I just drank whenever I could, tortured myself with dreams of getting him back, and forgot completely about classes.

With the end of the first term came finals. I wouldn't get up to go to my math final. Why go? I was going to fail anyway. I still needed to finish three or four papers, and I hadn't done my term paper for my third class.

I got a call over break, and my dean said that I had been suspended. So when I went back to school it was to pack. Dimly, I regretted it. I had been on my own out there, and I was just beginning to see that there was a lot I could have done, such as pulling my act together, being independent, and maybe learning to loosen up with people my age and have fun.

Mom was supportive of me, as were most of my relatives when I got home. I didn't really know what to do with myself in terms of getting a job, or going to the state university. I didn't really feel like doing anything. For about three months I stayed home a lot, cleaned, cooked, hung out with Mom and my brothers. I tried to escape from thinking about myself and what I would do. The only things I made an effort for were to go to Nebraska with my grandmother and to go to as many NAC meetings and powwows as I could.

I started to drink on the sly. I'd drink when there wasn't anything for me to do, or just to liven things up. One time, I had been slipping into the bathroom to take a shot of vodka every now and then, and I got carried away. My brother Rick told Mom that I was acting weird, and I remember sobbing as she rubbed my back. The next morning I woke up, and I thought, "Oh my God, what have you done?" I felt apprehensive, I couldn't remember anything, and I couldn't really believe that I had gotten stinking drunk like that.

Mom came home, and this is what she said: "Jean, you can't do this to me. This happened to your dad. If something happens to you because of drinking, I'm going to feel really bad. What's the matter? Why are you doing this?" And I didn't know what to say. But I realized that the parents are supposed to die first, not the kids. I saw in her face that Mom knew that she couldn't help me. I had to help myself, and drinking like there was no tomorrow wasn't going to do it. I saw how my not thinking had led me to so many things, and that somehow I needed to make sense of what was bothering me. I said how sorry I was, and for the first time in my life, I meant it.

So I enrolled in a religion and psychology class during the evenings and I got a job tutoring math and English at an inner-city alternative high school for Indians. Most of these students were from the reservation and had come from North and South Dakota, Nebraska, and Montana. Indians flock to Bismarck for jobs or for excitement. Most of us are poor, lots are alcoholic, and many come from dysfunctional families. What smacked me in the face was seeing that abuse was a way of life, the only way of life they knew and accepted. Their education: poverty; alcohol; drugs; emotional, physical, and sexual abuse.

There was a girl named Sharon who did her work and was quiet. When people picked on her she would cower. When she was called on in class her voice shook and she wouldn't look up. If I told her she was smart or looked pretty that day, she'd say, "No I'm not." If she had to ask me for some help with some problem she'd say, "I'm so stupid, I can't do this." I heard Sharon's boyfriend sneering, "Why am I even with you, I could have any woman I want." Sharon said, "I'm sorry, please don't be mad. I'll be how you want me to be." When I heard that I winced and ran into the bathroom. I tried to block out the echoes of her beseeching him. Those were my words whenever anyone was mad or displeased with me. I knew how that felt in your gut.

They had nothing. So those that still had any fight left in them latched on to being tough, independent, and reckless, all for pride. Everyone needs something. I don't know why the kids talked to me and told me about their lives so much. I don't know why they picked on almost all the other teachers and aides (to their faces most of the time) and left me out of their ridicule. Maybe it was because at 19 I wasn't that much older than them. Or because I was Indian. I liked to laugh with them or tease them when I could. And when they talked to me, I listened, because what they were telling me about was their lives.

All I could say to them was, "It doesn't have to be that way, you know." Those kids are the trapped, the bereft, the haunted. They are the reason I came back to college. I have to find a way to open up a life and world outside of their childhood so that they can at least get through high school and get an adequate education, one that prepares them for college. I have to find a way that doesn't make them feel ashamed about their pasts. I want to change the schools somehow. Schools and your success in them determine what kind of life and career you're going to have. I see so many kids weeded out, and it has nothing to do with their intelligence. Why is the path through high school to college so narrow?

Working helped me decide what to do with myself in terms of college. Since my return, I have done fairly well in classes. I still have problems in making myself go to classes on a regular basis and doing all the reading that I'm assigned. I'm more caught up in my family life and what goes on there than in my studies or the issues at school.

I don't aim for straight As, but for learning what I can that will be useful to me when I go into education, or what will help me understand people in general. I also try to learn as much as I can about the culture here, what kinds of ideals and standards motivate the students and professors. It's still a pain a lot of the time, because for all the advantages that most students have here while growing up, and for all their intelligence, there's an incredible lack of compassion or understanding that there are people who live hard, hard lives. Their worlds and lives are closed, too, and it disheartens me lots of times. Sometimes I think that academic knowledge is how they gauge the wisdom and respect of one another. It's something I don't understand, because what does academic knowledge have to do with who we are as people? As far as I can see, wisdom has nothing to do with books and theories.

For a while when I first came back, I joined a coed house, but I found that I still drank a lot to pass the time. I was hungover at least three times a week. I drank so much that I ruined something in my body. Now, when I have more than three beers or mixed drinks, I'm hungover really badly the next day. Luckily, I only get carried away once or twice a year like that. Now, I'll have a beer with dinner once or twice a month, and that's about it. I don't really miss it because I finally figured out that drinking solves none of my problems. It only wastes my time.

Since I have been back I have been an active member of the Native American Society and have lived at the Society's house whenever possible. It feels like a home. Most of my friends are Native American, not because I'm prejudiced, but because I'm much more at ease with them. I am still really quiet and shy when I first meet people, and I avoid at almost any cost participating in class. Just this past year I decided that I couldn't always be like that, and for now that's enough. I also fell in love for the first time. We were together for two years but broke up three months ago. It was so hard—it still is.

Peter accepted me for who I was, faults and all. He used to say that he wanted the two of us to be able to do what we both wanted, and then be able to tell each other about it all. But I didn't know how to accept myself, and I demanded so much from him. It was as if I expected him to make up for things lacking within myself, within my life. Now I know that there's no one in the world that can do that for me but myself. Until I met Peter I was always lonely. With him I learned how to actually reach out to another person instead of being someone who just dreamed about love. He reached out to me and I learned to trust.

One time I went out with a high school friend, and she was talking about how her father went to meetings for abused children and children of alcoholics. She named off all the symptoms that these children have. And you know, as she listed off the characteristics, she described me. I sat there with my mouth open, and it felt like I had been punched in the stomach.

I saw a lot of the abused child behaviors in myself throughout the whole time Peter and I were together. It's like there was a lightness in me after I realized it. Even when I was with Peter I often felt hopeless and depressed. I was always afraid he would leave me. I never understood what he saw in me, so I would try to be what he wanted. I couldn't stand getting into fights with him, and if I was ever mad at him, I'd sulk around and keep it in because I was afraid to express it. I was so insecure with myself. Things would build up, and when we finally got it out in the open, I wouldn't even know myself what I was mad about. Somehow I felt inarticulate and that I didn't even have the right to be mad. I still have some of these tendencies.

I see how I turned him into a kind of addiction and couldn't give him what he gave me, love and acceptance. When I told Peter about the fact that my brothers and I had been abused, and that I wanted to do something about it, he held me. My voice was shaking, and I could barely get across what I had found out. Peter asked if I felt like crying, and when I said yes, he said, "come here" and hugged me. But I couldn't cry. And when he asked how I felt, I said I felt ashamed. He said,

"Oh babe, you don't have anything to be ashamed about. It wasn't your fault." And then I cried.

As time went on, when we were apart I became more and more insecure. I demanded that he put me at ease and hounded him to keep me a part of his life. I smothered him. Slowly, I lost confidence in myself and in him. Then I knew that I had a long, slow battle to feel good about myself and to not revert to my victim reaction. Oh God, I just wish we had met years from now when I was normal. I wish I had not been abused. But that is not going to change the past. I need to deal with how things are now, and slowly get rid of the things from my childhood. At least now I am aware, unlike many people who never have an inkling about what beneath it all is really bothering them.

Graduation is finally in sight. I plan to go on to graduate school for Indian education. I want to work in curriculum and administration, but I will probably teach first so that I can get some practical experience. I find that because of my experiences away from home I've gotten a lot of perspective that has, in the end, allowed me to appreciate my heritage. I will always do my utmost to keep family ties, NAC, traditions, and powwows in my life. I want all that, or something like it, for my children.

I've learned to think about myself as important and to know that I have strengths. I'm finally starting to be at ease with myself and with other people, and I look forward to the person that I'm becoming. It's been a long, slow haul. When I walk down that aisle for graduation I want my relatives to be there with me, and I'll walk proudly. I would do everything over again. I wrote this poem that speaks for me and for others:

> *I wear a coat. I wear tennis shoes.*
> *I play a game and I am winning.*
> *I go to school. I feel the worth*
> *in the knowledge of my relatives.*
> *I play the game, I do not live it.*
> *Knowledge from all areas . . .*
> *My thought, my hope:*
> *someday that all my elders will be proud*
> *respectful of the little ones who follow them.*
> *I dream . . . to make a way for the small ones not yet here.*
> *The younger ones to play the game in a skillful manner.*
> *In a way that I never could.*
> *It is our wish, it is our wish.*

THINGS BEGAN TO CLICK

Jennifer is a first-generation Asian American who grows up in middle-class suburbia. When she returns to the United States from two years in Hong Kong with her family, she is in middle school, and she wants to be normal, to fit in, to belong. Invited by a friend to attend a youth group meeting at a local church, Jennifer finds herself engaged by the people, and, to her surprise, by the ideas of Christianity to which she is being introduced. After joining the church, she finds that she continues to compartmentalize different aspects of her life: friends, family, school, belief. In college, however, she makes the conscious decision to have Christianity "permeate" her life, a challenge on which she continues to work.

I am going to keep my eyes closed. I am going to stay calm.
"... And Lord, we just ask that your Holy Spirit would be upon us tonight."
Why are there so many people in here?
"God, as we enter into your presence now—"
Why am I here?
"Lord, we pray that you would show us your face."
Good God, this is taking long.
"We pray that our worship would be pleasing to you."
I wonder when you say amen.
"In the name of the Father, Son, and Holy Spirit. Amen."
Oh, there it is. Crap.
A muffled "amen" worked its way through the crowd as I looked around nervously. The lights were out now, and the girl behind the keyboard began to play a simple melody, eyes closed and clearly enjoying something, though I wasn't quite sure what. Others around me looked placidly ahead to the projector screen, and as the kid with the guitar began to strum, a chorus of voices swelled up around me, singing a song I did not know with words I did not understand. In my confusion, I instinctively began attempting to follow the melody, stumbling my

way through four very, very long songs until someone began to pray again and the lights flickered back on. As my pupils adjusted to the light, I began to wonder about the Friday night lineup I was currently missing for this.

Someone tapped my shoulder. I turned to my right and saw Hannah's smiling face, apparently encouraging me to do something. I looked beyond her and saw a sea of identically smiling faces. They wanted me to introduce myself. *Oh God. Do I really have to stand?* I mumbled something about sixth grade and Raleigh and sat down. This was going to be a long night.

By the time everything was over, I was exhausted. Names and faces blurred in my mind, and the newness and strangeness of it all made my head ache. I did not see myself coming back. Friday night television was definitely better than this.

I have always considered myself to be a fairly average person. I am middle of the road—average looks, average interests, average abilities. I am the Good Girl: I follow the rules, color within the lines, and avoid dangerous things. I am an expert at mainstream unobtrusiveness, a social chameleon.

At the same time, I have also always wanted to be different. As a young girl, I hated dolls. I hated dresses, skirts, the color pink, and the ballet class I was in for two days. Growing up surrounded by boy cousins, my boy brother, and all his boy buddies, I became convinced that boy things were cool and girl things were not. And yet, whenever I played with boys, I became acutely aware of my inability to make a decent catch, my disinterest in video games, and my poor knowledge of baseball cards and cars. So I didn't say anything. It was easier to follow them around wishing I could be cool like them than to deviate from the role of good, socially accepted little girl I had already established for myself.

These two somewhat conflicting character traits have been with me throughout my life and to a certain extent are still with me now. My desire to be Different But The Same has colored my story in many ways, influencing to at least a small degree the many life decisions and choices that I have struggled through and made, including my move from nonreligious person to Christian woman and from nonathlete to field hockey and lacrosse player. The interesting thing about life, though, is the fact that it is never just one personality trait or experience that reigns supreme over all that occurs. It is an intricately complicated weaving of people, places, events, and experiences that make up a life, and it seems inaccurate to point to one aspect of myself as THE reason for so much change and development, as influential as it may have been.

For the first nine years of my life, I lived in New Jersey suburbia. My parents both grew up in Taiwan—my mother in the city and my father in the country—and met the summer after their freshman year in college at an "adventure camp" sponsored by the military. (Somehow my mother, who is not what you might consider an outdoors person, thought it would be fun.) They dated through college, and after graduating in the late seventies, they both came to the United States to attend graduate school. They were married shortly after arriving, and five years later, I came along. At the time, we were living in a cute little house in a cute little neighborhood, right next to a not-as-cute little shopping mall in the suburbs of the glorious Garden State.

Though my parents were very proficient at English, they only spoke Chinese to me and to each other when we were at home. My maternal grandmother and paternal grandparents also watched after me at some time or another during those first few years, and they did not know any English. Needless to say, Mandarin Chinese was my first language, and evidently, it was very good. My parents would sometimes tease me later about how *good* my Chinese used to be! and about how I could just jabber *on and on!* I cannot attest to any of this myself, but I'll take their word for it.

I eventually learned English by being plopped down in the middle of a preschool class at the age of four and hanging around other little kids who happened to speak English. I was scared to the point of stunned silence the first day, watching in wide-eyed horror as twenty other boys and girls ran around me speaking nonsense. Fortunately for me, the teacher just so happened to be a Taiwanese immigrant about my parents' age, and she was able to help make my acquisition of English as smooth as possible. Within a month, I was speaking English as if it was my mother tongue. My parents continued speaking Chinese with me, but now that I spoke English all day at school, I started speaking more of it and less of Chinese at home. I was, however, still required to attend Chinese School every Saturday morning. It was there that I began to learn (and to detest) reading and writing Chinese.

When I had finished up with kindergarten and my brother was just entering his last year of preschool, my parents decided—in the grand tradition of many Taiwanese immigrant families of my area—to move to a nearby town with a better school district. The town itself was upper middle class with a population that consisted predominantly of Jewish, Italian, and Western European families, as well as a growing number of Asian immigrant families with backgrounds similar to our own. It was a more affluent area than where we had been before, but as a 6-year-old, the only difference I noticed was my bigger house and the huge amount of trees in our neighbor's backyard. I began first grade that fall, and thus began my illustrious career in the Raleigh Township school system.

In the middle of third grade, however, my father decided to accept an offer to become a professor at a university in Hong Kong. Needless to say, I was not happy. I was doing everything I was supposed to be doing—taking piano lessons, going to Chinese School, getting good grades. What was I supposed to do in Hong Kong? What about my life here? What about my friends? I didn't even know where Hong Kong was! After much goading, however, my parents finally convinced me that moving there might not be so bad. I even became a little excited as we packed up our house and slept on air mattresses the last few nights in America. I felt like I was going on an adventure into a crazy foreign land.

For me, living in Hong Kong ultimately became one of those extremely formative experiences that tend to be taken completely for granted until much later in life. Despite my initial excitement, I eventually did not see any of it as terribly special or out of the ordinary. I assumed that I was living an ordinary American life and just happened to be doing it in a foreign country. Our apartment was on a relatively sprawling university campus far from the cramped spaces of the main city, and my brother and I attended a private American international school. (One of the most amazing testaments to the insularity of our lives is that we got away with living there for two and a half years without learning Cantonese.) At the same time, however, the people with whom we interacted, the places we went, and the things we did exposed us to entirely new and different worlds, all of which inevitably, though perhaps subconsciously, had an impact upon our future selves. We were able to be friends with a truly diverse and international group of people. We were able to travel to places all over the world that I had never even dreamed of visiting. We were able to do ordinary things, like shopping for groceries, taking art and music lessons, and eating out, in a (in my mind) less-than-ordinary place.

Fast forward two and a half years, and we come back to America, back to the same town and the same school district. I was scared out of my mind. I had recently come to the horrible, horrible realization that I had missed nearly THREE YEARS of real American life, and I was about to enter middle school. I didn't know what clothes to wear, what music to listen to, or what movie stars to be drooling over. Who *were* all these people? Why did they care so much about clothes? Actually, where did they get those nice clothes? Why am I still wearing the Disney T-shirts and the—good God—*tapered* jeans my mother bought me? Despite coming back to America for at least a week every year, I felt desperately out of the loop and desperately uncool, and though I had attended elementary school with all these kids, I still felt like I was brand-spanking, very conspicuously new and painfully different. I panicked, slowly and silently, keeping my nervousness at a slow boil in the back of my mind. The first day of sixth grade, I latched onto two old friends, Cara and Angie, as soon as I could find them. Cara was the first friend I ever made in first grade, and I had come to know Angie through Chinese School and because we were in the same third grade class. I slowly made my way into their different friend groups: Cara's was a mix of girls linked by band and who knows what else, while Angie's consisted chiefly of more "bookish"—though not what I would consider nerdy—Chinese girls. I started by sitting at the appropriate lunch tables and moved slowly on toward the sleepovers and birthday parties. Thankfully, sixth grade was the lowest grade in the school, so I was not the only one making major adjustments. As I kept a vigilant eye on the other girls, fashioning myself carefully by subtly imitating the cues I picked up regarding fashion, music, and other important details, others around me were doing similar things. But I didn't know that, of course.

Many months later, I had reached what I thought to be a reasonable state of mainstream normalcy. Most of my clothes were from the right stores (or looked like it), my musical taste was appropriately sprinkled with boy-bands and angst-ridden women with acoustic guitars, and I was starting to feel less awkward and shy. I was not popular by any means, but I had found groups of friends who were like me, with similar senses of humor, similar tastes, and with some, similar family backgrounds. I had found my niche.

Somewhere in that settling time, one of those friends, Hannah, invited me to come to her Friday night youth group gathering. She, as well as a few other schoolmates of mine, attended a Chinese and Chinese American (the parents were mostly immigrants from Taiwan while the children were mostly born here) nondenominational Protestant church about five minutes from my house, where every Friday night the sixth through twelfth graders would come together for a small worship service, Bible study, talks, and hanging out. My family had never been religious, and my parents had raised my brother and me with the mixture of Confucian, Daoist, and humanist values they themselves had grown up on, along with whatever else they acquired on the way. As a result, I had never been to church before and had no idea what it was about. But Hannah was nice, and it didn't seem like it would be so bad. I never did anything on Friday nights anyway, aside from watching television and doing the Chinese homework I had neglected during the week.

The whole night was basically a blur to me—a blur of confusion, awkwardness, and nerves. I didn't know what was going on, and I didn't know anybody well except for Hannah. Aside from being completely lost and awkward, however, I think I had an okay time. The people were friendly and the singing, though confusing, was actually kind of fun. But I didn't plan on going back any time soon. Though I didn't have a terrible time, the exhaustion and headache from the newness and strangeness of the experience was too fresh in my mind to make a second trip worth it. I decided that church was "interesting" and the people were nice, but it definitely was not for me.

Thankfully, Hannah didn't mention anything about it the next week, so I was free to forget about it all. I did a good job of that and went on happily with the rest of my life, becoming more comfortable with school, getting more involved with after-school activities, and engaging in all the myriad activities vital to adolescent life (namely, going to the mall and hanging out with friends). Classes were going well, and I maintained my straight-A streak with relative ease. I began to grow closer to my friends as we banded together and began to grow up together, influencing one another's tastes, hobbies, activities, and classes. We rarely moved into any new realm alone, always making sure to grab someone along if we were brave enough to explore. I followed my friends into most of the after-school activities I was involved in. I joined a community service club, attended quiz bowl tournaments, participated in a research club, worked on stage crew, and even tried track for a while, though I quit that after realizing I wasn't ever going to make it to a meet. Though I did not have and have never had a "best friend" to whom I talked on the phone every day, I did not consider myself to be friendless. I enjoyed hanging out with the different groups I was in, and they could always entertain me and make me laugh until my stomach hurt. There were many lunch periods where I was barely able to finish my sandwich because I had been laughing so hard and talking for so long about things I cannot even recall now. I would sometimes get jealous of the pairs and subdivisions of my cliques, but I fought hard to get beyond that. I remember one time when a friend of mine called me up, upset and fuming about how so-and-so was always with so-and-so and about how she always felt SO left out because they would never invite her to do things with them. We whined and commiserated together about our feelings of abandonment and neglect, and though the resolution of that conversation is fuzzy now, I distinctly remember feeling incredible relief in discovering that my jealousy was not abnormal. As time went on, I began to be more comfortable with my lack of a best friend and even began to embrace the fact that I was not so strictly attached to anyone. My relationship with my parents throughout all this was fairly good, and I might even say that I was closer to my mother than many girls my age, confiding in her as I might have with a best friend. My father was my father, serious and somewhat boring some of the time, but joking and good-natured the rest, and my little brother was a little brother, unfortunately teased and slightly bullied, but loved all the same. Life seemed to be going the way it ought to be.

All the while, though, I still found myself lacking in that amorphous quality of "cool." I would label other people as cool, but never myself. My heroes were friends who could do the things I could not—sing, dance, draw, paint, play sports well. Especially the sports part. When a group of my friends began to play on school teams, a strange sort of jealousy began to eat at me. Why couldn't I be like them? Why couldn't *I* go out for these teams and be amazing and cool? Naturally, though, I found it easier not to say or do anything. I simply admired them quietly as I had admired my boy cousins and boy brother, continuing to plod along in my self-appointed role of "the average good student."

Some time later in eighth grade, I was invited, yet again, to that Friday night youth group gathering. This time, my friend Katie did the inviting, but her approach seemed less daunting than Hannah's had. She called me up one Friday afternoon.

"Hey Jen. What are you doing tonight?"

"Nothing really. Why?" (At this point, I was hoping that she would invite me to go somewhere with her. She was one of my hero-worshipped friends—I thought she was funny, cute, and awesome for playing field hockey.)

"I was wondering . . . if you wanted . . . to come to Fellowship with me?"

"What? Why?"

"Oh. Well . . . my brother keeps bugging me about it, and I promised him I'd go, and I thought maybe you could maybe come with me? I feel kinda weird going by myself."

"Oh. Ummm . . ." I thought for a minute. "I guess so."

"OOOH, good. Thanks, Jen! How about my mom drives us and we pick you up at 7:25?"

"Okay . . ."

"Cool! I'll see you then. BYE!"

"Bye . . ."

I wasn't too sure of what I was getting myself into. I vaguely remembered what my first visit had been like and was hoping that it would be different this time. Going with someone else who was new made me feel a little better, and going as that someone else's security blanket made me feel a whole lot better. Somehow, being the tagalong friend seemed like it would provide me with immunity from the hordes of scarily friendly people who wanted to know all about what I thought of God and Jesus. To be honest, I didn't even know. I kind of knew I believed in God and I kind of thought I was a good person, but I didn't know anything about this Jesus character or understand anything about trinities or blood of lambs, and I didn't really care. You might even say that I was in this more for the social scene than for the theology. So I went along, clinging to Katie, and not feeling as awkward as last time. In fact, I ended up kind of liking it. The people I met this time (who were actually the same people I met last time, only two years older and wiser) were hilarious and funny and seemed to be having a really good time with life. As the night progressed, I began to find myself drawn to them and, in the back of my mind, wanting to be like them, not unlike the way I was drawn to my hero-friends who could sing, dance, and play sports better than I could.

I ended up attending Friday night Fellowship rather regularly that year. Katie's mother would always drive us there, and my mother would always drive us home. Katie seemed to be getting into deeper friendships with those kids at church (many of whom we both knew already from middle school and Chinese School) and I was too, although I managed to keep myself more on the outskirts of the group. All the while, though, I wanted to be a part of it all. I wanted to be better friends with this extraordinarily fun and witty group of people, and to my surprise, I wanted to understand more of this Christianity thing. Week after week, as I began to listen more intently during the talks and think more about the Bible passages we studied, things began to click. Jesus as both God and man, the blood he poured out to restore humankind, the strength he gives to live every day of this unpredictable life, the enormous and all-encompassing love of God, the simple yet intensely complex idea of faith in what one cannot see—I began to allow myself to be immersed in this culture and vocabulary, and I began to see its truth. I slowly gained an understanding of what sin was, and I could see it in myself. At the same time, I was gaining an understanding of the perfection and love that God is, and I began to want to know that perfect love and draw close to it. I looked around me and saw people I admired, of sound mind and unquestionable intelligence, filled to overflowing with passion for this Jesus Christ whom they called Lord of their lives and who they said took away their sins so they could *be* with that perfect, holy God. It almost didn't make sense, but I knew I wanted that for myself. I wanted the passion they had and the love they experienced so evidently every week.

At the same time, I wanted in on what I felt was a club—I wanted to be part of this group of people with their joy and trust in someone greater. A tension began to grow within me between seeking God and seeking mere belonging. When Katie decided to become Christian, I was shocked, not by her decision, but by my own jealousy. All of a sudden, she was the center of attention, being welcomed with true love and happiness by those I admired so much, and I wondered if my supposed desire for knowing God was spurred on by a need for friendship or by real passion and curiosity. *Am I really seeking you, Lord? Is it you I want, or is it acceptance and popularity?* I prayed this prayer in the back of my mind as I continued searching for answers. I was so afraid that I wasn't being genuine with myself, and even more frighteningly, that I wasn't being genuine with God.

As I struggled and considered things, I kept quietly to myself. School and other various activities continued as normal, but I was becoming ever more conscious of the presence and existence of God and began praying at home and reading the Bible on my own every now and then. Though they were not religious themselves, my parents never objected to any of this and continued to drive me to church every Friday night and to pay for weekend retreats. During some of this time, my brother also began attending Fellowship and though we never talked about it together, I am certain that he was questioning and searching the way I was. He accepted Christ at a retreat one spring, and for a while, he was the one who had to drag me to church. A few years later, however, after I myself became Christian, he began to drift away. We have never been able to have a clear and emotionless conversation about it since, but from what I gather, the hypocrisies and betrayals he experienced within the church were enough to turn him away from God. To this day, even though I have seen and heard of this happening to many others, I am still often saddened and confused about his crisis of faith. But that's the stuff of a different story.

I ultimately had my own tears and altar call experience one warm summer evening at the end of eighth grade. Now, in Christian culture, what generally happens at the end of many sermons or speeches is that the speaker asks everyone to close their eyes so that they can pray. The lights are dim, everyone's head is bowed, and after a brief moment of silence, the speaker begins in a serious and contemplative voice, "Now, for those of you who don't know Christ . . ." After this follows an invitation to tell God that YES!, you believe that Jesus was his son who came to die on behalf of all our sins and was raised to life, thus conquering death and sin and bringing mankind back to its rightful place in communion with God. This is what is commonly known as an "altar call." I had heard them many times before that night and have heard it many times since so I make light of it now, but when you are on the verge of giving your life away to God, I guarantee you that the feelings of fear, excitement, and resonance with the speaker's words are immense. I was so sure each time I had heard this call before that my desire to raise my hand in affirmation was merely brought on by the pressure of the invitation (he's talking to me, that one person who doesn't know Christ, after all) and my desire for belonging, but something was different this time. Things were making incredible amounts of sense, and it all just seemed so right. Despite the perpetual presence of doubt in the back of my mind those past months, God had slowly been changing the way I thought about and conceived of the world. His Word had finally become true and real to me, and though I did not know everything about Him yet, I was now willing to begin a life lived on His terms and celebrating His goodness. By the end of that night, I had grieved over my sins, rejoiced in my new life, and taken that big step into Christian-hood. My church friends were incredibly happy for me, and as far as I can recall, my other friends were indifferent, neither happy nor upset. I am surprised and a little saddened to say that I remember nothing about how my family took this decision, nor do I remember how I told them. I do know, however, that this change was not met with any sort of opposition, and I was able to begin my Christian life freely and comfortably.

For many people, Christian conversion is equated with a complete change in lifestyle. Drug addicts become sober, the hardened and bitter become joyous, and rebellious teens stop cursing and start listening to their parents. I was none of these and saw, for the most part, none of these changes. Starting out as a Good Girl and becoming a Christian Good Girl doesn't really do much for noticeable behavioral transformation. I actually once asked my mother if she saw any changes in me, and she responded very matter-of-factly, "No. You've always been a good kid. I don't see how religion made you any different." Ouch. How was I supposed to be a representative of God's transformative power if even my own mother couldn't tell the difference between the me before and the me after? Though I was happy and content in my new relationship with God, I began, yet again, to resent how "good" and average I had always been and still was, wishing that my conversion story had the dramatic stuff of Sunday morning sermons.

In actuality, people rarely asked about how I became a Christian. Most of my friends just assumed I had succumbed to that weird (but harmless) Asian Christian cult and didn't mention the subject, and we went along our merry ways as friends. I became flustered and emotional when forced to explain my faith outside of church, especially to those about whom I cared deeply. I was under the impression (incorrectly, as I now understand) that it was entirely up to me to explain God and Christianity to them any time the topic came up. In leaving God out of the picture, I placed an enormous amount of pressure upon myself. I felt that it was up to *me* to defend the entire Christian religion on top of defending my own faith. In addition to that self-induced pressure, it didn't even seem as though my parents cared about understanding what I now believed and tried to live out. In an almost postmodern way, they saw Christianity as one of many possible truths and subscribed to the "as long as you're a good person, it's okay" philosophy, which made it easy to be a Christian around them but difficult to help them see why I cared so much about God and seeing other people come to know Him. It also didn't help to know that my mother was rather turned off to the idea of ever belonging to a religion herself, as she was altogether disgusted with the history of the Christian church and religious conflict in general. Because I still felt young, inarticulate, and unknowledgeable when it came to matters of faith, I reacted rather both frantically and selfishly when presented with opportunities to share about what it really meant to be in a relationship with God. The few conversations I had with my parents were so horrible in my mind that I can barely even remember what they were about now. All I do remember is my own anxiety at the time, which shows how much I was actually listening to them. My heart would beat absurdly fast, my palms would sweat, and I would be able to think of nothing but my need to perform well. True, much of what I said was genuine, but I rarely was able to hear the real needs that lay underneath their questions. I would speak at them rather than with them and become tearful as they failed to understand me and as thoughts surfaced in my mind of their continued separation from God, all because of my inability to say the right thing. After a few of those confrontational conversations, I resolved to simply not say anything anymore, unless asked directly.

Out of this time of initial adjustment to the Christian life came one of my greatest life-compartmentalization feats: God was in church and nowhere else. When He did make an appearance, it was in secret—door closed and ears listening for footsteps. I made a loud fuss about certain things (going to church and praying before meals, for instance) to remind my family and non-Christian friends about my "Christian-ness," but did little else. My Bible was generally in action only on Fridays and Sundays, and my deep contemplations of and conversations with God clustered themselves around retreats, Fellowship, and church. Yet, in spite of my half-hearted dedication, I was still growing and changing, learning more about God and wanting more and more (most of the time) to be like Him in His selfless love, goodness, and righteousness. When I wasn't paying attention, He quietly shaped me regardless, and whenever I did pay attention again, He would meet me powerfully and remind me of His constant faithfulness and love for me.

I remember this happening frequently at retreats, where we would spend an entire weekend listening to speakers, studying the Bible, and worshipping God. Inevitably, there would be one night where God would move especially powerfully in the worship service or the talk. I don't like to associate closeness to God with powerful emotion, but these were some of the few times where that was what happened. Generally, it would start out as a regular worship service. There would be a band up in the front, and we'd all be singing songs together. Then somewhere along the way, many of the people there would begin to feel especially moved. As more and more began to feel it, the worship service would transition into a time of prayer, with people praying hard, often tearfully, in little clusters or individually. (To an outsider, it would probably look weird and cultish.) Many times, these emotionally and spiritually intense experiences would center on repenting of our sinful behavior or of our neglecting God (hence the tears). It would blow me away every time—feelings of incredible sorrow, awe, and peaceful joy hitting me all at once, my heart aching, somehow breaking and healing simultaneously, as I saw a glimpse of this God who loved my wandering soul so abundantly, so unconditionally. But there were also times when we would simply be rejoicing in how amazing it was to know God and to know His love personally, with this essentially feeling like unadulterated bliss and absolute peace. It is somewhat difficult to put into words, and all I can really say is these were and still are experiences unlike anything else. While I do not regret that they often happened at retreats, I am now wary of the idea of using retreats to recharge one's "spiritual battery." I remember one speaker warning against this sort of "Tarzan Christianity," where a person relies solely on special events to meet with God, jumping from retreat to retreat to get his or her spiritual fill. At the time, however, experiences such as these really did a lot to combat my periods of doubt and apathy.

As my new relationship with God was developing, I began high school. To my utter shock and surprise, something miraculous happened. As the field hockey preseason was beginning, my friends on the team casually mentioned that the freshman team was in need of more players, and somehow, Hannah and I began to think about joining. *This is it*, I told myself. Finally, I was being given a chance to prove that I could do something outside of myself—outside of being typically good and typically smart. At the same time, I was incredibly unsure of my abilities. *What if I suck? Then what? Does this mean I will be forever doomed to being boring?* Looking back now, I think the growing self-confidence, comfort in my own skin, and all that good maturation stuff which generally accompanies getting over middle school made me really want to try something new. I was scared, but my budding desire to "go for it" conquered most of the fear. And so in the end, we both decided to join the team.

The first practice was horrendous. I spent most of it attempting to learn how to dribble the ball while being bitter about field hockey sticks being suitable only for right-handed people. I was depressed with how out of shape I was and at how uncoordinated I felt, hitting the ball two inches when I wanted to it to go two yards and left when I wanted it to go right. Everyone else seemed to be doing fine (granted, they had already had two weeks of practice and a year of play), and here I was, unable to even travel in a straight line. Yet as I started to get into it, I began to grow more and more determined to master those skills. I left that first practice more intent to succeed than I had ever been. A competitive spirit was growing within me, something I had rarely experienced before. As the practices continued and games began, my skills and abilities grew and I began to feel more and more accomplished. I, the girly klutz, was playing a sport and was actually kind of good at it. It was an amazing feeling.

I eventually did become quite good at field hockey and, in the spring, was even brave enough to try my hand at lacrosse. School was also going well: I was slowly figuring out the delicate balance between work, sports, and play, and I was starting to feel more and more like the mature and sophisticated person I had always envisioned high schoolers to be like. Things were good socially, too. I had three primary groups of friends during this time: my classmate friends (made up of people I had become friends with primarily in middle school and now saw mostly during school hours), my teammate friends, and my church friends. These groups overlapped a fair amount, and my closest friends belonged to all three or at least two. Most of these friends, as always, were Chinese American, with two or three "token white girls" and a few Korean Americans. From school, playing sports, and attending church, I was able to grow closer to these different people as we spent time together in class, at practice, at games, at church, and at retreats. Being the busy high school students that we were, most of that time together was spent on activities—we "did stuff" together, making jokes and discussing whatever we happened to be doing—but we did, on occasion (such as sleepovers or more serious sharing times in Bible study), discuss the big things that were on our hearts and minds. I would say the most frequent topics of serious conversation were school, college, the future, and—though perhaps more in jest—boys. We were growing up together, figuring out the world and figuring out ourselves, and I was able to talk and share easily with people in all the different friend groups, as varying as their worldviews may have been. It was amazing to watch the evolving desires and dreams each person had, ranging from toy designer to biology researcher, from saving the world to saving individual lives. As all these areas of my life were blossoming, however, I paid relatively little attention to my relationship with God. Sure, I would go to church service, Sunday school, and the weekend retreats (attendance has always been a strength of mine), but, as I mentioned before, it didn't amount to much more than that. Only rarely did I spend time with God on my own.

It was not until my senior year when I was invited to serve on the leadership board of the Fellowship that I began to think more seriously about my faith and walking actively with God. Serving there with a group of people so committed to God challenged me to rethink priorities I had set in my life. As I applied to colleges that fall and awaited the acceptances and rejections in the spring, I became more and more aware of my need to trust God—to trust that He would lead me to the right place for the right reasons. Talking to old friends coming back from college during their breaks, I realized the necessity of consciously striving to keep focused on God and His big picture as I made my decisions and entered college. Without this consciousness, I knew that I, being a perpetual perfectionist, could easily lose my center and fall into that endless race of striving to be the best, at the best school, in the best field. I knew that striving to do my best was not wrong; it was forsaking my relationship with the God who loved and saved me, all for the sake of my own achievement, that would hurt me.

As I began to take my relationship with God more seriously, I also began to grow closer to my friends at church. Much of it was because of proximity (Friday nights, Sunday mornings, Sunday afternoons for meetings, entire weekends for retreats, and other hangout times), but looking back now, it seems that much of it was also because of a certain likemindedness when it came to views on life and the world and ultimate purpose. As with friends from my teams and school, we shared similar life experiences and educational aspirations, but at the same time, we also shared a deep desire to know and follow God. We had laughed, cried, danced, sung, debated, and sweat together, not simply for the sake of being friends, getting into college, or athletic honor, but for the sake of becoming closer to the One who created us, loved us, and had a wonderfully unique plan for each of us. I loved my other friends and still do immensely, but the unique kind of closeness that developed with others who believed in Christ simply made for different kinds of relationships. At the end of senior year, as various sports, classes, and school-related activities drew to a close, I found myself seeing less and less of my friends who were not Christian and more and more of the ones who were, since church still happened every weekend. I cannot say that this drifting apart happened solely because of the difference between Christian and non-Christian—other factors, such as the ways different personalities click or simply the other friends and interests different people have, were critical as well. All the same, though, the relative split was rather noticeable.

The funny thing about entering college is that no one there knows you. These people have *never* seen you before. They don't know anything about you. Your past, your interests, your goals, your family, and your old friends—all of this is there, yet not there, implicitly informing the way you think and act but essentially a mystery to the new people in front of you. The blankness of the slate is remarkable, and you are drawing yourself anew, making (consciously or unconsciously) what people see in you and what you see in yourself as different or as similar to what you saw in yourself a few months before. As I entered my freshman year of college, I made several conscious choices about this personal revision. The most basic of these was to break down the little boxes and categories I had previously set up for my life. I was determined to let God permeate and touch every aspect of living, from the friendships I made to the major I chose. I wanted to purposefully involve myself in a Christian fellowship on campus and attend church every week, understanding that connection to other people who were seeking God was just as important as seeking God on my own. I wanted to self-identify as a Christian to whoever was curious and to try hard to live a life worthy of Christ that was neither hypocritical nor obnoxiously devout (in a hit-you-over-the-head-with-a-Bible kind of way). I did not want my faith to be just a Sunday thing. I wanted it to be real and living.

Following through with all this was a little awkward at first. For the most part, I found myself preoccupied with working through the typical freshman year adjustments. I didn't know what classes to take, what major to choose, how to work the dining hall, where anything was, or why I missed my friends at home so badly. Nevertheless, I did manage to begin taking steps toward putting God in the center of my life. I made a point of spending more time with God on my own time and tried to make prayer and the Bible parts of my everyday routine. This began first with attempts to read the Bible and pray before going to bed, but unfortunately, being tired and overworked does really bad things for concentration. I then tried switching to mornings, but as the year went on, I found myself sleeping later and later and eventually making the roll-out-of-bed-fifteen-minutes-before-class thing a daily routine. Needless to say, this left little time for pretty much anything. My goal of achieving regularity with the Bible didn't work out so well, but this irregularity was not "bad" the same way it was bad in high school. Because I was beginning to see God as part of my everyday reality, I began to see spending time in His Word less as a chore but more as an exciting opportunity to learn more. As a result, the feelings of "bad" that accompanied my lackluster results with Bible-reading were less often guilt-ridden than they had been before.

As that was going on, I also dutifully followed the advice of older friends and became involved with an on-campus Christian group. Because I had such a tight group of friends in my Christian group at home, I half expected similar friendships to spring up as soon as I walked into the room. Surely, we would be able to connect right away and be super best friends forever. Unfortunately, it didn't quite happen that way. In general, with all the friends I was making at college, the process was slower than I anticipated. While all of my friends at home could make me laugh until I ached, none of the friends I was making at college could. While my Christian friends at home and I would frequently stay at church for hours after Friday night meetings just talking, people here (and especially other freshmen) would bolt out the door as soon as the meeting was over. *Does no one here like me? Is no one on this campus funny?* It didn't make any sense! As the year progressed, however, I finally began to understand that not everyone in the world is the same and not every friendship looks and feels the same. I eventually embraced the friends I had made for who they were and the unique way we functioned as friends, and I also began making friends in the Fellowship, which helped me slowly begin to feel connected to the Christian community on campus.

This feeling of connection was helped along by interacting weekly with the group of people with whom I began attending church. Like many of my friends who went away to college, I went to a church consisting primarily of Korean American college students and young adults. Basically, the group of students I went with brought most of the "diversity" the church had at the time. Though there were some very Korean American–specific cultural elements (for instance, eating kimchee and noodles after service or the occasional reference to growing up Korean American in a sermon), I did not find it difficult to fit in with the congregation: more important to me than the ethnic makeup of the church body was the presence of God among them. I learned much from observing the genuine desire to bring God's restoration to the urban area where the church was situated, as well as the fervor with which they worshipped God. I also found myself being challenged to grow in my knowledge of God every week from the solid theological teaching spoken so powerfully by the pastor, as well as being challenged to reflect regularly on what His presence meant to my life.

Outside of church and Christian clubs, I became involved with a number of service-oriented activities, ranging from tutoring to assisting the blind. I worked hard to adjust to the intellectual demands of college classes (probably harder than I needed to), and I got to know my hallmates and classmates through things like barging in on each other's rooms randomly to procrastinate or going out to movies or parties. Though I loved field hockey and lacrosse dearly, I decided not to be on the college teams, mostly because of a fear of the time commitment and partly because of a fear of my relative inadequacy (it was college ball, after all). Much to my surprise, I missed sports quite a bit. Every time I saw a girl walk into the dining hall with her field hockey gear, I got that funny feeling of longing one gets for a favorite shirt that's been lost or an experience that has come and gone too quickly. I missed the camaraderie of the team, the intensity of the games, the crack of my stick against the ball, and my ability to climb up stairs without losing my breath (self-regulated exercising is often a challenge). My feelings of longing and slight remorse, however, eventually evolved into a greater appreciation and savoring of those past times with sports, and I do not regret my decision not to play in college. I see it now as part of my journey into other pursuits—religious, academic, and otherwise.

In these "non-Christian" realms, I succeeded in self-identifying as a Christian, though this was not as easy as I had hoped sometimes. "Yes, I am Christian," I would say to new friends, all the while hoping that they would not ask any more but also hoping that something brilliant would come out of my mouth if they did. Yet, even though I felt awkward, the more I said it and the more often I talked about God, the more natural the words became. As the years went on, and even just after my freshman year, I began to see God as more real and more relevant than ever before. He became (and is still becoming) a part of my everyday reality. I see His fingerprints on every part of my life, from the gorgeous flowers and trees outside, to the flowing prose I read in class, to the students, staff, and faculty with whom I interact.

You could say that all this growth resulted from my increased involvement in "Christian things." Yet, one could easily do all these things—go to church, read the Bible, and attend Christian meetings—and glean little more from it than a busy schedule. I could have easily gone on with my studies and friendships, graduated, and begun a career and a family without experiencing the fullness and realness of God as I did. My college experience could have simply been a redux of my high-school experience, with all the academic success, social happiness, and relative spiritual apathy attached, but, simply put, it was not. I have been at college for almost three years now and am soon to start my fourth and final one. Looking back on my time here, as well as the years before, I am amazed at the kind of work and orchestration required of God in producing *any* life story, mine included. I have come to see my yearning to be different as already fulfilled—not because of what I have accomplished, where I have been, or what I have seen, but because of the unique pattern of experience God has placed before me and the closeness with which He has graciously led me through it. I no longer consider myself simply average: I am a child of God with a unique story to tell, who hates dolls, loves good competition, and (dare I say it?) considers herself cool at least 95 percent of the time.

THE STRUGGLE OF
A LIFETIME

Born into small-town life, this college senior describes a lifelong confusion about who he is and what purpose his life serves. The kind of teenager pious adults point to as a "fine young man" who will "make us all proud," Jon conforms to expectations while longing to be a "regular kid." Lacking the ease and self-confidence to develop close friends, he experiences loneliness and isolation from his peer world. A religion of good and evil choices gives comfort and affirms his self-sacrifice and avoidance of typical adolescent pleasures. Beginning college away from home offers Jon an opportunity to re-create himself, but he repeats the lonely pattern of social and sexual avoidance. Through a change in academic focus to theology and involvement in campus ministry, he questions the moral certainties of his Christian beliefs, including its condemnation of homosexuality. He sees his future framed by the struggle of balancing service to others through a religious vocation with the need to be comfortable within himself and accepting of his human needs and imperfections.

My early childhood revolved around a close family, and Sunday dinner after church at my grandparents' house was a weekly ritual. Until I left for college, Nana and Gramps—my mom's parents—hosted a huge homecooked meal for our extended family. There was never enough room on the table for all the different dishes Nana made. Everyone had multiple helpings of mashed potatoes, ham, carrots, and strange things like turnips and parsnips. We would spend the afternoon talking, playing outside, and taking care of their two horses. My dad's parents would join us all on holidays, and since all four of my grandparents grew up in the same town, they loved to sit around the table telling stories about Bedford when they were young—and poor. "We didn't know we were poor," Nana would say. "We thought we had it good."

I grew up in Bedford, too, in the same green duplex as my mom. One of the many little towns in the so-called Coal Country of Pennsylvania, Bedford came into existence around the anthracite mines. All of the mines have been closed for years now, and things are not looking up for Bedford, which is the poorest of the nine towns in our school district. The population is almost entirely blue-collar, working-class families, elderly on social security, or various arrangements of people on welfare.

My family always pointed out the drunks walking up and down the main street, making sure I saw them falling over and looking dumb. I fully got the message when I was ten, when Gramps gave up alcohol for good after years as a borderline alcoholic. He owns a fuel delivery business, which was his father's before him. Now well over seventy, Gramps still works six days a week, more than eight hours a day, with no vacations, ever. His business is his life, and I know he'll work until he dies . . . probably behind the wheel of an oil truck.

Gramps started driving trucks when he was twelve years old, and at eighteen he borrowed $1,500 from his mother to buy his own coal truck. Now the business is worth more than two million dollars, and he worries about what will happen when he dies. He lives modestly, shares his profits with my mother and her sister, and makes special trips in the winter to deliver oil to people whose tanks are empty, even if they cannot pay. Though not a religious man, he is a kind of pastor to the community. He knows literally everyone and their family histories, and he spends time visiting with people when making deliveries. He buys their homemade pasties and pierogies, lends them money when they need it, and is an advocate for the working people with business and governmental bureaucracies. While growing up, I spent every Saturday working with Gramps, managing his office, riding on the oil truck, filling bags of coal and tanks of kerosene. His mother said he grew up too fast, and I realize more every day how much like him I am.

My own family is a strange one, inheriting from my dad's side the characteristic of not talking to each other. We stopped doing things as a family by the time I was in middle school, and since then my parents, my younger brother and sister, and I have each had independent lives. Trained as a nurse, my mom cannot work anymore because of severe joint problems that keep her in almost constant pain. For a while she was a teacher's aide in special education classes for children with emotional and behavioral problems. What I remember best about mom is her taking food and clothes into school for her kids, who often came to school hungry and without winter coats. I remember how frustrated she got at the administration's apathy. My father is a hospital administrator who hates his job. Work causes him huge amounts of stress, and he usually spends all his time at home watching television, which does not help the fact that he is overweight with heart problems and diabetes. I think he feels locked in a self-defeating cycle.

Though I remember family vacations and playing ball in my backyard, I was never really close with my brother, Luke, who is one year younger than I. Now a junior in college, Luke always felt that he was living in my shadow—he was "Jon's brother." Trying hard to be visibly different, for a while he wore only black clothes, and he still has long, unkempt hair. Now an accomplished musician and very happy with his life, Luke was always the outsider of our family. My sister, Rachel, is five years younger than I, and I remember helping take care of her as she grew up. Rachel is very different from Luke and me, an outgoing social butterfly who is constantly on the phone or chatting online with her friends to arrange trips to the mall or lament a boyfriend lost.

I was dubbed "the smart one" in my family early on. In elementary school, I loved learning and was excited to go to school. Education was important to my family, but the rest of the town saw it differently. Sports reigned supreme, and the other boys had been on mini-football teams, which their parents coached, since they could walk. My parents never got me involved with them, and though I was on a YMCA swim team for a while, I was awful at sports. Not able to throw a football to save my life, I hated recess and was always the last one picked in gym.

By fourth grade, I was bored to death with school, and my teachers persuaded my parents to transfer me to Bridge Street School for the "academically gifted" located three towns away in a community of upper-middle-class professionals. Students were bussed there from all over our district, but I was the only one from Bedford. At Bridge Street the classes were harder, and for a while I was lost. I got a C on a test for the first time ever, and I didn't win the spelling bees anymore. I was determined to excel again, and by fifth grade I had risen to the top of the class and regained the reputation as the one who always got the highest grade—and who was picked last in gym. Besides my natural shyness, I had a hard time fitting in because I lived in a different town from everyone else, and my parents weren't about to drive me all over. The other kids came from wealthier families, too, and I never had the right brand of clothes or backpack. But life was good, as my parents would remind me. I had a loving family, clothes on my back, food on the table—"some people don't even have that, you know."

For middle school and high school, everyone in the district came to centralized buildings, with heavily tracked classes to keep the "good" doctors' and lawyers' kids in the honors classes with the "good" teachers, and everyone else in the "regular" ones. Entry into that coveted honors group had taken a lot of work for me, and it took even more to stay at the top. I was thankful for making it and felt responsible to do my best. That's all my parents ever asked for, but my best kept getting better and requiring more from me. I felt guilty if I gave less than 100 percent and wondered how other people in my honors classes could totally blow off work.

For me, academics always came first, but in high school I took on a string of activities and leadership roles in school. Student council, newspaper, literary magazine, and chorus filled up my days, and then there were more and more positions in Boy Scouts, church, and community organizations. I worked constantly, and I was sure it would all pay off. I pressed on, earning the praise of adults and the certificates and plaques that covered the walls of my room. My résumé was growing at a frantic pace, and I envisioned that someday I would be valedictorian, get into a good college—maybe even Harvard—and be "successful." *Then it would all be worth it.*

Toward the end of the summer before my junior year, the choral director from a private school asked me to join his select choir for a concert tour in France. Jumping at the chance, I ended up singing in Notre Dame, Chartres, and Orléans Cathedrals. The music was spiritually moving, but the people were the most wonderful. Though I avoided going drinking every night with the junior and senior guys in the choir, it was okay. Everyone truly liked me for who I was, and I finally found a group of people that *I* liked. I finally fit in.

That experience made me disgusted with my high school, where no one, including the teachers, cared much about anything. Far from loving learning as I once had, I was now doing the minimum amount of work to get the highest grade, which took less and less effort as teachers and students became more and more apathetic. Overseas, I saw for the first time a whole world beyond my little town. I realized that life could be different from what I saw in high school, and I wanted to know and see and do more, to break out. I was convinced that I would go to college far, far away, probably never to return. Most of all, though, I wanted real school friends like I had found in the choir in France. I finally knew it was possible. When the choir director invited me to transfer to his private school, with a full scholarship, I *really* wanted to transfer, but my parents resisted until I just gave up.

When school started in the fall of my junior year, I felt that I had made the wrong decision and had forever lost the chance to change my life. By that winter, everything came crashing down; the stress I was feeling overwhelmed me. I felt unfulfilled by my work outside of school and hated being in class. More than that, my reputation had taken on a life of its own, and I hated the "Jon Davies" I saw in the mirror. I was supposed to be this responsible, honest young man full of integrity and honor, who would "make us all proud." I spoke at fundraisers, got put on boards of directors as the token youth, and was paraded around as Scouting's poster child. I didn't drink or party, have sex, or smoke pot. I was "trustworthy, loyal, helpful, friendly, courteous, kind . . ." just like a good Boy Scout. I did what adults think kids should do, but I was torn between the life I was living and an intense desire to "be normal." Why did I care so much what everyone thought of me? Why was this reputation so important to me? Why did I cling to it?

Because it was all I had to cling to. It embodied all my successes and the praise of adults. It was the source of my self-worth and pride. Now it was falling apart underneath me, and I was alone. For the next few months, I spent hours crying and talking to myself in my room, agonizing over my desire to go to that new school and start over sans reputation. I lamented my inability to tell my parents forcefully, "This is what I want." But I still am not sure I knew what I wanted—I was running around in circles and had to do something. I realized that I could not live up to that "Jon Davies" image that everyone had for me. For a while I thought I should say, "to hell with it all" and go be "regular" like everyone else—get drunk, go on dates, not do any homework, hang out, and just love living life without a care in the world. Forget the stress, forget the responsibility, forget being a leader. I wanted to be a teenager. I wanted my childhood back. I wanted to experience all these things for myself. But a nagging part of me said something different. The sacrifice would have been so high and would have cut off *everything* that made me who I was, however out of control it had become. My experience in France gave me hope that there might be some other choice, and there the story of my faith truly begins.

For most of my life, my family attended Second United Methodist Church, a quaint little place just a block from home. My mom taught Sunday school and my dad was on the board of trustees. There were lots of nice people who cared about each other, especially the children, and I did the typical Protestant things: Sunday school, youth group, Christmas pageants, and church suppers, in addition to the service on Sunday mornings. It was a great place to grow up, but by high school I was dissatisfied. The forty-five-minute sermons were boring and totally irrelevant to my life. By senior year, all the kids I grew up with stopped coming, and it was weird to lose all my church friends to jobs, girlfriends and boyfriends, and general apathy. I wondered whether church for most of the congregation was not just a social ritual that made them feel good about themselves. And I wondered about me. What drew me back week after week? Had church, too, become part of my so-called good-person image?

My *own* faith became important after it intersected with that stressful winter of my junior year. For the first time, I questioned the faith I was taught. I did what the adults said to do: I was a good person, I went to church. And look where it landed me: miserable. I somehow knew that turning into a wild and crazy teenager would not work for me, so I turned instead to examining Christianity *for myself*. I thought it might be the way out of my confusion. I began to listen to Christian radio and read free books from evangelical preachers like Billy Graham and Chuck Swindoll. I found a new message of sin and grace, pain and renewal, death and life spoken to people living in sadness and confusion, who did not always succeed, and who were not perfect—something I could identify with.

There was no one time when I was "born again," but that winter saw an important change. I found Bible verses that spoke to my need, especially "Come to me all you who are weary and heavy-laden, and I will give you rest" (Matthew 11:28). I had always had my church, but I had never learned to *be* a Christian. Now I heard a passionate promise of reward for the struggle and ultimate meaning far more significant than anything I worried about. I prayed those "asking-Jesus-into your-life" prayers, and I felt changed. The radio preachers and book authors were so clear and perceptive, pointing—it seemed—right at me. Most important, I found a sense of peace as a real gift of God. My life was mostly the same; I just had a new outlook. Faith was my way out of confusion, the source of ultimate meaning for my life, and a way to deal with failure.

As much as I used faith to get back on track, I still lacked friends. Evangelical talk about purity and walking the narrow path of righteousness made me judgmental of my peers at school. But by the senior awards ceremony, my achievements and ostensible success could not make up for what I was feeling inside. I got more prizes than anyone else, and new plaques joined the collection already covering my bedroom walls: National Merit Scholar, AP Scholar with Distinction, and my Ivy League admissions certificate topping them off. For a long time these honors were a confirmation from the adult community that I was on the right track, that I was the model to follow. But if loneliness was the cost of this kind of affirmation, I felt I had made the wrong choice.

At graduation, I was named valedictorian of my class—the ultimate prize toward which I had worked since sixth grade. But first the principal gave a long speech—to thunderous applause—about the baseball players who had won the state championship earlier that day. Then he quickly announced the valedictorian and salutatorian, offered his congratulations, and had us stand in our place amid the sea of 250 navy and silver gowns just long enough for the yearbook photographer to snap our picture. It was the ultimate hollow victory.

Coming to college, I had huge expectations. The wood-paneled library seemed the essence of the intellectual life I hoped to find. Here would be a place in so many ways far from home, where learning would finally be valued and where I would fit in because I was smart. More than anything, I wanted friends. In the basketball arena with the thousand other new students at our first class meeting, someone gave a speech saying, "Now's your chance to make a new start, to create yourself again, to be the kind of person you want to be." My parents were gone, no one knew me, and I could be just like everybody else. I would stop being shy and just go up and meet people. I would go to fraternity parties and drink, maybe even join a frat. I would get the girlfriend I never had in high school, be involved in sports for the first time ever, maybe try out for crew. I would see movies, take road trips, and hang around. But I never did any of those things. My freshman English professor called me one of the college's "closet intellectuals," and inside I hoped that there were others like me.

Freshman year was a replay of high school. I spent all my time studying, convinced that I had to get an A in every class. I followed college rules meticulously, so thankful to be at a great college. A near 4.0 GPA and two academic citations proved that I could make it, that I was good enough. I planned to double major in Russian and government and then work for the State Department. I decided to spend sophomore fall on a foreign study program in St. Petersburg, Russia, which was supposed to confirm my plans to enter the foreign service. But I was in for a big surprise.

Any illusion of self-sufficiency was gone after ten weeks in Russia. It was a totally different world. Fourteen students lived in little four-person apartments on the eighth floor of a broken-down dormitory whose stairwells smelled of trash and vomit. Sometimes we had hot water; most of the time we did not. The heat seldom worked right, the windows never closed all the way, our stove caught on fire, and the bathrooms smelled like sewage.

And for the first time I lived close up with people who acted my image of *normal.* My three roommates spent most of their time drinking, drinking, and drinking. They went to bars, clubs, or room parties more nights than not. It baffled me how they could do no work, sleep through class, and never study. How could they waste this opportunity? Most of all, I saw them drunk and hated it. I could never imagine being so *out of control.* Sure, I saw drunk students bumbling around campus, and heard stories of random hookups and "booting" in the bathroom. Even though I thought they looked dumb and immature, I had felt I needed to try all this out in order to be like everyone else. Now that I was seeing face to face the hangovers, vomiting, and vulgar drunken conversations, I wondered if I had to do it for myself to avoid feeling regret. I wondered if this was really the prerequisite for having fun and friends.

But it was also in Russia that I began to appreciate simple blessings of life. Beggars were everywhere—on the sidewalk, in the subway, in churches. On a cold November afternoon I will never forget, I was walking into a store to buy postcards, and an old woman in a wool coat and head scarf was standing in the entranceway. Her eyes were cast down, her hand outstretched, and she said *"Pom-ogitye!"* I knew the Russian word: "Help." Never before had someone cried out for help, right to me. More than a little shocked, I rushed inside but felt horrible the whole time I was shopping. It was the best kind of guilt. My ten postcards cost 22,000 rubles, a little over three dollars then, and though most people give beggars spare change, I handed her a twenty-thousand ruble note on the way out. She looked at it, put it into her pocket, and began to cry. *"Spasibo vam bolshoe."* Thank you, she said, and she began to pray out loud. She thanked God for me, and prayed that I might have every blessing, love, and happiness. She reached out, and I let her hold my hand. I remember the warmth of her skin so clearly, the tears in her eyes and mine. Over the next month I had many old Russian women pray for me, holding my hand as I looked into their eyes, and I know God heard them all. Their prayers truly changed my life, and all it took was to stop and look them in the eye, to see not a miserable beggar but Christ Himself.

As powerful as my time in Russia was, the routine of college life took over soon after returning to campus sophomore winter. One big change, though, was the resolution of my search for a church home. I spent all of freshman year "church shopping," often attending the United Church of Christ (UCC) in the morning and St. Andrew's Episcopal Church's student eucharist in the evening. The UCC was a lot like my church in Bedford, but I eventually chose St. Andrew's.

Entering college, I had a very evangelical understanding of Christianity: God created the world, sin came into the world by Adam, all are guilty of sin and should be damned, Jesus died to save us from hell, and if you believe in Jesus you will be saved, otherwise you go to hell. That was it: plain and simple absolute truth. Right was right, wrong was wrong, nothing in between. But I also had a passion to learn more about Christianity, especially Roman Catholicism, which was demonized among Protestants back home: "They worship statues, you know." I took religion classes, studied the Bible for myself, read the church fathers and contemporary theologians, only to find a Christianity I never knew before. Truth was hardly as simple as I thought.

At St. Andrew's, I found a church focused on Holy Eucharist and rooted in the historic Creeds. With a new appreciation for tradition and the work of the Holy Spirit, the Church in all its human frailty replaced a literal reading of the Bible as my source of theological understanding. In the parish there are feminist liberals, family-values conservatives, and everything in between. Side by side we share one bread and one cup around the Lord's table. Anglicanism has become my foundation for learning more about God, and I appreciate its freedom of ambiguity.

Soon after settling in at St. Andrew's, I realized that its college ministry, minimal my freshman year, was now gone altogether. Honestly looking for Christian friends for myself, I suggested to the priests that we start something up again, and found myself appointed as the student minister with the task of rebuilding from scratch a campus ministry. With no idea how to do that, I tried hosting dinners, getting speakers, organizing worship services, and a hundred other things, but hardly anyone came. I was working hard, praying hard, but nothing happened. The clergy talked about how I was planting seeds, but I was looking for some fruit.

At the same time, I very much felt the need to be "successful" in other ways: to make a lot of money and/or become famous. Preparing to be an important diplomat who would make a difference in the world, I received a Rotary Ambassadorial Scholarship to spend a year at Moscow State University in Russia. But deep down I knew this was the wrong path. For so long I had lived according to the expectations of others, and being an ambassador or international businessman was never something I actually wanted to do. I remember how my father always talked about hating his job and my mother about wishing she had gone to a music conservatory instead of nursing school. "Do something you'll enjoy," they always said, "don't make the same mistake." So when some typically Russian logistical snags gave me the chance to back out, I chose not to go to Moscow. Though my parents and mentors still are dumbfounded, it was a key decision that set the rest of my life into motion.

During that sophomore spring I had no idea where I was heading, but not going to Russia became the surprising first step toward exploring a call to the Episcopal priesthood. My first taste of ministry came in Scouting, where I led chapel services at summer camp. I loved studying the Bible, selecting songs, and writing prayers. Soon I was asked to do more than chapel services, though. When campers were homesick, they got sent my way. Staff with real problems ended up at my tent. The same happened in high school, when I heard about devastating breakups, arguments with parents, and complaints about teachers. There was nothing I could do to help, but I guess people found me a safe person who would take time to listen to them.

Though being a clergyman has always been on my mind, I never spoke about it to anyone. I was afraid of what people would think of me. I was afraid my parents would think they were wasting their money on my first-class education, afraid that my high school teachers would be disappointed, afraid that my hard-earned status as an intellectual would be in question, afraid that other students would think I was crazy. In this training ground for investment bankers, a future priest was definitely "sketchy."

But my choice of the Anglican church and a call to the priesthood were strengthened in the aftermath of the brutal murder of Matthew Shepard, a gay college student from Wyoming. Since Matthew was a devout Episcopalian, I impulsively contacted my college campus' homosexual advocacy organization about helping with the vigil they were organizing. When asked to make spiritual remarks, I spent hours in front of the computer trying to figure out what to say—how could I offer something meaningful that would touch the souls of people I knew little about?

When it was my turn to speak, I was petrified of offending someone and making the tense situation worse. There were already people planning, in the name of Christianity, to protest Matthew's funeral with "God Hates Fags" signs—and here I was the guy from the Episcopal Church. Midway through my remarks, which were vague because of the Anglican Communion's conflict over homosexuality and my own confusion about its morality, I knew I was merely making myself feel good that we bothered to show up. So I skipped to the prayer I wrote, and after a moment of very holy silence, began: "Eternal God, unsearchable and un-knowable mystery, our refuge from one generation to another. To you we turn with sighs too deep for words."

When I finished, I sat down, and I listened. For the next two hours, students told painful stories about their victimization that to me were unimaginable. I could not empathize, *only listen.* A Native American student, beaten up in a town park-ing lot for confronting someone about a sexually offensive homecoming T-shirt, a gay student who received death threats, African Americans, Jews, Latinos, all say-ing that life at this campus was not nearly as comfortable as people made it out to be. And I wondered what responsibility the Church had in causing their pain and the hate and fear that led to it. Do we in our rush to grab hold of and proclaim the truth end up causing evil, sin, and death? In that night of holy tears, I learned a great deal, most of all that God's people are not all like me, and that I have a lot more to learn.

In a Christmas card from my rector, he wrote that that night confirmed in his mind my "true priestly calling." But as I became more of a presence at St. Andrew's and prepared to take the first official steps of the ordination process, I realized the need to deal more directly with the most difficult questions in my life.

Living for so long as a loner, I value the freedom of independence. But my lack of good friends for the last twenty years has taken its toll. At school I was never close with anyone: I never went on dates, never had a girlfriend, and did not go to any of the proms. I came up with lame excuses, maybe because it was easier to make them up than to learn the social skills I lacked but everyone else seemed to have perfected. In high school, the stories of other people's sexual encounters became cafeteria and locker room conversation.

With my Boy Scout values and evangelical Christian sense of right and wrong, everything sexual seemed pretty wrong. The whole issue went unspoken in my family. And as much as I stuck to my beliefs, I began to wonder if I was the abnormal one. At Scout camp, one staff member my age, Doug—a vulgar guy who chewed tobacco—constantly asked me, "You get laid yet?" knowing full well the answer was "No." After a while, Doug made a little addendum to his comments: "If you don't get laid soon, I'll know you're a fag." Was I?

Without real-world experience of romantic relationships, I often sought re-lease from my sexual tension through Internet pornography. High-tech versions of newsstand magazines, what I saw on the computer screen in a dark room by myself was all I knew of sex. Partly *because* it was so detached from reality, it be-came my reliable outlet. I could distance my public self from my private desires and let them wander and explore, without risking my image. This was better and safer than really having sex, or so I told myself. All along it felt strange, though, and fake.

Sometimes I felt like a hypocrite, masquerading as someone righteous but with a clear sense of the sinful habit I allowed to entangle me. Pornography kept me trapped in a cycle of disappointment with myself, and I wanted for a long time to break out of it by force of will. At other times, I realized that sexuality would not magically go away and that creating another prohibition for myself, or another benchmark for personal moral achievement, was equally self-defeating and missing the point.

For the longest time, sexuality was bound up in my image of the wild and crazy teenager, and later with the "work hard, play hard" frat guy. At first fraternities were a secret world of carnal pleasure that appealed to me as a way to be normal for a change. Later I thought fraternities were the only way I could make friends. Maybe playing beer pong, the college's favorite drinking game, was a necessary rite of passage. So many times on a Saturday night, I resolved to finally go to my first fraternity party. I would get dressed and walk almost up to the house, see the line of people outside, and every single time I turned around and went back home. The yelling and loud music, kegs of beer, people dressed up and flirting, all seemed to say "This isn't for you." "But what is for me?" I wondered. "Is there another way that won't leave me full of regret or set me up for a midlife crisis?"

I always was a person outside of every group but with a foot in them all, and most of my relationships were one-sided: me helping people. I felt like I was their counselor or mentor, never a friend, but I also wondered how I could help people when I didn't share their experiences: bad relationships, divorces, single parents, drugs, suicidal thoughts, bad grades, and the list goes on. From what people tell me, they talk to me because I am a patient listener, actually care about them, and am a stable person they can rely on or use as an example.

That last part is the trick. In high school I took pride in being that example. As much as I hated my reputation as a "fine young man," I wanted people to believe that I could *really* help them get their lives straightened out, so they would be good, just like me. I constantly wavered between questioning my own normalcy and trying to get the people I was supposedly helping to follow my Scouting ideals and Christian morals, ones that I then believed to be universally true and good.

Giving up that need to make people be like me, admitting that I really need to learn a lot of social skills, and making time to spend with people instead of just working have helped a lot. But there still is more. Dan's questions, "Did you get laid yet?" and the implicit one, "Are you gay?" would replay themselves in my mind. So many girls in high school and college told me, "You'd make a great husband," but because girls have always been my closest friends, I could never conceive of them as a "hookup" or a "chick" or someone I'd "get with," like the more popular guys did.

But the longer I remained a virgin, the more suspect I became as a closeted gay. And I secretly wondered myself. I never met an openly gay person before college, and even then homosexuality was categorically condemned by evangelical Christianity and Boy Scouting, still my two main sources of moral authority. But my sexual fantasies were about both men and women, and bisexuality was an even more foreign notion to me. I wondered if I was deluding myself by offhandedly excluding a possibility far more dangerous to my reputation than I could imagine.

I got to know a lot of homosexual people in college, and that real-life exposure made me question the outright moral condemnation I had been quick to apply to them—and to myself. I felt locked in between the pressure of those who said "repent" and the ones who said "come out." But both seemed too like a prepackaged solution. When I was honest with myself, I realized that my homosexual feelings, directed toward heterosexual guys, were essentially envy masked by lust; I most wanted to *have* what they *had:* the muscular body, the popular girlfriend, and physical intimacy.

And so I set about exercising more, taking care of my body and appearance, becoming more emotionally self-confident, and asking myself what I truly imagined for my future. Part of me really longs for a family, but more often I wonder if I am called to a more radical service in a life of celibate singleness. Even within my religious tradition, that option is uncommon and strange. And though the mystique of "getting laid" has faded from its earlier importance to me, to others I still appear as a closet gay: a suspicion which has become more problematic as I encounter homophobic attitudes in my church and Boy Scouting. When I came to college I was offended by the term *homophobia,* but I realize now how much the fear of being called gay has interfered with my own life and the lives of other young people.

There is an Ojibway saying that I carry inside my appointment book: "Sometimes I go about pitying myself while all along a great wind is bearing me across the sky." The great wind in my life has been Boy Scout camp, where I have spent every summer since I was fourteen. There, away from my parents and school, the woods provided an alternative reality, a break from the discouragement and stress of the rest of my life. When I think I have no friends, I remember all of my close relationships on camp staff. We have shared late nights around campfires, deep conversations about the important things of life, the sweat of hard work, and days that never seem to end.

For the last two years, I served as program director of the camp, and my main goal was to create an environment in which the teenage boys who were campers there could be themselves. It would be a place that pushed their limits but supported them when they failed, where people cared about each other and could reveal their weaknesses, where approval was not conditional on fitting into images, and masculinity not dependent on performing physically, smoking and drinking, or making fun of people. It seemed a near-impossible challenge, but it has begun to work. And all the while I became more free, more confident, more at ease. I became my own true self.

I had just begun to curb the widespread practice of using "faggot" as a put-down, when midway through the season the Supreme Court ruled that the Boy Scouts of America was free to exclude homosexual Scouts and leaders from the organization. So when a camper said to me, "Boy Scouts hate gays, right?" I was at a loss to give him a good explanation without disagreeing with official policy and risking my job.

Can I be true to myself and still be a Boy Scout leader? Can I best advocate for change from the inside or the outside? Those same questions face me as I consider more seriously a call to ordination, which would place me squarely within the institution of a church which has lost its former appeal to me. Hypocritical, irrelevant to daily life, and bound up in bureaucratic infighting, the church seems very distant from the radical way of Jesus as self-sacrificing servant and liberator of the oppressed, which is now the core of my personal faith. Even the sermons of my priests at St. Andrew's, once moving and intellectually challenging to me, now seem like empty words. So what if "Jesus died for you and would do it all over again if you were the only one"? What does that mean? I want to know what *difference* being a Christian makes.

One day a Jewish student asked me, "Do we see God?" I answered with a presentation of the differences between the mystics and the scholars, but he interrupted and asked, "What do *you* say?" I never thought about that before. What *do* I say?

This year, I have begun to spend much of my free time at Royalton Heights, a low-income housing development just a ten-minute drive and yet worlds away from campus. As I come to know the children there by name, I see them living in the midst of sexual abuse, alcoholism, illiteracy and poverty, hunger, neglect, and violence. Looking them each in the eye, touching their lives, and allowing their lives to touch mine, I find the moral conflicts of my time in Russia coming back again. How can I spend three dollars on an ice cream cone, when children ten minutes away are going hungry? How can I worry about a perfect GPA when adults there can barely read?

It is a daily struggle as I think about my future. People who are poor, hungry, in prison, suffering from the captivity of abuse and neglect, these are the ones the homeless Jesus I claim to follow called "blessed." These are the ones in whose lives I find God, yet I know that my comfortable lifestyle depends at least in part on their suffering. I still want to preserve myself, to feel fulfilled, to somehow recapture that part of me that got lost in my growing up. But Jesus says that the only way to find one's life is to give it away for the sake of the world. What will I say?

I don't know. I still struggle with my simultaneous desire for close friends and the freedom to love everyone and avoid any exclusive group. I enjoy being independent but realize that I need a source of stability for myself. I have been working on the social skills I never learned growing up, and I am less shy and afraid of self-disclosure. I have some close friends, male and female, with whom I can freely talk about my life, both the good and the bad parts. I struggle with sexuality, but now it is symbolic of the larger question of how to live out my vocation, as a married or celibate person. Liberated from the burdens of adult expectations and my own academic and moral perfectionism, I am beginning to discover my true self. And while I believe deeply that the Kingdom of God is our true human destiny and that no one will be truly free until all are free from oppression, I struggle to let go of my need for security and live a life of service, with no guarantees. This will be the struggle of a lifetime.

THE HATRED WITHIN

This writer wrestles with issues of family, ethnicity, and self-esteem. José, a twenty-year-old Latino junior, whose parents emigrated to the United States from Central America, explores his early experiences at school and his growing belief that his academic success made him not only "different" from other Latino/Latina students, but "better." Only when he reaches college does he come to understand this attitude and his disdain for his parents' relatively humble origins as a form of internalized racism. Drawn into the major Latino organization at his college and assuming a leadership role in student government, he comes painfully to name and eschew his self-hatred and embrace his developing Latino identity.

We were always horrible to the poor old man, Mr. Connors. He was the stereotypical high school substitute teacher—scolding us in a voice that echoed off the back wall and putting us to work with boring written exercises. We would respond by acting up, throwing papers, talking back, and pulling practical jokes—tormenting him in any way we could.

"Poor old guy," I thought. No more than five feet tall, he was bald except for the fringe of white hair that circled his bare dome. He wore rectangular eyeglasses and always came decked out in a full gray suit. I think it was the only suit he owned because he seemed to wear it whenever he substituted.

One morning, only a few minutes into the tormenting, the national anthem began over the P. A. system. As always, we stood up while the music played. Usually we did a good job of being quiet, but this time my friend Andrew and I kept joking and chatting as the music played.

When the song was over, Mr. Connors did exactly what I expected the typical "old-timer" would do. He began to yell at us for showing disrespect to the nation, but instead of focusing his obvious anger at both of us, he looked dead at me.

"Why don't you try that in your own country?" he barked.

Silence. I was in absolute shock. Did he really just say that? Without a second's pause I responded, "Why don't you try that in yours?" I took a step forward. There was no mirror there, so I have no sure idea what I looked like. But knowing how I get, I'm sure my face turned a bright red, my eyes became narrow and angry, my eyebrows crouched down. When I'm enraged, I make it very obvious. And it usually has the desired effect of intimidation because it's such a contrast to my usual jovial expression.

"This *is* my country," he answered back without a pause.

I took a few more steps forward. Not rushing to him, but with a slow threatening pace. "Well, this is *my* country, too."

"Well, how about your parents' country?" he asked, seeming not to realize that he was pushing me more and more, and that with every comment he uttered he was becoming more and more offensive.

"How about *your* parents' country?" I snapped back in the same mocking tone.

"My parents are indigenous," he said smugly.

The word at the time was unfamiliar to me. Although I was mad at myself for not knowing it (I wanted to step above this man as his intellectual and physical superior), I shot back, "What the fuck does that mean?" I didn't know what had come over me. I didn't swear at teachers, even substitute teachers. I joked, I kidded around, but I was always as respectful as my sense of humor allowed me to be.

He answered back by saying that the word meant his family had always lived here. Since he didn't look Native American, I had to assume he meant his ancestors came aboard the Mayflower or a similar absurdity. At that point I was at the foot of his desk, an arm's length away from his gleaming dome. I had no idea what I was doing. How can you ever be prepared for a confrontation like that? What did I hope to do when I reached him? Hit him? Spit in his face? I stood there barely a second before Andrew and my other pal Dave came from behind me and pulled me away, yelling, "Come on, José, back off! He's not worth it." And I knew he wasn't worth it. But what was it? What had happened to me? What did I think I was going to do? Why was I so enraged?

I wasn't the kind of student who turned violent so quickly, not with students and especially not with teachers. But something had come over me. My shock and disbelief at his words had drawn me magnetically toward him. Did he really say that? To this day, it remains the first situation that comes to mind whenever someone asks me if I have ever encountered outright racism. It was a slap in the face. But in hindsight the incident reveals more about me than it does about Mr. Connors.

Why did he look at me and not see a student like any other, or even an annoying teenager who had little respect for his country? Why did he appear to view me as a brown-skinned foreigner who didn't belong and deserved to have his identity questioned by a high school substitute teacher? That day in my sophomore year I felt like a minority. I felt like a Latino student. I felt like I didn't belong. Every other day, however, I took pride when my friends told me, "José, you're so white."

I'm surprised that it isn't harder to admit. As I see it now, I was a sellout in high school. I was a box-checker. I was a coconut. Name the insult and I was the epitome of it. In college, a friend referred to Latino students who didn't recognize their background or culture as "those who didn't associate." That was me. I didn't associate.

My high school was pretty diverse. The students in the Honors and Advanced Placement courses I took, however, were almost entirely white. I was lost, along with a handful of other students of color, in a sea of white faces. Given the fact that my classes were full of white students, it's no surprise that my friends were all white as well. I occasionally hung out with the one other Latino student whom I had known since kindergarten, but he, too, didn't "associate." He dressed in khakis and corduroys, polo shirts and button-ups, clothes that most people considered "preppie." And in my high school, preppie was synonymous with smart, and smart was, with a few exceptions, white.

Daniel, my good friend from the fourth grade on, was white with blond hair and blue eyes. My two best friends at the time, Nelson and Sara, both had dirty blond hair and piercing blue eyes. The pack of a dozen or so girls I hung out with junior and senior year were, with few exceptions, white. All of them were upper middle class. Most of them owned cars when they turned sixteen. These were my friends and I was proud of them.

But it was more than just the fact that they were white. I don't think there's a problem with having a lot of white friends, and I don't think I sought them out because of their skin color. They were just the people I saw every day. But what *did* matter was the attitude and thoughts that grew from this valuing of whiteness. Why did Mr. Connors's comments hit me so hard? Precisely because I was in denial of the fact that I was any different from my friends. I was like them. They were like me. It hurt me to be singled out as a Latino because, deep down, I really did believe that I was better then most Latinos. I was smart. I was hard working. I was ambitious. I was successful. I was funny. These traits, I thought, were uncharacteristic of most Latinos. Mr. Connors brought me down, and I'm sad to say that that was the biggest reason he upset me so much all those years ago. He tore me away from my misconception that I was accepted and belonged in the white world, which I saw as the embodiment of the good, happy, and successful life. He forced me to confront my own racism.

I talked to my mom about this late in my senior year of high school. I actually complimented her on her parenting skills. I pondered how she had managed to raise us in a way that made us better than most Latinos. It never occurred to me how wrong this thinking was. I would never have dared to repeat my racist thoughts out loud. But at the time, I thought them. I saw other Latinos and would often assume the worst. It was easy to convince me that one was a drug dealer or a criminal, as I was already biased against them. And I always made that distinction clear: I, and for the most part my nuclear family, was not a part of *them.*

But these were all thoughts I kept buried deep down inside. I continued to check off "Hispanic" whenever forms asked for the optional race/ethnicity classification. I took pride in it then. With so few Latinos who aren't wastes, I figured I was helping myself. They would see me as an anomaly, I told myself. I was unique and that made me very happy.

So, besides the little box that I would check off from time to time, my culture and background meant nothing. In fact, I would treat it as a joke:

"Quit stealing my money, spic."
"Hey, don't look at me, I'm just a spic."
"Ah, those spics just don't get it."
"You're such a grubby, grubby spic."

These were words I spoke, phrases that sprung out of my mouth and the mouths of my closest friends. They were always said in jest and I always approved. I found it funny, because I thought being called a spic was pretty damned ironic. I recall a white friend telling me I was more white than he: I acted white, I dressed white, I talked white. In essence, to him I was normal, and normal was white. You're not part of a gang? You must be normal, you must be white. You don't shoot up every morning or carry a gun? You must be normal, you must be white. You don't speak Spanish in school, you don't know how to Latin dance? You must be normal, you must be white. And I laughed when he said I was a spic. How funny, I told myself, me . . . a spic? I thought I was anything and everything but that.

Besides these occasional insults, which I then thought were perfectly fine, my days at school had nothing to do with being Latino. I was normal, I told myself, therefore my ethnicity couldn't be my prime characteristic. I considered it a contradiction. This kind of thinking—this utter disdain for who I was—is something most people will never be able to understand. I think it's natural for adolescents to question their identity, but I did more than just question: I denied everything that was natural to me.

I would avoid the sun as much as possible late in high school. Why? Because I tan pretty easily and I didn't want to get too much darker than other students. A slight tan was okay, but I didn't want to get carried away. I didn't want to stick out. Sometimes I would actually fret over my darkening summer tan. How can I remain as white as possible? I would look in the mirror each morning and wish not just that my skin and features were different, but that my whole ethnicity could be washed away. My self-hatred lay at the core of my being. And that's where I kept it.

When I brought my friends home, I would be ashamed when my mom and dad, whose English was so bad, spoke to them. I would cringe when my dad tried to crack jokes because his thick accent made him sound like some teenager in a man's body. I would be embarrassed when my dad swore without pause and told them some anecdote. I would never bring my parents to school as other children did for events or programs. Worst of all, the superiority I felt over Latinos I also felt over my parents. They were older, and more experienced, but because they couldn't communicate on the phone with their mortgage bank as well as I could, or because I understood the seven o'clock news better than they did, I felt like I stood on a higher plane. I used to look at my best qualities as traits that were somehow incompatible with the language I spoke at home, the color of my skin, and the values my parents taught me.

My story, my struggle as a Latino student in a white community, is also the story of my parents. The two cannot be separated. I now realize that much of my journey is a continuation of what they began so many years ago. They immigrated illegally from Honduras to the United States several years before I was born. In Honduras my father was on his way to becoming an engineer; my mother was a teacher in the school system. When they came here, they lost everything and were forced to take menial jobs in a country where the language confused them. Within months they were caught and sent back by la migra. When they came to the United States the second time, they struggled constantly but they also thrived. My oldest brother Armando, who is nine years older than me, immigrated with my parents. My other brother Steve, five years older than I, was their first-born in America and therefore was given the most American name they could think of.

Until I was 7 years old we lived in the "poor" section of our city. Surrounded by black and Latino kids, the feeling I can most recall is fear. I was scared of riding the bus to school. I was scared of the other kids. I was much like the scared white boy in a black neighborhood. I was scared of the others because I saw myself as inherently different. Even in elementary school, I had begun to develop the self-hatred and racism I would carry with me throughout my adolescence. All I knew was that while I was home, I had to cover my head with my pillow to drown out the police sirens and gun shots. But when I went to school and sat with the "smart kids" in the reading and math courses, I was nestled in a peaceful, white community. When my parents were finally able to save enough money, we moved out of the poor section and into the white community I had held so dear.

My father was, and still is, a drunk. Drinking was more than just something he did; through the years it had become a part of the man. I cannot imagine him without a beer in his hand, just as I cannot separate the man from the violence he inflicted. I respected and looked up to my father when I was young, but perhaps most of that came from my fear of him; fear of what he would do if I misbehaved. He was a pretty intimidating man, with a big round beer belly and huge biceps and calves. Some of my earliest memories are of me hanging off his extended arms, like a skillful monkey swinging along the trees. He had a loud, booming voice. His Spanish was always rough and convoluted. It wasn't that he spoke poorly, it was just the slang or expressions he picked up and used like Standard English: "So I told him, 'Hey guy, fuck you, okay? Fuck you.' " He seemed always to be telling a story, always swearing, and, of course, always drinking. He was in his forties, but to me he sounded like a teenager trying to be cool. But as I grew up, I came to see him as a meaner, darker character. He wasn't just big anymore, he was scary. His resonant voice, which sounded like he was yelling even when he was in a good mood, often brought me to tears.

The last time my father hit me is still vivid in my mind. I was in seventh grade. I had a paper route all through middle school, and I usually delivered the papers right after school. One weekday after school I went to a friend's house instead of delivering my papers. We hung out the whole afternoon, playing cards and telling stories. I didn't get home until a little after five o'clock. I froze when I saw my dad standing on our front steps as I rode my bike into the driveway. He stared at me, clearly angry. My dad didn't even wait until I was inside the house to start yelling. "Que hora es esta para llegar?" He asked why I was late. Living in front of the high school, I was aware of the crowd of students staring at me as my father scolded me. I went inside, angry that my father would embarrass me like that. As soon as I was inside he slammed the door and continued his abuse: "Donde estabas, babosada?" In Spanish he called me a little shit, irresponsible, no good for not calling and telling him where I was. His face was bright red as his words tore through me.

As he stormed upstairs, I knew where he was going and what he was getting. The door to my brother Steve's room, which is down the hall from the kitchen, opened up and I saw his face pop out. I clung to Steve as little brothers tend to do. "If he hits me, I'm running away." I whispered, "If he hits me, I swear, I don't care, I'm running away." Tears were already streaming down my face and I braced myself for what I knew was coming. I heard my father pound down the stairs. He swung a belt and I foolishly tried to block the blows with my hands as he screamed to me to put my hands down. Again and again he brought the belt down across my thighs. The pain spurted in quick stings. There's no pain worse to me, at least in my memory, than the feel of a belt against my skin. I just wanted him to stop. I screamed louder, begging him to stop.

Eventually he stopped, probably tired of my screaming and tears; he turned abruptly and went upstairs. I remained crying, curled up in a little ball on the kitchen floor. I wished that I had the guts to actually stand up, grab my things, and leave the house forever. I had imagined and planned it so many times before—what things I would take with me, where I would go. But it was never meant to be anything more than a product of my imagination. Instead of making my plan a reality, I cried, just as I had done so many times before.

I'm not sure if he had been drinking that day or if it was just a bad mood. I mean, why hit your son for being late? My father, and the way he made me feel that day, became the personification of Honduras and my cultural roots. He was exactly what I wanted to avoid becoming. When he drank, I saw him as a stupid, pitiful fool. And it didn't take long for me to project those feelings on to all minorities around me. Except my mother—who I saw as different.

My mother is the sweetest woman in the world. She would do anything for me, including staying married to my father. She did it for me because she knew a divorce would hurt me. She did it for me because she didn't want us to have to move out of our nice home in front of my high school. She did it for me because she needed my father to help pay for college. I guess I take it for granted that it really was all for *me*. But there's no doubt in my mind that it was.

I was born with a heart murmur, which made me vulnerable as a child. My family took extra care of me, but more than anyone my mother was anxious for my safety. It was partially because of her personality, but also due to the circumstances. The combination of my sickness at a very young age and the fact that I was her last child—forever her baby—meant I was bound to be treated differently. She poured the last of her motherly instincts and care into me. Well into high school she would tuck me in at night and wake me up in the morning. Some nights I asked her to rub my back and, though she jokingly complained, she always did it. My closeness with my mother was a contrast to my father, whom I saw as the enemy.

As I grew up, my importance in the family and in her eyes grew. Armando never finished high school and failed my parents' dream of being the first son to graduate college in America. Steve failed similarly after only two terms away at the state university. I became their last chance. Out of thirty-two cousins on my father's side, I am the fourth youngest yet only the second to go to college. When Armando got into trouble, my dad unloaded on him in the only way he knew how. My father's mother had supposedly whipped my father into submission many years ago. A rope would have been a welcome change to some of the instruments he was beaten with as a boy in Honduras. Yet somehow he grew up loving and thanking his mother for every bit of punishment she handed to him. Similarly, my brother Armando has consistently defended my father for the pain he has inflicted on us. He, out of all of us, has stood by as my father's sole defender. For that reason, among others, my brother Armando and I did not often get along. Even though he knew my dad beat me, Armando felt he had gotten it much worse and viewed me as a spoiled brat.

My mother did not defend my father for most of their marriage, nor did she fight back. She quietly withstood his verbal abuse whenever he drank too much. Over time, however, whether it was the freedom she felt now that she was in the United States or her own personal growth, she began to speak up and assert herself. When he yelled, she would yell back. Usually, though, she was the voice of reason to his temper tantrums. Most of the time he didn't listen and kept on shouting, stalking off in anger and sleeping for the next few weeks in the basement, where he had a bed. Eventually, when I was in high school, my father moved most of his clothes down there and for months at a time would not sleep in his own bed with my mother. Through it all they stayed together . . . although *together* is a strange word to use for two people who never spoke, never stayed in the same room together for more than a moment, and were married, it seemed to me, in name only.

When they argued, my dad would say anything to interrupt her, to keep her quiet, to regain the peaceful life he remembered from Honduras. Her spirit took him by surprise. This wasn't the way it was in Honduras, he must have thought to himself. This wasn't the way it should be. The wife, he felt, was supposed to cook his food, serve him his drinks and meals, clean the house, stand by him always, and never talk back. But my mom, the wonderful woman that she is, would not stand for that. She knew that she was an American woman now and that things would have to change. Sometimes, crying to myself, I would hope that my mom would just give up and stop arguing back. I respect her now for being strong, but as a little boy I just wanted the shouting to stop. But no matter what, I always blamed my father. He was exactly what I didn't want to become and yet he was also the biggest male presence in my life. In my mind he represented Latino males, therefore I had no desire to grow up and become one.

As easy as it is to blame my father, another side of him, a gentler one, surfaces in my memory. He isn't always the man who beat me and yelled at my mother;

sometimes he's the man who sacrificed so much for his family. During my sophomore year in college I was profiled in the college newspaper as a campus activist. The article described everything I'm involved in and all of my accomplishments. I referred to my mother as the "force in my life." A few days after it was published, I sent the clipping home. I was worried how my father would take it. When I finally spoke to my mom about it, she said they had read it together and they both had cried. He was not angry or jealous, as I would have expected him to be. She told me that my family had had a barbecue and invited all my family members. Sometime during the party, my father pulled out the article, which he had already taken to work to show his friends, and translated the article into Spanish for my relatives. My mom told me that everyone was so proud of me, but my thoughts were with my father. This is the man I call my dad, this is the man who, along with my mother, I strive to prove myself to each day in spite of his harshness to me. When I look back on my life, I won't see it as a success unless both of my parents see it that way as well. In the back of my mind is the knowledge that if things had gone differently twenty-odd years ago—if my parents had made just a slightly different decision, or if my father hadn't worked half as hard—my life would be completely different. I owe something to them, whether I like it or not, and that knowledge drives me to achieve, even when I feel that "I have too much to do."

That's why my narrative can't be separated from my parents' story. Their journey to the United States didn't end when they arrived for good, or even when they finally became citizens. The two stories continue in tandem, and just as important is the extended family they left in Honduras and the extended family that traveled with them. Growing up, I was often surrounded by my many aunts and uncles, cousins and second cousins. Just as my father became the embodiment of the Latino man—everything I didn't want to grow to be—my extended family also represented my ethnicity, my culture, and the target of my racism.

I saw my nuclear family as different from their little clans, and as I grew up, *different* also meant *better*. We Garcias were somehow special. My aunts were either single, divorced, or remarried. My cousins were constantly being arrested, having children out of wedlock, causing their parents grief. My cousins were the only Latinos I had any close connection to, so, to me their behavior exemplified all Latinos. They got into trouble, broke the law, stole, cheated, lied, and were disobedient. Although my brothers and I occasionally exhibited some of these behaviors, I nevertheless saw us as above it all. My female cousins got pregnant, moved in with boyfriends, married and divorced early—all the kind of behavior that I considered "subwhite." To do the wrong thing, then, as I saw my cousins do the wrong things, was to be less than white, to be *not* succeeding in America.

It is true that my brothers and I were generally better behaved, and better educated, and better mannered than many of my cousins. But instead of leaving the comparison there, I took it a step further and said that this was because they were Latino and were acting it, while we were Latino but we had somehow overcome our heritage. Overcome our heritage! This idea disgusts me now, and yet there was a time I didn't even question it. I didn't think of my family as successful because we were Latino or in addition to being Latino, but *in spite* of that fact.

The notion of overcoming my heritage recalls a poignant incident that occurred during a family vacation to Honduras. On the road, a small child around my age came up to our van and asked for a ride. We told him we didn't have any room, but as we started to drive we noticed that he had climbed on the back of the van and was prepared to ride with us, at fifty or sixty miles per hour, holding onto a ladder. At the time I disliked the little brat; I couldn't believe he had the nerve to try and hitch a ride from us. A dozen years later I think of that kid and can't help but see myself. If circumstances had been different, I could have been him. That notion would occur to me again and again, but at the time, and even as I packed bags for college, I still looked at that boy—at so much of my identity—with disdain.

My parents didn't pressure me much to succeed; I put the pressure on myself: I was the one who had to bring respect to my family after Armando dropped out of high school and Steve dropped out of college. Armando and I constantly argued, and he refused to come to my high school graduation. I think my success only highlighted his failure. My parents' pride in me was a sharp stab at him. He had been expected to be the first one to do so many things that I was now doing. Steve was more complacent, always assuming he would return to school and catch up with me. And that's how I left for college—angry with most of my family, convinced that I was better than my family and my heritage, and bearing the burden of bringing home what my parents wanted to see: a good report card and a college diploma.

For the most part, college was everything it was supposed to be: I was having the time of my life and meeting so many amazing people. It wasn't until my first meeting of La Unidad, the Latino student organization, that I had my first confrontation with the hate inside me. I had gone to the meeting because I felt an obligation to go. Despite my belief that I was better than my background, I was also confronted by the feeling that my status as a so-called box-checking Latino was what got me into college. Why else would I have identified myself as such? *Associate, identify*—words like these meant the difference between being seen as an outsider to the Latino community or a link within it. If you identified, that basically meant you acknowledged your heritage, you went beyond your box-checking status.

I went to that first Unidad meeting because I felt an obligation, not because I felt I would gain anything from it. I didn't want to be seen as a Latino student by the mainstream but I also didn't want to be seen as a sellout by the Latino students. My self-hatred and hatred of my ethnicity was deeply buried, and I had no intention of making it known. I barely thought about it, and that's the way I liked it. But my first weeks at college were characterized by a sense of exclusion, a sense that I didn't fit in anymore. Dressed in Abercrombie and Fitch, attending their parents' alma mater, most students seemed so different from me. I was afraid someone would suddenly discover that I didn't really belong. I had an overwhelming feeling that I had to start my life over again, build myself back up, yet I didn't know who I was or how to go about it.

That first Unidad meeting we all sat in a stuffy room, the Latino students on display for one another. I was immediately hit by the feeling that I was very *unLatino.* The others somehow exuded more Latinoness. It was in their accents, the speed of their speech, the Spanish words they mixed into their English. They all talked about home cooking and dishes that they loved, and although I loved my mom's home cooking, I didn't know the correct names of the foods she prepared. But most important, they all seemed to know more about their individual cultures. They were more culturally, socially, and politically aware than I ever thought I could be. What did I know about Honduras? I couldn't even tell you what kind of government they have there, let alone how "my people" are doing. What did I know about Latino culture besides what I learned in school, which was nothing? My cultural ignorance had never even occurred to me as a problem; suddenly it became a very big one.

The worst moment was when we went around the room and introduced ourselves. One by one they spoke, pronouncing their names with a full Spanish accent. Some people I knew always did so, but a few caught me off guard. *Drew* became *Andres, John* became *Juan;* the speed at which people said their names increased, and as we quickly went around the circle, I didn't know what to do. Of course, I could easily have used an accent, but I never did and I didn't want to do so just to fit in. I even had a fear about doing that. What if it came out badly? What if I couldn't even say my own name right? I didn't want their eyes on me, them to snicker and know that I was only a fake. I just wanted to come to the meeting, sit back, and feel like I had made up for the fact that I checked *Hispanic/Latino* instead of *white,* which is what I wished I were, or *Other,* which is what I felt like.

When the introductions finally came around to me, I blurted out my name, *José García,* with a full accent. I felt like a sellout, not because I didn't want to be Latino, but because I was willing to hide my true self in order to be accepted as Latino. I was more confused than ever. Inside I knew that I thought poorly of Latinos and that my racism was deeply rooted, yet I was willing to act unlike myself in order to be accepted by my Latino peers. I didn't know who I was or what I wanted. I only knew that I wanted to be accepted. I wanted to please everyone, and was finding I couldn't please anyone.

My confusion got worse before it got better. I had gotten involved early freshman fall in my college's student government. Representing the student body, the organization constantly worried about whether or not they were truly being representative. So they would literally take a count based on gender and race/ ethnicity. I wasn't just a normal involved student, I was the token Latino, or so it seemed to me.

The word *token* was one that I would get to know well as time went on. Token Latino, token minority, people of color versus minority, ignorance versus racism, the relationship of power in racism, prejudice, institutional racism . . . these were all terms and phrases that I had never been acquainted with before my first year at college. I had a crash course in being nonwhite. I'm convinced that if you asked a white person, half of those terms would draw a blank response. It's not simply because they're white, but because they have had no contact with these issues. I'm a great example. I had never considered any of these issues, yet I was that person of color, I was that token minority. I was *supposed* to know. That lesson came to me during a student government meeting when I was asked to give my opinion as a Latino. I wasn't asked to give it as a student who happens to be Latino, but to give the official Latino opinion, as if all we Latinos got together one day and took a straw poll on a number of issues, all of which came out unanimous. There is diversity among races, but there is also diversity within races. I wanted my friends to be color-blind. I didn't want to be seen as Latino or ethnic or other. In a short time I went from hating my ethnicity to not minding it, but still being grateful when people could ignore it. The inner hatred I had grown up with was gone, but something rotten remained. I still had a way to go before I would embrace and actually be proud of my culture, rather than just tolerating it.

I continued going to Unidad meetings, continued struggling through my ignorance. I heard other students of color talk about the racial issues they had confronted growing up. I began to find more and more aspects of my childhood that related to their childhoods—similarities in being the children of immigrants. Most of all, I was surrounded for the first time by students who shared my skin color and also shared my academic success. I was no longer the exception in a sea of white faces. The wall I had built up between myself and my ethnicity began to break down. Despite being 70 percent white, my college introduced me to diversity. So before I realized it was happening, that lifelong correlation between *white* and *successful* stopped making sense to me.

I recall a late-night conversation with my friend Jake who is half Latino and half white. He casually mentioned that he was against affirmative action, that he saw it as reverse discrimination against white students, and felt that it only served to emphasize racial lines more. As he put it, "Why should white people today have to suffer for what white people in the past have done?" This comment led to a passionate debate. I argued that, despite what he believed, there was a racial divide in this country. It was social, as evidenced by my high school substitute's behavior years before. It was economic, as evidenced by the poor section of my hometown that bussed me in and out when I was younger. It was educational, as shown by all the white faces in my upper-level classes from elementary school through high school. It was cultural, as witnessed by the isolation I felt at my first Unidad meeting. "You're right," I argued. "Most white people of today have nothing to do with what happened years before. But that doesn't erase the problem. That doesn't change the fact that minorities are still suffering because of what happened years before. Furthermore, whether whites are directly at fault or not, it doesn't change the fact that whites have benefited. Because others have lost, whites have gained. It's not a question of right or wrong—it's just the way things are. But that doesn't mean we shouldn't try to change things." Jake kept arguing that minorities just needed to "stop feeling sorry for themselves."

That night I developed my own theory on this subject: "Look Jake, it's like life is this one big long-distance race. Ever since the race began, the minority runners have been oppressed, kept back, slowed by slavery, by conquest, and so on. And all this time the white runners have been getting ahead. Suddenly, all restrictions are dropped. No more slavery. No more segregation. Everything is made equal. But is it really equal, Jake? All that equalization under the law doesn't change the fact that all these white runners have had centuries' long head start. How does that translate to real life? In economics, in education, in social attitudes? These are all big problems and they call for big solutions. I don't think affirmative action is the best long-term solution, but it is a temporary one until people are willing to make the bigger commitment."

Jake said that he used his Latino background to get him into college, just as he used his running talent (he was recruited by the college for cross-country). That was all his identity as a Latino meant to him. With my mind entrenched in issues of race and ethnicity, I was outraged at him for saying something like that. And yet just a few months before I could have said the same thing.

At college, once I began to deal with the long-suppressed issues of my ethnic identity the floodgates opened. Sometimes I got in serious arguments and found myself saying things I couldn't believe I was saying. In those moments I claimed all white people were racists or the United States border should be completely open all the time. But that was part of my learning process, of pushing forward. I was in the process of testing, trying things out, seeing where thoughts would go and then evaluating whether I still believed them or not. I was trying to find myself under years of buried ignorance, self-hate, and prejudice toward my own culture.

In another late-night conversation with friends, I recalled that small boy who had wanted to hitch a ride with us in Honduras, whom I had disliked so much. "What's so different from me and so many of the naked kids I see running around in Honduras, begging on the streets? Sure, I think my drive and my work ethic have been important, but I think the key difference has been the opportunities I have had—attending schools that are leaps and bounds above anything in Honduras and pursuing so many things that my parents never had the chance to. And yet it might have been completely different. It could be another kid sitting here today and me in Honduras. That's why I don't think I'll be happy in life unless I'm helping them realize their own potential. I want to give others all the opportunities that I had." And the minute I said it, I knew I believed it with all my being—I knew I would never look at my role or purpose in life in the same light again. I was never religious, and yet I felt I had found my calling. I knew then I could never be an investment banker or businessman. My place was in service, in education, in any field where I could use my skills to improve the lives of others and help them open doors.

In spite of my new insights, the same demons remained inside of me. When you look at yourself in the mirror for years and see someone who is unattractive because of his skin color, hair color, speech, and other characteristics, those negative feelings don't go away easily. I felt I had a big nose, that it was too round and not slim enough. I hated the fact that I would always be a good four inches below average height. I even came to dislike my boring brown eyes and black hair. My own insecurities about how I looked and fit in remained. Even though I was growing intellectually and emotionally, I had not yet purged many of the old thoughts that haunted me.

My self-hatred was also hatred of my background and my relatives. My perception of myself and others had been altered by all the new people I met at college. Generalizations I had held to—that all Latinos are lazy, all students of color are inferior to whites—were shattered while I was at school. My relationships with members of my family and their relationships with each other had also been forced to change as a result of my absence. My leaving home was exactly what my family needed.

Just how far the healing had progressed is evident in a radiant photo taken at Armando's new apartment, which he shared with his fiancée, Molly. In the photo, we're embracing each other tightly. My father has one arm extending far to his right to reach my brother and the other hand is tightly grasping my mother's shoulder. My mother is smiling beautifully; it's a genuine smile. She seems truly happy—happy to have her family all around her. You can almost read her thoughts: she has her family together again, different than before, but together. Caught in that photo is me kissing my brother. For no other reason than because I was feeling happy and wanted a funny picture, I embraced Armando's face and kissed him on his right cheek. He remained smiling while looking at the camera, his arm tightly around me. After the photo was taken, Armando wrapped his arms around me and pulled me in for a full hug. Steve came over as well. And right there, in the kitchen of my brother's new house, with my parents and his fiancée watching, Armando began to apologize to me for mistreating me for years and years. As we embraced, Armando sobbed, "I'm so sorry, José, I'm so sorry for everything I put you through. But you know I did it because I loved you and wanted only the best from you. You're my little brother, there's nothing I wouldn't do for you." He then opened his arms to Steve, and with the three of us wrapped in each other's arms, forming a little circle, Armando continued, with tears in his eyes, "You guys are my brothers, my little men. I love you two so much. So fucking much! I'm always going to be there for you guys, whatever you might need. You fucking come to me, all right? There's nothing I won't do for my brothers." The tears were coming down my cheeks now, and Steve, usually calm and reserved, also began to cry. Our coming together in love and reconciliation was the climax to what I had slowly been developing the whole year—my acceptance by and of my brothers after years of alienation. While we hugged, I remember hearing my mother tell my father to look over at us. I sensed her deep inner happiness. She was so proud to see her sons finally come together.

Several months later I took another step forward in my journey. I interned in Washington, DC, working as a research assistant for a nonprofit organization focused on strengthening the Latino community. I found myself surrounded by people who had centered their lives around making a difference in the Latino community. Two men in particular, leaders in the organization, further altered my views on Latinos. Both had gone to Ivy League schools and their résumés were packed with incredible experiences. They could have done anything they wanted to in life, but they chose to give back to their respective communities. I met many prominent Latinos through them and my perceptions of Latinos, which had expanded exponentially since high school, was further improved. Any significant prejudices I had were eliminated by the success of these two men. I admired them *and* they were Latino. In the past, I would have joined these two facts by thinking, *in spite of* their being Latino. It's such a small detail and yet reveals so much about how I thought.

I was still working in DC when I flew home for the weekend to see the production of a musical in my high school. I saw the show with Dan, my friend since the fourth grade. I told him about my involvement in student government, my increased activism, and life in general at my small liberal arts college. But since I was in DC at the time, I also mentioned my internship and the great time I was having. With pride, I pulled out my business card. "Empowering the Latino community?" He read off the card, smiling at me and waving the card to a mutual friend from high school. "Look Chris, José is Latino now. Look at the card. Our little brown friend's creating community!" His tone was mocking and they both began to laugh as they gazed at the card. "This is the biggest load of PC bullshit. I can't believe you're a part of this crap!" He laughed louder, staring at the card in disbelief.

I felt crushed. This had been my childhood friend? This had been the life that I had enjoyed so much? I was ashamed of who I had been and what I had believed, but I didn't think the shame ran so deep. Was there anything I could turn back to? Was there anything that didn't stink of my racism? It had been a while since I felt so uncomfortable, fidgeting in place, wanting to be anywhere but there. And right then I was struck with a realization that came just before I would have begun feeling sorry for myself. "Hey Dan, fuck you," I said. His mouth opened in disbelief, his laugh stopped in midbreath. I continued, "Just because you haven't grown up in the last two years, doesn't mean that I haven't."

"Hey Mr. Latino, don't take it personally. I just think that doing this sort of thing is very unlike the José I knew in high school," Dan said, handing the card back to me.

"A lot about me is unlike the José you once knew. People change, Dan, and ya know what? I'm happy with the changes I've made." I gave both of them one last look in the eye and then returned to my seat in the theater. I don't think I was particularly articulate or eloquent, but I got across what I wanted. I didn't back off.

As the show continued, I recalled that late-night conversation with Jake and the passion with which I spoke of privilege and racism. An image of that boy from Honduras came to mind and I again imagined myself living his life. I then remembered Mr. Connors, the substitute teacher, and the anger he had made me feel. I reflected on the dozens of conversations in which I called myself a spic and spat on my culture. Finally, I thought of my mother and father and all they had given me and continue to give me. Dan, who silently took his seat next to me, had accused me of being "very unlike the José he knew in school." I smiled, happy that he was right, proud that I didn't joke along with him and deny what I had spent two years forming, what is still forming, what I hope never stops forming.

UNA MUCHACHA DECENTE

Jessie, born in Puerto Rico, emigrated to New York City with her family when she was a young child. She explores in this case how her strong family ties, others' belief in her, and her own commitment helped her avoid the possible dangers and complications of her urban community. She describes how she remains connected to her friends and family, despite her experiences with gang violence, indifferent teachers, and under-resourced schools. She watches friends drop out of school, deal drugs, and become involved in local gangs because they seem to lack the support systems she has. College provides a new set of challenges, as she faces the ignorance of others and the impersonal academic demands of the institution. Jessie's determination to succeed makes us believe that indeed she will.

I was 17 years old the first time I considered purchasing a gun. Many of my childhood friends were dealing by the time we entered high school and had already established contacts with gunrunners and black market dealers around the city. There was nothing to it, I thought. I would use what was left of my summer earnings to cop a gun from one of my boys and still have a little extra cash to thank them for their services. It would be as easy as going to the bodega to buy my mother a can of Goya beans. It was only a matter of stepping out of my house and speaking to Joey, Red, or Edwin and everything would be set. A gun guaranteed security, ensuring I would never have to prove my physical prowess to individuals who mistook my reticence for an inability to defend myself. I was tired of fighting. A flash of my gun would emphatically demonstrate my capabilities without necessitating the physical and emotional distress that every altercation induced in me.

One crisp Saturday morning when I was 16 years old, I was buying my mother a birthday present at a nearby mall when two female gang members attacked me. I can still hear my glasses crash against the floor as the first attacker struck my face with her fist. Disoriented at first, I quickly caught sight of my assailant's face and employed the most crucial defense strategy my older brother taught me during childhood: never stop swinging. By the time the cops arrived on the scene, the officers had trouble distinguishing the perpetrators from the victim: one of my attackers fearfully stood over me while I threatened to take the life of her comrade whose neck was firmly locked underneath my arm. A female officer demanded that I loosen my grip but I would not budge. Two officers then restrained me while another officer helped the first attacker to her feet. After a few witnesses intervened to help explicate the situation, the officers arrested the gang members and advised me to press charges. I refused. Moments later the girls were released. The first attacker sauntered away, tears streaming down her cheeks while her sidekick cupped her hand over her bloody nose. I sat listlessly on a bench watching their figures diminish as the distance between us increased. A part of me wanted to catch up to the dynamic duo and apologize for their injuries. Another part of me wanted to keep swinging. When the girls were no longer in sight, two officers accompanied me to my apartment. My heart sank as I realized this incident could potentially mark a succession of violent attacks. It was only a matter of time before I would confront gang members seeking revenge for their kin. Gang violence never ends.

When I was 17, my attention dramatically shifted from myself to my family's welfare. The day before Mother's Day, I was practicing how to parallel park a few blocks away from my neighborhood when I received a frantic phone call from my mother—she walked into our apartment moments after a band of robbers had burglarized our home. Minutes later, I arrived at the apartment. I embraced my mother as she stared blankly at the debris concealing much of the floor. I slowly inched my way to my bedroom remembering I had purchased my mother's present earlier that morning. I searched through the rubble hoping to find my mother's necklace. It was gone.

Perhaps the most troubling aspect of the entire incident was unveiling the robbers' entry and escape routes. We live on the first floor of our apartment building. The burglars climbed through our living-room window, adjacent to the courtyard of our building. Our courtyard is one of the busiest spots in our neighborhood. People constantly pass through this area, play handball, smoke, drink and have barbeques and birthday parties. Needless to say, there were countless witnesses who were either in cahoots with the suspects or unwilling to speak up. A few days after the robbery, my brother's friend informed us that the attack was a mere warning. Local gang members in our neighborhood were after my brother. My brother was spotted wearing a sweater with yellow lettering during his last visit from college. Yellow was a Latin King color. Luckily, my brother returned to school the night before the robbery. Nevertheless, it was only a matter of time until our apartment was robbed again or any one of my family members was attacked. I refused to sit back passively waiting for the cops to notify us once they apprehended any suspects. My family was in imminent danger. I had to take matters into my own hands.

Although I had never officially joined a gang, I knew plenty of individuals in my neighborhood who would fight for me in the event of an altercation. My brother's "boys" assured me they were more than willing to defend me when and if "anything went down." Nevertheless, I did not want to get anyone else involved. My family's welfare was my responsibility. On my way home from school, I found my friend, Red, at a pizzeria across the street from my building. Red had dropped out of high school two years earlier and started dealing when he was 16. He had heard about the robbery and asked if there was anything he could do to help. It was at that moment that I informed Red about my interest in purchasing a gun. Surprised at first, he asked what I planned to do with it. I did not know how to respond. I arranged to meet Red and his "affiliates" three weeks later in front of my former elementary school building. When the time came for the exchange to occur, I was nowhere to be found. As much as I rationalized my intentions for owning a gun, to the point of neglecting the potential consequences for purchasing an illegal weapon, something inside kept me from taking that final step. When the time came to protect my family, I was ready to put my life on the line. Nevertheless, I could not fight fire with fire.

Decisions, decisions. Verdicts like yes, no, maybe, sometimes, always, and never were shaped by the values and experiences that have influenced my upbringing. My life experience has taught me to value integrity, respect, and honor in any decision I make. My parents raised us in a pious home where these values were instilled in us from the moment we opened our eyes. Speaking respectfully and honoring our elders, believing in things unseen, caring for those in need, learning that love does not have a face, color, or creed shaped our perceptions and interactions with the world around us. While we did not have many material possessions, these principles were priceless as they carried us through difficult times and had even more significance when life was blissful. As I grew older, my love and respect for people and my faith enabled me to chase dreams I sometimes had trouble envisioning. Others' faith in my abilities was also a catalyst for my drive to succeed and make decisions that would not compromise my sense of responsibility and would bring me closer to my goals.

My friends, teachers, and loved ones believed I possessed the ability to change circumstances that threatened to undermine my quest to succeed. I had the potential, capacity, and intelligence to make it. There were "no ifs, ands, or buts about it," as my third grade teacher would often say. However, it was up to me to use my God-given talents without having to resort to the same methods and philosophies that many of my peers and family members were utilizing to resolve immediate needs they felt their parents, teachers, government, or society routinely neglected. While I grew up in an area where violence and criminal activity tainted my childhood with the uncertainty of a brighter tomorrow, at the end of the day there was a home I returned to—a support system that was unlike anything I would encounter throughout my daily treks to school or my childhood masquerades with neighborhood peers. I learned the greatest lessons about life within my Brooklyn tenement, our second home since migrating from Puerto Rico. Mom and Dad lived a life of faith that taught me I could move mountains—and over the course of my life, I would.

I was born amid a flickering light dangling from the ceiling of maternity ward C12 in *Hospital de El Distrito De Aguadilla,* in Puerto Rico. To my left was the vast Atlantic—the waves slapping against the surf as gentle zephyrs pulled the tide further onto the shore. To my right sat my father, his rugged hands enveloping his face as he stared blankly into the eyes of his creation. Mom cradled me in her arms, her cheek pressed against my rosy forehead as she whispered a prayer. How could he possibly manage to support a family? There was no money. Nevertheless, in the midst of all the uncertainty, there was hope.

When I was living in Puerto Rico, my grandmother and I often sat outside right before the stars emerged. We would start counting *las estrellitas* one by one until the sky was flecked with a mosaic of radiant white flecks. By then there were too many stars to count. I remember wishing I could fit the sky into my pocket when I was a child. When we moved to New York City, the sky changed. At night, my Brooklyn sky did not reveal the sea of stars that poured out of my Puerto Rican sky. Nevertheless, sunny days were still as bright as my grandfather's sapphire eyes. Rays of sunlight glistened, reflecting from bottle caps and shards of glass strewn across broken sidewalks—remnants of street-corner brawls from the previous night. Although my surroundings were remarkably different, it was only a matter of time until I called my Brooklyn apartment home.

My first home in New York City was the maroon monolithic housing project at Mott Haven Avenue in Brooklyn. The streets were peppered with empty crack vials discarded from the binges of the previous night. Over the years, I became familiar with the colors of the caps: red, blue, green, and purple. The red caps were the most common. When my father had saved enough money from working as a custodian, we moved to another area.

Our situation moderately improved. The smell of urine in the halls of 2364 Decatur Avenue was slightly less pungent than in the Mott Haven projects. Unfortunately, the proportion of stabbings, shootings, and drug use in the area had not altered. Our apartment was broken into my senior year of high school and my older brother got mugged three times before turning 18.

I still remember the challenge of writing with mittens on my hands. On cold days it was the only way to finish the multiplication tables in my CIMS book. The orange glow of the space heaters was our only source of heat besides our coats. My father had explained that the landlord sometimes forgot to send oil to the building. Nevertheless, we needed to complete our homework, not because my parents nagged us but because it was the thing to do. To my siblings and I, it was what every child did before watching TV or going to church for *Missioneritas* or Royal Rangers (religious equivalent to Girl/Boy Scouts). The way I understood it, everyone in my family served a different function. As a child, my function was to complete my homework and tidy up the house before my parents returned from work. My parents' responsibilities included working, cooking, reading bedtime bible stories, and singing hymns and reciting prayers in the morning before we were off to school. Nothing got in the way of our roles and duties because we each contributed a vital component to our family's upkeep.

When we faced hardships, Mom taught us to count our blessings because "as bad as things get, they could always be worse." Mom and Dad knew all about worse—before being orphaned at 13 my father suffered years of abuse from his father, and he did not own a pair of shoes until he was 8 years old. Sometimes a cup of warm orange tea (made from orange leaves in his backyard) was the only meal he and his eight siblings would have for days at a time. One of fourteen children, my mother grew up on a small farm in Puerto Rico. She was pulled out of school by the sixth grade to help my grandmother maintain her household. Mom has also experienced her share of hardships over the course of her life. My mother's advice continues to shape my perception of the world today. In light of my mother's counsel, I thought my apartment was just as good as any. I did not mind the nights I slept in the coat I received over Christmas with the matching scarf and hat Abuelita (grandma) gave me for my birthday. Home was home. I was happy to have a roof over my head, clothes on my back, and parents who loved me when life was good and loved me harder when life was not so good.

Growing up, I viewed my block as my playground. My friends and I played hopscotch and freeze tag in the courtyard of our apartment building and invented new games when old ones became boring. Sometimes we would sit on the front steps of my building describing the shapes, animals, and people hiding amidst the clouds. My younger brother, Manny, always saw puppies—most often Chihuahuas or baby pit bulls chewing on toy bones.

Before church service on Sundays, my friends and I waited for Mr. Frosty, the ice cream truck, to stop by. Sometimes the myriad of options overwhelmed us—there was the snow cone, the Mario Pop with a gumball nose in the center, strawberry shortcake, the choco-taco, the banana split, chocolate, strawberry or vanilla milk shakes, etc. So many options, so little time before Sunday school started. Most of us chose the timeless classic, the Mr. Frosty special—a vanilla ice cream cone with multicolored sprinkles. One afternoon I discovered that twirling the cone fast enough created a "rainbow tornado." From that moment on, in remembrance of that momentous occasion, my friends and I would twirl our cones and admire our rainbow tornadoes before taking our first bite into Mr. Frosty.

When we walked home from school we were careful to tiptoe past Juanito's spot as he slept in front of the bodega, holding his plastic "change cup" imprinted with a faded Domino's Pizza logo—the red and blue ink was still vibrant, the green ink faded to a yellowish hue that reminded me of my elementary school's chicken noodle soup. When Juanito was awake he shook his cup like a maraca, his coins ringing like church bells that awakened me in the early morning when it was time to say my prayers and get ready for school. He told us stories of the good life in Puerto Rico, when he still had his right leg and would climb up palm trees to knock down ripened coconuts. Although he never told the same *quento* twice, his stories always ended with the same moral: "Be good to the ones you love, finish school, and never join the military."

Summer vacation was the happiest time of our lives. When school was out, games of "hide-and-seek," "steal the bacon," or "kick the can" filled our summer months. Only the kids whose parents *both* worked made trips back to Puerto Rico, Santo Domingo, or Florida for the summer. Nevertheless, when the sun beat down on our backs and plumes of steam began to rise from the scorching asphalt, nothing could beat dancing in front of open fire hydrants. When the sun hid its face, we spent most of our summer nights teasing the sky as we tried to outrun the moon. It did not matter how long or how fast we ran—it seemed as if the moon was sitting on our shoulders the entire time.

For years this was my childhood. I lived to be outside with my neighborhood friends, cousins, and brothers discovering new adventures. However, as I became older my mother began to restrict my outdoor privileges. By the time I turned 12, I was forbidden to hang outside with my friends as I was "becoming a young woman and the streets were no place for *una muchacha decente* (a respectable young girl)." To this day, while I understand my mother's intentions, I can still feel remnants of my resentment as I relive that brisk April afternoon when my friends stood in our courtyard patiently awaiting my arrival. I never showed up. In my eyes, this was probably one of the most abominable decisions my mother ever made. It was a source of contention between my mother and I for years thereafter. Why couldn't I go outside and play with my friends? *Muchacha decente?* At 12 years old, who wasn't a *muchacha decente?* I just wanted to play handball, basketball, stick ball, or freeze tag. What was so vile about playing hide-and-seek in our apartment building? I could not see how these recreational activities could threaten my status as a decent and respectable girl.

For months I would stare outside from our first-floor window watching my friends play in our courtyard and longing to once again be a part of their world. They were only about five feet away from where I sat, and yet they seemed so far away from me. Sometimes my buddies invented basketball games where they used my arms as a basketball hoop. I held out my arms in the form of an oval from our living room window as Luis, Eddie, Tony, and Stephanie took turns shooting the basketball into my arms. They stopped playing when my friend Stevie accidentally missed my arms and busted our living room window. Nevertheless, I could not give up. Sooner or later I knew I would once again be allowed to hang outside with my comrades. I convinced myself that this was probably just a phase Mom was going through—she would get over it in no time.

Days, weeks, and months passed and there was still no sign of change. When I grew tired of waiting for my mom to come to her senses, I attempted to sneak outside on numerous occasions. Not surprisingly, there was always a neighbor or a *comadre* who would stop me dead in my tracks because my mother had already notified them about her decision to restrict my civil liberties. After a while I grew tired of fighting with my mother because I knew she would not relent. From that moment on, my block never looked the same. Over the years the friendships I had developed throughout my childhood subtly altered. I would often see my neighborhood friends in passing but as we grew older, the glow of our childhood innocence dulled to a subtle glimmer as handball and kick the can evolved into the formidable behaviors and activities we were too afraid to talk about when we were children. I realized that the girls whose parents allowed them to chill outside with their friends adapted to lifestyles that often undermined their safety and well-being and severely limited their prospects for success.

Throughout the years, many of my friends became the people we spent much of our childhood trying to avoid—the men who promised to buy us candy if we delivered small packages in our backpacks; the feeble women with tracks of blood running up and down their arms who begged us for train fare or cigarettes; the gunrunners and gangsters we were too afraid to look at when we ran into the streets to retrieve our lost basketballs or handballs. Others died tragically before the age of 17. Some were killed during drive-by shootings, run-ins with rival gang members, or drug runs gone bad.

Unlike my friends who involved themselves in activities and behaviors that jeopardized their lives, my choir buddy, Anthony, was different. My sophomore year of high school, my chorus teacher invited me and three other students from our class to audition for the Brooklyn Academy of the Arts Program. Mikey, Anthony, Janelle, and I were told to arrive at the local community college one chilly Saturday morning to audition in front of six directors. When we arrived, there were approximately seventy-five to eighty students anxiously waiting to audition. We watched each student walk one by one out of the small auditorium, some with pink slips, some without. We soon learned that pink slips meant you made it. Luckily, for Mikey, Anthony, Janelle, and I, we all walked out of the audition with pink slips and bright smiles. Every Saturday thereafter we would arrive at 9:30 A.M. sharp (or risk being sent home) at the community college performing arts center for approximately four hours of vocal training and two hours of violin lessons. If we acquired more than two absences over the course of each semester, we were immediately removed from the program. There was no question—our Saturdays were grueling. Our directors were tough and oftentimes unforgiving. If any section was flat during a rehearsal, every individual in that section was required to sing the entire piece ALONE, until the culprit was discovered. Nevertheless, it was a small price to pay for making beautiful music. We learned about operas, symphonies, and other magnificent pieces of music created by composers we had never heard of before. We rehearsed classical pieces in foreign languages we didn't understand. And we loved every minute of it. Our chorus was well-known throughout the city and we would often perform at various functions and assemblies. We were on television on numerous occasions and in newspapers. We felt important. Mikey, Anthony, Janelle, and I looked forward to every Saturday (albeit with some apprehension). We were so thankful to have the opportunity to engage with a different type of learning experience and ultimately create something at the end of each semester that would make our friends and family members proud. Our performances were worth every embarrassing moment or seemingly endless rehearsal. We understood that at the end of every semester, our hard work paid off in a way that we never expected. Unlike school, where the benefits of our hard work were often not so clear, creating music in the All-America choir enabled us to embrace the fruits of our labor and show others a side of us we never really knew existed.

Although Anthony was ridiculed by many of his friends for spending his Saturdays *singing* in a choir, he felt the program kept him busy, away from his block and out of trouble. Anthony was determined to make it without dealing or engaging in illegal activities, and he involved himself in programs he felt would keep him "focused on doing right, you know?" We had "bright futures in our hands," he would often say. By our sophomore year, Anthony dubbed himself the "best tenor," while I was only a "mediocre soprano." Our beautiful music ended the morning I received the call that Anthony had taken his life. That afternoon I turned in my uniform. I could not bear the thought of seeing Anthony's seat empty during rehearsals. Young people are not supposed to die—especially not like this, I thought to myself.

Over the years, as familiar figures in my life continued to fade, it took some time to accept that death meant coming to terms with the reality that I could search every corner of the earth and never find these people again. As difficult as it was to say good-bye to people and memories that I cherished so deeply, I accepted these losses as something that would only make me stronger in the long run. I came to the realization that this was life and I needed to accept it in order to move on. My family's support and my mother's guidance helped me to keep moving as she reminded me *"hay remedio para todo menos la muerte"* (there is a solution for everything except death). I decided that nothing except death itself would stop me. I prayed that my loved ones and their families would find the strength to keep moving. I understood that such tragedies have a tendency to eclipse hope with anger as unanswered questions and grief oftentimes evolve into a bitterness that compels many to seek revenge, thus perpetuating the cycle of hate that news reporters and journalists so easily publicize in newspapers and two-minute news segments that depict the ghetto as a lost world without hope—without real people who hurt, feel, speak, live, and breathe like everyone else.

As the years progressed, I witnessed many of my friends lose sight of their goals and aspirations amid trying circumstances that rendered their determination futile. As hard as I tried, I could not figure out where it all went wrong. Many of us believed we would grow up to be doctors, astronauts, scientists, lawyers—bigtime people who worked downtown and donned fancy business suits. Others dreamed about becoming hip-hop singers, actors, and actresses—people we only saw on TV and on magazine covers. There was no doubt in our minds; we were going to make it big. However, there were others whose parents believed they would "turn out just like their fathers—no good, lazy, good-for-nothing, low-lives who will probably die young or spend the rest of their lives in jail." I can still hear Darren's mother yelling over his music: "that's right—you gonna meet yo father in jail—good fo' nothing, bastard." I believe many of my friends internalized these negative perceptions and were afraid to try because they were convinced they were going to fail. Darren wanted to be an artist but he dropped out of high school and started dealing at age 15. He has been shot on numerous occasions and has been in and out of jail since the age of 16.

Unfortunately, our schooling experiences gave us the same impression; we were not expected to succeed. I attended a large, overcrowded public high school made up of about five thousand students. Gang violence haunted my freshman year. My high school was a hotbed for violence between rival gang members who often clashed during our lunch periods. We were often forced to hide behind parked cars as we waited and waited for police officers who never showed up to secure our surroundings. Metal detectors, security guards who unjustly criminalized us, and dilapidated facilities were part of our daily reality. From the outside, our school resembled a prison. All of the windows above the first floor were barred with aluminum gates. Our lab rooms were a joke. Half the time we did not have materials to carry out experiments and would have to "estimate" our results. Our schools lacked essential resources and suffered from teacher deficits that tainted our educational experiences with disappointment and strife. We were lucky if our teachers showed up to class regularly. My senior year of high school, my physics teacher often walked into class about half way through the period and after taking attendance would take an "extended lunch break"—he would not return until halfway through the period the following morning. Furthermore, we were blessed if our teachers were qualified to teach the subjects they taught. Given these conditions and the varying needs of the student population, our schools were ill-equipped to manage the obstacles affecting students' lives outside of the classroom. Many of my friends walked into their schools carrying a world on their shoulders that kept them from seeing any tangible benefits in schooling. Their motivation to adhere to school demands dissipated in light of difficult circumstances that skewed their perceptions of a brighter future. Broken homes, neglect, physical and sexual abuse, and drug and alcohol abuse were but a few of the challenges that marred students' life experiences.

School environments that are incapable of assessing students' needs and experiences cannot provide students with an effective educational experience. Many of my friends and family members could not engage with school culture because teacher expectations and academic standards were sometimes inconsistent with their needs or experiences. School, the one place where students could escape the negativity surrounding their lives, if only for six hours, was not prepared to deal with their needs. Our school conditions told us we were not worth the expenditure because we were destined to fill the ranks of our predecessors. While there were not enough math textbooks to go around for everyone, metal detectors greeted us at the entrance of our schools supervised by security guards who treated us like the gang bangers, drug dealers, and criminals we were destined to replace. Our schools helped reaffirm our place in society—and our place was the streets, jail, or death.

Despite these circumstances, I enjoyed participating in my school's social scene. During our lunch periods we were allowed to eat outside on the main avenue made up of numerous stores and restaurants that overflowed with students when school was in session. When Foot Locker and Footaction publicized the release of new Air Jordan sneakers, Timberland boots, or Nike classics, we were always the first ones to know. During my freshman year of high school many of my friends and I found after-school jobs. I was employed at a pharmacy in Manhattan where I worked as an expert gift-wrapper and a stock clerk in the cosmetics department. At the age of 14, I was able to begin to assist my family financially. There was no greater feeling than being able to contribute to my parents' financial needs. My overtime also gave me the opportunity to purchase clothing my parents could never afford to buy me. I felt so independent and confident.

My best friend, Frankie, was my better half throughout my public school educational experience. We had known each other since the third grade and over the years had grown closer than sisters. We were involved in everything together. From hanging out, studying, attending club meetings and outings, tutoring each other in areas we struggled in, and attending church services and youth group meetings, we were one another's sidekicks—we were "joined at the hip," Mrs. Ruiz, Frankie's mother, would often say. Our temperaments also complemented each other. While we were both shy, somewhat quirky, I was a little more assertive and at times more impulsive than Frankie. She would always encourage me to step back and analyze situations and "slow down" before making any brash decisions. Throughout elementary and middle school, Frankie usually stepped in before altercations at recess erupted into fights. I was quick-tempered when it came to defending myself and Frankie often encouraged me to utilize positive strategies to resolve conflicts. Conversely, when I felt Frankie was being too much of a pushover, I encouraged her to stick up for herself and take risks. We were a dynamic duo who would one day become "famous physicians and discover the cure for AIDS and cancer." We were each other's support network. While many of our friends and family members were not as involved or engaged with school, Frankie and I kept each other grounded because our goals and aspirations were in the same place. We wanted to succeed to be able to help friends and family members who were unable to make it. We believed getting an education was the only way to make our goals come to fruition. A couple of days before going off to college, Frankie and I made a pact that we would "use whatever skills, talents, gifts, God has blessed us with to change the world and make it a better place—for everyone." We called this pact, the "No More Ghettos" contract.

Although many of us came from different ethnic backgrounds, we all came from the same kinds of neighborhoods and many experiences united us. There was no such thing as a social hierarchy. We were all working-class people of color going through many of the same struggles and challenges in our daily lives. Many of our parents were immigrants escaping a past of destitution and despair. Our parents pursued dreams and goals that might someday become manifest in the lives of their children. However, many students did not have a support system that helped them buffer much of the negativity surrounding their daily lives. It was all the more difficult for my friends who came from single-parent homes, who were foster children who experienced abuse and neglect, who were victims of domestic violence, or whose parents were substance abusers. Many of my peers who lacked a support system that would enable them to envision prospects for a more promising future just lost hope. Crystal Ruiz, one of my closest friends during middle and high school, dropped out and started dealing drugs because she did not believe that school would help her get anywhere. Crystal needed "money now to help my family, myself, and my mom—aint no one else gonna do it for me—I can't sit on my ass waiting for school to get me what I need . . . what my family needs." Crystal felt she did not have time to wait around for diplomas or college degrees because she felt she was neglecting the immediate needs in her family. She had four younger siblings to look after and a mother who was mentally ill. She never met her father. Her family's well-being was her responsibility.

Although many of the students in my class dropped out of high school before graduation, some of us still worked hard toward envisioning prospects for a brighter future. Something always told me there was more to life outside of my present reality. Although I did not know what that reality looked like, I hoped for a better tomorrow, dreamed of a brighter future just over the horizon and always tried to change the circumstances I had control over. When I was a child I imagined I had the world in my hands—I could change almost anything so long as I worked hard and prayed harder. I carried this blind determination with me throughout my life believing there was always something I could say or do to change situations that had the potential to undermine my goals or aspirations. Nothing would get in the way of my future. As I grew older, and the situations surrounding my life continued to change, I sometimes struggled to accept those things I could not change. When circumstances threatened my sense of responsibility, my determination to secure important aspects of my life would skew my rationality.

When it came to college, I had no idea what I was getting myself into. The fact that I was going to college was already a huge step for a young woman in my family. Not only was I going to college, I was going to one of the best liberal arts colleges in the country. I had no idea what that meant. It was not until I arrived that I felt the sting of isolation that accompanied my awareness of color and the implications of difference that separated me from the majority of my peers.

Move-in day at college was an experience I will carry with me the rest of my life. Just as I crammed the last box of my belongings into the trunk of my mother's Mitsubishi Galant, my brother drew my attention toward a fern growing in a tiny fissure between the sidewalk and the wall of my apartment building. "See Jessie, that's you right there. You gonna make it." I stared at the fern for moment wondering how life could sprout in such a miniscule, virtually arid world. I admired the fern for its strength and determination—for its ability to thrive despite such unfavorable conditions. Nevertheless, I realized the fern stood alone. Questions began to flash through my mind: Where did everyone go? Where was my brother? My cousins? My childhood friends? Growing up, I was convinced we were all headed toward the same goals, destined for a chance at a better life. Enmeshed in my quest for success was the safety and well-being of my loved ones. When I arrived at college, I realized I was alone. All of the familiarity that surrounded my everyday existence at home was gone. I was dreadfully alone.

When I reached my dorm room, I remember standing amidst my belongings not knowing where to begin. My roommate's family all joined in to help Olivia get settled. Mom left the instant I transported all of my belongings into my dorm room. One terse good-bye and she was off. No surprise there. She was afraid I would see her cry. Out of the corner of my eye, I observed my roommate and her family as they unpacked and organized her belongings. My bedroom at home was nowhere near the size of my dorm room. Where would I begin? Making my bed seemed like the simplest feat to accomplish at the moment. As I unpacked my bed set, I stared off into the distance for a moment as I remembered my mother's final words: "Don't ever forget who loves you, who you are, and where you come from." At the time, my mother's counsel seemed more like an admonition than a word of advice. I awoke from my reverie when my roommate's sister tugged my shoulder and offered to help me arrange my belongings. I do not remember responding but sure enough Nicole began to help me set my bedsheets. A few moments later I began to converse with my roommate and her family. I learned that my roommate's father was an engineering professor at Dartmouth and her mother was a stay-at-home mother with a college degree. After asking me a couple of questions about my neighborhood and background, Mr. Hanneman immediately commented on my use of *slang* in my vocabulary: "so—what exactly do you mean by *mad* hot?" Silence. What didn't he understand?

"Well, umm, I mean that . . . umm—I mean it's like . . . its really warm."

"ohh . . . ha ha ha . . . Ok—well then," he replied as his wife interjected:

"And your parents . . . what do they do for a living?"

"Well, my dad works as an assistant cook at a hospital. And my mom, she's a cashier at a pharmacy downtown, " I responded.

"Oh, ok. That must be nice . . . uh . . . to work in Manhattan."

I mean if you enjoy being treated like a second-class citizen, I suppose it would be nice to work on Madison Avenue. Customers often denigrate employees like my mother because they are perceived as dim-witted, incompetent, and altogether uneducated ghetto trash because of their accents. Yes, Ms. Hanneman, I can see how working downtown would be nice for individuals who enjoy that type of maltreatment on a daily basis. As much as I wanted to speak my mind I held my tongue. I merely nodded my head after her response. I was beginning to get accustomed to the awkward silence that followed my responses to their questions. I did not understand why, but they seemed a lot more uncomfortable than I was. Mr. Hanneman and his wife left later on that afternoon. Mr. Hanneman's final words: "You might want to write down some of those slang words and definitions you commonly use—I have a feeling Olivia will return home sounding a little like you." I smiled and shook Mr. Hanneman's hand.

A couple of hours later my hallmate's mother invited me into her daughter's room. "I saw your picture in the student directory—it says here that you are from Brooklyn . . . I am so happy my daughter lives right across from you. You are Latina, right? Maybe you can teach my daughter Spanish, I dunno—teach her about your culture . . . I'm so excited!" Once again, I responded in silence. I nodded my head, shook my hallmate's hand, and walked back to my dorm room. I never felt so confused in my life. That day set the precedent for the interactions and events that would shape my college experience thereafter.

My relationship with my roommate and hallmates started out fine. I treated and spoke to them just as I communicated with my friends from home. However, it was not long before I began to understand the implications of our difference. I could not relate to many of the subjects they discussed because I never encountered many of the authors they studied throughout their educational careers. They often made references to American classics that I had never heard of: *Anne of Green Gables* was among the most popular. They were astonished to hear that I had never read or watched such a "timeless classic."

I was told I had a Spanish accent, that I used "interesting street vernacular," that I spoke "urban." I was asked if I was ever shot at or stabbed, if I was "mixed or half-black," if I had any children. One student also asked me how it felt to be a product of affirmative action. I tried my best to ignore many of these comments. I needed patience because I realized I was also learning from their experiences and backgrounds. However, when I was called a fugitive, my relationship with my roommates and hallmates changed indelibly. That afternoon I had my headphones on as I worked on problem sets for my math class. My roommate and a couple of hallmates trotted into our dorm room. "There's my little fugitive," my roommate blurted out. One of my hallmates intervened and inquired why she called me a fugitive. "I mean, she's Puerto Rican. She understands." Everyone giggled and laughed and I ripped off my headphones. For a moment I feared my temper would get the best of me. I did not understand what one thing had to do with the other but something inside me burned. Nevertheless, as much as I wanted to say something, anything, I could not utter a word. I was perplexed. Why am I a fugitive? Because I am Puerto Rican? Or is it, I am Puerto Rican because I am a fugitive? Does being Puerto Rican somehow imply that I am a fugitive? And if so, HOW AND WHY?

I lost trust in my roommate and many of my hallmates after that day. While we all remained friends, I kept them at a safe distance and our conversations did not deviate from normal everyday exchanges. As different as their experiences were, I never made generalizations or erroneous interpretations about them or their backgrounds. I resented the comments they made about me, my experience, my ethnicity, my speech patterns, my style of dress, etc. I hated every minute of it. The majority of the time I simply did not understand how anyone could have such perceptions about my people or me. I also could not believe how such intellectually gifted people could make such misguided generalizations and assumptions. What I found most frustrating was their attitude toward my annoyance at their ignorant statements. They often chastised me for being "way too sensitive" and assured me that they could make such comments because they were my friends and meant no harm.

Those initial interactions with my roommate and hallmates affected my interactions with my peers thereafter. As the semester progressed, I heard more and more comments that undermined my self-esteem. I was no longer as confident as I once was. I became much more reticent and reserved. I did not want to share my perspectives with anyone because I was afraid it would give people more reason to judge me. I just wanted to chill with my peers and not worry about difference. I did not want to be different any longer. My difference made me stick out like a sore thumb when all I desired to do was chill and fit in.

When it came to academic life, I quickly learned that my best was not good enough. Quite frankly, my best could not get me a D in chemistry. I came into school wanting to be a doctor. That was my lifelong dream. However, when our chemistry professor informed us he would start the semester operating on the assumption that we learned chapters one through five in high school, I knew I was in for trouble. I was lost from day one. However, I was determined to learn what I did not know and ultimately catch up to my professor's lectures. Lab work was another story. I had never seen half of the materials and gadgets we were using to conduct our experiments. When I asked my lab instructor how to use certain tools or equipment, she would not bother to answer my questions. She often shook her head and told me to "hit the books" and get a personal tutor. I dropped chemistry after failing the numerous quizzes and lab exercises that I tried so hard to pass. I had never tried so hard at something and still failed. I became angry at college for taking my dream away from me—for making me feel incompetent and lazy. I also struggled in my other classes because I did not having the writing skills that my professors expected.

After a while, I stopped caring about my education. I felt so guilty for leaving my family and friends only to enroll in an institution I did not fit into. After a while, I did not want to fit anywhere at this college. I wanted to leave and forget all about my disheartening experiences. If this was what college was really supposed to be like, I wanted nothing to do with it. After my freshman year, I decided I would drop out and get a job to continue to support my family. This decision seemed sensible at the time. I knew I was capable enough to work. I had worked since I was 14 years old. I was tired of putting my all into something that failed me time and time again. College showed me I could not measure up to my professor's expectations even when I gave it my best. It was not my fault that the schools I attended were underfunded and that the math, science, and English curricula were consistently watered down to help more failing students pass state exams. When I arrived at college, I could not think, speak, or write like my peers. Who was I kidding?

At the end of my freshman year, though, I got to know students like me, some of whom came from neighborhoods that were in close proximity to my home. It was refreshing to find people who had experienced many of the same hardships upon arriving at college. It felt good to know that I was not the only one. I was not making things up. By my sophomore year of college there was a group of about ten of us who ate, studied, made *arroz con habichuelas* (rice and beans), watched movies, went bowling and often vented about our experiences at Swarthmore and our struggles to balance our sense of responsibility back home with our academic obligations. This support network helped us to stay focused on the greater goals ahead of us and overcome the difficulties that often demoralized our efforts to succeed. We were destined to make it—no matter what the cost.

The second semester of my freshman year I also took my first education class, where I started learning about students like me who came from inner city areas and attended public schools that lacked essential resources and suffered teacher deficits and administrative support. I also came to know professors who were willing to help me learn how to write and think about concepts that were important to me. When I interacted with these professors, I did not feel dumb or incompetent. A precious handful of professors helped me to understand that my lack of preparation prior to college did not reflect my intellectual capacity and that it was only a matter of time before I would be able to compete confidently at the level of my peers. My professors' drive to help me write, think, and speak college helped me to embrace the reality that I had the potential to achieve anything so long as I was determined to work hard and keep moving.

The morning I decided to meet Red for the exchange, I could hear my mother reciting the psalms and hymns she loved so much. As hard as I tried, I could not shake off one verse: "Even though I walk through the valley of the shadow of death, I will fear no evil . . . for thou art with me." When all was said and done, I realized I was far more afraid of the consequences of owning a gun than I was of anyone harming my family members. In the hood, violence never ends. I refused to feed the cycle of violence that claims the lives of thousands of children, young people, and adults living in hoods like mine across the United States. I had faith that my family members would be safe and I prayed for their protection every morning and every night. Today, while we live on the same block, in the same apartment, my family is still safe. In one form or another, purchasing a gun would stand in the way of my future. I simply could not let this happen.

There is no question: I will succeed. My success is based in the hearts of myriad friends and family members who continue to live out their hopes and aspirations of a better tomorrow through me. While I do not think I am special, I am loved by many people who believe in me. I cannot fail. I will not fail. There is just too much at stake.

WHAT IF I DON'T
WANT TO WHISTLE?

This is the story of a young black man who grew up living with his mother and half sister in modest circumstances in south central Los Angeles. In spite of economic hardships, his mother is determined that her children receive an excellent education. Orion attends a succession of mainly white private schools that prepare him well academically, even while they undermine his sense of racial pride. His struggle to achieve a sense of self, compounded by his battles with anxiety and his insecurities concerning relationships with women, makes for a very challenging adolescence. Only late in his college years does he open up in his relations with others, question his internalized racism, and align himself positively with the black community.

It was a bright California morning, but at 7:55 my classroom with its high ceilings was still cold, and I shuddered at the prospect of discussing race that day. In my senior English class at my boarding school outside of Los Angeles, I was the only black student in a class of eight. On most days the color of my skin was not an issue, but I dreaded the times when we talked about racial matters. Although no one voiced the thought, I knew that my comments on the subject would be assumed more valid than others'.

We had been assigned two essays to read the night before. The first was a paper explaining what the term *nigger* meant for black people, and the second was about the life experience of a black man in New York City. In the latter essay, the narrator had adopted a strategy of whistling classical music during his evening strolls in order to prevent whites from crossing to the other side of the street as he approached them. My muscles tightened as I anticipated the discussion, not wanting to hear ignorant remarks about race and then have to bear the weight of correcting them without appearing overly sensitive, angry, or condescending.

The class discussion began with the essay on the word *nigger*. Students searched desperately for a politically correct way to speak about the reading. "I thought it was interesting," said John tentatively and noncommittally. Brian added, "I guess it was good, but I just can't understand why black people would call themselves a name that is so insulting."

I remember the look Mr. Manson gave as he shrugged his shoulders in response to Brian's question. It was as if he were struggling to keep a straight face—like he had selected this particular reading as a practical joke. With his knowing smile, he seemed to be pointing out the stupidity of "those niggers" who don't even have enough sense not to insult each other.

I didn't know how to tell them any more eloquently than the essay had that the term *nigger* was not insulting coming from one black to another; especially when spelled with an "a" and not an "er," it was completely dissociated from the way racist whites used it, as far as my black friend Carter and I were concerned. I felt like a person of a religious faith trying to explain to nonbelievers why it was that I believed: Some things just can't be explained logically.

Not wanting to enter the conversation, I averted my eyes. My anger built; if the teacher had not understood the article and could not even regurgitate the arguments provided by the author, then why was he teaching it? Feeling powerless, I wondered what would have happened if I hadn't been present. Would the discussion have become an open forum for everyone to voice his or her condescension for blacks?

"Well, do you understand it?" Mr. Manson, as expected, asked me. I nodded in return. "Do you mind trying to explain it to us?" Even though it was a lost cause, I tried to make it clearer. Attempting to explicate the various connotations of the word *nigger,* I tripped over my words in anger and confusion for five minutes before I finally gave up all together and we moved on to the next essay regarding whistling classical music to put white people at ease. Everyone agreed that it was unfair to be black in New York and get treated as a thug. Then my friend Jay added, "Yeah, it's too bad, but at least he found a good way to get around it." There were nods all around, and I felt blood rush to my face. "That is not a viable solution to his problem," I blurted out. "The guy wasn't free! To be treated civilly you have to whistle? That means you are assumed guilty until you prove your innocence." I likened the situation to having to show someone a list of credentials, or having to shuck and jive, whenever you wanted to be treated with respect. "Can you imagine a nation of 'free men' who have to sing and dance in order to show that they aren't dangerous and be treated fairly? What would happen if you couldn't whistle? Or God forbid, didn't feel like whistling?" But I was the only person who saw how this was problematic. Reading the facial expressions around me, I could tell people thought that I was causing unnecessary trouble by being "too sensitive" about the issues, so I silenced myself.

In many ways, I fit the demographics for the stereotypical black male. I grew up in the inner city raised by a single mother without ever knowing my father. Yet, in other important ways, I do not fit the profile. My mother was an attorney, and as children my sister and I attended elite private schools on 90 percent scholarships.

My sister is three years younger than I am. We have different fathers, neither of whom ever married my mother; she tells us that at a certain age she wanted two children and then she got them—by two different men. My sister has had more contact with her father than I have had with mine. He lives in the same large West Coast city as we do, and my mom and sister run into him once every couple of years, often to my sister's embarrassment.

I do not know my father at all. I am told I met him once when I was 3. I'm not sure if I actually remember it or if I have constructed my memory of the incident: I just picture him lifting me up in the air in our front yard. The only photograph that survives of him is his driver's license. I know that he was 6' 2", weighed 201 pounds, and shares the same last name as me.

My mom used to drive me by an apartment building, pointing and saying, "That's where I met your father." That statement always left me uneasy, and I struggled to make sense of the motivations behind it. What exactly did it mean? Was it supposed to comfort me? Did it comfort her? From time to time, she would drop one-sentence descriptions of him into our conversations. "Your father was a salesman," she would say. Or, "Your father used to run track." But I never knew, for example, at what level he ran—was my father a champion? "Your father busted his leg open riding a motorcycle," she would tell me. But I didn't know if that meant he had a limp or any other physical, emotional, or psychological trauma because of the accident.

I don't think of my father too much, but as I write this I sometimes think that I might remind my mother of him, perhaps when she sees me from afar, walking toward her. At times, I reflect on which of my qualities, positive and negative, might resemble his. I wonder if my mom misses him, if she ever loved him, and how long they knew each other before they slept together. I wonder if my mother told my father and my sister's father about how she wanted children. If my father is anything like me, I can imagine him doing my mom a favor and supplying her with a child. But I can't imagine what was going through his head as he agreed. Did he even care that he was going to have a child?

In the end, all I could do was try to make the very little I did know about my father fill the great void where the images and memories of him should have been. When I was in third grade people would constantly ask me, "Don't you miss not having a father?" And eventually I was forced to liken it to not having a tail. "Do you miss not having a tail?" I would respond. How can you miss something that you never had?

My mom and I have always had a contentious relationship. I think now, at the age of 21, that a possible source of this friction was the dysfunctional relationships she had had with men—and her consequently negative attitudes toward them—which she projected onto me. My mom may not have properly dealt with her "issues" with the men in her life, including her children's fathers and her own father as well. Oftentimes when arguing with my mother I felt like the topic at hand had the emotional baggage of wrongs done to her years before my conception. Growing up, I could not communicate with her without her seeming to take everything as a personal attack. I think this lack of communication may have led her to sense that I wasn't appreciative of all she was doing for me—which may have been true.

My mom valued education and insisted that I go to private schools. She saw how much energy I had and knew that public school would be too trying on my patience, so she sent me to the Jordan School, an overwhelmingly white campus of five hundred students from kindergarten to eighth grade. I went to school with the sons and daughters of doctors, lawyers, business people, and movie stars. My family, however, lived in a one-bedroom house that was really a garage converted into a home. Above all, my mother was a single mother supporting her family on a single salary. Although she was an attorney, she was honest—and thus not rich. My mom, my sister, and I shared one bed, which I often wet as a child. Our home was a perpetual mess, and I hated not having my own room in which I could be neat and organized, like all of my wealthy, white academic peers. I didn't care how big or how nice our house was as long as it was clean and acceptable. I never wanted to show off: I just wanted to pass by unnoticed.

Our house was in south central Los Angeles—only three blocks away from where the Reginald Denny beatings took place—and I hated returning home to it. When we got out of the car and walked to our house, me carrying my sleeping sister over my shoulder, we would have to duck behind parked vehicles when cars drove by for fear of being shot. We were never the victims of such crimes, but I do remember going to sleep with the sounds of helicopters circling around the house as if we were in a war zone. Those helicopters, I thought, were undoubtedly hunting down a black man for some asinine crime. The noise of the propellers made me think of a plantation owner thundering on horseback through his fields just to instill fear in his slaves.

We drove one and a half hours each day to get to and from school. Our 1979 blue Toyota Corolla looked like a relic from World War II, recently hauled out of a junkyard destined to spend the remaining years of its life as an embarrassment to two black children going to an affluent white school. It was the single most potent symbol of the divide between our peers and us. I didn't care where I lived because the kids at school didn't have to see that; but they did see our car, and it was like a huge propaganda machine announcing the arrival and departure of the two poorest kids at Jordan. At the traffic circle where everyone stood waiting for friends, we would get out of the car and bowls of cereal and other junk would fall out, creating an embarrassing mess.

All through my time at Jordan I stole from my peers—things like electronic games and portable audio devices, not for the enjoyment of the goods themselves, but to wield some social clout. I wanted to walk around with an accessory like all the other kids who had Game Boys and Casio watches that functioned as calculators and stored phone numbers. After stealing, though, I'd usually feel so guilty that I tried to throw the stolen items away.

I was constantly comparing myself to the students of my school. I remember in kindergarten asking my mom questions about myself as we drove into Jordan. I once wondered, "Why can't I be white?" Somehow, I already felt like my identity was unsatisfactory. In fact, until I was 12, my experiences were such that I had concluded that all white people were rich and all black people poor. When I revealed this to my mom, she was shocked.

From an early age I was frustrated by our family's financial situation, which neither my mother nor I could change, and at school I felt isolated and cut off from any maternal protection. As a result, I felt as though my mom were the reason for all of the injustices in my life, and so I resented her. She in turn began to resent the situation she found herself in—a single mother working very hard to send two children to an elite private school, one of whom, a son, who would openly tell people that he disliked or hated her.

I remember being disappointed in kindergarten and first grade when at schoolwide recitals I would perform in front of an auditorium filled with nicely dressed parents and not see my mom. It became worse after the recital. "Perhaps I just missed her," I'd think to myself. "She'll come through in the end. She's my mother." I would rush out of the back doors of the auditorium and run toward the front with all of my peers expecting to see my mom walk out. But she didn't. I was introduced to a strange new world of being alone.

In third grade we had a Thanksgiving potluck at school, where everyone brought in a dish and the children dressed up. I remember the children laughing at me and the way I ate, saying I was making a mess. I felt so bad and embarrassed that I began to cry and didn't finish the meal. When my mom came and asked why I looked so down, I told her that I hadn't gotten to eat any of the pumpkin pie that I had brought in; one of the teachers explained what had happened and how the kids had made fun of me. After hearing the story my mom went out and bought me a pie, thinking it would solve the problem. But it didn't, and I had learned my lesson: When I needed my mom to be there she would not be. I knew that she cared, but I also felt that she knew nothing about and had no influence over the world I was living in at school.

In the mornings I would occasionally arrive late, which I thought was a situation to be worked out with my mother. Yet the teacher still chose to call me out and humiliate me in front of my peers, telling me to be on time. In the afternoons, sometimes my mom had to come late to pick me up, and members of the faculty would have to stay after school and wait until she arrived before they could leave. I felt guilty when this happened; the teachers' body language and curt sentences were as loud and powerful as any insults they could have said. I knew they were mad at me and my mother, but what could *I* do?

In the new environment of school, my connections to my family and home-life seemed to be severed and to serve no purpose; so I had to teach myself how to survive and adapt. My mom was like a god. She had created me and the situation I found myself in, but she was rarely present. To trust in her after experiencing the pain I felt in her absence would have required a faith so immense that I would have been crushed under its weight.

In light of the distance between my mother and myself, relationships with others became more and more relevant in my life. In south central Los Angeles I had only a handful of black companions; the Hispanics were all friendly and they were mainly who I hung out with. My most lasting impressions of black people were of the couple of black neighborhood bullies who had beaten me up and stolen my bikes multiple times. Meanwhile, the black kids at the Boys' and Girls' Club I belonged to made fun of me for the way I spoke, saying I sounded "white." I began to view young blacks as threatening and unaccepting of me. The problem wasn't that I myself did not feel I was black; a quick glance at my exposed arms and legs clarified that. It was more a question of how everyone else viewed me. In the black community there is always a concern that successful black people are trying to deny their "blackness." Certainly some blacks feel that once they are successful they have nothing to do with the black "struggle." But this was never how I felt.

In the sixth grade my mom signed me up for the Big Brother, Little Brother program in the hopes of providing me with a long overdue source of male guidance. A long period of time elapsed before I was officially assigned a Big Brother, so in the interim my mother located a co-worker who was willing to temporarily act as one. Sherwin was a very friendly older black male in his early fifties. We were both interested in computers, so we spent all of our time playing video games and building machines. He was probably the best black male role model I ever had: he was intelligent, patient, honest, and friendly. However, three years after we had applied I was finally officially matched with a Big Brother; when this happened—and when he started coming on to my mother—Sherwin was phased out of my life.

My new Big Brother, Jim, was a 30-year-old, white, Jewish male. Over the eleven years that we have been paired together, Jim has provided me with a considerable amount of financial aid and has always been there for me emotionally as well. However, there has been a lot of tension and little communication between Jim and my mother. On my mother's part, the conflict lies in the fact that Jim is a male and wealthy, which has led her to believe that I would immediately assume that whatever he says is of more worth than what she says.

I went to high school at Blair, a mostly white, affluent boarding school of 250 students, and my first year there was marked by an increasing sense of anxiety. I was tired of being pigeonholed as black and seeing the contributions of my "race" over the pages of history being limited to slaves and uppity freedom fighters. There seemed to be only three blacks worthy of study: Martin Luther King, Malcolm X, and Rosa Parks—as though blacks had made no contributions or changes outside of the civil rights movement. I felt that these heroes lived in a social and political climate far different from my own and I found it very difficult to incorporate their lessons into my daily life. I was also reluctant to accept any of the alternative black role models the teachers presented to me because they didn't speak to any of my personal interests; they were not meant for me specifically but for any black person, and they were not appreciated solely for their talents. Their first achievement was that they were black and whatever professional accomplishments they had made came second. I wanted the order of appreciation switched: I wished their professional talents to be appreciated first and foremost, with their race mentioned as a trivial afterthought.

Another source of the increasing sense of anxiety I felt upon entering Blair was the socially challenging environment. At boarding school, for the first time I spent protracted periods of time with my peers outside of an academic setting. During my freshman year I was bothered by a group of kids who seemed rebellious and claimed to be thuggish in spite of the fact that they were attending an elite boarding school. As a result, my style of dress changed from the tough boy gangster image, with big, baggy pants and basketball jerseys, to one of well-fitting khakis and polo T-shirts. This decision was of some importance to me because I felt that in rejecting that thuggish style of dress I was rejecting my culture. But dressing in a way that seemed through association to glorify drugs, money, violence, ignorance, and the mistreatment of women wasn't a true reflection of what my life was about. Similarly, in seventh grade I had stopped listening to the rap and hip-hop radio stations because the deejays presented themselves as ignorant. I wasn't rejecting black culture or music in general, but I was rejecting rap's nihilistic messages and what the deejays were choosing to define as black culture. I was not a "sell-out" or someone filled with self-hatred. Viscerally, I just could not accept negative images that harmed my sense of self-worth.

During my time at Blair, my only black friend was Carter. He had a short temper and an aggressive personality. His outlets were poetry and basketball. Although we were the only black males in our class, I did not feel closer to him as a result. In fact, our sociocultural differences made me feel somewhat estranged from him. I did worry sometimes that I gave blacks like Carter the impression that I wasn't proud of my heritage because I spoke so differently.

During one spring break, my mom invited Carter to visit our house. This was the first time a friend of mine had ever come to stay at my home and I did not know how he would react to our circumstances. Also, although we were of the same race and from similar economic backgrounds, it was difficult for to me decipher Carter's speech. With the language and cultural barrier between us I began to lose faith in the belief that all blacks could understand one another due to skin color. My skin color did not help me decode the strange words that permeated his vocabulary, like "yo," "B," "tap," "chill," and "bitch" (which was used to refer to all women).

On the first day of spring break we rented movies from the public library, and as we watched one around midnight, we began debating the movie's story line. Soon our debate escalated into a heated argument that moved beyond the movie's plot. Eventually Carter became enraged and screamed, "You don't even trust me!" He told me that earlier that day he had asked me what kind of music I listened to and I had told him rap, but when he looked through my CD collection he found that I also listened to classical and alternative rock. He seemed hurt by this, which shocked me, as I didn't think I had the ability to upset anyone at all—let alone Carter, who seemed so tough on the exterior.

I hadn't told him what other music I listened to because I still wasn't secure enough in my identity, racially or otherwise, to openly share who I was and what my interests were. Some of the music I listened to was made by white people, and I didn't want him to consider me a "sell-out." I didn't know how to tell him that I had been beaten up and made fun of as a kid for acting and talking "white." At the end of the conversation, he made me confident that he was not going to judge me based on the genre of music I enjoyed, and I felt comfortable opening up to him.

By the end of the vacation I was using his lingo nonstop. Once he referred to my mom as a bitch but then immediately apologized. "That's alright, I know what you mean," I said. But averting his eyes, he said, "Naw, that's not cool. I really do like her." And I believed him.

Throughout our time at Blair, Carter and I continued to grow closer, especially after I spent a week at his apartment. I felt I understood him better after seeing where he was from, yet I still wondered what he thought about my blackness, as race rarely came up as a topic between us.

Because of our close relationship, I asked Carter to write me a peer recommendation for college. It was at this point that he finally allayed some of my insecurities by telling me that he did not feel that I was a "sell-out." Still somewhat unsure, I asked him about the way I spoke. He considered for a moment and replied, "That's just the way you speak. You change when you are around me and when you speak to a Mexican and when you are in French class. You just have a knack with languages and you change accordingly. It's just about learning how to adapt." These words were some of the most comforting I have ever heard.

Besides Carter, my two other best friends in high school were Phillip and Jay. Jay and I were extremely similar. We both enjoyed math and were rather serious. We used to exchange stories about how we would both wake up on Saturday mornings during junior high and spend the first couple of hours in bed just thinking. We had similar conceptions about society and the same insecurities about what qualified as intelligence. Both procrastinators, we bonded over our consequentially sub-par performances on papers and final exams.

Regardless of grades, Jay was implicitly considered one of the smartest guys in our class and most everyone respected him. He was extremely logical and did everything for a reason, whereas I would act on instinct and impulse. Jay understood me better than anyone else and taught me a lot of lessons about what it means to be a friend. I had misguided ideas about the nature of friendships: I thought that the minute you got into an argument or a fight that you should call it off. It was hard for me to entertain the idea that you could be mad at someone you still liked. Jay realized that if I did something that appeared to be done out of malice it was probably because I didn't really know the source of my anger or that I was trying to get attention. He was a good listener and I could tell him about very personal things.

Phillip joined us during our sophomore year. The grandson of a famous playwright, Phillip was bright and good-humored and had impeccable taste in literature and music; and he would never lower his standards to suit the politics of skin color. When I stumbled upon a black hip-hop trio in his CD collection, my curiosity was piqued. I had not been impressed when I had heard one or two of their songs before, but seeing that Phillip owned their album led me to reconsider their merit.

When Phillip took a course on "Black Authors" while I opted for a class on "The Boarding School Experience," he approached me curious as to why I hadn't taken the course he was taking. I didn't know how to explain to him that I felt estranged from schools' representations of blacks. However, as the term progressed and he read books by Toni Morrison and Ralph Ellison and insisted on how good they were, I wished that I had taken the course. In these ways, Phillip helped me to find my way back into black culture, music, and literature.

One of Jay's most important contributions to our friendship was encouraging me when I decided to start seeing a counselor for my anxiety during my freshman year. In fact, to my surprise, all of my friends fully supported me in this. I saw the counselor once a week for half a year, and though she didn't cure me of my anxiety she did help me cope with it. One of her best suggestions was that I keep a journal. I began writing almost daily to loosen the grip of emotional paralysis through self-expression.

I remember the first day I began writing. It was a free period and rain was falling outside the library window. I was feeling anxious but started writing in my spiral-bound notebook anyway; and before long the words just flowed out of me. I felt like I was in the throes of mania. There was something magical but at the same time sort of sickening to me about the whole process—as though it were an unhealthy happiness. My thoughts were definitely me, but they were frightening. Excuse this comparison, but I related my journal writing to the work of Goya: beautifully dark and complicated pieces that reflect an intelligent but tortured mind.

Writing became my outlet; I wrote about everything. I let my friends read my journal until junior year of high school—it felt good to get things off my chest and share them with someone else. I felt that I was being my true and honest self in my journal entries, and I wanted everyone to know the part of me that never got a chance to surface in daily conversations. At one point, Phillip had stumbled across a passage where I admitted to feeling somehow incapacitated by my skin color. After reading the entry he approached me confused, wanting to talk about it more. He felt for me, not in a pitying way, but as a friend, and the way he approached me made a huge impact on the response he was given. Had I been approached in a condescending way, I would have been defensive about the inquiry. Although we never got around to fully addressing the issue, it was his concern that mattered most to me.

My close guy friends and my writings helped me to develop and further understand myself, but I still wasn't comfortable around girls. I never would have asked out Karen, my first girlfriend, left to my own devices. I hadn't much experience with girls and I didn't quite know what would be required of me and what role I was supposed to play. When Karen told me after dinner one night in tears that she liked me, I wasn't sure what to do. I either didn't believe it or didn't know how to take it; I think a lot of this had to do with the lack of love I had for myself.

Karen and I dated only for a short while freshman year (although I never told my mom about her, because she had said that I couldn't date until I was 30). Suffering from acute anxiety at the time, I ended up saying things like, "let's just go out on weekends," thinking that over the weekends, without the pressures of school, I could be a better boyfriend to her. But this suggestion made me seem shallow—and even sleazy. My behavior was sometimes aggressive and cruel, and I realize that this was, in part, a result of my frustration for feeling forced into the relationship. It wasn't just Karen; I couldn't cope with the idea of going out with anyone. I felt that it was another part that I would have to play that I didn't have the lines for.

I do not feel that my relationship with Karen, or with any other girl, was complicated by my race. Sometimes I wondered if girls were attracted to me because of my skin color, but I am fairly positive that no one dated me to live out any sort of fantasy about black men.

Although I didn't understand this at the time, I feel that my *own* insecurities about my race did permeate my relationships and other aspects of my life, however. It took my Asian American advisor to point out to me the importance of being aware of your own race. Sophomore year, he wrote on my report card that he was concerned that I had not begun to address the importance of race in my life. My mom agreed with him and brought the issue to my attention, as race had always been a vital component of her life and she wanted to make it important in my life as well. My mom made whites seem like the enemy, but in attending primarily white schools my whole life I did not see how being race conscious was going to help—especially when *I* was the one who would have to negotiate life amongst whites, without her there to support me as I treaded alone on enemy territory.

Instead of making enemies of whites, I tried to minimize my differences by ignoring the issues surrounding race. I was afraid that if I confronted them I would suffocate under the pressure of a problem I had no means of resolving. So when my mother and my advisor brought the matter up, I didn't know how to react.

I didn't *know* what it means to be black. I didn't feel *black*. I felt like me. I didn't think that I had any contributions to make to any discussions about "blackness" that would aid in a white person's understanding of the concept. I had always attended white schools and I had not thought that the people there were racist; I had white friends who seemed to like me. Looking back, I think the truth was that I thought we *were* somehow inferior; I hadn't yet learned what a black person had to be proud about. What I associated with black culture were dashikis and dreadlocks and other things that weren't a part of my daily life.

When I went back to school the day after my advisor had spoken to me, I ignored his suggestion. I didn't know what to do about my "problem," so I avoided confronting it. I did make advances on the relationship front, however. I began to realize that I didn't have to treat women the way I had treated Karen. The turnaround was mostly precipitated by my love for my sister, with whom I had an ideal relationship. I thought I should try to model a relationship with potential girlfriends after the one I had with her: one of mutual respect and understanding. My love for my sister became a mantra for the rest of my high school career. She earned my respect because she was always there for me, well-spoken, and able to get along well with my mother.

My next serious relationship occurred during my junior year in high school. Her name was Nicole, and she was a freshman and the youngest of three sisters, all of whom lived fairly troubled lives, dealing with the stigma of coming from a divorced household and the fact that their mother was dying of brain cancer. I probably would never have asked Nicole out, but she waited patiently and let me come around in my own way. Nicole was important to me and I was determined to learn from the lessons of my relationship with Karen. I decided that no matter what I felt, I would not allow myself to take out any undue aggressions on her. Throughout our time together, I felt that I was able to accomplish this, but we broke up nonetheless due to extenuating circumstances.

Nicole's mother died the summer after we broke up. We tried to get back together my senior fall, but it didn't work. She kept referring to jokes that we made during our last year of dating. It felt like she was trying to return to the period of our past when her mother was still living; until I told her, she hadn't noticed this. I explained to her how much I cared for her and that I didn't think it would be healthy for us to see each other under the circumstances. She agreed that it would probably be for the best to break up.

Overall, I enjoyed our relationship; it taught me how to identify and channel my feelings and to treat people appropriately. Although sad, I left Nicole feeling good about my ability to maintain a healthy relationship with a woman. With that in place, I moved on once again to the issue of race that I had been putting off confronting.

One day after sports practice, my friends and I went to visit Benson, a sophomore, in his dormitory. He had all sorts of expensive digital audio-visual equipment and told us how he had caught his friend Tony on tape falling off a couch and hitting his mouth against the coffee table, and that we should watch it. He added that Tony had said some pretty offensive stuff in the video and that he didn't want us to take offense, eyeing me warily. We assured him that it couldn't be that bad, so he began the film. When we saw our friend hit his head against the coffee table, we were left so amused that we asked eagerly what came next. Benson said that the following part was offensive and he didn't want to show us, but we pushed and he reluctantly played it.

In the video Benson had asked Tony, who was white, to say something, and he chose to say, "The Negro should go back to Africa." Given that Tony's style—his dress, musical tastes, and parlance were all strongly influenced by black culture—it was shocking that he purported to hold these racist beliefs. Once we had seen the clip, everyone turned to me, expecting me to be vehemently upset; but I didn't know what to be. I was surprised and speechless and tried to shrug it off. Was this racism, I wondered? Did this often happen when I wasn't in the room? And if it did, what was there to be done about it? I began to feel helpless. If this was racism, who was there that I could tell? And what would *they* do about it? This was one of the first experiences where I learned a harsh reality about the way others viewed my race.

I also learned a lesson about a condescending dimension of affirmative action during a school assembly my junior year for the highly selective National Merit Scholarships. The headmaster read the names of the winners, and to my surprise mine was called. I was wary; surely I had not done as well as the other people being called up. When I was handed my award, I immediately noticed that it was of a different size and color as the others: My award was for noteworthy achievement in the African American community. I was incensed and embarrassed. Why the special attention? No one else noticed this discrepancy, but I wanted to be treated fairly and not judged by a different measuring stick. It made me feel that society had decided that my race was inferior and that we should be rewarded for whatever work we could produce, regardless of its quality.

I graduated from high school without having resolved how I felt about race and what it meant to me to be black. When I arrived at college, I was still very unsure of my own identity. Conversely, my freshman-year roommate, who was a Native American, was very proud of his culture. He felt no shame about his heritage, and would tell me about going to the Native American Society and how he took part in a powwow. I admired the way he spoke confidently and respectfully about his people. I had thought that any society that was not completely in sync with mainstream white culture would feel ashamed of their differences. I was surprised that he didn't feel this way. I wanted to ask where he got his pride, hoping that it would rub off on me.

Inspired by my roommate, I joined the African American Society (AAS) on campus. Although I had long felt distanced from the black community and feared that they might not accept me, I participated timidly in their events, and, in spite of the fact that I felt a little awkward, I never stopped. I had joined the AAS not in order to have fun, but out of a sense of responsibility. I felt like I owed it to the black community. Still, I didn't know how to "behave" with other members of the AAS. I was afraid that my awkwardness would once again evoke emotional abuse and that I would relive my childhood experiences at the Boys' and Girls' Club.

A turning point in the formation of my racial identity occurred my sophomore year during an off-campus program in Barcelona. There, I found out, much to my surprise, that I would be living with a black Spanish family with three brothers close to my age. I was shocked. Up until that point, the members of my biological family in the States had been the only black people that I knew of that spoke Spanish.

I do many things that most stereotypical black people would not—and every time I find others of my race doing the same thing I am shocked. It's as if doing something positive or unique makes me an outsider in the black community. It could be that there are lots of blacks who don't like violence, like to read, are fond of the idea of falling in love, and enjoy theological debates. I, however, have not met them. With the way mass media implies that the only way a black male can succeed is if he portrays himself as ignorant or violent, I don't think that many blacks believe that they can do otherwise: it wouldn't be black. Although aware of these messages, I was not impervious to them, and I felt that when I met my Spanish brothers I had to act rough to show that I was worthy of their camaraderie.

At one point when I was on the verge of proving my toughness, my younger brother stepped back with a surprised look that seemed to say, "What is this guy doing?" The looks on his older brothers' faces betrayed similar sentiments. Although they did seem sort of impressed with my bravado, they did not make generalizations about my being just another rough black American. Instead they said, *"Pues mira que fuerte Orion es*—Look how strong Orion is." It was like being looked at as if I were an individual human being. It made me realize that blacks in the States, or at least myself, tended to look at other blacks as if they are animals incapable of acting otherwise.

My journey to Spain was the first time since seventh grade that I attempted to formulate a different definition of "blackness." I decided that the concept of blackness was an illusion. I decided to free myself from any definitions of blackness and to simply live and be whomever I wanted. I decided to pursue whatever interests I had without fear of them not being the "black thing" to do. In Spain, I felt free to define myself, to learn to snowboard, to read, to write, to learn French, to skateboard, and to play guitar. When I returned from Spain, I told my family and friends how blessed I felt for having had the educational opportunity to travel to Europe.

Yet, while I had come much farther in comprehending myself, I was still having trouble understanding the opposite sex. By senior year, I had not yet had a steady girlfriend my entire time at college and I was still a virgin. I called Jim, my Big Brother, who insisted that finding a girlfriend was not as hard as I was making it out to be. He suggested that perhaps I should start considering that there might be a more serious issue at work. I started thinking seriously about all of my sexual and romantic experiences. I then told him how many of my baby-sitters and I had abusive sexual relationships when I was younger and that I was concerned that this might affect how I related to women. Although I had written about being sexualized by my twenty-something-year-old baby-sitters in my journal, I had never mentioned it to any adult. After a short silence, Jim replied that he felt this new information was beyond his training as an amateur psychologist and that I should seek professional help.

So in the fall of my senior year I went to see a counselor at school about my love life—because I was 21, in college, and a virgin. I was prepared to open up and talk about my baby-sitters, my mom, my sister, Nicole, and Karen. I wanted to be as candid as possible so that the counselor could see the situation as clearly as possible.

As it turned out the psychiatrist was a black man, which was helpful to a certain extent because I felt I could tell him openly about my recent concerns about dating someone black. He asked me if I thought it mattered or if I had any preference about dating one race or another, and I told him no. If I liked a girl, then I liked a girl; it just so happened that most of the girls I had an interest in were white. I did, however, think Hispanic, Indian, and from time to time black women were attractive, too. I thought that the relatively limited number of instances in which I had dated or had had interests in black women was due to the scarcity of blacks in my educational environments. For the greater part of my life, I have been surrounded by whites. And the blacks I did see tended to have different social backgrounds from me and so I didn't always get along with them.

I told my counselor how I felt uncomfortable pressure to date and marry a black woman. I had overheard my mother in an argument with one of my older cousins about interracial marriages. She was yelling in the kitchen that she would not even speak with my wife if she were nonblack. My cousin was asking her, "But what if your son met a nice Asian lady in college and wanted to marry her? Would you still disapprove?" My mother responded that she would not allow her to come over to the house. She began referring to my wife-to-be as my "decision." She said, "Well, he and his 'decision' can stay and live on one side of the city, but if he wants to come visit me, he'll just have to leave his 'decision' at home."

Although my counselor didn't really help me solve my insecurities about feeling pressure to date a black woman, a good Hispanic friend of mine, Ivan, told me not to worry about what others thought, because a relationship involves just two people. I asked him if he felt pressure from his parents to marry someone Hispanic, and he said no. He said that his mom would probably prefer it if he did, but she wanted him to be happy more than anything. He encouraged me to understand that my mom might be acting out of love because she thinks it would be easier for me to marry within my race.

I feel certain that, in general, the representation of my race in my school experience has had negative effects on my self-esteem. I hated discussions that singled me out as different, and perhaps inferior, to my peers. I have mingled in educational communities that are predominantly white, and this racial isolation led me to endure long periods of insecurity about my blackness. I eventually formed a sense of color-blindness, believing that race is irrelevant in human relations. The merits of blacks are so rarely praised by the dominant social group in America that it is often hard to be convinced of our self-worth. Up until my senior year at college, my education took me away from a culture where my ethnicity is seen as a source of pride.

Still, my private education was in many ways helpful in providing me with opportunities. I am currently a week away from graduating from an elite college that I may never have attended had it not been for the unbending will of my mother, who insisted that I attend a secondary institution of rigorous academic standards. I feel indebted for the many experiences my education has given me: running in the country, camping, rock climbing, horseback riding, deejaying for a radio station, and teaching and living abroad. I am grateful that I can read, write, and express myself eloquently; but most of all I appreciate the confidence my education has granted me in terms of my academic ability.

Now, one week before my college graduation, I look back and reflect on my journey from being a black child who wanted to live without race to becoming a person who is beginning to formulate a valid racial identity. I have come to realize that in the United States a black person cannot grow up healthily without reconciling himself with his race. Although my own reconciliation with my race is not yet complete, I want to share the conclusions I have reached so far on what it means to be black with the community around me; I believe I can do that by teaching elementary school students in public school in Atlanta, which I plan to do after I graduate.

My choice in going to Atlanta is partly based on my wish to finally connect with and be surrounded and affirmed by people of my race. A Hispanic friend of mine told me that it is silly to choose where I live according to skin color, but it makes sense to me. I feel that with my personal experiences and interests I would have a lot to offer no matter where I went, but I feel that it is particularly important to provide a positive role model for other black youth perhaps in the midst of negotiating their own racial identities. I wish to counterbalance the negative portrayals of blacks with positive, truthful ones—ones that aren't created and selected by someone for financial gain. I would like the children I teach to come to whatever conclusions they want, but I want them to have more than just one definition for being "black," one that is broader than the media's portrayal. After all these years, I believe black is not incompatible with peace and happiness. Blackness is what I want it to be.

IN SEARCH OF MY VOICE

Born in Bombay and living in Malaysia for part of his childhood schooling before returning to India, this college student tells of the path that brought him from the East to a small liberal arts college in the American Northeast. Eager to be accepted by American society and his college peers, Devneesh is devastated by the racist and misogynistic attitudes his first-year roommate harbors. He is compelled in this hostile environment into a period of profound self-questioning and self-contempt, viewing himself as a tan dog paraded around by the college trustees to make his predominately white college seem more diverse. Only when he has forged close bonds with a young Jewish man and an East Asian woman does he begin to discover his own voice and reconcile his ethnicity with his environment. He emerges from his college experience with a new acceptance of his identity as a "wanderer" and with a strong desire to contribute to American society and make part of this country his own.

I was a complex ball of pride and insecurity as I passed through the immigration post at Boston's Logan Airport. I remember standing, bags and passport in hand, in a patch of sunlight streaming through a window, surrendering to the moment and feeling like the emperor of my life. I felt exhilarated. Liberated. Accepted. Welcomed. Now I could finally try to realize my dreams, I thought. But the truth is, I was running away, away from the shadowy patches in my memory. Ashamed of the person I knew myself to be, I was far from being the person I wanted to become.

I was alone for the first time in a strange land of beautiful, graceful white people. I was taken by how structured and controlled the faces around me at the terminal were. They all looked so smart and mature. So civilized and polished. I felt suddenly immersed in opulence. The abundance and obvious prosperity, however, struck me as being somehow cold. There was also a curious strain on these faces. What burden could these Children of Fortune possibly bear that would explain their placid, dispirited demeanor? They smiled out of habit and laughed occasionally, but it seemed their hearts were not in it. I figured people must just get bored when they have everything they could possibly want.

I was picked up at the airport by Sunil. My father and his had known each other for decades, and though we had met only briefly before in the security of my home in Bombay, I was delighted to see a familiar face and kept close to his heels. The cab we rode in was huge. I worried about how many precious dollars would be spent on this lavish form of transportation. I was beginning to feel the strain of my journey. My mind had been in a state of alert for quite a while, absorbing, observing, learning, unlearning, listening, tuning, and mostly worrying. Sunil was talking rapidly, about the rich history of Boston, his two years as a graduate student, and the developments in his research since we had last met. I could see him talking to me, but his voice began to fade away. My mind was fatigued, and I was getting weary of the adventure. I wanted to be in the comfort of my mother's presence, and I longed for the soothing smell of her saree.

Nevertheless, I was excited and anxious to meet my roommate-to-be. Jon arrived at Sunil's humble apartment the next day in a BMW and we shook hands, expectantly. His palm enveloped mine, his grip was firmer than I was comfortable with. Although I had nibbled on some breakfast, Jon and I set out to grab a bite. I couldn't help but gaze in wonder at his brown eyelashes. His fingers were so fat. His manner so stiff and controlled. His voice so monotonic. And his expression so condescending. I soon found myself fighting the thought that to Jon we were clearly not equals.

We zipped around Boston and came to a cafe he was obviously familiar with. I was taken by the name, Au Bon Pain, which I dared not try to pronounce. I followed him closely, picking up a tray and looking at the menus, just as he did. I was in for a shock: "What? Two dollars for orange juice! Even more for a muffin. What the hell is a muffin anyway? You have got to be kidding. I don't want to spend that much especially when I'm not in dire need of it." Resolved not to drain my wallet, I picked up a carton of milk, and sheepishly told him that I wasn't hungry. He was visibly irritated, and offered to treat me. When I declined, he was provoked further, telling me I had no reason not to be hungry, and that I shouldn't have eaten before, since we had arranged to have brunch together. His derisive tone left a strong impression. I would have liked him to be more understanding about my obvious embarrassment at not wanting to spend the money. No doubt it was an awkward situation for him as well, but there was clearly a significant difference between Jon and me.

I had thought about all the things we could do as roommates exploring a new college setting for the first time together, making friends, playing games, and talking about women, but now I began to feel a little worried. He was asking me if my mustache was a "normal" thing for people in Asia. He was curious to know if I was a hero back home among my villagers, since I was coming to an institution that was obviously superior to anything within their reach. Surely, he surmised, I must come from one of the richest families in India to be able to afford an education here.

On the ride back to Sunil's we were briefly interrupted by Jon's mother calling him on his car phone. Later in the year, casting his caution away, Jon would joke to me about how his mother had asked him during that phone conversation if I smelled like curry. I did not suspect it at the time, and noticed only that he was uneasy and eager to denigrate his mother to give me the impression that he was less dependent on her than he really was. I wondered if Jon and I would ever grow to see each other as individuals, past the obvious differences that distracted us. In all my excitement about college and the wonders of partaking in the American melting pot, it had thoroughly escaped me that I might be an unwanted intruder, an alien entity from a backward planet, whom some Americans, out of generosity and magnanimity of spirit, had allowed to study and work here, and to marvel at their superior, evolved nature of being.

I was greeted in Hanover the next day by a brief respite of beauty, where these concerns receded again. The Environmental Orientation Trip was perfectly suited for a wide-eyed novice to nature who did not know what Gore-Tex shoes and sleeping bags were. Eternally thankful for every moment of the experience, I was taken by the untouched purity of nature around me—the clear river water, the age-cracked pines, and the cleansing mist in the mornings. The hope that the natives of such a heavenly abode might also be pure in their spirit of humanity seeped back into me. I especially liked my trip leader, and two others—a gentle Vietnamese girl and a quiet Puerto Rican guy. I was happy to have them as friends, with whom I ate my meals, trekked the woods, canoed the placid river, and even did some good old-fashioned bird watching. Rationalizing that they were both naturalized Americans, and therefore not too far from the people I would soon live among, my optimism that Dartmouth might indeed accept me grew stronger, and therefore more dangerous.

I met many people the next few weeks, attended many orientation sessions, and took many tests. Throughout the whole first week, Jon and I never managed to say more to each other than a polite greeting. We agreed he could take the bigger of the two adjacent rooms that made up 102 Sage. He brought in decorators, including his mother, to carpet his room, wheel in the television, VCR, and music system, and help him put up posters of cars, women, and all the different types of condoms one could ever want to use.

A lot happened that fall term; Jon positioned himself as J.J., and Devneesh shied away into Dev. Calling myself "Dev" eased the burden of enduring introductions, but I soon started feeling like a cheap imported car. I felt stared at and patronized in social gatherings, and learned to make clever excuses to avoid them. J.J. found a few like-minded males to bolster his image and soon used alcohol and his critique of those things called women to pretend he was at ease. Ironically, he was seen as the mature, sensible guy who carried his wealth in style and was magnanimous enough to bear the burden of living with "one of them alien types."

J.J. was a key figure in my process of adaptation. I would occasionally wake up to his morning mantra, "Dev's a fag." He introduced me to his buddies, who would poke and test my cultural beliefs. "Dev the Man, tell them why you don't eat meat." "Devdom, tell them about why you don't drink." "Dev, is it 'cuz it's bad Karma or something?" And they would chant "Karma Man" for painful lengths of time. I once retorted that I didn't need alcohol to bring down my defenses. "But don't you just wanna let go for a while?" they asked. Let go from what? I thought then that these defensive pink angels were all playing a game none really wanted to be part of, but that societal and parental expectations forced them to play roles from which weekend binges provided brief relief.

As J.J.'s pictures of his family disappeared from his room to save him the embarrassment of showing attachment, mine surfaced from the folder I had kept them hidden in, to keep me from giving up. I finally felt I could bear to see them without breaking down. Oh, I missed them so! But I couldn't let myself admit it, lest I shatter to pieces. I was working in the College Cafe, learning to flip omelets, make sandwiches, mop the floor, and run the dishwasher. When I returned from my shift on Friday nights at midnight, looking to sleep off the strain of the week, there would inevitably be a party in our suite. I would sob into my pillow while I held it over my head to muffle Axel Rose's disturbing "mother-fucker" and "bitch" and Nirvana's anguishing screams that made me shudder with fear. I would try to quiet my mind with a little prayer, and then lie awake wondering if at any moment J.J.'s friends were going to barge into my room and beat me up as a way to release some of the aggression their music seemed to breed. I would curl into my ten-dollar polyester blanket and peer through the holes I had made in it.

I did not exist to J.J. and his friends. In the room that always had its door closed, there was no human being, no feelings that hurt, no intellect that mattered, and certainly no one who was being kept awake. Nothing. They could blare their music, flaunt their phobias about immigrants and "faggots," and all would be well. J.J. would tell me how he felt international students at Dartmouth—heck, in the whole USA—should all just go back home. They were leeches that took away valuable slots that local students were denied. They drained the financial aid that his parents were indirectly paying for. I, as an "import," was just getting in his and other people's way.

While peering through my blanket one night, I saw the door swing open, and in walked a few of J.J.'s friends. They seated themselves on my bed, used my phone, ate my chips, and tottered around for a while completely oblivious of the curled-up bump under the blanket. They appeared to me to be shouting in argument about something, but that could just have been my fear exaggerating their intimidating presence. They left eventually, and I tried impotently to find relief in sleep.

When I expressed timidly to J.J. that I hadn't slept much the previous night, he said, "Dude, it's a party. Dude. Everything is cool." I desperately hoped I had appealed to his sense of pity, and scrambled away thanking him. Soon after, however, it happened again. I came back from the cafe, my bones feeling brittle and my nerves throbbing, to a smoky, noisy room of judgmental eyes. My confusion and fatigue gave me an extraordinary temper. I lay in my bed, fuming and humiliated, for a couple of hours. Then I picked up my courage, opened the door, and requested that they turn the music down. "Oh, sure thing, Dude," replied a sniggering voice, and after I closed the door, the music got louder.

"I have had it with you, J.J.," I raged to myself. I put on my jeans and rushed out of my room, heading across the green toward the campus police office. But as I got closer, my courage seemed to abandon me. By the time I crossed the green, I was contemplating giving them a few more hours to enjoy themselves before I went back. After all, I reasoned, I was only an import. They had a right to their fun, and there was no sense in my getting in the way.

So I curled up on a bench and tried to snooze away the growing lump in my throat. A black dog with a red collar sauntered around the green and soon settled itself comfortably near me on the ground. Though I have been afraid of dogs from a very young age, this dog felt like my soul mate. He understood me. He was me; I was he. My position at Dartmouth College was like that of a tanned dog that walked on two legs. When my owners, the college trustees, pleased, I would walk around, parading myself, contributing to their vision of diversity. In return they paid for my college expenses. The humiliation and worthlessness that I felt that moment on the bench still make me very angry. I had reduced myself to a state in which I was glad just to be patted on the head, fed now and then, and allowed to wander freely, as long as I didn't bother anyone. The indignity numbed me. I curled up, defensive and weak, too empty for tears.

But I asked myself a fundamental question. Why did I let them do this to me? They are not to blame, really—I am. I let them taunt me. I didn't have the courage to face them, to ask for what I deserved: basic respect, not for special accomplishment, but for the simple reason that I was a human being. And something changed in me that night. I saw myself for the proud, arrogant, overachieving geek that I was. I deserved every bit of the abuse I had gotten. What a coward I had been. In my desperation to make America my home, a place where I would be accepted, I was giving in too much. But I was going to take it no more. The lesson was learned, and it was time for me to raise myself up, for my own life, my own happiness, and my own free will.

I returned to my room feeling empowered. It was deserted, and I slept. The next morning, I firmly told J.J. there would be no more parties in our room. And to my amazement there were not. I slowly began to change my accent, listening intently to those around me and practicing my American voice in whispers. I put on a mask of the stoic male that I felt would keep the curious at bay. My classes became the focus of my attention. It was time to start bridging the gap between who I really was and who I wanted to be. I had reached the nadir of my existence, and now felt cleansed and ready to undertake a process of building. For the remainder of freshman year I erected my scaffolding for this ambitious construction project that I intended to last a lifetime.

While I struggled to handle my roommate's bigotry, I fought another battle— a crush on a woman I imagined would be the answer to all my problems. One of the first acquaintances I made at Dartmouth was with Farha. On the first day of fall term, I was eating alone in the dining hall, contemplating a bland salad and wondering if I would be able to sustain myself as a vegetarian much longer. When I got up to surrender the dirty plates, my eye caught someone else sitting alone at another table. She looked Indian, and I was struck by the radiance of her face and her shiny black hair.

I excitedly went over to her table, trying to appear casual and comfortable, and introduced myself. She said she was Farha from Pakistan. To me she was Sunshine from Good Land. She spoke with almost childlike mannerisms that betrayed her full, bright red lips and big shining teeth. I shook her soft Vaseline hands and helped myself to a chair across from her. We talked about simple things, like adjustment difficulties, and she responded with the most sympathetic eyes I had ever seen. After I left, Farha grew on me, like a fungus.

I thought of her constantly, using the memory of her soft manner to bolster me during the first few difficult weeks of that fall. In my imagination, I told her my deepest fears and secrets, and confessed that things weren't really as good as I pretended they were. When we finally did get together, though, I would tell her she was naive and unrealistic and portray myself as experienced and practical. I looked upon her with disdain as a mere romantic who wouldn't survive in the real world. But when we played pool, I would stand at a distance looking at her wondering if she would ever see through the masks that I skillfully put up to distract her. Would she ever see the aching, sentimental, romantic part of me? I fired a spear at her now and then that punctured any desire she might have had to try and get closer to me, and sure enough she stopped trying to understand me altogether. I thought less of her for having let me win in the battle to defeat myself. I gave up the hope that Farha and I would ever be close friends. J.J., in sympathy with my failed hopes, explained that I needed to find myself an American woman who wasn't going to hassle me with "all this Islamic shit."

J.J.'s bigotry, Farha's rejection, and a growing feeling of academic incompetence made me miserable that year. I vividly remember one afternoon in that first winter, when I went down to the river, lay on a hammock, and contemplated walking onto the frozen river, not caring if I would fall through and freeze. As I lay there, I asked myself a key question: "Why should I go on—what is there for me at Dartmouth or anywhere else?"

I don't think I was serious about doing anything drastic to endanger myself, but it was the possibility of suicide that spurred me to think of reasons to live another day. I was working hard, plodding away at physics and math classes that I did not care much for, and also working grudgingly at the cafe. What was it all for? To graduate from Dartmouth and work myself up the ladder so that J.J. and I could one day sit at the same table, drive the same cars, and live in similar houses? I knew that, beneath my insecure shell, material respect was not what I craved. The overachievers and super-competitive people at Dartmouth that I lived and worked with were not role models for me. And if their lifestyle was all that my time spent in Hanover was leading up to, then I didn't really care if it ended or not.

As I lay there, my mind wandered into the depths of my latent childhood memories. Although it felt like I had come such a long way from places I had once called home, in another sense I was still facing the same conflicts. I remembered that there were actually a few times when I had pondered taking my own life. These times came invariably when I did not meet the standards that I or others had set for me. My right to live in this world, I thought, was earned every day by my achievements, failing which, it only seemed natural and fair that I should forfeit that right.

I think I must have made the connection between parental affection and high achievement during my first few years of schooling in Bombay. Report Card Day was easily the most important time of the year. It surpassed birthdays, festival days, and certainly vacation days. There was a ritual that I practiced every Report Card Day. I would be playing in the street outside my house, growing excited in anticipation, waiting for the sight of my father returning home. Just as his car turned the corner, I would abandon my game and my friends to race home, wildly, and hide under my bed, clutching my brown report card. As he entered the house, exhausted and hungry, he would hand over his briefcase to my mother, Amma, and with a twinkle in his eye would play along with my game, asking Amma where I was. She would call out for me, and I would emerge from my hiding place, pretending to be afraid to face my father, hoping to mislead him into thinking I had done poorly. I would look down at my feet, report card hidden behind my back, trying to act grief-stricken. Amma would tell him it was Report Card Day, at which point I would unveil my hidden treasure, flashing the gold star pasted on it that indicated I was first in my class, the passport to my father's affection. He would chuckle in satisfaction, beckon me to him, plant a noisy kiss on my cheek, and shower me with a string of nicknames. They made little sense, but they made my year worth living.

This annual ritual was altered one day when I stayed indoors on Report Card Day, shaking genuinely with fear. I had gotten a silver star instead of gold, and was at a loss as to how I could possibly face my father. Would I be beaten? Or perhaps just bitterly scolded, which was usually worse. Maybe he would cast me away, disowning me, and renouncing his ties to a failure like me. Instead, he simply washed up, sat down for dinner, and conferred the title of "The Second One" on me. I was taunted and teased for being "The Second One," and the newcomer who was first that year became my prime target of hatred and competition. I held him responsible for taking away my father's loud kisses and nicknames, and made sure that I never relinquished my gold star again. After that year I never heard "The Second One" again.

The thought of losing my father's attention and affection gave me the motivation to achieve and earn my parents' pride. I also saw my achieving as fulfilling my *dharma,* or duty, as the way to assure them that their generous investment in me was not in vain.

When I was younger, my father ruled the house with firm discipline. The hierarchy was very clear: The decisions were made by the head of the household, my father. My mother had the right to voice her views, and my sister and I had the right to voice a suggestion, but it was my father's firm nod of the head that made legislation. I loved my father dearly and longed to be strong and wise like him someday. He had no qualms in showing affection and would often make me laugh by playfully wrestling with me, dancing around most awkwardly, and making faces impossible for me to replicate. I relished his barrage of affectionate nicknames and squirmed with delighted embarrassment when he got into those affectionate moods. And I felt that on each Report Card Day, I extended my lease on the right to be his son for yet another year.

Soon, though, my father's scrutiny extended into everything else in my life. He felt he needed to correct my habits, my etiquette, my speech, my English, my posture, my behavior, my temper, my style of handling situations, my need for tact, the volume of my voice. He helped me develop an introspective view of myself, to know how to identify my weaknesses and improve upon them. That trait helped me a lot when I found it necessary to stop, take stock of a situation, evaluate where I was headed, and then make the changes I felt necessary, all without inflicting too much pain on my bloated ego.

However, my father's constant vigilance also made me very self-conscious. I had to put up the front of being the ideal son in his presence. When we moved to Malaysia after my seventh birthday, I came to associate this "ideal" identity with my academic performance. Indigestion before exams was my measure of sure success. My other Indian friends chose to keep a distance from me, as I became unpleasantly competitive in every field. On Report Card Day, I beat all my enemies, as well as all my fears and insecurities. I earned the bronze medal for my class every year, and prided myself in being the top Indian student.

The Chinese believed they were naturally a superior race, and established themselves as the hardworking, deservedly prosperous ruling majority in Malaysia. The darker races, Malay and Indian, were lulled into a submissive role as lesser peoples and accepted what little came their way. But I was never an easy person to suppress. I had a mouth too big and a voice too loud, which made many people uncomfortable. I was spurred by parental pressure as well as by the need to champion my race. I built my life around competition and achievement.

In sixth grade I was faced with a mammoth challenge to these aspirations. My parents had set their sights on St. Joseph's Institution (SJI) as the best place for my secondary education. Now it was up to me to work toward getting into it; I hated that whole year. I had nightmares for months before the nationwide exams that determined who got into which school. I spent the majority of my time at my desk, mostly worrying. That year, my indigestion gave me little comfort that I would be able to succeed. I needed something alternative to fall back on in case I failed to get into SJI. For years I had walked across a bridge over a canal on my way to school. I decided that if I was not accepted at SJI, I could easily climb over the green sides of the bridge and put myself at the mercy of the cars and the canal below. The thought of thus escaping facing my father comforted me at night, and I waited for the day of the results. As I went to school that fateful day, I marked the spot on the bridge that would be ideal to jump from. But I had indeed gotten into SJI—the premier secondary school for boys in Malaysia.

Until then I had largely been ignorant of my life as a pawn in the success story that my parents had designed for me. But now, as I approached age 13, I was beginning to understand more of the world around me, and came to realize that for the most part, that world did not include me. I saw that I was entrapped in this game of parental expectations, but did not have the courage to try and change the rules.

My first week in St. Joseph's was spent in admiration of its traditions and its hundred and sixty-odd years of high achievement. In my first year, I was initiated into the various conflicts that plagued the remainder of my years in Malaysia: fighting for my space, defending my race against the Chinese, struggling to relate to the other Indians who were of a different worldview, trying to sustain myself on a vegetarian diet, and struggling to live up to my father's expectations.

My Indianness centered mostly around classical Carnatic music, vegetarianism, and my newfound interest in meditation. The other Indian boys, because of their different interests, stuck together, spoke in their slang, idled on the stairs, and did badly academically. Although I found myself defending them to the Chinese, I didn't really identify with them either. I found myself rationing my time and efforts among all the groups, not wholly respecting or belonging to any one, but trying to fit in with all of them.

One aspect of my lifestyle that set me apart was my *mridangam,* a drum that is played in classical Carnatic music. The tradition is strong in my family, and many relatives hoped that I would follow suit and become a famous Carnatic percussion player. In Malaysia I began taking lessons. I enjoyed the first few years, and basked in all the attention I got. I performed on stage and on TV and radio a few times in Malaysia. However, once I entered SJI, academic excellence became my foremost concern and *mridangam* was relegated to a mere hobby. In my second year at SJI, I got tired of making excuses to avoid the required two hours of daily practice. Complaining that schoolwork was just too hectic, I turned away from *mridangam.* My father soon came to accept my change of heart, although he predicted that after I grew up I would look back and regret having quit.

My father was right. I do regret it. I could have grown to relish cooking up rhythmic patterns in my head, to revel in expressing my creative energy. But there was one glitch that made me stop. I had tried hard to get the exercises right, but it wasn't easy. I would practice till my hands bled on the rim of the drum, but I just couldn't seem to get it right. The thought that I could try so hard and fail at something was devastating to me. I had built the illusion of being a super-achiever. Everything else came easily to me, and *mridangam* had to as well. When it didn't, I decided to pack it up. My father bestowed on me another title—"The Quitter."

My father came home soon after with news that when I finished the school year we would have to relocate to India. We had lived in Malaysia for nine years, and it had affected my view of my homeland. India, with its lackluster economic performance, was a frequent butt of jokes in Malaysia, where material success was the all-important element of survival. Even to the local Indians, I would try to defend India, talking about its history, its benign nature, the endearing humanity of the people, and so on. But now, faced with the idea of going back and living in Bombay, I found myself quite opposed to the thought of ruining my career prospects, stuck in a rut in an unknown corner of the world.

Knowing that I was going to be gone soon, my ties to friends became stronger and more sentimental. I cried through my entire farewell ceremony at SJI. When our departure day came, I was touched to find twenty-three of my friends at the airport to see me off. As I walked to the plane, I turned to take a last look and saw a line of dark faces lining the windows of Gate 34, making me feel like the most loved person in the world. They gave me the confidence that I was indeed ready for India, and I tried to look forward to my first breaths of winter air in as long as I could remember. It would be a stark difference, I told myself, and I must try to make the best of it. In retrospect, I am glad that we moved to Bombay. The tough streets of Bombay were an ideal classroom to have my identity and core beliefs bolstered in preparation for my giant leap across continents to an American college. In the two years there, my own voice grew louder and more confident both within my family and in school; indeed, Bombay ultimately helped show me who I was.

We landed in Bombay on January 9, 1989, almost ten years after we had left. My initial reaction was one of simple shock. We landed at night and were guided through the airport and the streets to the hotel. I still see the images: a mass of dark oily faces pressing themselves on the glass windows of the airport; the taxi cab, an arcane remnant of the 1960s; the empty, narrow, dimly lit streets of Bombay; and the hotel room that served as our home for a month as our apartment was renovated far behind schedule. It was a tough experience for all of us, and tensions grew.

One evening my father returned from the office and noticed that I had left my sweater unfolded on his bed. The smoldering volcano finally began to spew lava. He began shouting at me about how I was completely irresponsible, uncooperative, and an utter pain in his rear. Finally I emerged from the bathroom, fed up with the abuse. I don't know what came over me, but I just didn't feel like hearing my father's inconsiderate noises any more. "It's not fair, Appa. I'm only 16. There's a limit to what I can take, too," I answered back.

For the first time I had found my voice and stood my ground, though fleetingly. We argued about the sweater for a while, and then I let him have the last word. He then asked us if we were ready for dinner. We normally alternated lunch and dinner between a Chinese restaurant in the hotel and a South Indian place farther down the street. The latter was my father's favorite, as it was the closest place he could get to home-cooked food. But being quite tired of the same Indian fare, I asked if we could eat Chinese for dinner instead. Old Faithful vented his steam yet again. "Don't you talk back at me. You either come with us, or don't eat at all."

I retorted, my voice quivering in fear, "It's just not fair. Not fair. We have our problems, too, you know. It's tough for all of us. You're the one who got the transfer to Bombay, and you go to the office and that's it. I have no idea what's going to happen from here on. I'm scared too. You're not the only one with problems."

My father gave me the look of a predator, too angry for words. He was beginning his strongest attack on me yet when the phone rang. While he talked my sister said that it was all over for me, and that the only sensible thing for me to do now was to apologize to father after he got off the phone. "Apologize for what?" I asked. And she said, "Just tell him you weren't thinking." He got off the phone and there was a cold and uncanny silence. I walked over meekly and told him I wasn't thinking. He looked up, and with his next words raised himself from being a mere policing benefactor to an adored role model. "That's not true. You were thinking. And you're right. It is tough on all of us. We'll go eat Chinese."

My sister couldn't believe it. My mom, glad to see the storm pass, bravely went up to my father and placed a supportive hand on his shoulder. At that moment, I loved my family. I believed that we were now ready to take whatever lay ahead for us in Bombay, for we were finally beginning to act as a unit that shared its fears and respected one another's needs. I understood, and even felt, my father's pain: He was scared, too, of what was going to happen to all of us. That incident represented a remarkable victory for me. I had taken a big risk in speaking out for something I felt strongly about, and the reward was quite sweet. I had been scared out of my wits, yet had taken a leap of faith, trusting my instincts that the just outcome would prevail. This incident, though minor, stuck with me thereafter. It flashed before my mind before I finally confronted J.J. at college, and again before I mustered up the strength to express my feelings toward Farha.

In the next couple of years my father and I became good friends. My sister attended university in Australia, and that left just three of us at home. My father had his frustrations and his lessons in adaptation at the office, and I had my daily trials at school. We brought them to the dinner table, where we shared our thoughts and grew to respect each other more. Knowing that I was trying my best to adapt and survive in school, my father didn't pressure me as much. I was discovering a confidant and a role model in my father.

Father also made no attempt to hide his pride in his son. He was happy with the way I was flourishing and maturing, growing in stride with the incremental measures of freedom given to me. I know that my growing older must have had something to do with it all, but I'm convinced that it was the softening of my father's nature that made Bombay bearable. Gaining his approval and making him proud of me, for who I was, for my ideas about people, for the way I dealt with situations, gave me tremendous encouragement and confidence.

Bombay went beyond just being a catalyst in the changing relationship with my father; it shaped my understanding of myself and of the people around me. It's a tough thing, becoming disillusioned with people. And I was disillusioned, over and over again, by the people who I came into contact with in Bombay. It was especially hard, since I had looked to India to fill a void that I felt in my identity. I went back to India thinking I was finally among my own people. We would understand each other, and we would be better accepted for the values and common faults we shared.

In short, I had been convinced that I would meet more like-minded people in Bombay, that I would develop strong connections that complemented my connections in Malaysia. I just had to! It was my culture—I was Indian, wasn't I? I had read the Mahabharata and Ramayana, hadn't I? I was initiated and reasonably religious, right? Put together, in my head, that meant that India and I shared a common "culture." I was to learn, much to my dismay, that culture goes beyond books, food, songs, and religion. It strikes at the core identity of a person, and Bombay and I were clearly not cut from the same cloth. The educated middle class in Bombay seemed to be caught up in living for societal approval, mainly by accumulating piles of money. I saw a society that was immensely cynical in its fatalistic surrender to suffering, and surprisingly aggressive, given its nonviolent modern history.

I soon found myself at Bombay Public School (BPS), the most expensive private school in Bombay. What I saw at BPS was nothing short of appalling, and it did not reassure me that I would soon fit in in Bombay. The students would sit quietly and attentively when "Sir" or "Ma'am" was around, but the moment the authority figures left the classroom, mayhem broke loose. Chairs toppled, bodies clashed, as the boys, all younger than I, got together to play a game that they had invented, hitting a tennis ball against the back wall. There was absolute pandemonium at the back of the class where I sat.

A large part of my time was spent worrying about the state of affairs in Bombay. The education system, with its blind emphasis on pure percentage points and admissions tests, coupled with parental pressure, was wreaking havoc on the character of the students. All anyone cared about was grades. Character mattered not; as long as a student had the grades, every misdemeanor in the world could be justified. This bothered me a lot, for many reasons. What were these boys going to be like when they grew up? What kind of a society were we going to have? It was such a shock that I was going to be living with people like this; I was terrified that in a couple of years I would grow to assimilate and take on characteristics that I did not respect. Even if I didn't want to, the pressure to perform, given the yardsticks that others measured me by, would demand that I cheat on exams, and take every opportunity to push someone else down in order to climb a little higher myself. The survival game, played by trees and insects in the Amazon, was being enacted "live" in Bombay Public School, and I was probably the only person there detached enough to see it.

I had to do something. Anything. I stood for elections in my class and became a representative of the Students' Council. I decided to start with the smallest unit— my own classroom. I convinced my classmates to be more organized in maintaining and caring for our classroom. Soon they got the desks put in orderly rows, the floor swept, chalk for the teachers, and we started to actually feel proud being Class 11-F. Spurred by my success, I ventured into other classes. Soon thereafter I was walking up the stairs from recess when a group of boys "escorted" me into the bathroom; there they beat me up. "Just who the hell do you think you are? Just go back to Malaysia or Hong Kong or wherever it is that you came from. This is India, okay, and we like the way things are just fine." I was able to stare down their leader, again finding a determination that I did not know I had. This boy then actually apologized for the "misunderstanding," pulling something straight out of a Hindi movie. "Hey, man, we could use someone like you in our group. Why don't you join us? Here, take my hand in friendship." Although I turned down his invitation to join their gang, he went on to buy me a mango drink, apparently convinced that I was worthy of more respect than he originally thought.

After that, though, my attempts at organization slowly fell apart. I had hoped that the momentum of my early success would inspire others to join in and start contributing positively. Instead, as my energy waned, so did the condition of the classrooms. I was attracting more cynical derision than I was inspiring, and I soon learned to bear down and start working toward my escape from what seemed to me like Alcatraz.

The first year of Bombay, with its encounters with prejudice and closed-mindedness, took its toll on me. I grew cynical and aggressive—emotions that I felt I needed to get by from day to day. I also picked up the important Hindi expletives and managed to keep a few friends happy once in a while buying them drinks during recess. I met up with some of the more sophisticated girls, and was invited to dance parties; repressed and socially unknown as I was for much of my time in Malaysia, I thoroughly enjoyed the popularity I received in Bombay. But that was the public image of Devneesh in school. On the way home, I would release my tension and anger at the hopelessness around me by punching and kicking the back of the seat in front of me. By the end of the two years, that bus endured a lot of abuse from me—the metal seat was dented and mangled by the time I graduated from BPS.

I should say, however, that I was a markedly different person at home. I thought about each day, satisfied that I had pulled it off. Whew! I saw myself as playing a role in school to survive. It wasn't really me. Oh, no. The real me had to be securely hidden away. I nurtured myself at home, in the evenings, by meditating, in private, with the lights off, floating away to a distant place buried deep within me. I was amazed at the extent to which I learned to perfect the art, and soon grew to look forward to the two or three hours in the evenings when I sat by myself and worked diligently, toying with my thoughts, emotions, and beliefs. Meditation helped show me my strength and nurtured my idealistic beliefs, just as BPS helped to show me how low I could stoop.

I didn't really live in Bombay or go to BPS after that. I was distant from almost everybody I met and soon retreated into an inner shell where nobody was allowed. I rarely spoke in class and liked to spend recess on my own. There were not many strong connections of my liking to be made in Bombay. Taking the SATs and running away to an American college or university seemed like my only real option. Dartmouth was the only college for which the early decision deadline hadn't passed when I received the forms, so I put all my effort and prayer into that application and waited for the decision. When I was notified that I had been accepted, I shouted and jumped in my house for twenty minutes nonstop, for this represented an escape from Bombay and what the city had come to represent for me.

It is difficult to put into perspective the influence that Bombay had on me. It gave me a lot of strength and confidence in myself, as a person with mental ability and social skills. However, it also took away from me a certain mirth I had. Life became an endless struggle against suffering and disappointment. Defending myself against the challenges that faced me every day, I also learned to broaden my views about other human beings. I had never before been exposed to such magnanimity of spirit, or such depravity of morals. In Bombay, my ideas about what humanity and suffering meant gained broader, deeper definitions. But it had become clear to me that Bombay would not nurture the person whom I thought I wanted to become.

As I flew over western Asia and the Atlantic on my way to Dartmouth, my excitement and anticipation grew. Dartmouth was my final chance, my final hope for finding a place where I belonged. Turning away from Malaysia and now India, I looked to America to fill a void of identity and acceptance. Would I find a home? Would I find friends? Would I both give and receive love and respect? I admit it was a lot to expect from a new land, but Dartmouth was to be my very own unhindered opportunity to realize my ultimate goal—to know myself.

Which brings me to that afternoon in the winter of my first year, when I went down to the river, lay on the hammock, and contemplated walking onto the frozen river. In the calm of the frozen riverside, where the trees were laden with snow, I vaguely remembered a song from what seemed a long-forgotten distant past. During my second year at St. Joseph's the senior assistant used to lead us singing:

If I can help somebody, as I pass along.
If I can do my duty, to a world upwrought.
If I can spread Love's message, that the Master taught . . .
Then my living shall not be in vain.

That song had always made me feel happy, and it did this time, too. It made me think about what use I could be to a society and about what really gave me happiness. If I could make a difference to somebody or someplace, sometime, I thought that would make me happy. It would satisfy my need to do something lasting and productive. I could go on at Dartmouth, doing all the things I was supposed to, obeying the ingrained habits of my upbringing and my present company, but secretly hoping to make a difference, in my own private way, in my own private time. In doing so, I could perhaps know myself and be happy with what I knew.

The Devneesh that had been bred to succeed and achieve, for security and recognition, finally allowed another Devneesh some space to breathe and grow. The second Devneesh wanted to do what made him most happy—to try to live unconditionally. That day a small battle started between my two halves—one side accountable to my parents, seeking their approval, and the other stressing my independence, accountable only to itself and the few selected people that it respects. Foremost among the selected was Michael, who was my closest American male friend. I looked to him for a gateway into American life, and he always explained as patiently and sincerely as he listened. He did it without being condescending, as though he recognized that it was an effort for me to adjust. I wondered how Michael came to be so different from the other males that I had met. He was the reverse image of J.J., and I was eager and hopeful that our budding friendship would grow with time, and that we would continue to respect each other as we came to know each other's strengths as well as weaknesses.

I longed to be seen as an equal by Michael, for I saw that he was a good person and I wanted to have him accept me as such as well. I couldn't identify it then, but we shared a common thread: Both of us had been through times that were painful and that made us look beyond the immediate, requiring us to grow and shape ourselves to deal with the pain. Perhaps both saw ourselves as outsiders at this college: he, a Jew from Texas, and I, a Hindu from Bombay. As a result, we both had a certain measure of confidence and respect for ourselves, which not only enhanced the quality of our conversations, but also made us look to each other for understanding and empathy.

Friendship with Michael was played by strict rules. And I often worried that words spoken during a disagreement or in a bad mood would permanently come between us. There were many times when Michael saw me in one of my more insecure or defensive moods. He would see me put on airs to impress someone, or be rude to a mutual acquaintance. He saw me be socially rough around the edges, and saw me make my blunders. Sometimes he would say something about it: "What was that all about, Dev? I didn't really understand why you did that." Caught in the act, I would find myself scrambling to hide my nakedness. Realizing that defensive explanations, regardless of how creative, were probably not going to fool him, I'd find myself discussing my faults with him. As a result, he got to see me more completely, and the fear that he would reject me for my faults was slowly assuaged.

The other person who has commanded my enduring respect is Farha, who has since evolved from being a "fungus" in my imagination to becoming a part of my every day and night, my daily thoughts and feelings, my anger and my tears, such that I feel incomplete when she's not around me. I love her dearly, and she has given me what nobody else has before—honesty, trust, and respect. And she brought out the same qualities in me, which I never really gave anyone else before either. She has become the active part of my conscience, which keeps me in check. She gives me the warmth of a mother, the support of a friend, the attention of an equal. We learn every day from each other, as we grow to understand each other more.

Yet as I explained earlier, it wasn't always like that. Our present relationship, cordial and occasionally intimate, began in the fall of my junior year, after I returned from a summer internship in San Francisco. After our dismal interaction during freshman year, we hardly met or spoke to each other during the fall of our sophomore year. That winter though, I decided to take the initiative to break the ice. It worked, and we cautiously experimented with getting to know each other as friends. Because of my friendship with Farha, I threw away an application for transfer that I had requested to MIT. There was too much I could potentially lose, I felt, if I left Dartmouth now.

After reuniting with Farha I got a summer internship, and the next few months turned out to be the most important three months of my first two years at college. It gave me relief from Dartmouth—from its fraternities that I felt excluded from, and from the constant competition and politics that plagues me there. It also gave me a chance to be alone, working hard, earning money, resting well on weekends, and cooking my own food. For the first time I started to feel I had a niche where I was cozy and comfortable. I also learned a most important lesson that summer.

It was a Saturday that summer, when two friends and I made a trip to Mount St. Helens. As we hiked up the volcano, we soon came to a point in the trail where a patch of snow lay dead in our path. If we were to go on to get a glimpse of the open top of St. Helens, we'd have to cross that patch and walk on for about an hour more. I looked down and saw that if I slipped while trying to cross it, I would slide for about a hundred meters and then fall right off the face of the mountain. I could feel my legs preparing to mutiny. I wanted so badly to get across, but was entrenched in the belief that I couldn't do it. I would fall. I would slip. I would die. I would look like a fool. I couldn't do it. It was a dumb idea. What would father say? He'd say it was a dumb idea. He's right, he's always right. Turn back now—and there won't be any trouble. No risk. No danger.

I wasn't going to look like the coward to my friends, though. Halfheartedly, I started to try to cross the iceberg. One step, left foot forward. That was okay. Next, move the right foot. Good. Now, move the left foot over. . . . Oops! . . . My foot slipped, and I panicked. I still had my right foot in place, and so I dug my fingers into the icy slope to keep from falling. Then my fingers started to freeze and I realized I had to do something fast. This was it. I was going to die. I began to run through a list of the things that I thought I would regret if I were to fall from that cliff. I wouldn't realize my dream of helping India out of its poverty, and I wouldn't live to give Farha the silver ring that I had made for her birthday. I remembered my parents, and thought to myself that they were going to be heartbroken at my death. One of my friends steadied me, and we inched our way backward off the snow. I was only too glad to be on firm ground again and thought that it was best to give up and head back.

We reluctantly turned around and started walking back, and I faced head-on the realization that I had given up on myself. It was my fear that had enlarged a simple patch of snow, not much different from those abundant in Hanover, into an imposing iceberg. I realized I was running away from an opportunity to do something that was within my reach because I was inhibited by my fear. And that patch symbolized many fears: my fear of never being completely independent of my family, my fear of failure, my fear of letting down those important to me, and, yes, my fear of not being able to face Farha without worrying about rejection.

I decided to try again, trying not to think of my fear of falling. I instead recited the Gayatri Mantra to calm myself, to remind myself of who I really was. I pushed away other thoughts, inhibitions, warnings, and fear signals, and just thought about getting across. Much to my amazement, in my newfound courage, the patch appeared no greater than a harmless speck on the ground. Before I knew it, I was across, and so were my friends. We went on to get a wonderful view of the side of the mountain that had been blown open, and I was amazed at how easy the whole thing had been. On our way back, we came across it again. There were a couple of middle-aged women trekking across it. Ashamed as I was that such a simple thing had almost gotten the better of me, I vowed that once I got back to campus, I would give Farha the ring, and I would tell her all there was to tell, tossing my defenses to the wind.

And that is exactly what happened. I told Farha quite plainly that much of the person I had shown her in the past two years was a hoax. I revealed that I had been scared of letting her see me in my natural state, lest she reject me. Vulnerable though I now was, I felt my affection for her flow through me. Farha, who had never been intimately involved with a male before, took some time to get used to the idea that she was interested in a guy. Given her family's strict objections to her being in a relationship, especially with a non-Muslim, it took inordinate courage on her part to take the steps that she did to get to know me better. She ventured out of her cocoon, and we spent days and nights finding out about each other, and finding ourselves in the process.

My upbringing was not geared toward taking risks. I am from a traditional conservative background that would have been only too happy if I had turned out no different from the generations before me—mild, passive, salaried, educated, and none too ambitious. But the events in my life, coupled with the impulses of my soul, ended up taking me out of that cozy cocoon, so much so that to go back would be akin to incarceration.

All through my adolescence, I have been struggling to find a community outside my home, struggling to find my own voice, to define my own dreams, to carve my own path. My parents will always be a part of me, even after they are not physically around to comfort and guide me. However, I still am looking, in earnest, to build a community of close friends who understand and stimulate me.

I struggled in Malaysia through my first ten years of schooling. Just as I was beginning to adapt adeptly, just as I was venturing out of my shell, learning the rules of the society vastly different from that in my home, I moved to Bombay. I thought I'd finally be home, but that too soon turned out to be a mirage. Unwilling to give up looking for a nest, I came to the United States, attempting to find that elusive community that would nurture me. Have I found it here in the four years that I've been looking? The answer perhaps lies in the fact that I know I can't go back to either Malaysia or Bombay now. I couldn't give up my links with Michael and Farha. I couldn't give up feeling hopeful again that my goal is still reachable. Here, in America, I am free to chase my goal of growing endlessly. I am free to give my voice freer reign than it ever had before. And as a result, I am the least cynical and unhappy that I remember ever being.

Still there are times that I feel America will never really be home either. I can be happy that I am around friends I love, but to most people I meet, I will always be a "legal alien." Alas, the age of the immigrant is over in America. A community of English-speaking Europeans have lived here long enough for their indelible cultural stamp to dominate. I fear I will be a member of a minority group wherever I go. Such is the life of a wanderer. Some enjoy wandering and may look upon my state with envy. I, however, am tired of wandering and want to feel a link to the land I am in, to the people I am with, and even to the air I breathe. I want the words I voice to be familiar to people around me, to have a deep relevance to their core being.

I want to feel like I helped build this American community. Helped it grow. Helped shape it so that it is better off in the future. I want this for me. I was born too late to fight in the American Civil War, too late to struggle in a sweatshop in New York during the Great Depression, too late to work alongside Gandhi while he built modern India. But my generation will also have its struggles, and I am perfectly poised to contribute a lion's share in the drama of the twenty-first century. So I continue in pursuit of this mirage, except I am, for the first time, enjoying the chase, relishing the risks, and loving scoping out the next opportunity that will give me a strong sense of connection with the people around me.

Trying experiences help one see oneself and know oneself better. My experiences have helped me get to know and love myself, and I'm more capable of respecting and loving others because of it. I know I have my own battles, my own challenges, my own red devils in the night, my own snow patches on cliffs, my own childhood fears and inhibitions, but I'm trying to grow out of them, one at a time, painstakingly moving toward a more fulfilling time, as I know and respect myself more. I am trying. I am doing it with a certain honesty and courage. And I can't give myself a better compliment than that.

THE GIRL IN ME

Emily is a twin, and determined to avoid her sister's tomboy image. She works hard at being a girl, from using nail polish to having crushes on boyfriends. She finds, though, that she silences herself everywhere except in the journal she keeps throughout adolescence. As she gradually comes out as a lesbian, to herself, her friends, and her family, her internal, written self emerges as a public person, someone who can engage fully with others through humor, conversation, and physical relationships.

I tried—God knows I tried. No one can accuse me of going down without a fight. I began shaving my legs at the appropriate age (around 13), I applied lip gloss every few minutes, and I composed long, prosaic diary entries about the depth and color of various boys' eyes. I giggled and went to sleepovers and wondered when I would get my period. My hair, though plain and often unkempt, was long. Also, I had low self-esteem and worried a lot. No one ever had to ask me whether I was a boy or a girl. I was, like so many adolescent girls, clearly working my way toward Alpha Female status.

I never made it.

Oh, sure, I had the normal feminine accoutrements: besides the diary, the makeup, and the hairless (if not shapely) legs, I indulged perpetually in crushing on boys, and I even managed to snag a boyfriend when I was 14. James was quite a catch by eighth grade standards, in that he was only a little greasy and occasionally even punctuated his grunts with complete sentences. Our relationship began one balmy April night in that breeding ground of all great romances, the middle school gym. He asked me to slow dance; I acquiesced; and, midway through the song, he confessed his months-long crush on me. When he asked me if I would go out with him, I knew what to do—I said yes. And when the song ended, I knew what to do—I ran and told all of my friends about it, and didn't stop talking about it for about three weeks. James was great and all, and I couldn't wait to spend time with him, but right now I had the very important duty of sharing this amazing news with every single one of my acquaintances. They provided the appropriate shrieks.

James and I dated for five months—eternity for eighth-graders—but things didn't go very well. Though we often held hands, and though I placidly accepted his occasional peck on the cheek and quietly listened to his analyses of the merits of various television programs, he wasn't satisfied. I didn't understand. I sat around waiting for his phone call, and when he did finally call, he insisted I turn on the same TV show he was watching, so I would understand and appreciate his witty commentary. I watched TV for him—on a *school* night. I'd never done that before. What more could he want?

And yet he wanted more. He told me he loved me, and I said, "Um. Thanks." He told me he wanted to French-kiss me, and I said, "Um. No." I wasn't a complete slut, after all. But then he called me a prude, and I didn't say anything; instead I French-kissed him. It was disgusting. Adolescents should be made to sign a contract saying they will not stick their tongues in anyone's mouth until they are at least 16 or 17 years of age. But we had no contract; we had a terrible slobbery make-out session on his mother's couch, instead.

Soon after that, he dumped me. I went to high school single and ready to meet boys. I had contact lenses. I had confidence. I practically had *breasts* by now (I was a late bloomer). I was going to find a new boy, a cute boy, a nice prude boy.

This turned out to be problematic. And the problem was not the quality of the male population at my high school—there were plenty of new boys, cute boys, even nice prude boys. The problem was me. Something inside me wasn't working right. The girl in me—the girl who wore lip gloss, shaved her legs, and loved boys—was broken.

* * *

From an early age, maybe 4 or 5, I knew what a girl was. "Girl" was the nail polish my baby-sitter carried in her purse, the bras my mother wore, the splash of shiny curls on TV. I was girl. My twin sister was girl, but she was bad at it.

We were fraternal twins, and I knew instinctively this was a good thing. It wouldn't behoove me to look like her. Tina refused skirts and threw tantrums over dresses. She tagged after our brother—our elder by three years—and played cowboys with him, and followed him to the tops of trees. She could beat me up; often she *did* beat me up, and not without good reason. When I learned the word "tomboy," I decided to adjust the phrase to better suit my boyish twin. Hence the nickname "Tina-boy" was born.

"Tina-boy," like all good insults, stuck hard and stuck fast. Even her own friends used it against her (and when they did, she would turn around and hit me, returning, I suppose, to the source of the word). Like many twins, I struggled to create an identity clearly separate from that of my sister. And perhaps one easy way to do this was to verbally demonstrate my disgust with her masculine tendencies. Not that I was ever really "girly-girl" in my own behavior—I climbed the same trees Tina did, and I caught the baseballs she threw at me. Nevertheless, the taunt persisted: "Tina-boy!" upstairs after dinner, when our parents wouldn't hear. "Tina-boy" during recess at school, where her friends could hear. "Tina-boy!" in the backyard, as I ran and my sister barreled after me in a mix of rage and tears. I couldn't have said why I called her that name; she couldn't have said why it made her cry. We were 6 years old.

But we both knew gender. Gender was everywhere.

Our parents did not pressure us to be "normal" girls—nor did they insist my somewhat solitary brother give up his reading and hiking for sports like baseball or football. My sister almost never had to wear a dress, and we both joined the local softball team. Mom and Dad were liberal for a reason: Mom had been a tomboy herself, as a child, and she remained uninterested in fashion, cooking, and other stereotypically feminine trimmings. Dad was happy, after realizing his son wasn't interested in baseball, to discover two little girls more than willing to run after his fly balls.

Our parents also encouraged all of us kids to think independently and do what made us happy. For instance, my parents didn't watch television. My mother read mysteries because mysteries made her happy, and my father listened to opera because opera made him happy. If these examples of my parents' independence do not seem noteworthy, that is because my parents were not exceptionally weird. We were not an aggressively eccentric family. Our parents taught us to be respectfully nonconformist, docile in our differences. Like them, we were not to be different for the sake of being different; we were to be different if and when being true to ourselves meant being different from what the majority did or believed.

My parents certainly didn't have to worry about me being different for the sake of being different. As a child, I spent much of my time striving to minimize the discrepancies between myself and my peers. It wasn't difficult to figure out who I was "supposed" to be. We lived in a very homogenous town; most residents were middle class, white, and politely but deeply conservative. The public schools were superb, but many parents chose to send their children to private institutions. The farmlands between neighborhoods were gradually overtaken by more neighborhoods and bigger houses. I grew up with the implicit belief that most people in America lived in a town exactly like mine.

Because everyone looked and acted roughly the same, I became obsessed by differences between my family and everyone else that felt huge—insurmountable—but were in fact quite small. My parents were middle class, white, and, interestingly, in spite of their own forays into nonconformity, politely but deeply conservative, just like everyone else. But as an insecure child, I did not see these similarities—these were the elements of my existence that were so ingrained as to be invisible. I saw the differences.

My family didn't go to church or visit friends or watch hours of television—instead, we read books. I became addicted to books long before I realized that compulsive reading was not a universal obsession. But I quickly became aware that my family read much more than other families and that there was a word for this. We were "nerds." And so I found a way of articulating the difference between myself and the rest of the world. I was nerdy.

I assumed it was this nerdiness that made me unable to live like a normal girl, to French-braid my hair and find a skirt that felt natural on my body. It did not occur to me that these could be separable issues, this love of reading and this inability to do gender properly. I was 8 years old; I was not exactly in the habit of analyzing the social fabric of my identity.

I knew that I couldn't give up reading; reading was without a doubt the best thing I had going for me. Books were a welcome respite from the stress of trying to live in a world so rife with stressful situations. When you read, you don't have to make decisions about anything, about what pants to wear or who to sit next to. You just let yourself go—you didn't exist—you just get pulled along by the current of words.

At this particular point in my life, not existing was often as close as I got to happiness.

So I read, and reading was my real life—the Baby-Sitters Club, then Sweet Valley High, then *A Tree Grows in Brooklyn,* then Steinbeck, Willa Cather, Harper Lee. When I wasn't reading, I went mutely through the motions of having an existence. I did not talk. I understood the power of words, and I wasn't ready to commit to have words of my own—not out loud, anyway.

On paper was a different matter. From fourth grade on, I kept a diary, a jumble of complaints, gossip, and secret thrills. By middle school I was obsessed with—and doing absolutely nothing about—the disparity between the "real me" who appeared in my stories, poems, and journals, and the pale shadow of a person who stalked the edges of other peoples' lives.

*   *   *

There are multiple strands to this story, multiple strands that became braided into the singular problem of who I was. It is hard now to express how unified everything felt to me during childhood, how naturally and unconsciously I connected reading and silence and gender. It's hard to express now, with my adult (and decidedly collegiate) habit of analyzing, breaking things down, examining the miniscule. But people forget: childhood is not like that. When the boys rode past my house on their bikes and called me "Mute Girl"—a clever tribute to my unresponsiveness—it was not merely my silence they mocked. They mocked my books, my journals, my plain hair, my athleticism, everything.

In a way, though, I was lucky. They did me the privilege of affirming my femininity, of calling me "girl." My sister was not faring so well in that department.

If the bulk of insults hurled my way reflected on my silence—if that had become my defining feature, my biggest weakness—my sister was far more likely to hear remarks about her gender. Kids called her a boy, and later, when they learned the words, a lesbian, a dyke. Sometimes they said it to me: "Is your sister a lesbian?" I was ashamed of her.

My shame only increased with age, and by middle school, I was ashamed of most things; I could have made a list. I was ashamed of my brother (he was too nerdy); my sister (*was* she a lesbian?); my parents (everything about them, just *everything,* was embarrassing); and myself: my grades, my silence, my lack of friends, my flat chest, my hair, my glasses, my voice, my eyebrows, my handwriting, my fingernails, my everything.

I was unable to look people in the eye. I was unable to speak. I was too ashamed.

And so I wrote. I wrote obsessively, fumbling through the questions I couldn't bear to take to another living person: Why didn't this boy like me? Why had that girl stopped speaking to me? Why hadn't I been invited to this party?

I wrote bitterly about an incident in sixth grade, when my best friend at the time did grave insult to me. We were sitting in English class, done with our work early (we had been thrown together by our status as the smartest kids in the class, and, in fact, we would graduate from our large public high school as valedictorian and salutatorian), and Shereen was complaining about her lack of friends in class. "I wish I had more friends," she said.

"Why?" I asked. "You have *me*, after all." I was half-joking, implying that I spoke in jest but actually meaning it very seriously: Was I not enough?

"Yeah," she said, unconvinced. "But, no offense, you're kind of boring."

Later, I wrote furiously: *I am boring. She's right. Of course she wants more friends, better friends. I have no personality. I don't talk. I just sit there like a lump.* This was true. Even among my few close friends, I spent the majority of my time acting as if I was trying to achieve status as an inanimate object. There was some part of me that did not feel as if I had friends at all. In eighth grade, I bitterly announced during French class that I had no friends. I personally offended at least five different girls, girls I sat with in class and giggled with at lunch; it was a callous thing to say (I was not yet aware that anyone besides myself could suffer or feel insecure). But in a way it was true: some part of me, the part with which I most closely identified, was not connecting with other human beings. In a sense that felt very real to me, I *didn't* have any friends.

This was the part of myself that came out on paper. In fact, it wasn't the fault of my classmates that I didn't consider them my friends; it wasn't because they weren't smart enough, kind enough, or good enough. It was my own fault for hoarding this self, for keeping it limited to pen and paper, for not having the courage to share it. I recognized this fact, but I didn't know how to translate this "real me" off the page and into the world.

And there were other parts of me, deeper, more frightening parts that I could not even bring myself to write about on paper. I never wrote that I was ashamed of my sister, ashamed of my association with her. And I certainly never wrote that I thought I might be gay.

But it was there, a shadow of a notion lurking inside me: *I might be gay.* It surfaced once in a while, but I chose to bury it again. I couldn't face it; it was unbearable. The idea started when I was very young; then, it was inarticulate, because I didn't know what gay was. My sister and I played with our troll dolls, taking on the identities of our favorite trolls, and our characters were always male. Our trolls drove around in fancy sports cars, lived in mansions, and seduced and won countless women. It was always more fun to play at being boy trolls, because they got to do the things Tina and I wanted to do. And if they had girlfriends, well, that was only because we both wanted romance, and if our characters were male, it only made sense that they would fall in love with women. It was a game.

Still, we never played trolls with our other friends.

I remember the first time I really *looked* at a girl. It was seventh grade. My friend Anne and I were standing at our lockers, chatting, when I suddenly looked at her lips and wondered what it might be like to kiss her. I had never thought about kissing in quite that way before; certainly I dreamed of my first kiss, but that was with a boy, and it was hard to imagine. I always assumed that was just because I didn't know anything about kissing—how could I imagine what I didn't know anything about? But here I was staring at Anne's lips and feeling like I could imagine it. They were soft and full, not at all like a boy's lips. They were *kissable.*

Then the moment ended, and I decided never to think about it again. I went back to daydreaming about various boys, and in fact, I really did believe, if a bit too resolutely, that I was in love with whatever boy I happened to be thinking about. I thought constantly about dating different boys—so how could I be anything but perfectly normal? I would never have thought to identify my feelings about certain females as crushes. That idea didn't occur to me when I looked at a girl in my gym class and admired the ease with which she played dodge ball, or when I couldn't stop staring at an older girl on my volleyball team, the one whose face was so beautiful.

I never wrote about these instances. Instead I described in detail the face and habits of my crush and future boyfriend James. When he finally asked me out on the night of that fateful dance, I turned, after shrieking to my friends, to my journal: *Is this real?* I wrote. *Can this be real?* Dating was something that happened to other girls. For the several months of our relationship, in fact, my life felt unreal, no longer my own. This was a clue. Dating James didn't quite fit with the rest of me. I assumed this was because I had never dated before, and perhaps this was partly true. But I did not consider that I might be dating the wrong person—or, worse, the wrong gender.

I did write about my misery when one of my close friends got a boyfriend— somehow, although I was dating James by then, it seemed as if she had betrayed me. I had never lost sight of my priorities even after I started going out with James. I still stuck with my friends first. But Michelle was actually spending more time with her boyfriend than with me. In other words, she actually *liked* her boyfriend. This was baffling; it made me feel vaguely insecure. Was I supposed to like James as much as she seemed to like Chris?

It was mostly a relief when James dumped me, though I sobbed after I got off the phone with him. I no longer had to force myself to enjoy his presence in my life or his tongue in my mouth. And anyway, what did it matter? I was starting high school.

I hoped to achieve the following modest accomplishments during high school (as articulated in my journal the summer before): I would acquire a close-knit group of male and female friends who would enjoy books and the arts; I would acquire a boyfriend who would enjoy books and the arts and also pass for moderately attractive; I would get good grades.

My efforts were not a total failure. I did get good grades.

The main problem with high school, besides my general inability to relate so-cially to my peers, was the utter lack of crush-worthy boys. It was rather astound-ing. Were my standards so high? Was it normal for a high school with a population of some twenty-five hundred students to house within its walls not a single at-tractive, intelligent boy? Did the census know about this? Did the other girls know about this? But that was part of the problem. All around me, girls were routinely developing crushes on and entering into relationships with these very same boys. They did not seem at all dissatisfied with the quality of the males in their lives. Even my sister asked a boy out (he said no). Something wasn't right. Mustering all of my willpower, I developed a half-hearted crush on Jason, who was in my sci-ence class. He didn't talk much, and he had nice eyes. In my journal I attributed to Jason all sorts of positive attributes: he was sensitive and passionate; he read books; and, most importantly, he secretly adored me.

Meanwhile, in math class, there was Katie. Katie was the most beautiful girl I had ever seen. Her eyes were so *big.* I would look at her in class and wish fer-vently that I could be like her. That was what I repeated to myself like a mantra: I wanted to be like her. I wanted to be like her. It wasn't that I liked her—it wasn't that. She was just so smart and pretty and nice. Everyone probably wanted to be like her. I tried to gauge whether other people admired Katie as much as I did, but as usual, the general population did not seem to share my sentiments. So I kept my thoughts to myself and watched Katie from afar. I *really* wanted to be like her.

One day in math class, we were assigned to work in the same group. I was terrified. I was wearing the wrong sweater. Katie pulled her desk over and began talking to me—talking to me!—and writing things down. I nodded mutely. I had no idea why my stomach was making this moment into such a big deal. It wasn't a big deal, it was just a class assignment, it was just some girl.

At random moments during the day, or at night, when I was falling asleep, Katie's face would materialize in my mind. I pushed the thought away.

Meanwhile, Tina and I were trying hard to establish ourselves as separate en-tities. We now shared the same group of friends, although she was more estab-lished within the group than I was. I felt, as I always had, vaguely ashamed of my sister, even when no one else was the least bit troubled by her behavior. But it was more problematic now, because I knew this shame was wrong; I knew it made me a bad person. I couldn't help it, though. I wanted her to stop being so . . . so *much.* Why did she have to keep her hair so short? Why couldn't she dress like a normal girl? Why did she laugh so loudly? Why did she talk so much? I tried to emphasize the differences between us by keeping my hair long, keeping quiet, and keeping my clothes as normal as possible. I couldn't quite meet her eyes in public.

One of our friends once told me, in strict confidence, that she had overheard boys in her gym class discussing which one of "the twins" was the hottest. Every boy had cast his vote for me. My friend waited for me to squeal; they had picked me! But I could only stare dully at her, the storm inside me made inarticulate by its intensity. How dare they insult my sister. *How dare they?* At the same time, I felt a prick of pride in my chest—they had picked me! And then, I was nearly bowled

over by my shame; I was taking pride in beating my own sister, in something superficial and cruel. I didn't know what to say to my friend.

Maybe that was why I didn't talk, all those years. I sensed that my feelings—
about my sister, about myself, about the pretty girl in math class, about anything—
were not quite right. I wasn't sure I deserved to speak.

It wasn't all bad, though. I was often miserable, but I wasn't *always* miserable.
I made some friends with whom I could talk; they were sarcastic, smart—bookish,
even. I began to notice that I could be funny, that my friends laughed when I
played up absurdities. Here at last was a method by which I could consistently relate to people. Never mind that my parents were concerned that I didn't take anything seriously. Never mind that my father called me a wiseass anytime I made a
joke. I had discovered a way to break this silence that had gagged me mute for
years: I was funny. Mine was not exactly a humor born of happiness, or even good-
natured silliness, but it was something.

Now, of course, after years of using jokes to get through social situations, I
understand that jokes can be another kind of silence: they are another way of keeping myself one step removed from people. Sometimes I make jokes and I don't
even want to; I want to say something genuine, something about how I feel. But the
joke rises most naturally to my lips. I don't mean to denigrate humor, though: it
got me through much of high school.

The summer after my sophomore year, I went to an academic camp. I was
terrified and certain that I wouldn't make any friends, but luck was with me. One
girl, Amanda, singled me out from the beginning. Amanda and I were inseparable
for those three weeks; we wept at the camp's end. Every night she would sneak
into my room, and we would sit on my bed and giggle and whisper for hours after
lights out. Everything was funny with Amanda, and for once, my jokes didn't feel
dry or bitter—they came from a sincere happiness.

Amanda and I stayed in touch, and during my junior year, I went to visit her.
I had been at her house for about twenty minutes and was looking through her
bookshelves when she said, "So, I've been thinking. I'm not really interested in
boys anymore."

"What, you?" I joked. Boys were her favorite conversation topic. "What are
you going to do with yourself if you don't talk about boys?"

"Well," she hedged, "I'm just not that interested in boys."

I remember the moment I began to understand. I was holding her copy of *A
Tree Grows in Brooklyn*—I had been paging through it, only half-attending to her
words—and my throat felt suddenly thick.

"I just don't think I'm feeling very heterosexual right now," she said. She actually *said* it. Out loud.

I stared down at the book. "Oh," I said.

"Is that okay with you?" she asked.

"Oh, yeah," I said quickly. "Yeah. Sure."

I couldn't even joke. It was that familiar feeling—there was too much going
on in me, I couldn't even begin to address it out loud, so I shut down. I nodded
vaguely as she explained that she had come to this realization a few weeks ago and

was still trying to decide whether she was *gay*-gay, or just bisexual. She hadn't determined whether she actually hated men or just didn't find them particularly attractive.

"Well, that's good," I said when she paused. "I'm straight," I added, somewhat irrelevantly.

"Of course," she said. "Peter and all." Peter was my latest crush. He was a boring, chubby boy with a bowl-cut, and I was obsessed with him.

"Yeah," I said. Right about then her parents called us down to dinner, so we obediently trudged downstairs, though not before she informed me that neither her parents nor her sister knew she was gay, so I should probably not mention it during dinner.

She really didn't have to worry. I wouldn't have ever mentioned it again, if she hadn't kept bringing it up.

It wasn't that I was homophobic. I believed very strongly in gay rights, a vague term whose meaning I did not fully grasp, but whose importance I would quickly defend. Theoretically, gay people were perfectly fine. There were some gay gym teachers at my high school—or so it was rumored—and that was fine. I heard that gay people lived in cities, and that was fine. Gay was just fine by me. But Amanda was not just any gay person—she was my *friend*. She was my very, very close friend, with whom I had giggled and shared a bed. I decided that Amanda was mistaken about being gay. I tried to explain this fact to her, but she seemed convinced. Somehow, during the course of my visit, she determined that she was, in fact, very gay, and not bisexual. I rallied hard on behalf of heterosexuality.

"Maybe you're just *afraid* of boys," I suggested.

She raised her eyebrow. "Oh, really," she said.

I looked away. Amanda was, if anything, the least fearful person I knew. It was unlikely that she was afraid of boys.

I left Amanda's house feeling shaken, but it was easy to stop thinking about the whole thing once I was home again. I could sink back into the usual routine: jokes, boys, homework, boys, and, of course, Melissa.

Melissa was my newest friend, and, I decided, a much better friend than Amanda. Melissa and I just related on more levels. We both worked on the newspaper, for instance, and we both shared a similarly absurd sense of humor, and, oh, yes, we both liked boys. We really had quite a bit in common.

Our friendship was incredibly exclusive; my acquaintances dribbled away as I realized I didn't need them anymore, because now I knew what true friendship was. Melissa and I giggled constantly at private jokes and raged together against the loneliness and frustration of being a dork in a middle-class jock high school. I sought her out in the hallways and went to her house every weekend. In math class, I didn't pay attention: I wrote her notes and drew her little pictures.

For the first time since I could remember, I was genuinely happy. Days were bearable because I had class with Melissa, because I would pass Melissa at her locker, because Melissa existed with me in the same building at the same time. I could get through history class, and bus rides, and lunch, by thinking of her. This did not seem particularly strange to me; this was what friendship was. If there was a small part of me that wondered about the intensity of my feelings, it was a very quiet, submissive part. It kept quiet if I wanted it to. And I wanted it to.

Melissa was funny; she was intelligent; she understood me. When my sister understood me, it felt suffocating, like she was pinning me down, like my genes were giving me away, like I would never escape from her knowledge or her shadow. When Melissa understood me, it felt liberating. Like I was in love.

When a thought like that slipped past my careful censors, I rationalized: Well, sure. I do love Melissa. She's my friend. Friends love each other.

I don't know exactly when I began to face it. There was no special moment when I had a revelation—there was no instance when it became suddenly and irrevocably clear to me. But it became harder and harder to ignore the fact that I would pass up a date with any boy on Earth, even if he were perfect in every way, to spend time with Melissa. But I didn't just want to spend time with her. I wanted to look at her. I wanted to kiss her.

Part of the reason I was able to acknowledge my feelings was because I was fairly confident Melissa felt the same way. She gossiped about boys, sure, but so did I. She liked me better than anyone else, that was obvious. She wrote me notes during school, she e-mailed me obsessively, and she invited me over all the time. "I'm crazy about you, Emily," she wrote once. We were clearly in love. It would be hard, of course, but it was bearable because we would do it together. I didn't particularly think of myself as gay at this time—I thought of myself as in love with Melissa. We were beyond labels. Eventually we would admit our feelings to each other, and we would be even happier than we already were. I settled back to enjoy the ride.

When I told Amanda about my feelings, it was because I wanted her to confirm that yes, it sounded like Melissa was crazy about me. She seemed more interested in the fact that I was attracted to a woman, which confused me: this wasn't about women, or even a woman. This was about Melissa. I just wanted to know, did she think Melissa liked me? Didn't it sound like Melissa liked me?

Amanda couldn't say whether Melissa liked me. She had never seen us together.

Yes, but didn't it *sound* like it?

Well, maybe. It could be.

For weeks, months, I bombarded Amanda with e-mails, relating another incident that I felt demonstrated Melissa's obvious affection for me. Amanda bore my obsession well; she wrote back, she counseled, she consoled.

And consoling was in order. One day in January, Melissa informed me that she had a date with a college boy. I was stunned. I tried to take it lightly; I tried to brush it off, she was curious, she was experimenting. But the date turned into another date, and another, and dates turned into late-night phone conversations and visits to his campus for the weekend. They made out; she told me about it.

Suddenly I was very much alone with this *thing* that I had assumed we shared. I didn't know what to do. For the first time, I began to realize my feelings had implications: *I might be gay.* I might have to live that life. And I might have to do it without Melissa.

*   *   *

Even now, describing a part of my life that is over five years old, describing a fear I have long since shed, I tremble. I had no idea how to be gay. I didn't know any gay people, except the gym teachers, and who knew if they were really gay? And who wanted to be like them, ugly, mean, mocked? I knew Amanda, of course, but she wasn't an adult; she didn't know anything more about living a gay life than I did. She hadn't yet told her family about her orientation, and she had never had a girlfriend. We were equally clueless. Now, of course, I know how much it helped to struggle with her, but at the time, her presence in my life seemed singularly unhelpful.

I became obsessed with renting gay movies, sidling over to the gay section of the bookstore, looking at gay websites online and then deleting the Internet's history so my family wouldn't find out what I'd been looking at. I wanted to understand how gay people existed, how they got through the day. How they stopped hating themselves. I began to try out the word, repeating it silently to myself: *Gay.* I still couldn't quite handle *lesbian.* It sounded so ugly. It was tinged with the brutality of an insult, the word hurled at my sister for so many years. I wasn't ready to identify myself with that word. I was ashamed to think of those boys laughing at her, at me, at us. I was furious to think that I had the very flaw they had pinpointed in my sister.

I was somewhat consoled by the fact that Tina was not gay. In a way, it even made me happy: I was *different* from her now. We were distinguishable.

I applied to and was accepted by a college known, among other things, for its student population's liberal attitude toward homosexuality. I read stories by and about gay college students; I began to understand that I might be able to be gay at college. Not now, not in high school, but soon. Meanwhile, I tried coming out. I told Melissa about my orientation, half-hoping she might be jolted by my confession into one of her own. No dice. She was very comfortable with my sexuality, far too comfortable to be hiding behind her calm façade some struggle of her own. It was her total inability to relate to my feelings that made her so supportive. I understood this. I remembered how I'd reacted when Amanda had come out to me. When I tried to tell Amanda she wasn't gay, I had something at stake—my own sexuality. Melissa had nothing to lose, nothing to fear, and she meant it when she told me she believed me, supported me, and remained my best friend.

For the remaining months of high school, I tried my hand at girlhood one last time. I might be gay, I reasoned, but I could still be pretty. I didn't have to be ugly, or—I practiced my new vocabulary—"butch." I attended the prom with a male friend and did the whole thing, makeup, dress, hair. I was extremely pleased with my appearance. People noticed. "Oh, Emily," someone said, "you look so *nice.* I didn't even recognize you!" I had stopped plucking my eyebrows, but I kept my legs smooth and my shorts well above my knees. My hair hung to my shoulders.

College changed me, of course. Most of my friends now would never believe I wore a dress to my prom; they are dumbfounded when I mention that I once plucked my eyebrows, shaved my legs. They try—and fail—to imagine my hair anything but short and neatly combed. I have become, in other words, butch. I am a lesbian, a dyke, I am every word those boys could think of. I am ugly, by their standards—standards that were once my own. I wear baggy pants. I think I own a skirt, but it is buried in the back of my closet, irrelevant.

I came out to my friends in college, as soon as I could muster the courage to do so, and I have not had to pretend here. I got a girlfriend. We broke up; a few months later, I got another one. It was absolutely amazing to me that I could have relationships, and we could walk around on campus holding hands without hearing slurs. We could have dinner with straight people. I could be friends with straight people—and gay people. I could cut off all my hair and dress how I wanted and feel, for the first time in my life, as if I had a body. Not just that I was attractive, although I did feel attractive. I literally finally felt like I had a body, like I *was* a body. I had never realized it: I had been invisible to myself for years. I had been afraid to look like what I was. I had been ashamed of what my body wanted.

I began to talk, too. I made friends far more easily than I had anticipated, and people liked me. I could talk seriously with my friends; I didn't always have to make everything into a joke. I began to turn my writing into poems, and I took classes, submitted my work to publications, and participated in readings. The yawning gulf between my public and private selves began to diminish.

The summer after my freshman year, my sister came out to me. I was the first person she told; she knew about my sexuality, and she turned to me because she expected me to understand and support her. I failed her. Instead of listening to her, I was angry with her. Instead of talking to her, I scoffed at her and condescendingly assured her that once she gained the wisdom and experience I had gained from a year of being "out," all of her questions would dissolve. I was secretly fuming at Tina. I didn't want her to be gay. Didn't she understand? Now we would be the Gay Twins. Now our parents would have two gay children (though at this particular point, I had not yet informed them that they had even one). Now the one thing that made me different from her, the one thing I owned for myself, I had to share with her.

I stayed angry for a long time, though I tried hard to squash my feelings, and I never told her what I felt. Instead, I scrambled to come out to my parents first; I'd be damned if I was going to wait until coming out was cliché.

My parents took it admirably. I have many gay friends, and I know coming out to one's parents is often rocky. But my mother, whom I told first (on the phone) tried hard to hide the fact that she was crying, and my father called later to tell me they would always love me, no matter what. It was uncomfortable, but it wasn't unbearable: I was lucky. My parents are nothing if not consistent: they love their children quietly but deeply. They think for themselves. They are not the kind to be lured into hysteria over their daughter's sexual orientation.

I was having a good time at school, especially with the burden of coming out to my parents lifted from my shoulders. I had stopped shaving my legs and wearing makeup. I cursed; I spit. I just didn't feel very girly. I felt more like myself and more attractive than I ever had before, but I didn't know what I was anymore. The word "transsexual" was tossed around a lot at school, and I wondered if perhaps my breasts were a mistake; maybe there was a boy inside me just waiting to come out. But I checked, and I didn't find one. I still identified with the emotional inner life most of my female friends described. The few male friends I had were gay.

I was often uncomfortable when I found myself in a group of heterosexual men and women. I was openly gay, so males didn't flirt with me, and I had no interest in flirting with them. I wanted to flirt with my female friends. But they were less interested in "playing along" with my flirtation once men came into the picture. I resented their attention to the opposite sex. Worse, I didn't know how to act. Even in a group of friends, there are sexual undertones based on potential attraction, and when I was surrounded by heterosexuals, there was no potential attraction. I felt like I had no allies. Hyper-attuned to these undertones, I sometimes submitted to silence rather than fight to create a space for myself. These moments were among the few when I still felt the familiar gag rise to my mouth and muffle me.

*   *   *

I am going to graduate in a few weeks. My college years have already taken on a distant quality; I think constantly about the future. But I see the logic of my future, and I see how squarely it rests on the experience of my past.

I will be certified to teach English to middle-school and high-school students soon, and as part of my certification, I completed a semester of student teaching. I think reading and writing have an incredible power to shape our idea of what is possible for ourselves and for the world; I can't forget the comfort I found, as a lonely teenager, in books about gay adolescents. *They existed.* I want to share this experience of finding myself in books and on the page, of discovering the power of my own voice. I want to help kids who close themselves to possibility because the possibilities are unacceptable or unthinkable; I want to show them books where people do the unacceptable and the unthinkable—and then prosper.

I never came out to the students I taught this past semester. Sometimes I wanted to. Sometimes, when a student asked if I was married or if I had a boyfriend, or when a student called something "gay," I wanted to stop everything and tell them. I didn't; I couldn't. They liked me, and I was scared to risk losing their affection and respect. And I don't know whether I will find the courage to take this risk with future classes.

I did tell one girl, the first person under 18 to whom I have come out. This was not a girl from school but a girl I tutored through a program at college. April was 12 years old. We worked together all year, and she talked to me constantly about her struggle with her sexuality. I listened but said nothing about myself, believing she was too young to handle this truth about me. Finally, a few weeks before our sessions ended, she asked me whether I was gay, and I decided to be honest. Maybe it would help her; maybe she could handle it. I introduced her to my girlfriend, and I told her how happy I was, how my parents knew, and my friends. She asked question after question: How did I know I was gay? When did I tell my parents? Who was my first girlfriend? Why did I try to look like a boy? What was wrong with boys, anyway? Did I hold hands with my girlfriend in public? Did people harass us on the street?

People called her a lesbian sometimes, April said. Did people ever call me a lesbian?

I told her the truth: I explained that when I was growing up, people often called my sister a lesbian, and I said I thought that was the worst possible insult. I said I had become the very thing I feared, but I had discovered it was not an insult and not something to be afraid of. Or ashamed of.

For the last few weeks of tutoring, April was not the same. She seemed a little afraid of me. But she continued to ask questions, and she continued to insist that she did not want our sessions to end before the semester ended. Sometimes she asked me about my male friends and then suggested I dump my girlfriend and go out with them. Each time she made this suggestion, I calmly explained to her that this was not who I was. I'm happy this way, I told her.

I don't know what April's eventual preference will be—she's still young, much younger than I was when I first began to consider the possibility that I might be gay. But I wanted her to know that gay people existed and could find happiness. I wanted her to see what I had not seen as an adolescent.

*   *   *

My sister and I attended the Philadelphia Dyke March last summer. We tried to "out-dyke" each other as we prepared our outfits; her hair was shorter and spikier, but my pants were baggier. She got points for her baseball cap; I got points for my necklace, designed for men.

"Let's go, lesbo," I called when I was ready.

Our parents looked us over and raised their eyebrows; they knew about both of us now. They had tried giving us razors for Christmas, a subtle encouragement to shave our legs. The packages remained unopened.

"Be careful driving," my father said as we breezed past.

We will.

"Have a good time," my mother added.

We will, we will.

We walked out. We got in the car.

"Let's play gay music," I said.

We did.

FALLING FOR SOMEONE

In this case, Graham traces his personal journey from withdrawn and awkward young boy—interested in girls but not knowing the "rules"—to self-possessed young man who values honesty and communication in his relationships with women. In a middle and high school culture where sex is viewed as a goal-oriented activity, Graham insists that for him emotional connection is an essential part of physical intimacy. He describes the significant romantic relationships he has had in high school and college, assessing why the yearlong relationship with Sarah ultimately failed and why the burgeoning relationship with Nora holds more promise.

I wrote a poem about the first night we went to get coffee together. A couple of weeks later, on Valentine's Day, I printed the final copy and spent an hour making it into a card. We were in a play together at the time, so that night at rehearsal I set it slyly amidst the things on her dressing-room table after everyone had gone to warm up. When I saw her again, she was waiting out in the hall, smiling. "Thank you, Graham," she said breathlessly, eyes gleaming. "I'm almost in tears. I couldn't let everyone in there see me lose it."

"So you like it?"

"I love it." She threw her arms around my neck and gave me a fierce hug, and then she squeezed my hand again, smiling, before reluctantly slipping back down the hallway to finish costuming. We didn't know what to say to each other the rest of that evening, so backstage, we just smiled at each other and blushed.

A week later at senior cocktails, she pulled me aside. "I started writing this the same night you did," she said, placing an envelope into my hands, "but it's taken me longer to finish." She sat and watched me as I read it, the noisy crowd just around the corner. Both of our poems described the same feelings, the same lovely moments. She wrote more than I had dared to include in mine; it made me dizzy, reading and re-reading the lines, the subtext too strong to ignore but too good to be true. All I could do was blush and smile and giggle like a schoolboy; she started, too, and there we were—two college seniors on a couch around the corner from a large cocktail party, rocking and giggling like children.

Her name's Nora. She's pretty, she's funny, she's talented, and she's smart. We've got common interests, common viewpoints, common tastes in music and food, and the same sense of humor. We're attracted to each other, and you can tell by the shine we both get when we're around each other, the lovely little flirting that goes on. The kicker is that she has a boyfriend.

I'd come a long way from the shy boy I used to be. Throughout my childhood I was shy, quiet, and withdrawn. Most people find it significant that I'm an only child and that I am adopted. "Oh, really?" they murmur, with a click of their tongue. "That must be rough." Well, no, actually—it hasn't been rough. I can't remember a time not knowing I was adopted, and I can't remember a time when the concept has ever caused me any grief. My parents are my parents, and if you get to know them it becomes immediately apparent how like them I am. My parents treat me as an equal, and for that I respect them.

I've always felt as though I had a high degree of responsibility and freedom in my family. They never gave me the sex talk, though: I learned all I knew about sex from the kids at school between third and fifth grade. I was not one of those sexually precocious kids who leapt right into the act and got it out of the way. I saved myself for as long as I felt I could and still gave away my virginity at seventeen. That was pretty old by the standards in my town—there just wasn't much else to do. I hit an early growth spurt and was five-foot-ten going into junior high. I towered over everyone and was husky in build—not exactly fat, but pushing the limit. I was clumsy with my size. I slumped. The subtle ways of fashion were mysterious to me—what to wear, what to say, how to posture myself—and my attempts at conforming to them seemed immediately transparent to the popular kids, who ridiculed me.

I've liked girls for as far back as I can remember, but I missed learning the rules somehow. I remember one time, when I was in seventh grade, at someone's birthday party. The room was darkened, and everyone was being social. I was standing with my back against the wall, watching it all, when I caught my own gaze in a big portrait-sized mirror hanging on the opposite side of the room.

I vividly remember feeling as though I was seeing myself for the first time: I stood head and shoulders above the reflected people, my lank and longish hair parted sloppily down the middle, with my bangs tickling my eyebrows. My almost-too-small shirt was open at the collar, and I wore a thin gold chain around my throat. My expression was blank, noncommittal; the corner of my mouth kinked up slightly in an expression of universal dismissal, but I held my own gaze for a long time. Dismissal was a safe expression to assume. People who seemed not to care about anything were the least fun to ridicule.

It was still common at that time to talk about sexual intimacy in terms of baseball: Making out was "first base," intercourse a "home run." Everyone was eager to know how far someone had gotten the weekend before. The analogy of a game was perfect, because it neatly removed emotion from physical intimacy; it reflected a perfectly goal-oriented mentality. This was a game I wasn't playing, partly because I didn't know the rules and partly because all that my parents had told me about physical intimacy as far back as I could remember was that it was something that you only did with a person that you loved.

Enter Melissa Reynolds, someone I had placed on a pedestal all through seventh and eighth grade. It didn't dawn on me until after the fact that we had been considered "an item" for about two months, which was pretty cool to me in retrospect, considering she was a year older and a grade above me; older loosely equaled cooler. Nothing ever came of it physically: Had someone suggested that I kiss her, I would have laughed in that person's face.

I saw Mel as untouchable, all encompassing. I was physically attracted to her, yes, but at that point in my life physical affection was a symbol of love, and I was so certain that I was unworthy of her love that any desire to hold her or to kiss her was buried by self-doubt. It *never occurred* to me at that stage of my life that I could be desirable physically to a girl who was physically desirable to me.

This leads me to think that physical and emotional development are related but ultimately different processes. In many of my friends, the desire for sexual release seemed to develop before the desire for any interactive emotional context, but I recall my desire to feel loved as dominant over the urges of my flesh. What did I want from girls? I certainly experienced simple physical lust, but in another sense I longed for emotional support, personal validation. These physical and emotional desires felt somewhat disconnected in me. Physical affection from my early girl-friends became a reflection of my self-worth, showing that I was attractive enough or witty enough to merit their attention.

Anyway, Mel must have eventually gotten tired of me because the next thing I knew we weren't speaking—it was as if we'd never met. This didn't surprise me greatly, and since I had never felt as though we were bound together by anything mutual, all I felt was disappointment. The advantage of a pessimistic attitude toward something is that when it goes wrong, you've been anticipating it. I suppose I thought pretty little of myself; I had no confidence with my peers because I felt as though I didn't understand them, didn't belong. I spent a lot of time talking about these issues with my best friend, Jeff.

Jeff is an only child, as I am, and we've ended up being like brothers. I guess I call him my best friend because I feel as though he is the one person who understands me the most completely. There was very little that I didn't share with him emotionally throughout high school, and he never judged me. He just accepted me for who I was. I could be completely honest with him and not fear his scorn or reproval.

Until high school, the female mind remained largely mysterious to both of us, a combination lock to which the cool guys seemed to share a secret code. They treated girls like trash, but the girls seemed to eat it up. All I knew was how to be polite, honest, and friendly. Self-deprecatory. I was the "nicest" guy everybody knew. It was in this mind-frame that I met Missy, My First Girlfriend. I asked her out on Valentine's Day of my sophomore year; she was a junior, and it was with her that I abandoned virginity.

My introduction to intercourse was somewhat anticlimactic, so to speak. In the back of my car, almost nine months after we had been going steady, we decided to "just see what it's like." The October leaves swirled in the dark parking lot behind the public library. We had parked beneath the farthest lamppost, which some kid had shot out with a pellet gun some months before, and the light across her anxious brow was silvery and dim. She nervously brushed a strand of her long blonde hair out of her mouth. Her blue eyes were wide and fixed on me. I was fumbling with my belt. She was as tall as I was, and the tiny backseat was cramped and uncomfortable. We were already more frightened than curious, and the sensation of momentary insertion was so unbearably sweet that it pushed us immediately over the edge into panic.

We leapt apart, buckling and zipping furiously until we were safely tucked back into our pants, and then we held each other tightly for a few moments, panting, before jumping into the front seat and zooming out of the parking lot and onto the well-lit streets of town, windows down, the night breeze cooling our damp faces. The next day we were terrified that she was pregnant, even though our contact hadn't been but three or four seconds. The biological facts of the matter didn't seem relevant to us; no matter how brief, the mere pleasure of the touch seemed enough to doom us.

As our fear faded, however, our desire deepened, and within a week we couldn't get enough of each other and began having intercourse in earnest. At the time, I truly believed this was Love: "the real thing." I spent all of my free time with her, to the point where my parents began to suggest that maybe we were seeing too much of each other. This enraged me—I felt that they didn't understand our feelings for one another, didn't realize the depth of our connection. I began to feel as if I didn't need anyone else's affection or approval—I had all I needed emotionally in Missy.

Over the summer, I kissed another girl. I was disgusted with myself morally because my physical desire had gotten the better of my desire to remain faithful to my girlfriend. At the same time, though, I was overcome by the physical thrill of my bravado. Things between Missy and me deteriorated, and we broke up after she went off to college that fall.

I had a silly little relationship with a sophomore my senior year, but I was more concerned with college applications and with getting out of Dayton than I was with her. My first sexual encounter here at college, though, is worth mentioning: I was a bright-eyed, first-term freshman in this brave new world, and hence easy prey. A junior named Alice asked me to her sorority formal, and I accepted. We drank quite a bit and danced suggestively enough to earn catcalls from her sorority sisters. She came on to me very aggressively and brazenly, which I don't recall as particularly *arousing*; I was dizzy, and I remember a vague excitement of being in uncharted waters, the thrill of having someone come on to me like that. I didn't encourage her advances, but then I didn't discourage them, either.

When we got back to campus, Alice asked if I wanted to stay in her room that night rather than walk home. I was tired and drunk, so I went up with her into her room and collapsed on the bed. I lay there watching the ceiling slowly spin, and she suggested that I'd be more comfortable without all of my clothes on. This was undoubtedly true. She helped me undress and heap my clothes on a chair in the corner, and then we both crawled into the bed and pulled up the covers. Soon we were kissing and rolling around, and although we didn't have intercourse, things got awfully passionate. I remember vaguely the point at which it seemed to be over and I could drop off into an exhausted sleep.

I awoke the next morning around seven with mixed emotions. Alice was the first sexual predator I had ever dated, and I was realizing that it wasn't such a great experience. The complete lack of emotional substance to the whole affair depressed me, and I was angry at myself for having done such a thing. I got dressed and Alice walked downstairs in her nightshirt to the door with me. As I remember it, I never said a word the whole time; I just sort of looked at the floor and got out of there as quickly as I could. She made light comments, trying to start a conversation, I suppose, but all I really remember her saying was "give me a call" at the door as I stumbled out.

The irony of this, to me, is the gender reversal in this scenario. Isn't it supposed to be the older frat boy who asks the shy young freshman girl to the formal, gets her liquored up, and then convinces her to spend the night in his room? One difference is that I don't feel like I was taken advantage of; I never felt like any of the responsibility for my actions lay with anybody but myself. I didn't *have* to drink or stay in her room, I decided to. One thing I'll say to Alice's credit: She was clear about what she wanted, and maybe that kind of communication is better than none at all.

Communication is imperative. I think a major reason that my relationships at college have seemed different from the ones I had in high school is that people communicate more. For example, my buddies here are all important to me, yet there is no significant sense of hierarchy; no single one of them fulfills my every interpersonal need. That being said, my happiness still seems to some degree dependent upon my relationships with others. I get depressed when I feel unloved or unnoticed, which leads me to think that I *need* other people, I *need* friends around me. Is it possible to be completely self-sufficient? Is it desirable?

As a kid, I spent a good deal of time by myself. I guess I was lonely but then I never really remember being unhappy, as such. I often enjoy being alone; I *need* to be alone sometimes. Ideally, I have a balance of quality time with my friends, quality time by myself, and activities that combine social interaction with independent work.

For example, I like to act. I like to get up on stage and impress people. I like the attention and the freedom of my body on the stage—the freedom to expand my personal space until it encompasses an entire room. I unleash my voice and express my energy. I love the applause, washing over me in its thunderous *yes*. On stage, I can be graceful and funny and tragic; I control the dynamic. I can feel alone in a room full of people, letting them in and out of my life as I wish, and then enjoy their approval.

I am most exultant when I am living a scene moment by moment, never anticipating the next, not inhibited by the sequence of emotions I'm scripted to experience, but rather living a fictional story line as spontaneous, as now, as if I were the character. Acting is a strange mixture of awareness and spontaneity; I have the chance to figure out how my character will behave before the action takes place.

When I walk onto the stage and into the world of the play, I'm living spontaneously in a self-controlled moment; there is nothing to be unsure of, so I can experience a range of passionate emotions without doubt, without unpredictable repercussions—everything's safely scripted beforehand.

I met Sarah the spring of our sophomore year. She was beautiful; she had dark, thick hair that fell to her jawline and big, brown doe eyes. When I looked at her, she'd smile and sometimes glance away and blush.

We began spending more and more time alone together. We'd go for a jog, grab a bite to eat, take in a movie, or just walk around and talk. At some point I realized we were sitting on her bed in her room one night, and the conversation had fallen into one of those comfortable silences. It occurred to me to kiss her, but then I thought I'd better ask, just to make sure. When I did, she smiled and blushed and said yes, and we kissed and it was bliss. It felt like chemistry; it felt right. "Why did this take us so long?" she smiled, as if she'd been thinking about it for a while. It occurred to me then that maybe I had, too. I suppose things happen at the pace they happen, and that's part of the beauty of courtship.

We saw more and more of each other. By the end of the term, we were going steady. I don't recall ever being that happy in my life, in the sense that *nothing* mattered. It was a mindless kind of happiness: The world could have ended and I would have been content to go down with it knowing that there was Sarah and me.

The romantic clichés are clichés for a reason—because they are indeed Fantastic, they are Magnificent, they are 100 percent true. It's bliss, it's beautiful—it's walking on air; it's as light as a feather. She was radiant, and when I looked at her I couldn't *stop* looking at her. I wanted to touch her and hold her and hug her close and melt right into her body, fuse like that, curl up like a kitten inside her and wrap around her and weave through her hair and fall into her eyes. I don't know if that's the healthiest phase of falling for someone, but it is certainly an exhilarating lack of perspective.

Every time I looked at her, I was struck anew. With other girlfriends, that sense of astonishment diminished over time. I'd "get used" to them, so to speak, in the sense that my aesthetic attraction to them became internalized, accepted, understood, not thought about consciously. But with Sarah, it was like seeing her for the first time every time I looked at her. She was also the most intelligent girl I'd ever dated; she thought in a wonderfully straightforward, logical way. We could discuss issues and never lose each other; our processes of deduction seemed to mirror each other's and work in exactly the same patterns. This is not to say that we never disagreed; rather, I mean it always seemed that we understood one another.

In her eyes I was funny, talented, intelligent, and diverse—"Is there anything that you *don't* do?" she asked early on—so different from the other boys she had dated before. She described me as passionate, inexplicable, dynamic, rational, emotional, ridiculous, sophisticated, sophomoric, artistic, communicative—unlike anyone she'd ever met. And my willingness to go head-over-heels, hopeless-romantic crazy for her was probably exactly what she was looking for at the time when a fling with another frat-boy, Econ-major, cookie-cutter, blue-blazer, third-generation-legacy stereotype had fallen through in her life. I fit. She fit. We were perfect for one another for impermanent reasons. We spent that summer together at school, and the whole term went by in a happy blur.

In the fall I went to study in London for two terms. Sarah took the winter off to go ski and work in Colorado. There was a general feeling of unease in me; I feared that she might get into an exciting new environment and fall for someone else. I also feared meeting some nice British girl and breaking my word to Sarah; I'd not yet been successful in a long-distance relationship. I came home to the United States over break and flew up to see her after Christmas; she was going to meet me in the airport. I wasn't sure what to expect—would she feel the same?

I was one of the last people out of the plane, and as I walked across the tarmac in the bitter night's wind, I felt a strange calm come over me. I was excited to see her, but perhaps I was steeling myself for a letdown. I walked through the door into the bright terminal.

She was sitting in a chair against the wall, leaning forward with her elbows on her knees when the crowd parted and we saw each other. Her hair was longer and I was again struck by how lovely she was. She rose and we embraced—it was wonderful; that sense of gently trying to pull the other person completely into oneself. For me, it was an ecstatically silent affirmation.

We drove home to her house in Albany, New York, and tried to catch up on what had happened in the time since our last letters, the last phone call, the whole term in general. There was so much I wanted to say, but somehow we just sort of sat smiling in silence as we drove through the dark. I could smell her favorite perfume, the scent of her hair, the fabric softener she used on her clothes. The sound of her voice was so much different in person than it had been on the telephone.

We ended up spending almost the whole time with her parents. They were all better skiers than me, and they all looked like one big, happy family. Her parents always seemed a *shade* distant toward me. I wasn't sure if it was just that I was their daughter's first "serious" boyfriend, the fact that I was a creative writing major, something specific about my personality, or a combination of these things that inspired this coolness. She was Daddy's Little Girl, and I suspect that part of the odd feeling originated in the psychiatrist's evaluative eye he always seemed to be examining me with.

I think from those four days, I wanted definite confirmation of her feelings for me. Sarah wasn't the best at articulating her emotions. "The more we try to pack everything into four days," she said, "the harder it will be to go without it again." I wasn't sure what that statement implied.

Sarah was uncomfortable with the idea of her parents seeing us in any physically intimate way. We were very comfortable with one another when nobody else was around, but with her parents it was an almost visible fear, a tension that lasted the whole four days. When the day came to have her take me back to the airport, I was still confused.

I went back to London; she went to Colorado. I enjoyed hearing how animated her voice became over the phone when she told me about the crazy high jinks she had gotten into while working on the mountain that week. I was having a better time myself, meeting people and traveling around Britain. All seemed well until that fateful day when I talked to her, perhaps two weeks before the end of the quarter. We talked for an hour, but I never felt like she was actually in the conversation.

"You know, Sarah," I suggested, "I've been wondering if maybe this relationship is going to be the same when we both get back to campus in the spring."

"You know, I have, too," she replied with audible relief. "I mean, it's been so long and we've both been through *so much*. It's strange, isn't it? I'm not really sure how to feel about you any more." All of this in a light, *thank goodness we agree!* sort of tone. Well, I had to sit down.

". . . Are you *serious?*" I asked, after a moment. "What exactly does that mean?"

Silence on the line.

"I thought you wanted us to be honest with each other," she said.

"Well, yes—I do. I do. But Jesus, maybe not *this* honest." I was floored. It felt as though a deep hole had opened up somewhere inside my gut, and everything was getting sucked down into it. My center of gravity had suddenly become a black hole. I couldn't let myself believe what seemed to be happening, not after all this time, not this way.

"Well, we can talk about it when I meet you in France, right?" She seemed to want to wrap up this discussion.

"You still want to do that, then?" This gave me some kind of hope.

"Of course I do! I wouldn't miss that for the world." Sarah's family and another family had a tradition of going to Europe biannually to ski. Sarah and I had made plans to go to Paris before their trip was scheduled to begin.

I mumbled a few shaky good-byes, and the conversation was over. I went into my room and lay down on my bed and stared at my ceiling for about two hours. I couldn't get over that hollow emptiness inside myself. A strange detachment came over me, and I was sort of marveling at how interesting a sensation it was. *I haven't just been dumped, that's for sure. She never said we aren't going out anymore—after all, she's still going to meet me in Paris over break, like we planned. That must mean something. We'll talk about it. She'll see that she still cares about me when we meet again face to face. This is not a disaster.*

Cut to a wide-angle shot of me two weeks later, sitting alone in Gatwick, waiting for her to deplane. I'm having a coffee and reading *Bleak House*. The crowd parts and there she is, walking toward me, smiling. She is deeply tanned from the slopes of Colorado, and her teeth are brilliantly white. She carries a large duffel sack over her shoulder, which she swings to the floor as I stand up to greet her.

A grandmotherly embrace. A dry peck on the cheek. There could be no doubt anymore, but somehow I managed to convince myself otherwise. It's amazing what things we won't let ourselves believe when we don't want to believe them. The taxi ride back to my room was mostly silent, uneasy.

We spent a day and a night in London. It was immediately apparent that things were different between us, but I denied the signs of this. There was no physical affection beyond the casual or the accidental—the few times she made contact with me were sisterly, almost reluctant. When we got to Paris, it was worse: She didn't want to talk about it; she didn't want to acknowledge that there was anything to discuss. "Less not spoil our time here," she said a couple of times. It was terrible.

The city of romance was gray and wet. A cold wind blew through the streets. We slept in the same bed, but she would not be touched—if I brushed against her, she rolled away. This was not done in a cruel way, which somehow made it worse. Her absence of emotion was harder to handle than love, hate, or anger: Anything would have been better than her wistful distance. It was as if I was fading out like an old photograph, slowly losing cohesion until light itself began to bleed through me; I could almost feel myself becoming more and more translucent and ghostlike.

Even when I would grab her and pull her close to me, hug her fiercely as if to say "See me! See me!" she would look into my eyes and smile vaguely, sadly, until I thought my heart would literally crack. She never wanted to face it, to discuss it, to admit that this was happening. I felt like she was lost, but she was always there—I'd look up from the bed while she was gazing out the window and it was *her*, in the *flesh*, and that kept alive in me a strange kind of hope.

Her family and their friends arrived in the city; we all spent the day together, and they all looked knowingly at me. That evening I left alone for London, as planned.

I spent the spring term at school, where it finally ended, almost a year after we met. Ultimately, I had to do it myself. We both arrived back on campus and got in touch; a week or two went by during which we ate lunch, met for coffee, and did the usual sort of things together, but as in Paris there was no spark at all.

Finally, I went to her room one afternoon. She was lying on her bed reading. I sat down in a chair next to her and said, "I think it's really time we talked about this." She stared at her book. Her tension was palpable; I wanted to make it as painless as possible.

"What do you want to talk about?" she said.

"I get the feeling that you don't care about me anymore," I replied.

Pause.

"That's not true. . . ." She was struggling with the words. "I just don't think I care about you in the same way that I used to. I think things have changed." I explained to her why it was important for me to *hear* this from her, to actually have it *said* and *deal* with it once and for all. I told her that not knowing for sure was the worst thing and that it was wonderful at last to be communicating sincerely again.

Her relief was visible and immediate. From then on, I asked if she was still interested in being friends and she gushed that of course she was. I hoped we could still spend some time together, and she assured me that she wouldn't want it any other way. I was so happy that she seemed at last to be looking *at* me rather than *through* me, that I seemed to finally *exist* again in her eyes, that I forgot about what was really being *said* here: We were breaking up.

It was maybe a day and a half before it began to sink in that things weren't going to be like they had been before. When I'd suggest activities, she always had other plans. She told me that she was sorry, that if she could make herself feel the same way that she had before then she would. I asked her if she had fallen for one of the guys she was living with in Colorado, and she flew off the handle. *That's not important. That's none of your business. I can't believe you'd ask me that.* Panic. A week later she's dating Kevin, a guy from school she'd met while out West. She began avoiding me.

I began to see Sarah in new ways, began to hear the things my friends were saying (that perhaps they had been hinting at all along) about our incompatibility. Had our relationship been doomed from the get-go? I wondered just how much of my affection for her had been based upon my emotional needs at the time. It seemed in my life that I just bumped into these girls I was serious about and that fate dictated my relationships. Not my own emotional state, but the chance meeting of one special girl. For a while after Sarah, I looked at it as almost entirely dictated by my own emotional state: I thought that if I was emotionally ready to have another big relationship, I'd find the girl to have it with and convince myself that it was destiny. As I see it now, big relationships in my life have probably been just as dependent upon my emotional needs at the time as they have been upon who it was I happened to meet during that period—a combination of chance and internal readiness.

I loved to hold Sarah, I loved to be close to Sarah, but did I love *Sarah?* What exactly was I waiting six months for? Why did the lack of physical intimacy over both of our vacations strike so fundamental a chord in me? Was she purely a beautiful object with whom I sexually validated myself?

No. The lack of physical intimacy at vacation time was a problem because it was the way in which we communicated. Since she didn't discuss her feelings very much, I read them in her body language. An affectionate hug around the waist was one sign that she cared for me. Being apart had a preservative effect on our relationship, then: Without communication there could be no unified evolution, and a relationship in stasis eventually goes stale. I got used to not seeing Sarah for so long, but without the physical we didn't communicate. We spoke on the phone but very seldom about how we felt, about "us" or what was going on emotionally. When I saw her in person, then, I needed that physical communication. Not because I couldn't stand going without the sex—I had done fine without it for three months—but sex would have given me a document to analyze, a script from which to interpret her feelings. I could have found affirmation in her physical interaction with me, but our halfway vacation was stifled by her parents' constant presence.

We never said that we loved each other. It didn't make sense to; I had told other girls before that I loved them and then proven myself false by breaking up with them. Telling someone that you love them is all very well and good, but where do you go from there? It's a rut. Once you say it, it immediately begins to lose its meaning. It fades. There is no greater emotional profession, but there are many types of love. I told Missy that I loved her, and I still believe that I did—I was madly, hopelessly, Romeo-and-Juliet in love with her. I wanted to surrender myself completely to our love. It was ridiculous. Wonderful, but ridiculous in the way only first love can be, with its talk of forever and eternity, of magnitudes beyond the mortal.

Sarah never got that into it. I don't know how Sarah saw love, but my guess is that she was saving it for later. This was fine by me, since I'd said it too often to other girls and soured it in my mouth. Clichés don't mean much, so we used little body language haiku. It felt like love, but perhaps both of us knew deep down that there was something missing (an element of clear and fundamental communication?), that there was some kind of unwritten expiration date between us that made it "not love." Further, although I feared it might expire within me, I now believe that from the beginning it was doomed to expire within her. That didn't stop us, though, from falling happily into whatever it was for the time being.

Looking back, I don't regret a minute of it. The experience changed my perspective on relationships. For a while I dated around, hooking up with friends and acquaintances, fulfilling the desire that flesh is heir to, but emphasizing the transience, the lack of emotional substance to such behavior. My partners and I would talk beforehand, making sure that what was about to happen "didn't mean anything." It was fulfilling physically and convenient emotionally—a handy kind of disposable love, you might say—or like instant coffee, one cup at a time. But after a year of that lifestyle, I began to feel a little hollow and hunger for something more emotionally substantial.

I often need someone to remind me that there is a broader perspective from which to look at my life: a girlfriend, a buddy, a parent. Usually, there is an element of understanding that exists between myself and my male friends that I don't think exists between myself and my female friends or my parents. I feel as comfortable with a girlfriend as I do with a best friend—I freely share my inmost thoughts and feelings—but sometimes there is some doubt in my mind as to whether or not they truly understand where I'm coming from in the same way that, say, Jeff would.

With Nora and me, it seems like an entirely new experience. Three weeks have elapsed. She broke up with her boyfriend a few days ago, and we've been seeing even more of each other since then. Both of us are happily in that phase of exultant exploration with which relationships characteristically begin, but I'm approaching this with a mixture of skepticism and hope. Will it be possible to develop our ongoing physical attraction as well as our actively evolving emotional and intellectual relationship? She tells me I'm unlike anyone she's ever dated before, but I've heard those words before. Still, she can explain her thoughts and feelings in detail, and I do feel as though we connect in a unique way. I don't want to kid myself anymore—I don't want my actions to be dictated by my emotional needs.

I'd like to behave in complete accordance with my moral and rational convictions. I often catch myself doing otherwise, but I continue to make the effort. For example, there was a period of two days when the chemistry between Nora and me had become undeniable, but she had not yet formally ended her relationship with her boyfriend—"overlap," she calls it. I urged her to deal with that situation, even though I knew how difficult it must have been for her, remembering the pain and sadness I felt when Sarah was not straightforward with me. She discussed everything with him; she explained her feelings and why she felt the way she did. It wasn't easy for her to do, but he's an extremely mature and friendly guy, and she tells me that although he was hurt, he appreciated her honesty.

I hope that I'm better equipped to deal with this relationship because of what I've been through with Sarah. I'm very happy getting to know Nora, although I am wary of being hurt again. Communication is important to her, too, which is refreshing, and overall I feel good about the direction we've been taking. People may never meet Mr. or Ms. Right in their lives; the very concept of the perfect partner may be unrealistic in and of itself. If we all communicate, if we are willing to work at it, I do believe that any relationship can be an ultimately productive and therefore positive experience in our lives—and besides, isn't it almost more fun not knowing?

PART II

RELATIONSHIPS

THEORETICAL OVERVIEW

This section of the book focuses on relationships, specifically family and peer relationships. Until the 1970s, psychoanalytic and neopsychoanalytic theories yielded the most prominent and influential explanations of the processes by which adolescents' relationships with their parents and peers change from childhood to adulthood. Anna Freud and Peter Blos described the process of adolescents' individuation from their parents (Blos, 1962; A. Freud, 1946, 1958), and Harry Stack Sullivan wrote about the development of intimacy through best-friend relationships (1953). Since that time, social science research has often contradicted these theories, leading scholars of adolescent relationships to evolve new ways of thinking about adolescent relationships. Psychoanalytic views on adolescence have changed (Blos, 1979), with some new perspectives, such as attachment theory (Allen & Ladd, 1999), drawing on elements of earlier psychoanalytic theory. Other theoretical models of adolescent development center on aspects of adolescent relationships that were not the focus of the psychoanalytic perspective. For example, cognitive developmental theory (Kohlberg, 1969; Selman, 1980; Smetana, 1988, 1989) focuses on how children's understanding of their social world becomes more organized and complex as they proceed through adolescence and clarifies how more sophisticated cognitive skills may change parent-adolescent, sibling, and peer relationships. Evolutionary theories discuss how both cognitive growth and pubertal development propel the child from dependence on parents to connection with sexual partners outside the family (Belsky, Steinberg, & Draper, 1991; Gray & Steinberg, 1999). Most current theoretical models of adolescents' development now recognize the effects of changing environments on adolescents' social relationships. Critically important social contexts include school and work sites, as well as changing social expectations of adults regarding teenagers (Collins, 1995). This introduction explores some of the most important issues in the study of adolescent relationships that are raised by these theories and related research studies, and mentions some ways in which the cases in this portion of the book may be used to foster discussions of these topics. Students who are interested in more in-depth study could read a number of excellent overviews of current research and theory on parent-adolescent relationships, such as those by Collins and Laursen (2004), Collins and Repinski (2001), Grotevant (1998), Steinberg (2001), and Steinberg and Silk (2002), and peer relationships, such as that by Brown (2004).

Family Relationships

The psychoanalytic understanding of adolescent-family relationships has traditionally viewed adolescence as a time of profound inner turmoil and outward conflict—a time of "storm and stress." Explosive conflict with family, friends, and authorities was thought of as commonplace. This view was based, to a great extent, on the theoretical work of the psychiatric community in the 1950s and early 1960s (Blos, 1962; Erikson, 1959, 1966, 1968; A. Freud, 1946, 1958). Largely on the basis of their experience with adolescent psychiatric patients, these clinicians and theorists described adolescence as a time of extreme psychic and interpersonal stress. Emotional crises and upheaval were viewed as appropriate responses by the adolescent to major psychological and societal tasks required during this phase of life: dramatically reducing psychological dependency on parents, separating from the family, and forming an adult identity. Adolescent turmoil was not only inevitable, but necessary for subsequent normal personality development.

This storm-and-stress perspective of adolescent family relationships is still perpetuated by the media and is often assumed by the public. Scholars of adolescent psychology, however, are in the midst of developing new ways of describing, explaining, and understanding adolescent-family relationships. These new approaches differ from the long-reigning classic psychoanalytic perspective in several ways. One way these new perspectives differ is in the assertion that adolescents and their families are more likely to negotiate changes in power, responsibilities, and modes of intimacy through a continuous series of minor, although significant, daily "hassles," rather than through tumultuous, warlike conflicts. The majority of conflicts in adolescence arise over mundane issues such as family chores, curfews, eating practices, dating, and personal appearance. Data from empirical studies with nonclinical populations of adolescents and their families from the past forty years have led to a radical revision in our understanding of how adolescents separate from and remain connected to their families. The majority of current research clearly refutes the notion that most adolescents undergo severe emotional stress and family conflict during this period of life (Collins & Laursen, 2004; Adams & Laursen, 2001). A variety of studies using such diverse methods as epidemiological surveys (Rutter, Graham, Chadwick, & Yule, 1976), phone interviews (Montemayor, 1983), and time sampling with electronic beepers (Csikszentmihalyi & Larson, 1984) have shown that for most families with adolescent members, serious conflict and disorganization are not characteristic states (Hill, 1987). Evidence drawn from various kinds of self-reports offered by nonpatient adolescents and their parents provides no support for an inevitable dramatic increase in family conflict from childhood to adolescence. In fact, the frequency of conflict with parents declines from early adolescence to midadolescence and again from midadolescence to late adolescence (Laursen, Coy, & Collins, 1998).

In general, the family is not at risk for great turmoil or disorganization during the adolescent years; the search for greater independence from the family is not usually played out in major battles between adolescents and their parents. Instead, current studies look for smaller, although still highly significant and lasting transformations in sharing of power and responsibility and in the nature of family intimacy through daily renegotiations. Adolescents usually value their relationships with their parents, and these relationships change and adapt as the adolescent becomes an adult member of the family (Adams & Laursen, 2001). It would be a mistake to conclude that conflicts between adolescents and their parents or siblings are insignificant or rare and that their presence indicates family or individual psychopathology. Any valued human relationship undergoes stress at times, particularly when the relationship must adapt to change within an individual. However, the majority of parent-adolescent conflict situations are not associated with lasting problems, although chronic and unresolved hostility between parents and adolescents does predict adolescent maladjustment (Hauser, Powers, & Noam, 1991; Smetana, 1996). Given this understanding of the experiences of most adolescents in the United States, how do the cases presented in this book help you to understand conflict and transformation between these adolescents and their parents? Cases 10, 11, 12, 13, and 14 may be used to clarify your ideas concerning what characteristics are important for an optimal parent-adolescent relationship. In what ways do these families hinder or foster their teenagers' independence, achievement, identity, or intimacy goals? Are there any problems that could be associated with a pattern of family interaction that exhibits no conflict? How can "normal" developmental tasks of adolescence, like identity development, occur in the context of extremely troubled family relationships, as seen in Cases 10 and 11?

In cases with severe family conflict, you might ask which adolescent issues trigger aspects of the tumult in these families and when is conflict a product of a long-standing family system. Case 11 provides a powerful description of a family under severe stress and an adolescent's extreme strategies for coping with that stress. Clearly, some of these strategies strengthen resilience (e.g., Chhaya's perfectionism reinforces her ability to succeed at many demanding tasks, including school), while other strategies (e.g., Chhaya's anorexia) eventually cause more pain than relief. Chhaya's case is a reminder of the variety of patterns that lead eventually to successful young adult adaptation and functioning. Cases in other sections of the book may also serve as examples of atypical family situations leading to severe stress in adolescence (see, for example, Case 1, "Someday My Elders Will Be Proud").

Contemporary approaches to describing adolescent-family relationships now also emphasize adolescents' continuing need for maintaining intimacy and connection with parents and siblings (Collins & Russell, 1991). In "The Family I Have" (Case 10) Myra realizes that she has a strong desire for a closer relationship with her brother. Earlier psychoanalytic theories focused primarily on the process of separation from the family. Results from studies that have observed adolescents' interactions with their parents have indicated the importance of family interaction styles that permit conflict between members in a context of support (Baumrind, 1987, 1989; Powers, 1988; Powers, Hauser, Schwartz, Noam, & Jacobson, 1983), acceptance, active understanding from parents (Allen, Hauser, Bell, & O'Conner, 1994; Hauser, et al., 1984, 1987), and parental expressions of individuality and connectedness (Grotevant & Cooper, 1986). Closeness is maintained through different behaviors and activities in adolescence than during childhood: close physical contact and joint activities with parents decrease during adolescence, but conversations that convey information and feelings increase (Hartup & Laursen, 1991). These conversations are more likely to occur with mothers than with fathers, most likely because adolescents spend considerably more time with their mothers (Steinberg & Silk, 2002). Most of the cases in this book are strong illustrations of adolescents' heartfelt need to be affectively connected to their families. Devneesh's case (Case 7) presents a poignant example of the struggle to maintain closeness and connections with parents and, at the same time, forge a new identity that is not wholly based on being the "perfect child."

Another important difference in newer approaches to the adolescent-family relationship is the strong effort to encompass descriptions of a *wide variety of patterns* of family relationships, rather than focusing on explaining one primary picture of how "normal" adolescents interact with their families. Instead, a wide range of adolescent family behaviors is considered relevant to understanding adolescent adaptive responses to growth in relationships. This new perspective seeks to include more diversity in the adolescents and families studied. For example, it is crucial to understand the varieties of adaptive family functioning in African American, Latino, Native American, Asian American, and other groups of adolescents in U.S. culture (Cooper, 1994). It may be helpful to contrast the family pictures described by adolescents of European American descent in this section with pictures of family life described by adolescents from different ethnic backgrounds (see the thematic index on pages viii–ix and Cases 1, 4, 5, 6, 7, 12, 15 and 20) and by other students in your class. Cases 4 and 12 illustrate the importance of adolescents learning skills from their parents for dealing with racism and discrimination. Scholars of adolescent psychology have also begun to examine adolescent-parent relationships within families with diverse structures, such as single-parent, stepparent, and noncustodial-parent families. Research findings show that the majority of children and adolescents that experience the divorce of their parents are more resilient than was once expected. An important factor for facilitating a healthy adjustment to the transitions that accompany divorce is the adolescent's relationship with at least one involved, caring, and authoritative adult (Hetherington & Stanley-Hagan, 2002).

Peer Relationships

Many cases throughout the book discuss peer relationships, and the reader is encouraged to look in the thematic index following the table of contents for cases that can be found in other sections but include material on peer relationships. For example, "Someday My Elders Will Be Proud" (Case 1) and "Seeking the Best of Both Worlds" (Case 20) describe the power of peer pressure when an adolescent's ethnic culture is different from the dominant culture. The sections on sexual identity are particularly useful for examining romantic relationships.

Peer relationships include close friendships, cliques, peer groups and crowds, and romantic relationships. In an excellent review of peer relationships during adolescence, Brown (2004) notes five major themes in research findings regarding adolescent peer relationships. First, adolescent relationships are characterized by instability (Connolly, Furman, & Konarski, 2000; Eder, 1985; Feiring, 1999; Strouse, 1999). Second, research has increasingly focused on describing the behaviors and processes by which adolescents manage conflicts in friendships and romantic relationships (Galliher, Rostosky, Welsh, & Kawaguchi, 1999; Welsh, Galliher, Kawaguchi, & Rostosky, 1999) and pressure and influence one another (e.g., Spracklen, Andrews, Patterson, & Dishion, 1996). Third, conflict is common in adolescent peer relations and can support both healthy growth in coping strategies and, under some circumstances, lead to maladaptive outcomes (Welsh, Grello, & Harper, 2003). Fourth, there are important links between adolescent functioning in different types of peer relationships (e.g., functioning in close friendships predicts functioning in romantic relationships) (Connolly, Furman, & Konaiski, 2000; Furman, 1999; Furman, Simon, Schaffer, & Bouchey, 2002). Fifth, peer relationships change throughout adolescence in accordance with developmental growth in the domains of cognition, puberty, and identity.

Cases in this and other sections of the book may be used to explore and illustrate each of these major themes. For example, cases may be analyzed to illustrate and understand some of the reasons underlying instability in peer relationships. Sienna's case (Case 12) provides a window through which to view the importance of close friendships in high school, while José, Devneesh, and Andy's cases (Cases 4, 7, and 14) illustrate the crucial nature of close friendships in the transition to college. José (Case 4) and his struggle to "fit in," can be used to examine how peers are used as a means of social comparison and how peers can be an important source of information outside the family. The role of popularity—fitting in with desired cliques, being rejected or neglected by peers—is acutely felt by all adolescents included within this section on peer relationships.

Current theory and research also underscores the importance of connections between the quality of family relationships and the quality of close peer relationships (Gold & Yanof, 1985; Parker & Gottman, 1989). The case of Chhaya (Case 11) provides excellent material for a discussion of the impact of family relationships on the development of peer relationships. Chhaya's ways of relating to her high-school friends mirror the way she relates to her family; she is afraid to show anything other than her "perfect" self. What are the aspects of close friendships and romantic relationships that the adolescents in this book value, and how do these values change as these adolescents mature?

THE FAMILY I HAVE

As a child, Myra loves her somewhat eccentric family. As she enters adolescence, however, she begins to distance herself from them because their eccentricity begins to seem "strange." She engages instead with friends, academics, and activist causes, in both high school and college. Her adopted brother's difficulties in and out of school lead her to reflect more directly on her relationships with members of her family and the family's general process of interaction. In college, she begins to renegotiate these relationships, holding onto her independent and separate self while exploring what it means to be part of her family.

The red-lit number on the face of our answering machine announced that the machine stored twenty-eight messages. I began to play them and quickly skipped through the first fifteen or so as I searched for a message from a friend relaying details on an activist event we were planning. As I slowed my advance through the messages, I noticed that many of them had been left by the same automated voice. "This message is to inform you that your ninth grade son has been reported absent from one or more classes. This absence has yet to be explained. Please call your son's grade level office—BEEP . . . This message is to inform you that your ninth grade son—BEEP . . . This message is to inform you that your—BEEP . . . this message—BEEP . . . this message is—BEEP . . ."

I sighed with exasperation at the fact that no one but me had bothered to delete the messages and clean the tape. Yet, I paused to reflect on my brother's attitude to school, which was significantly more bad-ass than mine had been. "Michael sure figured out that it doesn't matter if you skip study hall faster than I did," I mused. By my junior year of high school I'd loosened up enough to occasionally cut a gym class to go grab lunch or finish my math homework, but I was significantly more uptight than my younger sibling, who had recently blossomed from a shy kid who liked watching nature channel specials on the emu and collecting Star Wars cards into a suave socialite, much cooler than myself.

Michael's social prowess, far more conventional than the silly humor and activista passion that I had used to build my own social circle, was just one of the characteristics on an unending list of the differences between me and my brother. Despite our polar characters, Michael and I had a friendly albeit distant relationship. The close bonds of our early childhood had ended abruptly with my entry into kindergarten, where I succumbed to the peer pressure of my classmates who informed me that little brothers were *not* friends. They were annoying. Before that Michael and I had been comrades in fun: cutting eye-holes in paper bags to create torso-sized masks, setting up tents in front of the TV where we could cuddle with each other and blankets while we watched "The Sea Gypsies." There had been none of the typical jealousy that comes with new siblings.

I attribute this initial lack of sibling rivalry largely to the ownership I felt over the decision to have another child in the family. Because giving birth is an unpleasant process, my mother claims, my parents chose to adopt their second child. While at two years old I clearly had no veto power in this decision, my parents gave me a sense of agency in the adoption process. "I want to adopt a girl from Brazil!" I proclaimed.

"Okay, we'll look into that," my parents responded seriously, "but we're not sure if it will work out. How would you feel about having a brother from Vietnam?"

"I want a brother from Vietnam!" I ordered. In addition to feeling that I had picked out the new person who would soon enter my life—unlike my unfortunate playmates who would be saddled with whatever sister or brother happened to pop out of their mothers—I relished the adoption process that must have been painful and painstaking for my parents. The meetings with social workers, the creation of books of photographs, and the purchase of stuffed animals mailed to Vietnam, each of these events was an adventure for me.

After Michael finally arrived, a warm April after his second birthday when I was 4, I quickly forgot that he was adopted. Having an Asian brother complemented our family's Judaism nicely in allowing me to share stories during the diversity lessons of my liberal education, but other than that, it didn't really factor into my daily life.

In fact, many of the factors that seem like they should have been of paramount importance at that time didn't seem to impact the experiences of my childhood. Maybe it's that childhood is this time when your family is still your first and sometimes only reference point. You haven't yet been exposed to all these outside influences that tell you which of your experiences are normal and which experiences distinctly aren't. The fact that my parents slept in different bedrooms didn't phase me—they both snored and would wake each other up all night long if they didn't! My brother's night terrors were just a problem that had to be dealt with, like an earache. My father worked until seven or sometimes nine at night, and my mother was a graduate student working through her courseload at a snail's pace. What other way could a family be? What was important were the raucous lab parties that took place on our porch; the globe game that Michael and I played identifying countries to win red-hots from my mom; the sound of *A Jar of Dreams* or *Fried Green Tomatoes* read by my mother before bed; the trips to the gas station with my

Dad when we got to pick out *whichever* candy bar we wanted. When I was a young child, I made a remark that later became famous in my family: "I have the best parents. I love Mama so much because she spends time with us and reads us stories and loves us. And I love Papa so much because he gives us candy and toys." As a child, I loved my family unconditionally, not picking up on the fact that some of the things that I regarded as wonderful or normal might be perceived by outsiders as problematic.

The proud love I'd felt for my family as a young child and in my elementary school years swiftly dissolved as I entered my secondary education. I began to notice more and more "strange" things about my family. I cringed when my mother insisted that I continue to call her and my father "Mama and Papa" rather than the more adult "Mom and Dad" because she didn't like the way "Mom" sounded. I couldn't understand why it was so difficult for my mother to pack me PB and J on white bread with a juice box and chips for lunch (I instead found myself with pickles, matzo, rye bread with nutella, and seltzer water). I could no longer explain to my peers why my house was atrociously messy, why my parents slept in separate bedrooms, or why my brother had more Pokemon cards than he had friends or As on his report cards. The fact that my mother was proud of her obesity—"no one wanted to get to know me for who I really was when I looked like Barbie"—suddenly became a huge issue in the appearance-oriented world of adolescent girls. My intellectual, eccentric parents were suddenly at a disconnect with the normalized teenage world that I had stumbled upon. In seventh grade, when I asked my mother for last-minute help on a report on an artist and she *insisted* that I write about Rubens instead of suggesting a more standard Van Gogh or Monet, I made a decision. I don't know if that decision was conscious or not, but from that point on I became as independent from my family as I could be.

That was the last time I ever asked for help on a homework assignment (with the exception of ninth grade biology, during which my cancer-researching father was a valuable asset). I completely ceased asking my friends over to our house, always going to their homes or meeting them downtown instead. I rushed through family dinners in order to meet my waiting homework. I struggled to stop asking for favors; I packed my own lunch and walked places or got rides from friends rather than from my parents. I had chalked up my family as dysfunctional and weird. By high school I had clear-cut goals: good grades, activist causes, and strong friendships. In my grand scheme of things, I felt that my family was only a liability when it came to tackling the challenges I placed before myself. More and more, my family dropped into the background.

The recession of my family's importance in my daily life was mostly simple, gradual, and unnoticed. Most teenagers assert independence from their parents; it's part of growing up. My father never commented on the fact that my withdrawal was perhaps more significant than that of his colleagues' children. Perhaps he expected me to skip family dinners for homework and to prefer spending my summers at camp over family vacations. Maybe the intermittent contact during help with biology homework or when we watched TV together and the relative lack of conflict were satisfactory to him.

At the time, I'm not even sure that I realized that I was withdrawing more than my other friends. It was the girl who stayed home from weekend get-togethers for family dinners who seemed lame and odd, not me. Spending time or thoughts on my family simply was no longer a priority; these had been usurped by worlds my parents seemed to know nothing about: friends and clothes, extracurricular commitments and SAT prep.

While my father didn't seem fazed by the changes in my time schedule and attitude, my mother was deeply affected. She sometimes articulated her unhappiness in the face of my abandonment of our family and my obligations to our shared household. Perhaps because she was upset about the changes in my behavior, our relationship became more and more antagonistic, which in turn caused me to distance myself further. Frequently, we would have long and intense verbal battles. They would start over something that seemed small, maybe tension had already been building, I don't know. I'd be sitting at the table doing my math homework, sleeping in bed, or for the first time in weeks relaxing in front of the television. My mother would interrupt me, to tell me about some dishes I had to wash, or a pile of stuff I had to move. "Look," I would say, struggling to assert that I *knew* what I had to do and I had my priorities in place, "I have an Algebra test *tomorrow*" or "I haven't sat down to rest in *weeks*. I'll take care of it after this." My mother would respond by asserting my selfishness or lack of responsibility and the disagreement would erupt into a volley of screams and cruel quips aimed to hurt the other party. Eventually my mother would say something that I found so horrible—you're a creep, a horrible daughter, you only care about yourself—that I would begin to sob and exit the room, slamming the door behind me. Sometimes the shouts would continue from separate rooms, but eventually, almost always after I lay crying alone my mother would enter the room and hold me and comfort me until I stopped crying.

I wondered why our fights always followed this pattern, why my mother would provoke me when she knew what the end outcome would be. I think sometimes there would be a reason behind our fights and some temporary consensus would be reached. Sometimes, whatever was really troubling me about our family would come out during the climax of the argument, or while my mother comforted me afterwards: "You and Papa don't really love each other." "You're *never* going to finish graduate school. Michael and I stopped you from getting a job." "You spend too much time taking care of me, Michael isn't going to do well in school." And then my mother would soothe me and inform me that this wasn't the case, that if I had just spoken to her earlier this misperception could have been cleared up. There would be momentary calm and the volcano would not erupt for another few weeks.

Occasionally, however, the fights wouldn't resolve in that manner. My mother would just go on being antagonistic and occasionally cruel and never come to rescue me. I remember one fight erupting during a five-minute car ride to a friend's house and her casting me out of the car in tears to ashamedly greet my friend with a red and salty-wet face. When my mother abandoned me in my misery at home, I would go find my father. "Don't you think she's being unreasonable?" I would ask. "Don't you think if she let me have some *input* into the way we organized the house I would clean it more?" And my dad would assure me that I was indeed the reasonable one and that my mother was indeed irrational. But he would also tell me that I just had to placate her and move on.

I was not a violent or angry teenager. I have never fought with anyone the way I fought with my mother. The angry words and outrage that flew were a release of energy, but they were not behaviors I liked displaying—so I distanced myself from my mother further. But maybe this strategy amplified the problem.

While my parents in general and my mother specifically provoked me to retreat from my family, the physical and emotional distance between us expanded to my brother as well. During these years, categorical observations all too often formed the bulk of my thoughts of Michael. I didn't think about him as a person I knew, but rather about him as an abstract unit of the family. I had a brother: he liked soccer. He was good at art. He was bad at school. He was adopted. These observations complicated my relationship to abstract concepts like race, talent, and academic success, but didn't really texture my day-to-day interactions with the boy I shared a house with. Our relationship didn't go very deep—I didn't particularly feel like I *knew* him that well, despite the fact that I felt a strong sense of love for the brother I'd watched grow from afar. At this point, my relationship with Michael was similar to my relationship with my parents, although I didn't feel the same strong, protective sense of love for my mother and father that I did for Michael, and in the case of my parents our distance seemed purposed rather than coincidental.

The space in my life and emotional consciousness that opened up when I distanced myself from my family filled so quickly that it seemed like I hadn't pushed away my family and childhood pursuits but that new activities and relationships had crowded them out. I clearly and consciously defined a personal path to success for myself that consisted of a mélange of typical teenage perfections: popularity, appearance, academic success; and more personal goals: political involvement, intimate friendship, having a unique character. My days suddenly filled themselves with school, hours upon hours of homework, the synagogue youth group, dance class, activist clubs, and other activities. I also began to fill my life with new people. The importance of friendship in my life grew tenfold. With the independence of adolescence came the ability to meet friends for dinner at downtown restaurants, to bike over to their homes unaided and later to go for long drives to nowhere. I quickly developed a steady and nurturing group of friends who were similar to myself.

Together we embarked on adventures and projects. In middle school two of my friends and I always walked home to one of their houses. There we completed our pre-algebra and French homework, ate dried cranberries, and watched movies. We made a project of folding one thousand paper cranes for my friend Emily's bedroom. Everyday after school we would listen to music and fold and fold and fold while we chatted about things that I don't even remember but that seemed incredibly important at the time. My friends were fun, and the things they liked and did seemed *so cool* especially in contrast to the bizarre tastes of my family.

In high school these types of friendships continued and intensified. My small group of a few girls who played stringed instruments and worked hard at school expanded to include about ten other kids who liked music and art, were intellectually engaged, and like to have silly and spontaneous fun. We had calculus study groups (renamed Algebra 4 to seem less intimidating) that degenerated into giggle sessions, and we ate every lunch together in the band room. I remember having incredible amounts of fun with my friends in high school: cooking dinners together on the weekends, going paddle-boating, filling buckets with water and bobbing for apples during lunchtime, taking easels to coffee shops and drawing the patrons, swing dancing and going to jazz concerts, playing ultimate Frisbee in the park, taking county highways to drive-in movies, embarking on photo-scavenger hunts that we designed ourselves.

This core group of friends—as well as other friendships that I built with other politically involved kids in the later years of high school—also shared my values (values that all of our parents also shared) and pushed me to think and develop those views. We'd bring the *New York Times* to school in the mornings, talk politics over lunch. We got angry when we saw discrimination in our school, we thought critically about our role in the world. In middle school my friends and I did every fundraising walk we could find, and by the end of high school we'd graduated to a 450-mile AIDS bike ride. My friends challenged me and together we explored our role in the larger political world. We formed clubs, and through those clubs I made new friends who were intrigued by political issues and power structures. Together we figured out what it took to learn outside of school, to implement recycling programs, and to pass city council resolutions. We learned about how, even as teenagers, our power in the world could be so profound, but also so limited.

I formed another important group of relationships at summer camp. Each summer I'd pack my bags and head to the wilds of upstate New York. There I had space to grow and develop on my own. My role models were college-aged camp counselors; there were no real grown-ups in sight. In a social world composed completely of my peers I stretched my wings and really felt like I grew. There were boys at summer camp with whom I flirted and felt normal. There were girls at summer camp with whom I could candidly discuss issues of body image, feminism, and superficiality. Isolated from the real world, we critiqued the messages the media, our schools, and our parents sent us about what it meant to be successful and what it meant to be good. I felt independent and loved in that environment.

I held on to my summer camp friendships during the year, too. I exchanged e-mails and paper and pen letters covered in collages and doodles. Every night my best friend and I would have long conversations via instant messenger. We'd exchange notes on the opposite sex, on the banality of high school, on whatever current event was big news, and on what Bob Dylan was like when he was our age. Every so often I'd take the bus down to the city for a New Year's party or a long weekend with my summer camp buddies. When we were old enough to drive these visits took on an independent and wildly fun flavor as we drove around the suburbs making surprise visits to friends and leaving poetry in the mailboxes of crabby neighbors.

In addition to being fun and challenging many of my friends were also steady and reliable. I listened to their problems and they would listen to mine. We discussed the typical troubles of adolescents: eating disorders, drug use, romantic relationships, friendship difficulties, the pressure to succeed academically, as well as simply recounting the events of bad days. When my family seemed weird or crazy or impossible I had people to go to. I never really talked to them about any serious issues with my family—fights were mentioned with flippancy, the oddities that bothered me were reduced to humorous incidents. But when life at home seemed impossible and strange I could usually count on a study date or evening of scrabble with my steady and level-headed friends.

This isn't to say that my friends were perfect—they were annoying or petty at times—and this also isn't to say that my family truly was completely dysfunctional and awful, or even that as a teenager I felt that way all the time. My adolescence was characterized by a disdain for my "weird" family and a quest for independence. But, I was also a fairly culturally critical kid. I knew from the social science books that I read in my free time that cookie-cutter normalcy wasn't all it was cracked up to be. I loved some of my family's idiosyncrasies. Who else did I know that had been brought to gay pride marches and counter-protests at abortion clinics since infancy? Who else's parents had lived together since college (despite the fact that they hadn't married until they were past thirty) resulting in the repetitive story of when it was Papa's week to cook and they ate borscht soup all week long? I was proud of my father's research—who else knew that cayenne pepper could cure cancer?—and the myriad of talents that my brother had, but didn't pursue: "Yeah, he was the best kid on the soccer team, but he didn't like running so he quit. You should see this flip book he made, though!" The feminist example that my mother set for me provided me with armor for many of the challenges that my female peers faced in adolescence, and my feminist identity stayed with me throughout all my years of schooling. I used the resources that my parents had to offer: a dinner with them and some family friends gave me advice on how to plan a rally—how long it should be, where tables should be set up. My father's job accepting graduate students to the university yielded advice (which I sometimes later discarded) about college applications.

I managed to deal with what I perceived as dysfunction and inefficiency in the family unit by distancing myself from it through high school and the beginning of college, yet I had a basketful of funny stories about my "weird family" that I'd whip out at a moment's notice. I had a penchant for the quirky and eccentric and during lulls in conversation wouldn't hesitate to mention that my parents lived together for twenty years before they got married—and when they did it was at the spur of the moment in Taiwan. By the time I entered college my mother finally had a job and my brother finally had friends. The house was sometimes clean! Things seemed to be stabilizing: my family didn't really consume much of my time, but they were a helpful conversation piece that I could use when I needed them and even appreciate in real-life interactions. I'd even started to be comfortable enough with my family that by winter break of my first year of college (following my brother's example), I was cool with bringing a few high school friends home to hear stories from my inebriated father about the kangaroo he was planning to meet on his next business trip to Australia.

But of course, as always happens, things changed that following spring. I thought that my brother's life was going well, judging from the crew of kind friends that seemed permanently glued to the TV in our basement and the sweet girlfriend he'd recently acquired. I chased any worries about his grades or school attendance from my mind by reminding myself that Michael couldn't and shouldn't grow up to be like me, that academic performance was only one measure of success. But that April my mother called me on my dorm room phone to check in and let me know that even though Passover was over, she still wanted to send me the Passover package she'd been planning as soon as she figured out how to ship pickled lemons. When I inquired about how my brother was doing, though, the tone of our conversation changed.

"We've been having some trouble with Michael lately," she said. She then went on to list a litany of issues that had recently come to her attention. Michael had completely stopped going to school, was failing all his classes, was hanging out with different kids, and was smoking pot every day, maybe even more than once a day. All this came as a shock to me. For some reason, I had assumed that my brother, like me in high school, didn't touch substances. I thought he skipped gym class—not every class, every day. I thought that because his friends seemed so clean-cut and nice, since they did fine in school, that they'd take care of him. But none of this was true. I felt bad and helpless because my brother was apparently in such a spot of trouble in his life. But I also felt guilty because we were so distant that I hadn't even realized it.

During childhood and early adolescence it had been the norm to have distant or even antagonistic relationships with siblings. After all, I'd ditched my lame-o little brother because of kindergarten peer pressure. In elementary school I went so far as to be mean to Michael, calling him stupid and blaming him for my misdeeds. ("I don't know where the candy on top of the refrigerator went. You should ask Michael.") By high school we were friendly but distant. It all seemed correct. But now, in college, I looked around and it seemed like everybody was best friends with his or her sibling. I was surprised by the long phone conversations my roommate had with her sister, by the fact that my best friend openly admired her older sister, who was clearly her role model. And it was hard to listen as my friends discussed how fun it was to watch their younger brothers and sisters undergo the same college search process that they had, and whether they thought their siblings should go to Brown or Pomona. Not only did I wonder if the suddenly abnormal lack of friendship between me and Michael was a shortcoming on my part, I also wondered what role I had played in causing his current difficulties.

At this point in my life, my everyday activities were colored by a sense of logical efficiency. The first thing I did was to tackle the problems in Michael's life the same way that I would tackle any other problem that surfaced in my life: by analyzing them. Who was to blame for these new problems? Was it my parents who had not been involved enough in my brother's upbringing? Was it me for abandoning my brother in favor of other pursuits? Was it me for encouraging my parents to do their parenting job from a distance and showing them that everything would turn out all right if they did that? Was it our large public high school which catered its attention and energies to highly motivated students like me, allowing students like my brother to fall through the cracks? Was it my father for the hands-off approach he took to parenting, leaving the important decisions about Michael's life to my mother's—perhaps unsound—discretion? Was it the attention deficit disorder with which Michael had only been recently diagnosed? Was it low self-esteem influenced partially by the way I called him "stupid" at the drop of the hat as a youngster? Was it the traumatic experiences he'd had in day care as a toddler?

As I moved back further and further in Michael's life searching for the root causes of his present difficulties, I stumbled on a series of factors that I'd only recently begun to consider when thinking about my brother. It wasn't until I was 13 that I looked across the dinner table and fully realized that my brother looked different from me. It was much later in high school when I first thought about the fact my brother's children would not inherit any of my genetic material—no one would ever say that my niece had inherited my eyes or love of dance. And it wasn't until college that I realized that my family fit the definition of a "multiracial family"— because up until now I had assumed that my brother's ancestors were the same French and Hungarian and Russian Jews who passed on their genes to me. All these startlingly obvious, yet belated and intellectualized, observations began to shape my conception of my relationship with Michael toward the end of my high school years and the beginning of college.

Now that Michael's life seemed to be spinning out of control, I wondered what role these factors played in his life. My school classes on race and ethnicity reminded me that my brother's growing-up experience, as a child with brown skin and Asian eyes, must have been significantly different from mine. I remembered the elementary school kids who'd asked Michael if he ate dogs, the kid at summer camp who had called Michael "chink" during a physical fight, the distant cousin from small-town Wisconsin who had told me that Michael must be very, very smart since he was Asian. I then allowed my mind to wander in a far less politically correct direction. Could some of Michael's problems stem from genetic factors? Had my work ethic and intellectual prowess been inherited rather than learned from my parents? And then, the worst question of all was raised in my mind: what if we hadn't adopted Michael and my parents had just chosen to have another biological child? Would that child be succeeding? Would that child be my friend? These thoughts were difficult and felt like a betrayal of the younger brother that I loved so intensely, albeit distantly. I couldn't imagine my life without Michael, with some paler, less athletic boy in his stead. I pushed the adoption questions out of my head and focused on the present.

As problem after problem unfolded in my brother's life, I watched from a distance and kept the issues secret from my friends. I was never home for more than a month at a time, and in that time I tried to be kind to Michael, observing the tension between him and my parents. Most of my information about the drama of Michael's late adolescence was relayed to me via phone conversations with my parents, not through phone conversations with Michael. Each time I called, it seemed like a new horrible thing had happened. In my memory their chronology is blurred, like the events of those years are an avalanche of horribleness and it didn't matter the precise order of when each chunk of snow and ice hit the ground, it just mattered that they were falling fast and that they were dangerous. And the chunks were scary. Over the course of the next year Michael got violent when he got drunk, ran away from home and was not heard from for months at a time, was arrested, lost friends, stole money, was beaten up, and broke up with his girl-friend—the only steady and positive thing in his life.

Like I said, I don't really remember when each event took place, and perhaps that's because I didn't talk with anyone about these incidents. My mother lost her job because of the time and energy she was spending dealing with and fighting with Michael. This was a huge blow to me; I'd been waiting since I could remember for my mother to finish graduate school, to get a job, to become a normal mother. To have this wonderful, normalizing thing taken away hurt me and thrust the gravity of the situation in my face. And my brother was missing. And I had homework to do.

I also had friends to see, friends who didn't know what was going on. I chose not to confide in my friends for a variety of reasons, I suppose. Because I'd never told my friends about the previous problems I'd had with my family. Because it would be awkward to say to them, "So, how was your bio test?" "It was fine." "Did I mention that my brother is dependent on marijuana and has run away from home? Oh yeah, my mom lost her job, too." Because I didn't want to dramatize the situation and make it about me and not my brother: "Yeah, did you hear about how tragic and dysfunctional my life is? Yeah, it's pretty bad . . ." Because I was embarrassed and ashamed of the way my family acted. Because I didn't want my friends to constantly check in on me, as if I were a fragile thing that needed help-ing. This was my brother's issue, and I wasn't quite sure where I fit into everything

That October, I took a day off of class to attend synagogue for the Jewish New Year. I reflected over the previous year, the goals that I had set and accomplished, where I had fallen short. I once again wondered where I fit into my family in gen-eral and my brother's problems in particular. I thought about the hundreds and hundreds of hours and all the energy I'd poured into activist causes over the pre-vious year: The Sweat-Free Campaign on my campus. My school's Committee on Equal Opportunity. Voter Registration. The AIDS Ride. How could I devote so much of myself to helping strangers raise their wages or pay for HIV drugs when my brother, who should be one of the closest people to me, floundered while I did nothing? I'd spent the last five years of my life ignoring my family, I decided. For whatever reason, I felt that this distance was wrong, incorrect. This year, I re-solved, they would be a priority, though I wasn't really sure what that meant.

It meant calling home rather than waiting for my parents to call me. It meant calling my brother's cell phone to leave friendly messages on his voice mail. It meant coming home for breaks to find that my brother had returned from what-ever friend's house he was crashing at in order to sit on the couch with me while I watched him play video games. Like I said earlier, just because my brother and I didn't have much in common, just because we weren't "close" the way some sib-lings were, didn't mean that we didn't profoundly love each other. He came home to see me.

By making small efforts, I placated my conscience. The family box could be checked off on my to-do list and I felt slightly better about the whole thing. But that didn't mean that Michael did. When he had run away, I couldn't even contact him to make an effort to be there for him. So I just waited and waited. At times, the waiting hurt. But day to day, it wasn't really *that* painful of a waiting. Despite the fact that I'd pledged to make my family a priority in my life, my life was filled to the brim with other things. We'd won the Sweat-Free Campaign, but I'd barely taken time to claim any victory before thrusting myself into the anti-Taco Bell movement. I was applying to study abroad. There was plenty of drama with my friends, who also were constantly urging me to "play more." School, as always, de-manded much time and energy. My boyfriend and I—or was he my boyfriend?—were going in circles trying to figure out if it made sense to be dating. I had baby-sitting jobs to attend to, and tours of the campus to give. I was organizing a large service-learning program for the kids at summer camp. So worrying about my family was an intermittent thought that surfaced occasionally when I called home, or when I read an article in the *New York Times Magazine* about the author's meth-addicted son that caused me to cry uncontrollably alone in my dorm room.

The thoughts of family surfaced again when I received yet another phone call. Michael had come home. He'd run out of other options, none of his friends would have him any more. I was glad. I bought a ticket to go home for spring break.

Despite the fact that it seemed like Michael had hit rock bottom and could now only bob to the surface, things were still difficult. True, it did seem that Michael could only move up from where he was—but he didn't follow a linear path upward—things were (and still are) like a roller coaster with him, and I con-stantly worried that he wouldn't get back on track enough. Especially since he had shattered some of the old mechanisms he'd used to deal with problems in the past.

Michael had always had a special, close relationship with Mama. He turned to her for advice and unconditional love. But upon his trauma and homecoming, his relationship with her degenerated to resemble the fights I'd had with her when I was in high school. But in this case, the fights were drawn out, never-ending, and sometimes physical. I sided with my brother, both because I felt that that was my role and my duty as sister, and because I remembered how our mother could suck you into a fight you didn't want to have, let it escalate and escalate, and then blame you for each action you took. I wanted her to put down what she was doing and fix my brother. Instead she engaged him in verbal battles. And when those battles turned physical, she took the drastic step of calling the police and getting my brother enmeshed in the legal system, an over-18-year-old charged with domestic violence. Michael retorted, for the first time, by insisting that my mother was not his *real* mother, and removing the photo of his biological mother from it's place on the piano in the living room to bring it closer to his lair, the TV room where he slept, played video games, and entertained friends.

Despite the overtures I made to my brother, and the fact that family now had a higher-up spot on the to-do list that was my life, my efforts did not always bear fruit. There were moments: good conversations on the cell phone, a carefully drawn out birthday card thanking me for being a good sister, a steady stream of "I love yous" and "I love you toos." But more often than not, my trips home to see him ended up being the two of us sitting in separate rooms, him turning down my invitations to accompany me out to dinner or to the grocery store, me watching him play Rainbow Six, and a couple intermittent conversations about how weird our parents are. Was it enough? What should I have done?

When my overtures didn't pay off, I found myself wondering if it takes two to tango. I never stopped assigning blame for the situation. I blamed my mother. I blamed my father. I wasn't sure if I should blame myself. What's a sister supposed to do? My parents told me that my job was just to love him and be his friend and be his ally. But how was I supposed to do that and what was that really doing? I knew that there was not that much that I could do, and gradually began to doubt how much my parents themselves could affect the situation without a willing partner. But assigning blame to Michael seemed fruitless and incorrect. I knew that with a few alterations in action (going to class, for example) he could have easily turned his life around and harnessed the reservoirs of potential harbored in his person. But those few alterations seemed impossible, given Michael's anger, fear, low-self esteem and depression. Who could I blame?

When Michael left, in some ways I became closer to both of my parents. There was finally something to talk about that we were all interested in, that I could only discuss with them: Michael. My parents negotiated a tenuous line: how much to tell me, how much to involve me. They knew I was Michael's sister and not his parent and didn't want to over-worry or over-involve me. At the same time, they knew that I was very concerned and no longer a child. My parents negotiated the line with skill, and I came out of the situation drawn closer to them by the information they shared and the responsibility they assumed.

After my mother lost her job and became embroiled in the battle with Michael, however, the oddities in her personality that I'd chalked up as (sometimes lovable) eccentricity seemed symptomatic of mental illness or at least out of touch with reality. The changes in her behavior—or maybe her behavior didn't change and I just noticed it for the first time—led me to remember the oddest symptoms of strangeness she exhibited when I was growing up: She loved being fat despite the health problems it could cause, and refused conventional diets and exercise in favor of "sleeping more" or "eating the foods I love so I am satisfied and will eat less." She seemed to be sick all the time, and would lie in bed all day. She was always starting some new educational program, never finishing and getting a degree. She would start projects around the house that she would never finish— the bathroom door, the drier duct, varnishing the floor. She changed her name legally because she never liked the way "Jeanne" sounded. She wrote her own version of "happy birthday" and banned the traditional version because it was annoying. These idiosyncratic projects consumed time she could be spending working toward a concrete goal. Instead the little details of life swept her away in their seemingly paramount importance.

I remember these problems and projects receding into the background when my mother got a job running therapy groups for children who had been sexually assaulted. Aside from the strange office politics in which she embroiled herself, the way she occupied her time seemed worthwhile: it helped others and brought home a paycheck. When she lost her job and became entangled in my brother's problems, though, my attention again swerved to focus on her strange ineptitudes. In the absence of work, she devoted time and energy and apprehension and nervousness to our local Yiddish choir, composed of almost-senior citizens from the various synagogues in my hometown who liked to get together once a week and sing old Yiddish songs about potatoes and the like. This laid-back, peripheral activity suddenly became the focus of her life: photocopies needed to be made, songs needed to be practiced, rehearsals needed to be held in our home, we needed to host the after-performance potlucks. Anything that got in the way of Yiddish choir was bad. Her spending habits also troubled me. She spent her money (which she didn't have in the first place) on a foam memory pillow or a pair of earrings for me that I didn't want. She insisted on practicing Spanish for three hours a day and got horribly upset when she was unable to. While the Spanish practice was intended to help her get a job doing therapy in Spanish, I wondered when she'd be proficient enough. She was fluent, but the job search never began.

With my mother strangely out of commission and my brother flailing, my Dad really came home from work for what seemed like the first time ever. Suddenly it was Papa who arranged the meetings with the school social worker, who hired a lawyer to get Michael out of the legal trouble my mother had put him in, who drove him to school each morning, who cooked dinner with him and slipped in wise, fatherly talks about what it would take to get Michael graduated from high school and into culinary school.

I'd always admired my Dad's efficiency and logic. Sometimes these traits would be displayed to me—but only after my mother came up short. I'd come to my dad, complaining about some complicated way my mother wanted to purchase my plane tickets or get me from extracurricular A to extracurricular B. My Dad would smile and tell me to calm down and, with the same logical precision and imagination that allowed him to run a lab, get large grants from the federal government, and discover cool new things about "junk" DNA, he would make a plan to solve the problem that my mother could only complicate. I loved having my father step in and clear things up, but this only ever happened after all possibilities with my mother had been exhausted. My mother was the chief-in-command when it came to dealing with the children, and when I came to my father first, I was redirected back to Mama.

So, when my Dad finally stepped up to deal with Michael I was relieved to have someone so level-headed tackling the problem. On the other hand, old resentments were dredged up. "What would have happened," I'd wonder, "if Papa had been this involved *before* things had gone so wrong? Would Michael have been placed in a better school for him? Would he have better friends? Would the problem have been caught and dealt with earlier?"

At the same time as my parents lives were realigning in terms of their relationship to Michael, their lives were changing in other ways. I often tease my father about becoming "bourgie" after I left high school. When a doctor told him that his weight could pose serious health problems, my dad started going to the gym for two hours a day, switched his diet from pork and steak to fish and salad, and subsequently melted from a Santa look-alike into a physically fit little elf. He cut the beer and joined a wine tasting class, where I'm sure he regaled his delighted peers with tales of his attempts to get flexible with the new spine ball class at the gym.

My mother, despite her apparent craziness and lack of a job, developed a new social circle—women from the synagogue who also happened to have sons undergoing problems similar to Michael's. These women also happened to be Weight-Watchers fiends so my dad fit right into the crowd. Their lives, which used to be dominated by children and work, suddenly took the empty-nester turn, and they organized a social life filled with kayak trips and dinner parties. But the nest was not empty. Michael, at 19 with 20 looming in the distance, had still not graduated high school, still lived at home playing video games in solitiude, or with the occasional sketchy friend dropping by.

In high school, I had one of those great, touchy-feely English teachers who related every book we read to the pubescent teenagers in his classroom. *Catcher in the Rye* was about casual sex, *All the King's Men* was about how the past affects your daily life, *One Flew Over the Cuckoo's Nest* was about the walls society puts around us, forcing teenagers to conform. One day when we were sitting in class relating some aspect of our mundane lives to some great work of literature, Ms. Scott turned to me and asked, "Do you like your parents? Are you close to them? Will you be close to them in the future?" I thought a little and responded, "I think I will like my parents a lot more and be closer to them when I get out of the house. The more independent I get, the more I think I'll be able to like and appreciate them. You know, when they don't control my life and are just people." I resented the control my parents had over my life; I truly felt that I was more capable of making decisions and running my life than they were. Perhaps this was true. I struggled to retain control.

I still struggle with the financial dependence I have on my parents. But other than that, I *am* in control of my own life. And now the struggle in our relationship is knowing where I am obligated to connect to them, and where I want to connect to them, now that our relationship isn't regulated by the control a parent has over a child.

With Michael, on the other hand, I struggle with my lack of control. Not only does it seem like if I knew the right words to say and the right actions to perform I could repair my distant relationship with my brother, it also seems like I could solve his problems. Even though I know, as the daughter of a perennial psychology master's student, that Michael must be the one to exert his agency and decide to fix his own problems, this is difficult information to process.

Every trip home seems like it uncovers some old piece of confusion or pain that I am unable to resolve. So what keeps me coming home and calling home? I have this picture in my head of a family I'd like to be a part of some day, when I'm grown up and have a job and am the mother. In that family, the parents display an unending love and admiration for each other. The children are the focus of the home, and they are carefully tended to as they grow older and stronger. In this family, the love is apparent and when time is spent together, fun is had.

This is the ideal family that American culture projects. But that family also extends to the uncle and grandparents my brother and parents will be to my children. How can I yearn for an ideal family for myself in the future, while abandoning the one that I have currently? And then the question becomes, what do I owe my family? This family who has never been perfect, and is not nearly always a joy for me to be a part of. When I was growing up, maybe because Michael was adopted, I remember talking a lot about "what makes a family." I learned that in some families there are two moms, and in some families there are no moms at all. In some families, there are just grandparents, or an auntie or an uncle. There are stepfamilies too. In Kenya, there are many families with no grown-ups at all. So what makes all these groups of people families? The answer that I learned so long ago, and the answer that remains true today is: it is the strong love that they have for one another that makes these groups families.

Not everyone is lucky enough to have a home filled with people who love them. I have had the incredible fortune of feeling a strong and profound love for my distant brother, my crazy mother, and my father whom I sometimes think did not do enough. The way they show their love for me can be unconventional and can make me unhappy or uncomfortable. But I think that I owe them love in return.

The question that remains, though, is what it means to be a part of a loving family and what my obligations to this group of people are. I don't know what my role was in Michael's downfall, but I'm pretty sure that I don't have the tools necessary to get him back on his feet. I think I can't mend the problems of my family members, and I know I'm not sure how to deal with them from day to day. This is a challenge that I'm sure will stay with me as I outgrow adolescence and move through adulthood. How are you supposed to be a daughter and a sister, but not a child? What is my role? All I know is that it has something to do with making my love available to my family. But I'm not sure how to do that. The only model I have, the model I dream of, is a sister and daughter in a very different, much more perfect family. I am learning to struggle to cast my notions of perfection aside in order to concentrate on loving the family I have, weirdness, dysfunction, and all.

FALLING FROM MY PEDESTAL

Living in a family characterized by disharmony and constant threat of divorce, this author traces her serious eating disorder to her attempts to compensate for her parents' unhappiness by being a perfect child. But no matter how hard she works or how perfect her grades, Chhaya's parents remain unhappy and even criticize her efforts. The emergence of adolescent sexuality creates a crisis in her sense of perfect self-control that is followed by the devastating news that despite her obsessive hard work, she will not be valedictorian. Drastically restricting her intake of food becomes a compensating obsession and means of asserting self-control and achieving perfection. Her health deteriorates and she is hospitalized. She learns that she must discover her own realistic goals and give up her "insane drive for perfection." Her recovery proves to be arduous and long, but by the end of her story she feels she has turned the corner.

So many people have asked me "How did you become anorexic?" that I'm about ready to tape-record my life story and play it back the next time the question comes up. I try to explain using the analogy of a rainbow. The entire spectrum of colors comprises the rainbow, but no single color can be extracted—they all blend together to form a continuum. The same can be said of the illness. Anorexia wasn't something that just "happened" to me—I didn't one day suddenly decide to stop eating. My problems ran much deeper than simply "not eating." The disorder was my desperate attempt to maintain some semblance of control in my life. It was a cry to establish who I was, to pick up the pieces of my shattered identity. To make sense of this insidious disease, and ultimately of myself, I must confront and examine the issues that led to my using the eating disorder as a coping mechanism to deal with the turmoil that surrounded and threatened to suffocate me.

I am convinced that my childhood represents the beginning of much of what led to the anorexia. My identity problem goes back as far as the elementary school years, and starts with my ethnic heritage. I come from what you might call a mixed background. My parents could not be more opposite in their histories if they tried—my father is East Indian and my mother is a typical WASP. As for me, I've gone through my entire life not knowing exactly what I was. I've always despised filling out standardized forms that ask for personal information, because I never know what box to check under "ethnic origin." The categories are neatly defined, literally black and white, and people who are "melting pots" like me present problems for this efficient form of classification. Technically, I'm more Indian than anything else, but I always feel deceptive saying I'm Indian when I'm really only a half-breed. Thus, I end up the perpetual "Other," an unclassifiable anomaly.

No one would guess merely by looking at me that I'm part Indian—my hair and eyes may be dark, but I'm quite fair-skinned. The one thing that gives me away is my name—my horrible, terrible Sanskrit name which I'm convinced no one on this planet can pronounce correctly without help. I have lambasted my parents endlessly for sentencing me to a lifetime with this albatross around my neck. I can't even count how many times people have completely massacred my name, either in pronunciation, spelling, or both—the number is utterly unfathomable. I'm forever giving what I call my "name spiel," explaining the origin and meaning of my name. Since such an understanding requires knowledge of my background, the subject inevitably leads into a discussion of my family, one of my least favorite conversational topics.

Even though my parents' relationship was tenuous (to say the least), they never fought in public. No one would have guessed they were anything other than normal as far as married couples go. At home, though, the masks came off, the farce ended, and the boxing gloves were donned. The match would usually begin at the dinner table. Supper was the only time we all came together as a "family," if you can call it that. It typically started with something insignificant like, "Why didn't you fix mashed potatoes with the steak," and escalated inevitably into the divorce fight. You could always tell when one was coming on. First, they'd bicker for a few minutes, then the voices would rise. The remark, "Why don't you just leave?" by either of them was the cue for my exit, for I could recite practically verbatim the arguments that would follow. Mom would snap, "You should go back to India. You haven't been happy since you left." Dad's bark ran along the lines of, "Why don't you move in with your parents?" In spite of all the fighting and all the threats of divorce that were made, though, it was always just words. Neither of the two ever acted upon their vow to end the marriage.

I think the instability and uncertainty of their relationship bothered me the most. The dark, intense fear always loomed in my mind—would this be the fight that leads to divorce? Is this fight going to be the straw that's going to break the camel's back? What if they're really serious this time? I'd be fraught with anxiety after every one of their quarrels. Within a few days, things usually returned to normal, meaning the usual strained relations in the absence of verbal brawls. Once I knew things were "safe," that divorce was not imminent and that we would remain a foursome, I could breathe a small sigh of relief, at least until the next argument.

When you're young, you think the world revolves around you. Given my egocentrism, I blamed myself as the cause of my parents' marital strife. I felt it was up to me to salvage their marriage, which I tried desperately to do. After each fight, I would ask myself what I had done wrong and how I could rectify the situation. Harboring intense feelings of guilt, I lambasted myself for not pleasing them and not living up to their expectations. Maybe if I'd cleaned my room like they'd asked . . . I wondered. If I could just be good enough, I thought, they'd love each other and, in turn, love me. I erroneously believed I could bring my parents together by the sheer force of my will. Frustration over my inability to positively influence their relationship caused me to feel completely ineffective and inadequate. My solution was to be more perfect than anyone could expect a child to be, to hide all signs of anger and rebellion, in order to deserve and gain their love.

Being achievement-oriented in school was my answer to many of the problems I faced. By making the grades, I was sure (or so I thought) to gain the love and attention I so desperately craved, not only from my parents, but from my teachers as well. Because my family life was like an emotional roller-coaster ride over which I had no influence, I turned to school for comfort and security. I knew that by working hard, I could do well—in the classroom, I could exert complete control. As the perfect student, people would respect and admire me. Only if others saw worth in me could I be truly assured of my substance and value.

Unfortunately, my plan backfired on me. The more As I received, the more my parents and classmates began to expect I would continue to do well. I strove endlessly (and fruitlessly) to impress my parents with my good grades. At the end of the marking period, I would rush home, report card clutched in hand, hoping to have glowing praise lavished upon me. Words can't begin to describe the crushing disappointment I felt when they merely remarked pointedly, "We knew that's what you'd get." Part of me was angry at having my hard work and accomplishment minimized. Whenever I mentioned my grades, all they did was preach about how "Grades aren't everything in life." Another common point they made was that "Common sense [which they felt I lacked] will get you farther in this world than will good grades." I felt I could never win with them. It seemed as though no matter what I did, no matter how hard I tried, there was always something lacking, something else I could and should have done better. I yearned for reassurance and affirmation of my worth, but because I felt that I could never be perfect in their eyes, I could never be truly convinced of gaining their love.

These traits I have described were present throughout my childhood, but no one ever recognized them as potential problems. On the contrary, my drive to be good, to achieve, to live by the rules, and to avoid disappointing or arousing the criticism of others was what made me a model child, even though I never felt like one. The severe misconceptions I held became dramatically apparent, however, with the onset of adolescence, for I was pitifully unprepared to meet the issues of this period.

As I entered high school, I became even more rigid in my interpretations. My self-doubt intensified and my self-esteem plunged even lower. I was convinced everyone else was more capable, both socially and intellectually, than I. Never comfortable with myself, I constantly devalued my abilities, thinking I wasn't good enough for anything. Striving for perfection, for being the best (and then some), became my all-consuming goal, my purpose in life, to the point where I sacrificed all else. I studied all the time, believing that if I let up in the slightest bit, I would inevitably slip up and fail. All of my flaws would then be revealed, and I would be exposed for the imperfect person and the fraud that I was. To me, failure represented the loss of control, and once that happened, I feared I would never be able to regain it.

I became petrified of showing any signs that could possibly be interpreted as imperfection. I felt compelled to live up to and surpass the expectations of my parents, teachers, and peers in order to avoid arousing criticism, which I took as a personal attack. While others may have expected 100 percent from me, I pushed for 110 percent. So driven was I to succeed—or rather, to be seen as a success—that I imposed the strictest of standards on myself. Rather than creating a sense of pride, worth, and accomplishment, however, my role as the good, obedient, successful student—the girl who had it all together (at least on the outside)—caused me to feel increasingly empty inside. Paradoxically, the more "successful" I became, the more inadequate I felt. I began to lose control of my identity more and more as I fell victim to the Perfect Girl image in all areas of my life. I had no idea of who I *was*, only who I was *supposed* to be.

I denied myself pleasure throughout high school, never allowing myself to simply have fun. To do something for the sake of enjoyment brought forth incredible feelings of guilt and self-indulgence. I think part of this conflict arose from my parents' disagreement over issues regarding my (non)social life. My mother always had a tendency to be overprotective. She tells me that when I was an infant, she used to peek in on me, sleeping soundly in my crib, and pinch me ever so slightly, just to make sure I was still breathing. I think her reluctance to let me out of the house had to do with her overriding concern with shielding my brother and me from the dangerous outside world. At the time, though, I felt she was trying to suffocate me. I would vehemently protest against her fears; what reason had I ever given her not to trust me? "It's not you or your friends I don't trust," she would respond, "it's the rest of the world." My father, on the other hand, pushed to get me more involved with my peers. "Why don't you invite your friends over here?" he'd prod. I always found that suggestion rather amusing, given the nature of our household. If I asked to do something with friends, I was always bounced from one parent to the other to obtain permission, and usually they ended up arguing over the incident. As a result, I ended up feeling guilty for being the cause of their marital strife, a position that tore me up inside. Rather than jeopardize the family harmony (or rather, lack of discord) I often didn't even bother to ask to go out. I tried to avoid the conflict by removing myself from the situation.

I had friends throughout high school, but I always kept them at a distance, scared that if I let them get too close, they would see that I wasn't perfect and reject me. Relating to my peers was extremely difficult for me as a result, because rarely could I talk about my inner feelings. I equated the expression of emotion with weakness and vulnerability, so I always remained deadly serious and kept things on a strictly superficial level. To others, I must have seemed frigid, removed, and detached. I myself felt lonely and isolated. I desperately wanted to reveal the true me, but my intense fear of exposure silenced me.

Two specific events, both of which occurred during the spring of my junior year in high school, catalyzed the emergence of the eating disorder. One of these two major happenings involved my very first romantic encounter with a member of the opposite sex. Prior to meeting Kevin, I had had no experience whatsoever with guys. My self-confidence being what it was (practically nil), I thought no one could ever possibly be interested in me. An extensive "screening" process, with stringent standards that few guys could measure up to, was a way of protecting myself from unnecessary pain and hurt. If in every guy I met I found some fault that immediately made him undesirable as a mate, then I'd never have to worry about him rejecting me. I could remain in control and would therefore be safe.

My encounter with Kevin changed things dramatically. I met him in March at a two-day science symposium held at our state university. I had mixed emotions about Kevin—on the one hand, I found myself incredibly attracted to him and excited at the prospect of what might lie ahead, but at the same time, I didn't want to open myself up for fear of getting hurt. I wanted badly to be "swept away," to experience all the wonderful emotions described in romance novels, but reminded myself I should remain calm and levelheaded. After all, I was treading on completely foreign territory. My intelligence was of absolutely no use here, and since I couldn't rely on previous experience, I had to make sure I protected myself. Despite all of my hesitance, I was able to let my guard down long enough to experience my first kiss. Kevin and I, along with another couple, parked in his car in a secluded area of the campus. As the two in the back seat started going at it immediately, I sat uncomfortably in the front, eyes focused straight ahead. I was afraid to even look at Kevin, sure I'd flush with embarrassment. He would see right through me and realize how inexperienced with guys I really was. He was definitely the one in control here, as I had absolutely no idea how to behave.

We talked for a while (with his friends in the back continuing their dalliance), and then it happened. By "it," I am referring to one of the most monumental moments in a person's life—the first kiss. I had wanted mine to be as passionate and romantic as they come. After practicing on pillows for so long, I thought for sure I'd be ready when the time came. All of my rehearsing turned out to be in vain, though, for in no way did it prepare me for the intense emotions I felt. I remember more the mixture of thrill and nervousness that jumped around in my stomach more than I do the actual physical interaction of our lips (which I simply recall as being warm and wet). Thinking back on the event, I have to laugh at how it came about. I had undone my seat belt while we were parked, and when we were getting ready to leave, I couldn't rebuckle it. As I fumbled with the strap, Kevin leaned over to lend a helping hand, but instead ended up giving me much more than just a hand.

I was exhilarated by the thought that this tall, intelligent, incredibly gorgeous guy actually saw something good in me, something more than just my grades. He validated my sense of worth, and I began to think that perhaps I wasn't such a horrible person after all. Maybe there was something inside me other than the empty space that all the As in the world couldn't fill. Whereas my academic accomplishments gave me only a transient sense of self-satisfaction, the knowledge that Kevin liked me provided a warm feeling inside me that didn't fade away. For the first time in my life, I felt truly happy just to be alive.

In addition to the positive aspects of the relationship, there was, of course, a down side. I feared losing control of myself, a worry that was intensified by the fact that I was in completely new and unfamiliar territory. The incredible power of my feelings scared me immensely. In my family, I had learned the importance of always being rational and logical, of keeping my emotions in check and exhibiting self-discipline. Now here I was being "swept away," throwing all caution to the wind and acting purely on impulse and desire. The guilt I felt was extreme.

When I related the incident to my mother (the fear of telling my father loomed so large that I never talked about the relationship with him), I was thrown totally off guard by her reaction. I had pictured her throwing a fit and saying I shouldn't be getting involved with members of the opposite sex at my age. But just the opposite happened—she was glad I had met a "nice boy." Perhaps if he had lived in our town she might have reacted differently. Given how far apart we lived, dating was never feasible, so she didn't have to worry about my going out late at night doing God knows what.

Kevin and I had been writing and calling each other on a fairly regular basis, and I began to entertain the thought of asking him to the junior prom. Though absolutely terrified at the prospect of rejection, the encouragement of my friends and mother (who actually offered to have him spend the night at our house!) finally convinced me to take the risk via the mail. At the post office, my hands shook and my stomach quivered as I took a deep breath, opened the mailbox, and dropped the letter down the chute. As soon as the deed was done, though, I thought, God, what the hell have I done?! I'm setting myself up for the biggest fall of my life! How stupid could I be to think Kevin would want to go with ME?!

I awaited his reply with nervous anticipation, checking the mail every day as soon as I got home to see if it was there. When the letter finally arrived, I was so nervous I could barely open it. My stomach was literally doing flip-flops as I began scanning the note for signs of his reply. When I read about how he would love to be my date, how he thought we'd have a great time together, and how he looked forward to seeing me again, I was euphoric. I was practically bouncing off the walls, so full of exuberance and utter joy that I thought I'd burst with energy.

Within a week's time, I found an outfit (gown, shoes, clutch purse—the whole works), made dinner reservations and a hair appointment, and bought the tickets. Everything was in place when the big night finally arrived. After I finished getting ready, I decided to risk taking a look in the mirror. I was worried that I would find a brainy nerd who was trying hard to fit in where she didn't belong. The image that reflected back at me, though, caught me by surprise. With my hair pulled up and with flowers in it, my mother's pearl choker around my neck, the teal-colored gown flaring out around my waist, and the rosy glow of my cheeks (due more to my excitement, I think, than to the makeup I had applied), I was actually not half bad to look at. I felt as though I was looking at a stranger, for I knew the elegant young woman in the mirror couldn't possibly be me, the same person who always felt awkward and ugly. I truly felt like Cinderella, transformed if only for one night.

I was anxiety-ridden about seeing Kevin again—it would be the first time we had seen each other in some months. Everyone, both family and friends, loved him as soon as they met him. They all thought he was attractive, intelligent, and an all-around great guy. I floored everyone as I made my entry with him—not only had I myself been transformed, but here I was with a gorgeous date at my side. Finally my feelings of inferiority melted away. I had always been recognized as smart, but now on top of that, people saw me as attractive. The culminating event that evening was my election to the junior prom court. Normally a popularity contest, I never dreamed of standing among the four couples who flocked the king and queen. When my name was announced, I arose from my seat, mouth agape, as everyone around me applauded. Again I had stunned everyone, especially myself—smart people simply did not make the court. Proving them all wrong gave me a sense of uniqueness that I cherished. I reveled in my now complete blossoming from a former ugly duckling into a beautiful swan.

In spite of all its magic, the prom experience stirred up the same mixed bag of emotions I had felt when I first met Kevin, only to a much greater degree than before. At the dance, Kevin's open display of affection bothered me tremendously. I felt uncomfortable expressing my emotions in public, especially since I wasn't even sure exactly what I was feeling. I had no idea how to behave, and so I distanced myself from Kevin. If he moved his chair closer to where I was sitting, I moved in the opposite direction. If he tried to hold my hand, I would fold my arms across my chest. I wouldn't even let him kiss me in front of everyone. He was probably totally baffled by my behavior—I know I myself was, but I couldn't help it. Since I felt out of control and didn't know what to do, I turned to the only defense mechanism that I knew from previous experience had worked—isolation.

After the weekend of the prom, Kevin and I stopped writing and calling each other. To add to my confusion, my mother and friends expressed their disdain for my handling of the situation. They reminded me that I had had the chance at a relationship with a wonderful person and had blown it, big time. My mother, who had thought Kevin was one of the nicest, most polite, handsome young men she'd ever met, laid the worst guilt trip of all on me. She made it seem as though he had done me this enormous favor, for which I should feel some sense of undying gratitude and obligation. "Here this nice boy drove all the way over here just to escort you to your dance, and how do you treat him? Like dirt." As a result of others' reactions to my behavior, I became even more miserable and disgusted with myself. This relationship represented the first time in my life that I had tested the wings of independence and trusted my own feelings, and I had failed. The incident reinforced my belief that I was worthless and incapable of making decisions on my own.

I mentioned before that the prom was one of two important events that helped catalyze the emergence of my eating disorder. The second event, which occurred within a month after the prom, was my guidance counselor informing me that I was not ranked as first in my class. My very first reaction was that some terrible mistake had been made. There was absolutely no way I could be anything but number one. I was the only person I knew who had maintained a 4.0 GPA, with nothing less than As on all of my report cards. Becoming valedictorian had become my life; every aspect of my identity was in some way wrapped up in it.

When I expressed my disbelief to my guidance counselor, he assured me that no mistake had been made—I simply was not first. That's when the shock set in. I sat in his office thinking, "I have to get out of here NOW." The walls were closing in on me and I felt as though I was suffocating. I quickly mumbled something about having to get back to class and practically ran out of his office and into the nearest bathroom, where I let the intense pain that had been welling inside me burst forth. My heavy sobs shook my entire body, and I was hyperventilating so badly I could barely breathe. I leaned up against the wall and slid slowly to the ground, clutching my knees to my chest and pressing my hot face against the cool wall tiles. "How could this be happening to me?" I screamed in my head. Why? What had I done wrong? Hadn't I sacrificed everything for the sake of the almighty grade? Wasn't I the perfect student? How could I pretend everything was normal when inside I was falling completely apart? Afterward I fought desperately to keep up my false image of control and stability, stuffing my pain down further and further inside me in the hopes it would somehow magically disappear. Everyone expected me to be number one—what would they think when they found out I wasn't? If only they knew. . . . I felt duplicitous and deceitful, as though I was projecting a false image that was just waiting to be debunked. I was falling from my pedestal, and I knew the fall would be a long and hard one from which I might never recover.

The fall was even more profound than I could have ever anticipated. It devastated my life to such an extent that now, five years later, I am still trying to put back the pieces and recover. An eating disorder, however, was the last thing I expected. In my mind, I had imagined people losing respect for me, devaluing my abilities, and seeing me for the incapable fool I felt I was. That didn't happen. The only person to turn her back on me was me. I was truly my own worst enemy, endlessly berating and cursing myself for being so stupid. Gone was the radiant, smiling teenager from prom night, so full of life and exuberance. In her place was an ugly, sullen person who could barely drag herself out of bed in the morning because she saw no purpose to her life. The change was dramatic, but no one ever commented on it, perhaps because I was so good at putting on a happy face, and perhaps because they felt (or maybe hoped) I was just going through one of the low points that characterize the average adolescent's life. What others didn't realize was that this was not simply a phase that would pass in time—it was to become a deadly disease that would grab me by the throat and nearly choke the life out of me.

I don't really know when the anorexia actually hit me. Thinking back, it seems to have been more a progression than an event whose full impact hits all at once. Why I turned to food as a means of establishing control in my life, I honestly have no idea. I had never been concerned with my weight prior to this time. I was always thin, but ate whatever I wanted—in fact, I was the ultimate junk food addict. Chocolate, candy, cookies, chips—if it was bad for you, I loved it. These items were, of course, the first to go when I started my downward spiral, and as time went on, the list of "forbidden" foods grew while my food intake gradually but steadily diminished.

The earliest recollection I have of anorectic behavior involves its isolation more than the self-starvation. During the spring of my junior year, I began skipping lunch. My friends and I usually sat together during the lunch period, eating and chatting. Instead of going to the cafeteria with them, I started holing myself up in the library, where I could be alone with my pain, as I felt I deserved to be. My friends immediately noticed my absence and commented on it. I told them I was simply doing my own research into the different colleges that interested me. I wasn't completely starving myself at this time, but what I now know were the early signs of my eating disorder went unnoticed at the time.

It wasn't until that summer that the disease began to intensify. With the school year over, I no longer had to deal with my teachers and peers on a daily basis. Thus, it became easier to isolate and confine myself to my own internal world, a jail cell out of which there was no escape. I felt I was divided into two separate personalities—one jailer and one prisoner, simultaneously beating myself up while begging for mercy. I would lie on my bed, behind the safety of my locked bedroom door, crying endlessly. One part of me was saying, "I hate you—you're stupid and worthless," while another part was pleading, "Please don't hate me— I'll work harder to make you like me." It was a no-win situation, though. There was no pleasing the jailer, no matter how hard the prisoner inside me tried.

As the prison walls began closing in on me, I fought desperately to hang on. I got a job waitressing at a nearby restaurant, and tried to keep busy by working as much as I could. My work schedule made it easy to hide my eating patterns from others. Since Mom and Dad worked full-time, I was safe for most of the day. "I ate something before going to work and then had dinner on my break," I'd lie. If anyone at work asked about my eating habits, I'd say my mother was saving dinner for me when I got home. I was really clever about deceiving others, as most anorectics are, and delighted in the thought that I was able to pull the wool over everyone's eyes. No one would be able to figure me out, I vowed. By keeping to myself, I'd be safe and protected and could get back some of the security that I felt had been brutally snatched from me.

I started cutting back on my intake with the initial goal of becoming "healthier." I'll look and feel better if I get toned up and shed a few pounds, I told myself. After a period of restriction combined with exercise, I lost between five and ten pounds, and did in fact feel better about myself. The source of my improved self-image wasn't so much being thinner as being able to accomplish something with tangible results as reinforcement. I could step on the scale and watch the number drop from day to day, just as I could feel my clothes getting baggier around my waist. Here was something I could do successfully! Maybe I wasn't good enough to be first in school, but I certainly seemed able to lose weight, a task that presents enormous difficulty for many American women.

I read every article on health, nutrition, and weight loss I could find. I sought the diets that offered the quickest route to losing weight, pulling together bits and pieces from each to develop an elaborately detailed plan of my own. I learned what foods were "good" and what foods were "bad," and became a careful label reader, comparing caloric and fat content for a wide variety of foods. Going to the grocery store was a big production—I would spend ages in each aisle, trying to hunt out the products that would give me the most food for the fewest calories. Almost paradoxically, food became my obsession, the center of my world. Pouring myself into losing weight became a substitute for pouring myself into my schoolwork.

As with all other areas of my life, I gave 110 percent to the illness (when I commit to something, I do a thorough job). My insane drive for perfection, however, once again turned on me, in the same way it had done with my schoolwork. Losing that first bit of weight left me feeling good about myself for a little while, but then I began to question the greatness of my accomplishment. After all, I told myself, five pounds really wasn't that much—anyone could lose that amount of weight in no time with minimal effort. Now, if I could lose ten pounds, *that* would be something—shedding that much weight requires more commitment and dedication. If I could do that, I'd really feel capable of doing something important. Thus, longing desperately for that feeling of self-worth, I readjusted my target and continued in pursuit of my new goal.

Of course, once I reached this new weight, the same thing happened, and a vicious cycle developed. No sooner would I finish patting myself on the back than a little voice in the back of my head would squelch my pride, saying okay, maybe you achieved that goal, but I bet you can't meet this one. . . . I found myself getting caught in a cycle of self-destruction. Even though I craved success, I would go out of my way to ensure it eluded my grasp. As soon as I reached one goal, I'd set a new, higher standard. I was doing to myself the very thing I hated my parents for doing to me. Whereas I could detach myself from my parents, however, I couldn't escape myself. I internalized the frustration of not knowing how to please them, to the point that I was unable to recognize and meet my own needs and desires. Because I didn't even know how to satisfy myself, I was forced as a consequence to look to outside indicators of my value. My life became dominated by the numbers of the scale, which governed all of my feelings and emotions. If the number fell, I was secure and happy (for at least a little while). If it moved in the opposite direction or not at all, I panicked and tried frantically to think of a way to regain control of my body. I based my every mood on my weight, not realizing that in doing so I was setting myself up for failure—though I didn't realize it at the time, self-worth comes from within, and can't be found outside oneself.

As I continued my quest for a "wholeness," an identity I thought thinness would provide, I failed to recognize the self-destructive path I was following. My body became more emaciated, but all I saw in the mirror was excess flab that I had to be rid of. I rejoiced when the skirt of my waitressing uniform became so big I had to use safety pins to keep it up. One day while going through my clothes (which were becoming baggier with each passing day), my eye caught a glimpse of my prom gown, sheathed in plastic and hanging at the very back of the closet. I decided to try the dress on, just to see how it fit. As I removed it from the plastic, I thought about how far away the dance seemed—almost like another era, even though in actuality only a few months had passed. I pulled the dress on and zipped it up, only to have it fall past my bare and bony hips to the ground. Gone was the elegant gown that had transformed me into Cinderella. All that remained now was a mass of teal-colored satin lying in a pile around my feet. Though somewhat wistful over my inability to recapture the magical quality of prom night, I comforted myself with the thought that at least I wasn't fat like I had been then. Thinness was the one measure I could grasp hold of to convince myself I was better now than I had ever been.

I deluded myself into believing I really was doing fine. Though I experienced all the telltale symptoms of the eating disorder—constantly feeling cold (especially my hands and feet), hair falling out, problematic bowel movements, insomnia, amenorrhea, dizzy spells, skin discoloration, and the gnawing hunger that penetrated to the bottom of my stomach—I brushed them off in denial. I can recall only one instance that summer when I was forced to face the gravity of my illness. I remember getting out of bed and heading for the bathroom to take a shower. As I reached my bedroom door, I got a swift, overpowering head rush that nearly bowled me over. The room started spinning and I had to clutch the door frame just to keep from collapsing. My heart started palpitating and I felt as though my chest was going to explode. For the first time in my life, I truly thought I was facing death. I leaned against the door frame and let my body go limp as I slid to the ground. Stabbing pains pierced my heart so sharply that they blinded me. Oh my God, I thought, what have I done to myself? I prayed to God to please let me live. I'll eat, I promise I'll eat. . . . I won't try to lose any more weight. . . . I'll go back to eating normally. . . . Just please make the pain stop and don't let me die!

Being faced with the all-too-real prospect of death shook me up enough that I did fix myself something to eat. The frightening impact of the incident faded rapidly, however, and within a few days I was once again back to restricting. I passed off this danger signal, reassuring myself that since I survived the episode, I must be fine. When I tightened my grip over the food, I was in control—I was invincible, and no one could touch me. The eating disorder gave me an incredible feeling of power and superiority, a sense of independence. I could prove that I had control, that I could accomplish something on my own.

You may wonder where my family was in all of this mess. Didn't they see me slowly wasting away into nothing? I vaguely recall them nagging me from time to time to eat. I don't feel any resentment toward them for "letting" me become anorexic, for not catching me before I got as bad as I did. They were, I'm sure, in as much denial as I was. Acknowledging my disease would (and eventually did) open a Pandora's box full of problems, ones that went far beyond my not eating to include the entire family. My mother did get worried enough toward the end of the summer to call my pediatrician. When she explained my situation, his advice was to get me to take vitamins (just the solution to an anorectic's problems!). His failure to recognize the severity of my illness made it easier, I think, for my parents to gloss over the situation. Having a doctor's reassurance probably put their minds at ease. The family problems could stay safely locked away, at least for the time being.

I somehow managed to make it through that summer, and the beginning of my senior year in high school soon arrived. My mother tried to warn me of the reactions people at school would have to my emaciated appearance, but I could see no difference in how I looked now as opposed to how I looked at the end of junior year, when I was at least twenty pounds heavier. She was right on target in her assessment of the situation. I'll never forget the looks I received from my classmates and teachers that first day of school. Their eyes bulged and their mouths dropped in horror as they stared at the withered, drawn figure before them. Three months earlier, I had been a healthy teenager and now all that remained was a skeleton covered with skin. I was incredibly self-conscious walking through the halls, certain all eyes were on me and that the topic on everyone's mind was my dramatic weight loss. Feeling like a queer anomaly, I tried desperately to cover my twiglike arms and hide my body under baggy clothes. My answer to the stunned looks was that I had been sick and was run-down as a result. Though I found it perfectly plausible, my explanation was met with skepticism. No one pushed the issue, though, probably due to my unwillingness to discuss the subject, evident by my curt responses to their questions.

Within the next few days, the nurse called me down to her office. Apparently, nearly all of my teachers had voiced their concerns regarding my health. I offered the same excuse to her as I had to everyone else—yes, I had lost some weight, but would be fine once I had a chance to recoup from being sick. She was skeptical at my insistence that everything was okay, but I promised to work hard to get back my health. I was, of course, lying through my teeth. I had absolutely no intention whatsoever of returning to what I considered my grossly fat previous weight. Did people think I was going to abandon my quest for thinness just like that, simply because that's what they wanted me to do? No way was I going to let all the hard work I had poured into this project over the past three months go to pot! I was annoyed with others meddling in my life. Rather than seeing their concern for its genuineness, I was convinced they were trying to undermine me. They just wanted to see me fail at something else so they could laugh in my face. Well, I wouldn't let that happen! I'd show them that I could achieve! They would marvel at how well I could shed those pounds and admire me at least for that, if nothing else. I thought that perhaps by being successful at losing weight, I could somehow make up for my intellectual flaw of not being valedictorian. I was knocking myself out to impress others for no reason, though. The only one who cared that I wasn't first was me, but ironically, that was the one person I was unable to satisfy no matter how hard I tried.

I remember one key experience that clued me in to the severity of my problem. While going through candid photographs for the yearbook, I discovered two of myself. I picked them up to examine more closely and gasped in horror as I looked at the ghastly image captured on film. Her face was as white as a sheet, her eyes sunken, and her cheeks severely drawn. The blue veins bulged out of her sticklike arms, and her clothes hung limply on her fragile frame. She looked morbidly depressed, a pathetic creature who seemed ready to snap at any moment. Surely that person couldn't be me! Tears started welling in my eyes as I looked at that picture. What had happened to the smiling, vivacious teenager of the previous spring? She was like a rose that had bloomed and then withered away. I bawled uncontrollably as I realized I was falling apart. The life was being slowly sucked from me, and I was growing increasingly weak and helpless. Please God, help me get my life back together, I prayed. I don't want to die!

You may think that, having recognized myself as having this disorder, I would be well on my way to recovery. I know that's how I felt—now that I really *wanted* to get better, to get back to a normal life, I would. I tried to convince myself and everyone else that I could tackle and overcome this problem on my own. The solution was simple, I thought—all I have to do is eat and gain back the weight I had lost, and I would be fine. Unfortunately, it wasn't quite that easy. Anorexia nervosa had come to symbolize seventeen years of emotional instability, psychological turmoil, shattered dreams, and bits and pieces of my fragmented identity. There was a lot more that needed fixing than simply my diet—all of the issues that permeated my entire life needed to be confronted and dealt with before recovery would be possible. It took everyone—my family, friends, teachers, and even myself—a long time to realize this and to recognize the full, devastating extent of the disease.

Though I really did want to get better, I was unable to regain the weight my body required. Having gone beyond the point of no return, so to speak, I continued to lose poundage. The nurse finally suggested my mother take me to a specialist, someone who might offer the assistance I needed to get better. I became absolutely irate at the very mention of the subject. "I am NOT crazy, and have no intention whatsoever of seeing a shrink!" I hollered at my mother. But she was adamant. The psychologist I went to see was unable to help me, though. My disease had progressed much too far by the time she intervened. About a month later, she told my parents there was nothing more she could do for me, and recommended I be evaluated for admission into the Eating Disorders Service at a nearby children's hospital. Though I strenuously resisted the idea of hospitalization, my mother calmly but forcefully put her foot down: "We can commit you without your having any say in the matter." My parents were finally taking charge.

In terms of my treatment in the hospital, Mom and Dad focused more on the outer me—my body and its weight—than the evolution of my inner self. Whenever I spoke with them on the phone or whenever they visited, the very first question was always, "How's the weight doing?" My recovery became framed in terms of numbers, the very thing I was trying so hard to get away from. I had based my entire identity on tangible indicators of my worth—grades, class rank, weight—at the expense of my true inner being. As a result, I never established a self-directed identity. My work in therapy to evoke an awareness and understanding of the impulses, needs, and feelings that arose within myself was incredibly difficult and emotionally draining.

Before my admission, I had been closer to my mother. She was always the more reliable one. If I had a problem or needed something, I always went to her first. My father, on the other hand, was a lazy bum. I couldn't count on him for anything except for material objects. When I was in the hospital, this changed dramatically. Mom was like an ice woman. All the other parents felt guilty, thinking they were in some way responsible for their child's eating disorder. Not my mother. She staunchly and promptly informed me that she was not going to take the blame for my problem. At the time, I saw her as cold and heartless. I *wanted* her to feel sorry for everything she had ever said or done that caused me to be the way I was. She *deserved* to feel guilty for creating the sham of a family life I had to endure. My father, on the other hand, was easier to deal with when I was heavily dependent on him, as I was when in the hospital. I think he needed to feel needed by me, to feel in control of my life. He called me every night, just to find out how my day had gone. On his frequent visits, he would always bring fresh flowers, and we would sit and talk, watch TV, or take a walk. I remember on one occasion, we even made the bed together. It was times like these when I felt closest to him. I wanted to be taken care of, and he seemed willing to do the job. The combination of my not wanting to grow up and his wanting me to stay daddy's little girl helped to sustain this dependence. Though at the time I saw his behavior as a form of care and affection, I now recognize it for the power game it was.

Paradoxically, our weekly family therapy sessions failed to reflect these newly developed interactions. During that one hour, the family roles reverted to their usual prehospital form. At first, I actually looked forward to family therapy, thinking it would expose some of the important and volatile issues that had always been buried underground. Finally, we would be able to resolve our problems and, I hoped, become a loving, cohesive unit, the perfect family I longed to be a part of. Unfortunately, this miracle transformation didn't occur. Our problems ran much too deep for even a therapist to tackle. The sessions became as much of a sham as our family itself was. Every week it was the same thing. Everyone, with the exception of myself, shied away from the real issues, the potent problems we faced as a group of four individuals collectively termed a "family." My parents always wanted to discuss specific aspects of the Eating Disorders program, details that were "safe" for them—for example, "Why isn't she eating any red meat?" or "When is she going to get back to eating normal foods?" Getting them to recognize that food was not the main issue, that the eating disorder cut far deeper, to the very core of my identity (or lack thereof), was the most difficult task I faced. I would try to bring up a particular aspect of our home life—for example, my parents' marriage or my brother's attempt to shut himself off from the rest of the world. Before I could even finish my account, though, my father interjected, shaking his head and protesting, "She's making too much of this and blowing things way out of proportion."

The dismissal of my emotions as trivial wasn't nearly as bad as what came next. "Our family life may not have been wonderful," Dad admitted, "but it was relatively normal until she began this whole mess and disrupted all of our lives. She's the one with the problem, not us." I sat dumbfounded, not believing my ears. How could he possibly lay the entire blame on me? Did he honestly believe I had planned on becoming anorectic, that I set out on some mission to destroy our family? I refused to just sit back and let him heap any more blame on me. I had meekly taken all the denouncing for so long that I had internalized and turned it back on myself, resulting in incredible feelings of guilt and self-doubt. I couldn't stand the torture any longer. "You're wrong if you think I'm the cause of everyone's problems," I told my father point-blank. "We had problems long before I got sick." To my surprise, my mother then spoke on my behalf, saying to him, "You can't blame her for everything. We're part of the problem, too." Finally, someone was taking my side! I looked over to my mother with gratitude in my eyes, silently thanking her for saving me from drowning in a sea of guilt and self-worthlessness. At least she was beginning to recognize my problem encompassed much more than a simple decision to stop eating. Throughout this entire scene, my brother remained isolated and detached from the rest of us. When confronted, he would usually just shrug his shoulders. He had a grand total of two standard responses to the therapist's questions—"I don't know" or "I try not to think about it."

After six weeks in the Eating Disorders Service, I returned to the real world—back to my home and family and to my teachers and friends at school. Everything was pretty much the same, though. My parents still fought and my brother still shut himself off in his room. I was still obsessed with food. Though I had gained weight and was now eating more, I still kept a meticulous log of every (measured) bit of food that entered my mouth. I refused to touch red meat, junk food, or any kind of fat whatsoever.

Eventually, I had to resign myself to the fact that I alone cannot repair the immense damage that exists within our family. Without the cooperation of others, my endeavor is doomed to failure. I have relinquished my role as the family savior, realizing I am unable to control the behavior of my parents and my brother. I can, however, change my own actions and reactions within the family structure. An important, and difficult, part of the recovery process has been extricating myself from the dynamics of the family in order to develop and accept my own independent sense of self.

I can't believe I'm almost through with my college career. So many things have changed since I was a clueless, teary-eyed freshman. Now I'm half through my senior year. Within the past year alone I have undergone a complete metamorphosis, beginning with my revealing my anorexia to the world. I had wondered for so long whether I would ever be able to overcome this wretched disorder, and finally, I have reached the point where I can eat when I'm hungry and stop when I'm full. My recovery has been due in large part to the drug Prozac, which has also made me less obsessive and less high-strung. My recovery, however, has had its ups and downs. This past summer I fell into a deep depression. I felt like my life was spiraling out of my control, that everything I had worked so hard for was falling apart. I spent most of my days crying and mulling over things. I didn't even want to go back to school in September to finish my senior year, but everyone convinced me to do so. I got treated for the depression, and finally decided to take medication for it. I had adamantly refused to do so in the past, though an antidepressant was recommended by two of my previous psychiatrists. When I think back to how bad I was this past summer, I'm so thankful that I got help in time and was able to turn things around before they got completely out of control. I'm finally starting to feel good about myself, comfortable with who I am, and actually happy!

A big part of the change in me is due to LOVE. Yes, I finally met someone who was as attracted to me as I was to him. He has stood by me through some of the worst times of my life, through fighting the eating disorder as well as depression. I started seeing him nearly a year ago. Things were rough at first, mainly because of my inexperience and the issues I was having to deal with about myself. I was freaked out about sex and mostly about opening myself up to someone. I had been so egocentric for so long that it's been hard to give some of that self-centeredness up. I also had my first sexual encounter with him. That was another issue I had a hard time dealing with at first, but now, after having lived with him for the summer, it seems pretty silly.

I thought for sure that we would spend the rest of our lives together, deliriously happy and in love. But this past summer really put our relationship through the wringer. We've been fighting a lot, but more than that, I think we've been starting to pull back from each other. We pretty much both know that June will bring with it not only graduation but the end of our relationship. It's been really hard for me to accept that what I thought was an infallible, perfect romance is actually not immune to problems. I really wish things had worked out the way we planned them, but I guess I should have learned by now that life doesn't always follow the plans you make for it.

So, you might ask, what happens next? Well, I have moved ahead, and after four long years, I have finally beaten this disease. I feel as though an enormous weight has been lifted off my shoulders (no pun intended), and that I am finally ready to move ahead with the rest of my life—to "live, laugh, and love," as they say. I'm optimistic about the future, for if there's one thing I've learned, it's that I'm a fighter. . . . And, more importantly, I'm a survivor.

THEY SAID I WAS BEAUTIFUL

Sienna's parents instill in her, at an early age, a clear understanding of the beauty, the strength, and the struggles of the black community. She takes this understanding with her into her interactions with her peers, her experiences in a predominantly black middle school, and her entry into a more diverse magnet high school. When she reaches college, she needs to draw on the strengths she has developed to hold onto a clear sense of her own gifts in a community that is so different and so challenging.

I took a class my freshman year of college that focused on race and ethnicity. In it, we did an exercise where we listed, in one minute, words that tell who we are. The sentence read, "I am . . ." and we filled in the blank with things like "tall," "a musician," or "an activist." According to my professor, the elements you choose and how you prioritize the elements follows a pattern for women and for people of color. Women across the board tend to place near the top of the list the fact that they are women, while people of color tend to place their race or ethnicity at the very top of the list. I followed the pattern for students of color very closely, placing the word "black" at the very top of my list. Of course, I had other crucial aspects of my identity on the list—things that informed my life in fundamental ways such as "Christian" and "musician." Still, I realize now how significant it is that I strongly identify as a black person, if for no other reason than the fact that it is both a natural and informed state in which I began to operate at a young age. This was not a major development that came about through a series of college experiences. It was not something that I had to "figure out." I would say that, throughout my life, my race has been an undeniable fact that I learned to negotiate within different contexts outside of my home. My parents equipped me with an awareness of my identity that prepared me to enter a world that had already determined for me who I am.

The atmosphere in my home growing up was perfect for producing individuals with an appreciation for this thing called blackness. My parents never presented blackness as an achievable state of being, but instead helped me understand it as a daily reality. It was a constant variable that I had to acknowledge, and one with which I must learn to be content, even if only because the world I faced outside my home makes being black an issue. The experiences I have had in my school environments alone—from elementary school through college—remind me how true their predictions were. It makes sense, then, that my parents explicitly cultivated my identity at home for reasons that even today are complex and intricately woven into the history of being black in America. When the time came, I left my home and entered my schooling with this foundation.

THE EQUIPMENT

I derive the strength of my black identity from the life histories of my parents, two members of the baby boomer generation who have peculiar and crucial perspectives on being black in the United States. Both my mother and father were raised in southern Louisiana among grandparents and great uncles and aunts who remembered being slaves. Their childhoods were spent in a culture of de jure segregation. My father served in the Navy and saw American politics at work in other nations, while my mother was in the midst of the fight for black civil and human rights on the home front. Both are now familiar with United States society post segregation, in which they have educated and observed two generations of black youth who have slowly, but surely, been disconnected from the ideas, priorities, and goals of the community of black people living in America in a history that is painfully recent.

While I count myself among the youth in these later generations, my orientation is heavily informed by my parents' experiences. There were times when their lessons were explicit and illuminated the nuances of an event that was occurring in my lifetime. Many times, however, it was the random narratives of earlier years, sparked by a picture, a news story, a call from "home" (Louisiana), or a question I had. They were not even talking to me half of the time—I was known for listening in on "grown folks'" conversations. I listened to their words intently, but I also studied their expressions and noticed the unfinished sentences punctuated by sighs and headshakes and distant gazes.

From my mother, I heard narratives highlighting black culture, The Movement, and her admonishing to be wary of white people. The subject of integration first came up when I was about 8 years old. I was watching *The Ernest Green Story*, a Disney Channel movie chronicling the experience of the Little Rock Nine who integrated Central High School in Little Rock, Arkansas. Ernest Green entered as an upperclassman and was the first of the nine to graduate. I doubt if I paid attention when the words, "based on a true story" appeared on the screen, so I believe my initial assumption was that the story was fiction. When the movie got to the height of the emotional and psychological violence exerted upon the nine black students, my mother began to sigh and provide commentary for what was happening on screen. She said something like, "Yeah, that's just how they did us too." I realized her voice came from more than textbook knowledge of the civil rights era that I began learning in my elementary school. She told me about how my grandfather essentially forced her and one of her sisters to integrate the all-white school located in the middle of the town in which they grew up. She told me how there were only four of them that committed to go and continued on—everyone else who agreed to go into the high school got scared and dropped out. She remembers walking to the front entrance of the school while the white students parted the way like water, and seeing, from her peripheral vision, the white students silently staring at them until they got up the steps. On the first day of school, they met with the principal, who told them, "You are going to have to do this. You have to go to classes by yourselves." My mother and the other black students were not necessarily afraid of physical danger. What weighed more heavily were the subtle, daily tactics employed by white students. Everywhere my mother and her friends went, there was exaggerated space between them and the white students, emphasizing white students' repulsion at the thought of touching black people. The unexpected attacks were what frustrated my mother the most. Because the students used cubbies instead of lockers, everyone had access to the blacks students' books and would write "nigger" on random pages. It was one thing to brace yourself to hear "nigger" whispered in the hallway, and quite another to turn a page to read in class and see "nigger" written boldly in the book.

Much of what I gathered from my father had to do with the nuances of the political system, the consequences of integration, and the perspective of a black male. His stories of living in Louisiana during segregation and his experiences of the all-black school he attended remain with me, but he mostly tried to demonstrate his strength and pride in daily interactions with people. So when the police pulled us over or when a fleet of cars from the sheriff's office raced down our street and began barking orders, he spoke. He asked questions. He asserted himself as a resident with the right to know what was going on in his neighborhood. Every time we received bad service (and it has been often), my father has spoken to a manager, called company headquarters, or written a letter. The thing I now realize is that he never did it secretly or masked his anger or frustration. He spoke about it openly and made phone calls and inquiries in front of me and my sister. His example let me know that I had the right to my intuition and could at the very least ask questions to help understand the situation better. And when it was necessary, I could take action.

The way my father chose to convey his concepts of beauty were really important to the way in which I saw myself and the people around me. He always stressed that appearance did not make people "pretty" or "ugly"; it was how individuals acted and treated other people that determined their beauty. Still, it made a difference that my sister and I were always "pretty girls" and my mother was always beautiful to him. This is also significant because there is a common expectation that black men are supposed to be more attracted to lighter skinned women with more European features. My father, instead, demonstrated an appreciation for the spectrum of color found among black people and valued the features that are devalued and hold negative characterizations in mainstream culture. This was especially important when it came to my sister and me. People always made distinctions between my sister and me because of our different skin tones. The variation was significant, but not necessarily uncommon among black people. Still, my mother tells me stories about how strangers would come up to her when I was a baby and say, "Is that your child?" When she would confirm that she gave birth to me, some would reply, "Oh. She must look like her daddy," implying that my color had to have come from someone besides this chocolate brown woman. Her flippant response to this was, "No, she looks like her uncle," referring to my father's brother, who is one of his more fair-skinned siblings. She knew what strange relationship this implied she had with my uncle, but she obviously did not care. My sister also had some confusion with my color when we were young. She remembers climbing up the side of my crib, looking down at me and asking, "Is it fun to be white?" She swears I nodded in the affirmative. She would go around to family members and tell them I was white. My mother would get really mad and say to my sister, "Look at me! She is NOT white!" My mother actually tried to sit me in the sun as a baby to give me more color, but I would just break out in hives because my skin was sensitive.

No one in my family criticized my skin tone, but as others made it an issue, in the more positive sense, my parents' efforts grew to make sure I knew that it really was not a big deal. I became aware of both the priority that people placed on having light skin, and the negative implications for people with darker complexions, which happened to be everyone in my household. Therefore, I become agitated when I encounter people who are, as we say, "color-struck." So in the fourth grade when my friend Pam kept questioning me about whether she had gotten darker as we walked in the sun on a field trip in Palm Springs, I replied in frustration, rolling my eyes and knowing the implications of her question, "Why do you care?! Either way you are still black!" (One of the teachers walking near us simply said, "Amen.") Another of my responses to this issue growing up has been to stay in the sun because I wanted to prove to nonbelievers that it was okay to get darker.

My parents consistently immersed me in black culture and surrounded me with black people. This meant choosing to remain in our neighborhood in South Los Angeles, participating heavily in my black church, and especially sending me to neighborhood schools. This foundation shaped my identity even as I branched out in the many different contexts to which my experiences in school led me.

THE APPLICATION

I have been in school for a long time. It has taken up a big chunk of my life. With all the social drama that goes on within school walls, many recognize school to be the place where a significant part of one's character is constructed—the place where you "find yourself" (I hear this a lot in relation to college students). From helping you to develop life goals (career day) and lifelong friends (cliques), to nurturing strengths and helping you learn to hide weaknesses (college applications), school plays a big role. Given all that I picked up from home and the ways in which my family's words and actions supplemented my social education, my experience in school has been more about negotiating my previously constructed identity than it has been about finding out who I am.

That is not to say that at every moment I was completely sure of myself or that I was isolated from the wonderful world of puberty and adolescence. I vividly remember being talked about if my mother combed my hair a certain way or if my hair was not straight. My full lips were always the choice physical feature to make fun of. The most public display of ridicule came during my sixth grade graduation ceremony. We were a class of maybe seventy students who all knew each other well. So as our teachers called our names to hand us our certificates, the rest of the class would do cat calls, which included nicknames, a chanting of the person's last name, or anything else they were known by. While some people punctuated my last name, others yelled, "Big lips!" I was so embarrassed, but I had to keep moving for the sake of the ceremony and for my own sake. Not even a year later in the first middle school I attended (with many of the same classmates from elementary school), there was one kid that kept calling me Bubba Gump, after the character in the movie *Forrest Gump*. By that time, I was really good at either ignoring those comments or staring hard and rolling my eyes. Eventually, the kid tried to engage me in a regular conversation and, again, I just stared at him. I don't know. Maybe he liked me.

Conflict on this social level meant that I had to learn how to fight and, at the very least, forced me to develop a quick tongue and learn to play "The Dozens," that game of insults that includes, but is not limited to, jokes about "Yo' mama." I was in an ongoing battle with a good friend of mine at the time over those types of insults. We had a crowd around us every day at lunchtime watching us go back and forth with insults and threats. We did not actually physically fight until about a week and a half after our conflict started, but I was always ready to defend myself because all the insults coming my way hurt. Even through that pain, though, I had the background commentary from my family who said I was beautiful—from my nappy hair and my full lips on down to my chicken legs and big feet. That helps me even today when I feel less than adequate, so I know that my family's words were important.

My elementary and middle school years were not difficult for me. Up until the eighth grade, I went to school in Inglewood, California (read: inner city) where the majority of my peers were black and Latino. I remember there being one Asian girl and maybe two white students who I, for the longest time, just thought were light-skinned black people. I can name and visualize the four white teachers I had throughout my elementary and middle school years. Two of the four were not even my permanent teachers; I was removed from one of the white teacher's classes because of overcrowding, and I went to the other one to get advanced work during part of my class time. Every other teacher and administrator was black. Everyday I saw people who looked like me in positions of authority, who not only handed down directions and rules, but who also talked to me in a language I understood and appreciated, whether it be a dialect, a particular saying that was known throughout the community, or just body language (like the look I got when I knew I was doing something wrong that made my body freeze, my heart sink, and all my insides shrivel up).

I did not realize it at the time, but I experienced a caring environment and the handing down of culture in my elementary and middle-school settings. My teachers were not afraid to take students aside for chastisement, nor was there any hesitation to hug students or get involved in their family lives. Teachers and counselors spoke to us as professionals and as members of the community who cared about what happened to us once we left school grounds. In addition to hearing my black teachers commentaries about our successes and failures, I took part in events that both marked my childhood and enriched my cultural understanding and the identity that my family continually reinforced. For example, we celebrated Mardi Gras at my elementary school. It was normal for many of us because so many families in my neighborhood were from the South, especially southern Louisiana (like my family). We had a whole day of games, a parade of floats that each class built (so creative!), and a rhythm band that marched to New Orleans jazz music (I played the sticks. They would not let me in the tambourine line).

Our games were hand games and double dutch. The rhymes we made up are hilarious to me now, but I am fascinated by the fact that even when teaching in a different inner-city community as a part of a community service project, I hear the same rhymes we sang, modified versions of these rhymes, or brand new rhymes that the younger generation has created (which I intend to learn). I am thankful that young people today are still jumping double dutch with phone cords and clothes lines just like I did. I do not know if I always considered these activities culturally black, but I know I associate these times and experiences with black people. Personally, I am shocked when I meet black people today who never had experience jumping double dutch; there were always those who could not jump, but they could at least turn the rope. I also get upset when I meet black folk who are surprised that I do know how to jump double dutch.

I know I was sensitive to the things we chose to make fun of with our classmates, what was generally thought of as "good" and "bad," and what was valued as authentically black. My home training made me a second-grader who defended the outcast. It was not the typical gravitate-to-the-underdog situation, because I understood the reasons why they were outcasts. I knew kids were targeted if their hair was short (for girls), if their skin was dark, or if they did not wear the right clothes. I could not connect with those priorities because I had a mother who, every time someone commented on how "good" her hair was and how they liked it long, would immediately go to the hair dresser to get it all cut off, her expressed purpose being to show that, "It's just hair. It will grow back." This is the same mother who made her clothes growing up and refused to buy things she could throw on a sewing machine and make in an hour. So we shopped for quality and discounts and, I must say, I looked cute in all the family albums. Even at that age, I wanted there to be a positive association with all that it meant to be black, hoping that this shared identity would be something to be proud of and not something up for ridicule.

My high-school environment forced me to negotiate my identity in ways I had never experienced before. I attended a magnet high school for science and math in Southern California. In my college education classes we talk all the time about the need for diversity in school. Well, I can honestly say that my high-school environment was the closest thing to diversity that I have ever experienced, even to this day. My school was centrally located on one of the state university campuses and drew students from eleven school districts within a five-mile radius. Students originating from Inglewood, Compton, and South Los Angeles to Torrance, San Pedro, and Rancho Palos Verdes ensured interaction across race, class, viewpoints, and experiences. Racial and ethnic diversity was an expected feature, given that the goal of the high school was to promote underrepresented minorities in math and science fields.

I had no idea how to operate in this environment when I started high school. This community looked nothing like what I was used to in my neighborhood. I came from elementary and middle schools where my experiences were shared with hundreds of black and Latino students. My elementary and middle schools were on a gated and policed urban site where there was violence in and around the school and where seeing a student run across the grassy field and hop the fence to ditch class or run from security was reminiscent of a prison break. I walked home every day and knew my surroundings, including the drug dealers to whom I said "hey" on my way home. I learned a great deal in those environments, in part because I was also insulated by my family. I was confident that I could relate to almost everyone in my schools because we lived in the same neighborhood and had black teachers who supplemented our lessons with admonitions that indicated a "knowing" of what we faced in the world as young black and brown people from the inner city.

In contrast to my elementary and middle school environments, my high school was in the back corner of a college campus in bungalows that we shared with regular college students. No gates. No security focused on us. We did not get a permanent building to call our own until my senior year. But limited facilities meant a limited number of students, which meant my class was made up of 160 students. That number shrank as time went on because students were only admitted in the nineth grade. So every time someone made the decision to go back to their home school, it was like a painful runaway story—we would hear of sightings of this person, but there was no telling when we would see them again. Our size forced us to know each other and to create a community.

For the first time, I went to and from school on a yellow school bus. I traveled on three major freeways to get to school, which meant I never walked home again. There were times when I was stranded at school, either because of a breakdown with the bus or in communication with my parents. By the time I reached tenth grade, many of my classmates had cars and those open spaces enjoyed by college students were even more accessible to us—ditching class was now more high-tech than hopping fences.

My high school introduced me to students who came from multiethnic schools where the dominant cultural representation was white. Still, I found myself in a space among people of different ethnicities where white was the minority. I never lost the consciousness of being black and what that meant even in this context, but I was faced less with a black-white dichotomy than I was with orienting myself in relation to other minorities who also carried a specifically imposed racial identity. At the same time, we were all encouraged to appreciate the diverse cultures around us. I was open to these new experiences mostly because teachers, administrators, and our own test scores told us how great we were. My high-school principal was an especially skilled motivator. Because her main purpose was to promote the school and raise funds and support for our facilities, we constantly had visitors come and "observe" us in our "natural setting." She always made it a point to announce to us how impressed our visitors were with us. In my elementary and middle school, not many people (except for a few faculty members close to students), talked about the schools and students in terms of achievement. To hear the expectation of excellence from the beginning was a big change. Many of my classmates who also felt that pressure to do well met the challenge, and we raised our personal expectations for our success in the process.

My high school introduced me to the word *multicultural* and made it mainstream. Every year there was a big school-wide event called the "Multicultural Fair." This was a chance for all of the cultural groups and campus organizations to set up booths in the dirt lot adjacent to our bungalows and sell food and jewelry, run games, and paint faces. There were performances on stage from groups doing cultural dances, singing, or reading different works. My peers exposed me to such a rich display of culture both on and off school grounds. It was in high school that I saw my Filipino classmates perform the Tinikling dance, where dancers hop between two bamboo poles in time to music. I also got to visit a booth where my Indian classmate put a design on my arm using henna. Outside of school, I went to Mexican, Puerto Rican, and Cuban Quinceaneras, and to a traditional Filipino Debut.

There were times when I realized how strange my high-school friends and I looked to others when we went out together. We were a rainbow when we walked through the mall or had a tennis match at our opponent's tennis club in Malibu. Other groups we saw had a more monolithic racial and gender composition. We were all over the place. The best experience that we all had together was participating in the Youth & Government program run by the YMCA. The program simulates a state government and culminates with a big conference in Sacramento where we represent positions such as senator or lobbyist. We even held elections for governor for the year. My first exposure to the training and general workings of the program happened at the two smaller camps that were held before the big conference. We got off the bus, I looked up, and there was a sea of white people. The only other YMCAs that had any color in them were the ones from Compton and the one near my home in South Los Angeles (the YMCA I represented was near my school and it was easier for my friends and me to get there after school). Sure we stood out for our diversity, but we also had tons of energy and we truly liked each other. No infighting, but a lot of joking and fun mixed even as we took our roles and our purposes seriously. At the conference in Sacramento, my friend Vicki went on the hotel's closed-circuit television in a too-small costume from the movie *Monsters, Inc.* Antonio decided to save money for the weekend by bringing economy packs of noodles to his hotel room and went on a manhunt when we hid them from him. Dan and Mark made it a point to be obnoxious during meetings for senate bills that they did not like and kept a tally of when they successfully talked the bill down. These are the people I go home to even today and none of them are alike.

I learned and was able to appreciate so much about my peers, but I was still sometimes frustrated by what I am now able to express as our wasted potential. Given the inclusive atmosphere, I expected that, along with the knowledge of their cultural wealth, my classmates would be more aware of their positions in society, realizing that the world did not look like our high school. As much as we talked about and were introduced to diversity, none of our classes really gave us an opportunity to talk explicitly about important issues surrounding multiculturalism. There were occasional days in economics or history class that we would set aside for discussion of critical issues. There were also after-school "open forum" sessions addressing topics that had to do with current events in the country or in the school itself. The most explosive conversation that made it into class discussion focused on affirmative action and occurred during our senior year, right around the time when everyone began receiving their college acceptance letters. It amazed me how four years of close-knit associations could disintegrate over college admission results. As letters of acceptance and rejection came pouring in, cries of "So-and-so took my spot" and "So-and-so didn't deserve to get in" made my stomach turn. Tears were shed. Bragging began. And among all of these students of color, you still heard the words, "You only got in because you're black/Mexican/Filipino." I knew then that there was something missing. There was a historical foundation that many of my classmates either ignored or did not understand.

I had this conversation many times with my good friend Alan, who began his educational experiences in the inner-city schools in Compton and who also had greater expectations of his peers' social and political understanding of the world. Alan and I together were a force to be reckoned with. The one year we had all of our core classes together (we traveled in cohorts each year) we would not let one questionable comment go unexamined. We shared similar worldviews and past experiences. His presence helped me, first, to know that I was not crazy and, second, to know that when I opened my mouth to speak in English or history class, he would add his voice to mine and help me make clarifications if ever I got stuck in my expressions. Especially in the discussion about affirmative action he was able to share his own experiences of discrimination. He described how the state of the schools in Compton demonstrated how racism and inequality still hinder people of color; even though many people think racism is not a serious issue, we are farther away from an equal society than we would like to believe. Our classmates began to expect to hear from us, and Alan and I offered our voices freely. I think we figured that we were in a small setting and we were stuck with the people there so we might as well say what was on our minds.

What surprised many of our peers was that when Alan and I were together we were often engaged in heated discussions. Our friend Shanelle would always look at us and say, "I don't see how you two are friends. You're always arguing with each other!" Alan and I understood that we did not share a brain—we especially did not share a gender. But we could sit together on the lunch benches and talk about any and everything that frustrated us, call each other names when necessary, and then remember there was a Lakers game on that night and agree that the Lakers would pretty much embarrass whomever their opponent was that night (keep in mind, this was the era of Shaq, Kobe, and Derek Fisher). We had other friends who joined in on our discussions who had different cultural and social references. Even today when we all get together we have good discussions and I feel validated and a sense of home, whether my friends agree with me or not. The idea is that in these spaces and with these people I had a voice, and at the end of the day they saw me as a whole person and did not rely on superficial judgments of my being. This interaction changed for me and for all of my friends from home after high school. I have had similar conversations with Alan and others who left for places like MIT and Yale about their adjustment to these environments that look nothing like our space in high school. I, too, noticed the difference and the fight for my own balance as soon as I left California and headed to college.

The campus of a predominantly white, elite liberal arts college was an environment for which my previous experiences did not prepare me. Before freshman orientation began, I attended the Students of Color Weekend for admitted students and familiarized myself with the location of the Black Student Union. My alternate universe was triggered once I found myself tied to my white roommate, my white hall, and the sea of white people in all of my classes. I had been around white people before, but not like this. I am thankful for the underappreciated commodity called *social skills*, for had I not possessed them, I would have shut down completely. So I kept smiling and made conversation: "How are you? . . . What dorm do you live in? . . . Yea, the food is great!" I also had to prepare myself for the ignorance that came my way: "You're from South Central? Oh . . ." "You have cool hair! Can I touch it? . . ." "There is no need for a black Student Union, especially when people would get mad if I started a White Cultural Center. The BSU is racist."

As much as the general campus complained about the exclusivity of our black student group, the Black Student Union is where I ran when the pot started to boil over. It indicates my personal state when I say that I was in the BSU every single day throughout my freshman year. I worked, slept, cooked, ate, socialized, and attended meetings in the BSU. Finals week after my freshman fall, I had more papers due than I ever thought could be written. I just wanted to go home and recover from the culture shock. I was so grateful for the movie marathons, the sleepovers, and the breakfast that some of the black students organized during finals. I did not want to see anyone else; I certainly did not want to go to professors' office hours to discuss the papers. I talked to black upperclassmen, got advice and guidance from them, and wrote. I escaped. My roommate freshman year (who is still my good friend to this day) thought I did not like her because I was never in our room. It had nothing to do with her, but had everything to do with my adjustment to this new environment. I often wondered, how do I as a black woman from the inner city, with a strong cultural identity and valuable experiences fit into the culture of this white institution? Is what I have to say in class relevant? Does the general student body even care to hear what my concerns are? Why am I here?

I asked these questions frequently. Even though I appreciated the challenging academic atmosphere and the commitment to social change among my peers, many times it felt like my classmates wanted to prove that they deserved to be here. They sometimes behaved in and out of class in ways that served to integrate them into campus culture rather than doing things that fulfilled them or making inquiries and comments that edified everyone. My freshman history seminar felt like "Look Professor, I Belong Here 101." There I was, a math and science student trying to transition to historical thinking in an eleven-person, four-hour class where I was the only person of color. I shut down. I did the readings, I listened to the brief lectures, and I took notes on both. I even smiled and looked interested when my classmates made comments. But something happened in me after that first day when we went around the room, said where we were from, and what school we went to. Lots of private schools. Lots of suburban living. When you are from Los Angeles, everyone either assumes you know movie stars or wants to know the specifics of what part of town you are from. I did not think everyone in this bunch was ready for the black girl from South Central, so I shut up. Towards the end of the semester we began to have conversations about topics that I really wanted to comment on, but I could not find my voice. I refused to say anything when we began talking about civil rights and black people. I felt the heat of stares and was ready to go off on anyone, especially the professor, had they asked me to make a comment just because I was black. I kept thinking, "I am not here to be your mouthpiece for the entire black community. Go read a book!"

I started to hate that class. It was every Thursday afternoon. I got anxiety attacks beginning on Tuesday nights and had great highs on Thursday nights because the class was over. When I had to write my seminar paper, I was in such a panic that I got headaches and could not sleep or eat. I called home every day and my mother threatened to fly to Philadelphia to get me. I lost a lot of weight that fall. To get through that, I did what I knew to do: I ran to my community. It was my friend Paula who helped me survive that experience. She was a senior history major from East Los Angeles, and, as a Mexican American, she knew my struggle in these classes. She told me about the department and her frustrations. She even told me about the professor for my seminar and how she was usually more conscious of the racial dynamics in her classes. So as I struggled to write this paper, Paula stayed up late with me doing her own work (in the BSU, of course), edited my paper, gave me suggestions and encouraged me in my thought process and writing.

This kind of support and encouragement is what kept me at college. I was not the only person of color struggling. Others were worse off than me, with the added insult of having professors expressing that they expected these students to fail. So we supported each other academically, socially, psychologically. There were many times where we just sat around after a weekend party and aired our grievances. We joked about things that could truly break us if we had to deal with them on our own. It is infuriating to hear that such a "progressive" and "safe space" institution would still have its college security asking random black males to show their IDs. It is equally galling to get asked, "Do you go here?" by every white alumni whom you encounter while working with a host of other students at Alumni Weekend events (all students had on shirts that distinguished them as student workers, by the way). I was thankful from the beginning that I found others who understood my situation and who wanted to exchange affirmations of our identity in a place that claimed to offer that support but was often unprepared to truly provide the type of assistance that matters to people who are not necessarily searching for themselves in a mystical sort of way, but are looking to know that what they have will be valued.

Thankfully, I did not quit. I had every opportunity to believe that I was not good enough and that what mattered to me was irrelevant to everyone else. It took me until the end of my junior year to be accepted into my major. At that point, I felt that even if they did accept me as a history major they were doing it more out of pity than because I deserved it. Once again, I allowed myself to be encouraged and guided by my community. I talked to the black and Latino former history majors that I knew. They told me to whom I should talk, which classes to take, and which professors to avoid. After I brought my average up from a B- to an acceptable B, those same people listened to what I wanted to write for my thesis and gave me advice on how to approach my topic with my professors. I wrote about black Americans' educational priorities during the era of integration. By doing primary source research into black perspectives during the 1950s and 1960s, I demonstrated that integration was not black Americans' preferred strategy for solving problems of unequal education in their communities. As controversial as even suggesting such a topic can be, I was able to do the research that interested me in a city that I love, and I was able to incorporate the life and cultural lessons that constituted the foundation my parents set for me. As difficult and frustrating as the entire college experience was, I grew by leaps and bounds, and I feel an even stronger sense of my identity and how that has informed the work I hope to do throughout my life.

My challenge now is to translate the experiences that have challenged and strengthened my identity as a black American into my work as an educator. I am committed to working with inner-city students and imparting the knowledge and experiences I have to help them navigate an ever-changing educational and social system. I understand what it takes to make it in a world that systematically hinders the progress of black and brown students from urban backgrounds, and I am convinced that education is a big key. I am intimately aware of the challenges that many young black students will encounter once they reach a crucial level that naturally exposes them to elitism and other privileges enjoyed by the dominant culture. I did not just read about underperforming schools, multiculturalism, or snooty liberals. I lived these experiences, and they have in turn tailored my identity and honed my skills to the point where I know what I know, and I know how to find out what I need to know. The good and the bad have made me more self-assured and my goals more meaningful. There are others like me who need encouragement to use their foundation and the core of who they are to ask the right questions and make lasting changes.

BEYOND THE EUPHORIC BUZZ

This author, a college junior, describes her double life as a high school student—respected student leader and secret weekend drinker. Growing up in a permissive family in Florida, Sarah slips into a pattern of binge drinking, drunkenness, and promiscuity. With utmost skill, she manages to keep her high school responsibilities and her drinking compartmentalized and for a while sees no need to change her habits. However, finding "common ground" and romance with a Chinese American man at college compels her to reassess her life and to master her addiction. Now a wife and mother, she commits herself to "a whole new appreciation for the sober life" and to caring for her husband and infant child.

Someone go find Luke! His girlfriend is puking."

I'm lying on the bathroom floor of the hotel room. Luke and I had been going together for only a month, when he had asked me to be his date for his junior prom. We drank together plenty in those four weeks, but this was the first time I had gotten sick. In my excitement at the after-party, I had veered from my "Beer then liquor, never sicker" rule, and that's how I came to be in my present situation.

I wake up to see Luke walking through the hotel room's bathroom door. "Oh, hi." I try to smile, but the room is spinning wildly. I can't make it stop. I close my eyes. Oh, worse. I grab the toilet bowl to puke some more. I hate vomiting. It feels like my guts are being yanked out through my mouth for everyone to have a look at. But there's nothing I can do to stop it. I keep waking up, feeling the room spin, puking, then falling back asleep.

At some point Luke decides I need to get in the shower. I argue with him because I can't move without the entire room turning into a carousel gone mad, spinning and spinning. Eventually, he ignores my whimpers. As he stands me up, dizziness overwhelms me. I begin to fall in slow motion. The world is tipping, like a bottle of tequila, and I'm inside, sloshing back and forth sickeningly. . . .

I am lying in the bathtub. Every movement creates another current in the water around me and the bottle sways back and forth. I slosh from side to side, bumping my head on the glass side. Luke is trying to hold the small plastic trash bin for me to puke into. I stop throwing up as the waves die down. I move my arm to get comfortable. More waves. More vomiting. I knock the trash bin on its side and vomit spills into the bath water. For just a moment I'm watching the room from above. I see myself lying there pitifully; sopping clothes, stringy hair, unable to control my bodily functions, bits of vomit floating around me. Then I'm back inside me, inside the bottle that almost finds equilibrium to stand up straight, but then something sets it rocking again. After what seems like hours I drift back to sleep, with Luke holding my head above the water. I'm too exhausted to keep up the fight.

Luke says I need to change into some dry, clean clothes. I look at him. He's never seen me without clothes on. But there's no way I can argue. I obviously can't go to bed like this, and I can't even stand up by myself. My body is not my own. He pushes my pants down to my ankles and sits me on the toilet to pull them off and to put on dry ones. I relax into his arms as he carries me to the bed.

Looking back at that night, I marvel that I never apologized to Luke. I remember feeling awkward because I had never become so ill from drinking, and I wasn't sure how to act. But apologizing was not my instinctive response. Instead, as soon as I had the realization that I had ruined Luke's big night, I began making excuses for myself. "It was only his *junior* prom," I told myself. My philosophy had always been that when I make a mistake, I should resist guilt and invest my energy in learning from the experience instead. But learning from my mistakes assumes some logical cause—something solvable. When drinking became the source of my mistakes, my already formed habit of avoiding guilt became a perpetuating force for my mental addiction. If I didn't feel guilty about the negative consequences of my drinking, what would motivate me to quit?

Today I can answer that question easily. I am finishing my last year in college, I am a wife and mother, and I comfortably identify myself as a nondrinker. But I cannot pretend that the person I am today is unconnected to my past. Just two and a half years ago I was driving home drunk, with a six-pack on the seat next to me, and I cruised into a tree in my front yard, putting a sizeable dent in my mom's car hood. So I must ask, how did things get so bad? Are there aspects of my personality that allowed me to sink so low or was this a simple case of alcohol addiction? And what keeps me from having a drink tomorrow, starting the whole cycle over again? What I've found is that the more I uncover in the complex networks of my mind, the more I see how this will be a lifetime process of realization and readjustment.

I am the youngest of four girls in my family. So, I learned everything about growing up from watching my sisters go through it. School, boyfriends, adolescence, alcohol, high school, drugs . . . I saw it all—first through the eyes of a little girl, and then later as I experienced it myself.

Lilliana, my oldest sister by six years, was my idol growing up. She was a cheerleader. She was on Homecoming Court. She was popular. She drank, she partied. After a while she even did drugs. Pot. Acid. Probably more. But I knew her only as my beautiful, glamorous sister whom I wanted to be just like when I grew up.

Her teenage years were extremely hard on the family. Lilliana was anything but subtle in her disobedience. She would yell and scream at my mother at the slightest cause. It was not unusual to find my mother chasing her around the kitchen table, out the front door, and around the rickety old station wagon parked in the driveway. She wielded a wooden paddle and a fierce look—intent not on hurting her, but on disciplining her rebellious spirit by punishing her defiant acts.

My parents learned a lesson in dealing with Lilliana—you can't force a teenager to do what you want. So they never took an authoritarian approach with the rest of us. Whereas my parents would try to tell Lilliana to come home at one and she would purposely stay out all night, I never had a curfew. Their strategy with the rest of us was to persuade us to do what they thought was best by reasoning with us, discussing the issues, telling us about their experiences. But ultimately, the decision was ours. They understood that sometimes hearing about their mistakes wasn't enough. We needed to experience and learn for ourselves too.

And that was our relationship, for as long as I lived in that household. I respected my parents, obeyed their few rules, considered their abundant counsel, and made my own choices. I could say that not having a curfew was conducive to excessive partying. I could say that being allowed to drink at home was convenient for heavy drinking. But I don't. I never blame my parents for any position I found myself in. I made my own decisions and I dealt with the repercussions myself.

As the offspring of genuine hippies, drugs were never a taboo topic. Growing up, I knew that my parents had lived on a commune with a diet consisting mostly of tofu and pot for the majority of their young adult lives. I was raised on all the "psychedelic" music of the 1960s and by the time I was 12 knew all about the allusions to drugs in the Beatles' songs and many others. But drug use was not a subject that I took lightly.

A memory is imprinted on my mind not because it had great meaning or emotional impact, but from sheer repetition. My mother would be doing something around the house and talking to me at the same time. Suddenly she would stop—always midsentence, sometimes midword. It appeared that she was just pausing in order to concentrate better on what she was doing. I would wait for her to finish the task, expecting her to then complete the sentence, but she never would.

"Mom. What were you going to say?"

"What?"

"What were you going to say? You were just telling me to do something."

"Oh," she would say with surprise. "I was? I'm sorry, honey, I don't remember."

"But *Mom!*" I would reply, drawing out the "o" in exasperation. "You were *just* saying it."

"I'm sorry, sweetie." And the conversation was over. Now for that to happen once is understandable, twice is forgivable, three times a little trying. But over and over and over . . . it's something you can't forget. Later when I found out that this is a typical symptom of being "burnt out," this memory served as the greatest incentive I could ever ask for never to try pot.

By the time I was 13, both Lilliana and Rachel, eighteen months my elder, were heavily into drugs. Everyone knew it, but there wasn't much we could do about it. I resented the huge role that pot played in Rachel's and Lilliana's lives. They totally dropped out of family life. Not just by neglecting chores, but also by retracting all emotional investment. They couldn't stand to be around the family without the buffer of being high. They only valued smoking and people who smoked with them. They were always off in their fairy-tale land where everything was cool and chill and nothing really mattered.

High school was a wonderful time, filled with new experiences, new faces, new challenges. Our freshman class was composed of six hundred students. Wandering through the halls I saw many familiar faces from middle school, and many new ones. I smiled brightly and said hello to everyone, without hesitation. During the second week of school I was in the attendance office and I saw sign-up sheets for anyone who wanted to run for Freshmen Board. Instantly, my mind was flooded with memories of helping Lilliana run for student office. Late nights spent making stickers that read, "Vote for Lilliana Fox!" with little legs and a bushy tail drawn around the "Fox." It sounded like fun! I put my name down for treasurer, a notable title without a lot of work, I thought. The following week I made posters and stickers that looked like a sun and wrote "Vote for Sarah Sunshine!" To my surprise, I won.

The following week a freshmen student assembly was called to introduce the Freshmen Board. The four elected ones sat in four lonely chairs on the vast gymnasium floor. The kids who filled the seats in the towering bleachers were full of that first-week-of-school, fidgeting, bottled-up kind of energy. The assistant principal spoke (for too long) and then began introducing the board. Finally, it was my turn! "And here is your newly elected treasurer, Sarah Fox." Applause, stomping, yelling. Wow! Was that louder than they had cheered for the President? It sure sounded like it to me. But as I approached the microphone, the mob before me was still daunting.

"Thanks for electing us to Freshmen Board," I said with a smile. "Our goal is to make school a more enjoyable place. And I think we've done good so far. We got you out of class today, didn't we?" Hooting, hollering! I was beginning to blush. They hadn't cheered during anyone else's speeches. As it was getting quiet again, Ted Williams, hunk of the class, yelled out, "We love you, Sarah Sunshine!" That started another round of rowdiness. Realizing that I could control this great throng, I willed my bashfulness to disappear. "Okay, okay," I said, as if I was used to this, unimpressed. I continued with my speech, and glancing up, I saw it. People were actually listening to me! With this reassurance, I flashed smiles at faces I recognized. When I came to the end of my note cards, I headed to my seat. The compulsory applause followed. But I couldn't stand such a mediocre ending. Just before I reached my seat I dashed back to the podium. "Freshmen class rules!" I cried into the microphone. They exploded! They stood on their seats, they went wild! But I wasn't a participant in the excitement—I was the leader of it. Yes, that's right, follow my lead, I chuckled to myself, as I sat down.

Looking back I see that this experience had quite an impact on me. That feeling of power over the multitude was intoxicating. Until then I had lived like a little girl, without a care about the consequences of my words and actions. But in the course of that speech I lived my first calculated moments. I did not smile or speak as I always had, out of an impulsive, friendly instinct. I acted in order to produce a desired effect. I was rewarded for my calculation with instant popularity. As my high school career progressed, I treated every action as a political statement.

Being on class board was not just about popularity, for me. I quickly involved myself in every aspect of the school's inner workings. The principal of the school once introduced me saying, "This girl runs the school. She holds everything together around here with her sunshine smile." I once let a curse word slip out in class and was sent to the office. "Look," I said to the assistant principal. "I've heard you use that word how many times? How are you gonna punish me for it?" Not only did I have administrative immunity, but I was making honor roll without trying terribly hard and all my teachers loved me.

I seemed to spread the fairy-tale glitter of my life over everything and everyone that I came in contact with. And the better I became at playing to the crowd, the better my life seemed to get. I couldn't have asked for more. This was every girl's dream of high school. So why shouldn't I become totally immersed in it? Yes, it required some acting, putting up of façades, surrendering of my hopes to live life with childlike innocence. But it was worth it. Hell, it was more than worth it. What I had was better than innocence. It was perfection.

Throughout junior high and freshman year of high school I never drank. I had always been firm in my refusal to drink, to the point that I never had to mention it; it was known. I was confident in my role and I felt I was being wise. So when I decided to get drunk for the first time I could honestly say it was a choice that I made for myself when I felt I was ready. I wasn't just following the crowd. *I* wanted to try it. I set the date in my head and then I told everyone else. "Next Saturday I'm going to get drunk," I said.

"All right! We'll have to get some good stuff, then!" That was Frank. He was two years older than me and had this incredibly charismatic personality. He had an air of relaxed confidence about him, as if he were so cool he could just relax about it. We were part of a group that hung out on the beach every night. He lived near me so he often drove me home in his jeep.

All that week I looked forward to it. On Friday, Frank asked, "Why don't you just do it tonight?"

"Nope. Tomorrow. Don't worry, Frankie, it'll be just as fun!" And was it ever! I drank a beer and felt giddy. I was talking and laughing, which is not uncommon for me. Everything just seemed to have an extra sparkle. Then I drank another and I was off and running. Weighing one hundred pounds, I knew it wouldn't take much alcohol to affect me. "Let's go down to the water!" I said excitedly. I met with groans and sighs.

"It's too far."

"Aw come on, Sarah, just sit down and relax."

"Come on, come on! It'll be fun!" I urged. "Come *on!*" I said pulling on Frank's arm. Finally Diana, who had not yet tried drinking, decided to go down with me. And then I convinced Frank to come too. "I'll race ya," I said to Diana and set off running. I arrived at the water's edge out of breath. Diana was trailing behind me, laughing.

"Sarah, you're such a nut!" she cried happily.

"Oooh!" I said, as I had another thought, "Let's go swimming!" And before she could respond I was running toward the water. As soon as it was deep enough I collapsed into the water. I felt it close in around me, hugging my body, making me warm. I moved and turned, feeling the water swirl around me. And after a while I popped my head out of the water, took a gulp of air, then let the water envelop me again. I just lay there this time. Letting the lull of the waves move my body for me, relaxed completely. And then I felt arms around me. Real, human arms. Someone was dragging me out of the water.

"Oh, hi Frankie!"

"Diana thought you were drowning," he said flatly. He didn't sound amused.

"Oh. Well, I wasn't," I explained. I began thinking how unfortunate it was that he had pulled me out. It was so much warmer in the water! He set me on the ground. And then I caught sight of the sky. "Ooooh! Diana look at the stars!" I said. "Let's spin!" I stretched my arms out, let my head fall back, and spun around and around and around, looking at the stars in the heavens. I was a little girl again. Grinning so widely that my cheeks bulged out to twice their normal size. No cares outside of the here and now. Ah life! What joy! I sat down and pondered with amazement, while the world slowly stopped spinning around me.

This is the story of the first time I got drunk. But it is also the story of how I fell in love with the drunken state of mind, and still love it today. Being drunk is like being a kid again. When I was drunk I could experience careless bliss. Once I tasted the forbidden fruit, I couldn't give it up. When I discovered that being drunk was like artificial childlike innocence, I couldn't resist. And why should I? I could have my cake and eat it too.

Sophomore year I was elected class president. I was passionate about the work I was doing to improve the school. The people around me seemed to sense my dedication. It was the same with all the people I worked with: facilities managers, administrators, students, teachers. They worked extraordinarily well with me and for me because they respected me professionally, liked me personally, and thought that the final results of my work repaid their efforts. My products were inherently more valuable because I put so much of my self into my work. I wasn't just the president anymore; I became a public figure. As much depended on my personal integrity as on my capability.

Sophomore year I was partying with all the most popular kids on campus. Yes, I stood out from the crowd, but only because when I wanted to have fun, I *really* had fun. No inhibitions, no quiet reservations. Everyone had a "One time

Sarah was so drunk . . ." story to tell at school the following Monday and I thought it was great.

I always drank to get drunk. And I usually passed out sometime during the night. I knew people thought it was a big deal to black out but it didn't make much sense to me. Passing out to me was just like falling asleep. And when can anyone remember the exact circumstances of falling asleep? I remembered my nights in the form of a flash: action, feeling. And the emotion washes over me, in that flash, with an intensity that can hardly be paralleled when sober. Why dilute that memory with specifics and particulars? In my eyes, I was sucking the marrow out of life.

From the second or third time I got drunk I began to think about alcoholism. I still wonder, was my instinct warning me, from the very beginning? Could I have known somewhere deep within my subconscious that I was *too* in love with being drunk—that it could become a problem for me? I wanted to find out more about alcoholism, but I was scared my political career would be over if my secret concerns became known. In eleventh grade the opportunity I had been waiting for finally came. I had to do a documentary on a topic of my choice. I immediately knew I wanted to interview recovering alcoholics and counselors for substance abuse; then take what I learned from them and apply it to students who were known as fun partiers. I wanted to show that what most people thought of as harmless fun was truly dangerous. Looking back I realize that I wanted to increase social awareness so that people like me would be taken seriously. The best definition of alcoholism I heard from those interviews was, "When your alcohol use begins having a negative effect on more than one area of your life and you continue to drink." The only problem is that the more addicted one becomes, the more subjective one's judgment becomes. The definition of what's "bad enough" keeps sliding.

Going into the summer before senior year I had it all made. I was managing to keep my school responsibilities and my drinking compartmentalized, balanced. At that time I was involved in my most serious relationship yet, over one-and-a-half years long. His name was Luke. His family was moving to Orlando at the start of the summer, about six hours upstate, and he was leaving for the state university in the fall. Lately, I'd noticed myself looking at other guys. I was just hoping to stay faithful until he left, and then I'd be free. I had already convinced him it would be better not to attempt a long-distance relationship.

Two days before Luke's departure, we went to a party. When I had become sufficiently intoxicated, I pulled aside Steve, a friend of his that I had always thought was cute. "So, listen," I said. "Luke is leaving on Tuesday. Why don't you give me a call and we can go party or something?"

He looked at me quizzically, peering into my face to confirm the implications he thought he had just heard. His face broke into a broad smile. "Sure."

Tuesday came and Luke left. Thursday came and Steve called. We went to a kicking party. The end of the night found us skinny-dipping in the jacuzzi. We made out passionately in the steamy water. He pressed himself against me, and for the first time in my life I seriously considered not saving myself for marriage.

Luckily, I was too nervous about the whole situation (nude in a strange place with my recent ex-boyfriend's good friend) to do anything.

A few nights later I went to another party at the same girl's house. There was an attractive guy there who I had my eye on. He had graduated from my high school two years earlier. When I introduced myself, he said, "I know. I used to watch you during lunch when you sat outside." I was flattered. He used to watch me from afar! I always wanted an admirer! As the party cleared out, Christopher and I were left on the fold-out couch. We started making out and it got pretty intense pretty quickly. At some point he asked me whether I wanted to "do it." I said I never had and he dropped it. A while later he brought it up again and after a few minutes of pondering I said sure. Just like that. That night seemed like it never ended. I don't know what girls are talking about when they say the first time hurts. I thought it was terrific. Over and over. At times I would forget his name, then the next time I woke up I'd remember it.

I awoke the next morning and knew right away that everything had changed. Why had I decided to go for it? I asked myself. I had no answer. Saving myself for marriage was such an integral part of my self-identity as a moral, good person. Without my virginity, I was left devoid of any positive self-image.

It took less than one moment to decide my response. I would not regret losing my virginity to Christopher. No regrets! I would make it a meaningful experience by developing a real relationship with him. And if that worked, wouldn't it be fantastic if I actually ended up marrying my first?

For the next month, there was little time that we spent together when we weren't drunk or having sex. But we were getting to know each other a little more. For instance, I learned he was much more uptight than I was, he had been a complete loser at school, he had been kicked out of two state universities in the past year, and none of his friends or family thought highly of him. In fact, anyone who knew about us tried to convince me that I shouldn't be with him. Not many people knew, though. If any of my friends from school heard I was with him, they might also hear that I was sleeping with him. And that, I knew, would be the end of my perfect reputation at school.

Our relationship was a constant roller coaster. Every time something came up that put us on less than good terms, I panicked. I could sense that Guilt was just out of eyesight, impending, threatening, and if we didn't stay together it would come barreling down on me. It got to the point that the simplest interaction, like calling him up, required having at least a few drinks to calm my nerves and rally up my courage.

After about five weeks I stopped caring. I found what I needed in my drinking. I finally ended it by kissing another guy. While we had been together, I told myself that Christopher would be the only exception to my sexual abstinence. But once we broke up, Guilt again threatened to overcome me. I still did not want to surrender to it. The only alternative was to keep going without looking back. That's just what I did.

All summer I partied every night. Drinking was starting to lose its excitement. My new thrill was hooking up with whomever I wanted. There was a certain satisfaction in knowing that I could seduce anyone. My conquests were always one-night stands and I never became emotionally involved. Looking back it was as if I became a completely different person when I went out drinking. Never would I have done those things sober. I knew they were wrong, and I would have felt too ashamed. But as the summer went on I could plan who I was going to get that night, before I ever started drinking. By the end of the summer drinking was not a necessity. Although it was a large part of my lifestyle, I didn't have to be drunk to carry out my conquests.

I was drinking more and more during the day. Partying all night left me depleted of energy during the day. Drinking made the daylight hours bearable, made me feel physically better, more energetic and happier. Not only was my physical health failing, but my emotional health was also deteriorating. My sexual conquests required cutting off all emotions. Once I learned how to cut myself off, I found myself doing it all the time. Not only was it easier to live life without a conscience, but there was a convenient aftereffect: since I didn't care about anything, even when alcohol was having a negative effect on all areas of my life, in my mind things never became "bad enough" to quit.

When school started in the fall I hardly paused. I was president of student council, captain of the debate team, and treasurer of the National Honor Society. I was enrolled in two AP courses and three honors courses. I stayed two hours after school every day, and sometimes arrived an hour early, to take care of the official business of my various positions. I was dedicated to my academics, but somehow I still found the time to drink. On Wednesdays I arrived home from school at four o'clock. My church orchestra practice started at six. On my way home from church, I stopped by 7-Eleven and bought some brew with my fake ID. A few of my nonschool friends would be waiting for me when I got home.

I was able to keep my reputation and positions at school because no one there knew about my drinking. I never partied with people from school. At the time it was because I thought they were superficial and their mere presence annoyed me, inhibited me. In retrospect I see that I was successful in the various spheres of my life, and in order to maintain that success while continuing to drink, I had to preserve barriers that would never be crossed.

About halfway through the fall of my senior year I started getting a bit bored by my drinking routine. It had lost its excitement. I felt so old and tired. I could feel myself getting numb. I decided to clean up my act. I wanted to start a real relationship. My plan was to build up a relationship slowly, and at the same time cut down on my drinking and partying. Eventually we would spend all of our time together and I'd have no need to drink at all. It was a good plan.

I picked out a sweet, innocent underclassman, Ted. By the next week we were passing notes between classes. Already I felt like a normal teenager again, excited at the mere hope of being someone's girlfriend. I could almost feel the spiritual calluses softening up.

And then came the big football game that Friday. I hadn't gone to a game sober in ages. At first I tried to make plans with some of my old nondrinking friends. But I hadn't even called them in ages. They couldn't just drop their new friends and welcome me back with open arms. Friday came and I couldn't resist. My drinking buddies bought a bottle of tequila and we drank a good portion of it before walking over to the field.

Before I could get very far I ran into Ted. What terrific luck! I was actually hoping I'd see him here. We saw each other from a few yards away and we both burst into smiles. I ran into his open arms. He picked me up and he swung me around. This is the way it should be, I thought to myself. I stood with him for a bit, until I spotted my friends, looking impatient as ever. I gave Ted one last hug.

The night was still young, the halftime show had just ended. I was beginning to tire of putting on fake smiles for my superficial school friends. Then I ran into an old acquaintance. Not just anyone, mind you. Rick Marciano. Wow! What a hotty! He had graduated two years ago, and he was still known as a legend amongst the lady folk. I greeted him with an extra close hug and barely stepped away after the embrace. We talked for a few minutes about nothing and then he told me about a party after the game. I already had plans, so he gave me his number to meet up later. "You'd better not forget my number!" he said as we parted.

Don't forget his number? Who was he joking? Did he really think he was the pursuant here? Or that any girl in her right mind would give up such a golden opportunity? I walked away feeling even happier than the eight drinks had made me feel.

And what about Ted? Well, I did think about him for a moment, as I walked away from Rick. But this was such a once-in-a-lifetime opportunity that I couldn't give it up. By this time I was so good at making excuses for myself that I hardly had to think twice to defend my actions. Ted and I hardly have anything going, I told myself. I mean, it's not like we're going out or anything. Plus, maybe it was a bad idea to try to have a normal relationship. Maybe I'm not ready for it yet. And that was that.

That night one of my only true friends from school was throwing his first big party. When I arrived, all the popular kids from his grade were there. After a few drinks, I called Rick to invite him over.

The next thing I remember Rick and I were making out in the bushes in front of the house. Of course, everyone saw. Wilson persuaded me to at least find somewhere more discreet to do whatever I wanted to do. So Rick and I hopped in his car and drove away. That was all that people needed to start the rumors.

It wasn't long until Ted heard the stories. He called me on Sunday night. It was horrible. He told me I was the first person who ever made him feel like a real man. Why did I do this to *him?* Was he not fast enough for me? He was crying. There was nothing I could do to make amends for what I had done. Not just to Ted, but to myself, my family, my church, God. I could feel the weight of the world bearing down on me, about to collapse. In that moment the gates opened up. Feelings of worthlessness, guilt, shame, sadness—all the emotions that I had been refusing to feel, that I had intentionally dammed up inside me by drinking alcohol, alcohol, and more alcohol—it all came rushing out in a torrent. I felt like Jesus Christ, all the sins of the world cast upon me in a matter of moments. Except these weren't the sins of the world, these were *my* sins.

Do you know what a shock it is to the system to feel so many emotions all at once, after not feeling anything—nothing—for months on end? It's paralyzing, to say the least. He was sobbing. What could I do? I was bawling inside. But I had forgotten how to express those kinds of emotions. Or maybe I should say I had unlearned it.

I slept for only two hours that night. I dreaded Monday. I considered staying home from school, but that would be a cowardly public statement. At school I could feel the stares, hear the whispers as I walked by. By the end of the school day I felt extreme blackness cover my insides like a blanket. It was too much to bear. I had to shut myself off again or else I would have a nervous breakdown. I was sure of it.

The worst part was the Student Council meeting. Ted was a representative. He sat quietly in the back row, like the martyr that he was. The meeting was complete disorder. Everyone thought they had the right and the duty to condemn me. This was their way of showing their disrespect.

Eventually things at school died down. I didn't get back my ability to feel, but I didn't really expect to either. I had undergone a trauma. I would never be the same again. Sometimes I pitied myself. I'm still a kid, I would say to myself. I'm not supposed to have to grow up this fast. But I knew I had only myself to blame for it all.

It took this harrowing experience for me to realize I had become obsessed with the powerful feeling I obtained from controlling men. Through it all, I never thought to quit my drinking. I knew that my lack of self-control was worst when I was drunk. But quitting drinking would disrupt my whole life. And I just wasn't ready for that. I needed all the comfort I could get at that point.

In many ways college was just like high school. I quickly got a reputation that I was fun to party with, and everyone had a funny, "One time Sarah was so drunk that she . . ." story to tell. The most important difference was Dan. I met him my second day on campus. The moment I saw him my heart started racing. He wasn't just good-looking, he was strikingly so. This guy was *gorgeous*. And as we began to talk I saw that his beauty was not just skin deep. Our friendship was like love at first sight. From that first night and every day after, my amazement, admiration, and enjoyment of Dan just grew and grew.

We spent all our free time together. We could be found lying side-by-side on the lawn doing homework, meandering through town, and eating breakfast, lunch, and dinner together. Not only did we have a terrific time, but I was constantly in wonder of how alike we seemed, despite our apparent differences. He from the Northeast, me from the South; he from the big city of Boston, me from the midsized tourist town of Sarasota; he Chinese American, me white, Cuban American; he the oldest of his siblings, me the youngest. But we seemed to find common ground in everything. We were like two puzzle pieces made of different materials, by the hands of different craftsmen, who had spent their lives adjusting to the fact that we would never quite fit in with the rest. Then all of a sudden, by some twist of fate, we discovered that we fit—together, perfectly.

It was three months into our friendship before we confessed our romantic love for each other. The ensuing months were heavenly. We were so in love and happy about it that the most frequent comment we received from friends was, "You guys make me sick."

The only thing we didn't have in common was drinking. Dan wasn't a big drinker. His social scene in high school had never included drinking as a regular activity. Our freshman year he went to the frats, because that was the main social activity, but he didn't derive his pleasure from drinking, like I did. About four months into freshman year—we had been together as a couple for only a short time—my partying became a problem for us. Dan was getting tired of staying at frats until midmorning, when he wasn't even having a good time. But this was my way of having fun and I wasn't ready to give that up for any reason. I don't think it was a matter of being addicted to alcohol at that point. I just enjoyed that scene— the people, the noise, the drunk intellectual conversations, and, yes, the drinking. But maybe that lifestyle is part of the mental addiction.

Dan and I never discussed these issues. About three months into our romantic relationship I kissed another guy at a frat after Dan had left. It wasn't a long, passionate kiss. A quick peck. But the guilt was overwhelming. I confessed to Dan the next morning. We talked about why it had happened, how I needed to control myself when I drank, but we hardly scraped the surface. The real conversation started when I confessed to a much greater sin. Two weeks after we started dating we had a one-month vacation. On my trip back home I slept with my recent ex-boyfriend, Keith. Dan almost couldn't handle it. We practically broke up. But my begging and pleading finally convinced him that *he* was the one I wanted to be with, that I would never let it happen again.

Other than those incidents, our relationship was wonderful. It was the happiest, healthiest relationship I had ever been in. We never came out of the "in love" stage. We were affectionate and snuggly and passionate, but we also had stimulating intellectual discussions and challenged each others' perspectives.

At the end of our freshman year, we were faced with a summer apart. I had an internship in Miami, about five hours from my hometown, and he had an internship in Boston. I knew I'd be spending several weekends at home, and a part of me wanted the freedom to be able to hook up with people at parties, if the opportunity arose. I explained that I wanted to be with him. In fact, I wanted to marry him, eventually. But I needed this last chance to be free and irresponsible, before I grew up and settled down. He couldn't understand how we could be anything but monogamous and still stay together. Finally he put his foot down. Either we stayed exclusive or we broke up. I agreed. We would stay exclusive.

All summer we talked every day. We talked on the phone at night, we e-mailed each other from work during the day. All was going well. I had visited home a few times and I was confident in my ability to stay true to my promise.

Fourth of July is always a big celebration in my town, and it's a huge drinking affair. By the time the fireworks ended, I was very happily drunk. I had invited a few of my old drinking buddies over, for old times sake. While we were all hanging out on the front porch drinking, I began to notice how attracted I was to one of my old friends. When everyone else had left, we began to kiss. One thing led to another and we ended up in bed. I didn't really want to have sex with him. That wasn't at all what I had in mind. But that's what happened. I was so drunk that I didn't really care. All I could muster was a questioning, "Um, Rob?" As if to say, what are you doing? But I didn't feel strongly enough about it, at the time, to put up much of an argument. Needless to say, it was terribly unenjoyable.

The next morning came and I felt like shit. I knew I had to tell Dan. That had been his one request. "Sarah, if you care about me in the slightest, you'll give me the respect of telling me if anything happens over the summer." I boarded the bus back to Miami and thought about how I was going to tell him. How I was going to explain that it wasn't passionate, it wasn't meaningful, it had just happened. Most of all, how was I going to keep him from dumping me?

I called that night. I cried. He was silent. He had expected it, he explained. He had felt something, a certain foreboding, about me going home for the holiday. He called me late on the night of the fourth, hoping that if the thought of him was fresh on my mind, it would stop me from doing anything. But it hadn't. He broke up with me. I said everything I could to win him back. Finally I told him I would quit drinking.

"Good! You need to. But that's not going to make what you did any better. And it won't solve the problem, either. I want you to want *me*. No one else. Whether you're drunk or sober, I need to be the object of your love *and* your lust. You need me, but you don't want me." Maybe he was right. But I had to do something. I called AA that night and found out where the meetings were held.

For twenty-four hours Dan and I were in Hell, separately. I called him the next night. We were miserable. I don't think he even liked me, at that point. I could hear the distaste in his voice. I didn't deserve him. We both knew it. I had caused him so much awful pain. But we were even more miserable apart. So he took me back. It was going to take a long time to mend his broken heart and regain his trust. All I could do was hope—hope that our happiness together wasn't over for good.

Quitting was the only thing I could actively work on to improve things with Dan. I stopped drinking cold turkey. It was easy while I was in Miami. I barely had a social life there, so I rarely had the opportunity to drink. My visits home were the true test. My family had become so accustomed to my drinking habits, that they questioned my sudden abstinence. Over the next few months, my sisters and parents each took their turn explaining that I need not be so extreme. A little alcohol surely couldn't hurt, they implied. But I knew myself. I knew I couldn't drink without getting drunk. I never had experienced that mentality. My mind only worked a certain way. Once I have the first sip, my only goal is getting wasted. I knew that my craving wouldn't be quenched by one drink. It wasn't the taste that I desired, it was the feeling. That euphoric buzz that leads to a numb semiconsciousness. No, I couldn't even have a sip.

When I first quit drinking, I felt like I was missing out on the best of life. Who can go back to a normal lifestyle once they've experienced the passion and extreme highs of living for the moment, completely rid of the inhibitions of societal norms and personal conscience? The memory of my fast-paced, extravagant lifestyle was not enough. I wanted to experience more. Being at a college where drinking makes up the bulk of social interaction did not help. When I saw crowds of drunk people meandering through frat row I felt so much hostility. I wanted to be there, I wanted to join them. I didn't want to grow up yet. And, damn it, I shouldn't have to. I'm 18 and I deserve to be still having fun, I told myself. What I knew had been fun and exciting. How could something else be anything but dull and mediocre?

To Dan, my decision to quit drinking on July 5, 1998 was a statement that I had recognized, at last, all the pain and injury that my alcohol use had inflicted on myself and those around me. But that's not what it was to me. To me, it was admitting that keeping Dan was more important to me than continuing to drink. Realizing the myriad of ways that alcohol had affected my life would be a long process.

Before I could see that my alcohol use was the cause of many problems, I had to admit that I had problems. I needed to admit that *by my own standards* my life had gone to hell. I had to admit that I had slipped so far from where I wanted to be. I thought of myself as a failure. The first step is admitting to myself that I feel this way and then recognizing that the source of these feelings is me, my perspective, the way I think life ought to be.

I feel like I have done a lot of harm in my day, to myself and to others. I've broken the hearts of guys who were foolish enough to invest feelings in me, during my alcohol and sex binges. And I never to this day even thought about what I had done to them. I've seen sides of myself that I never wanted to believe I was capable of. God gave me the ability to influence people, to captivate them, and I desecrated these gifts by using them for sexual conquests and to further myself politically. This is not religious guilt, put on me by someone else. It's the way I feel inside.

It took me two years just to gain enough distance to be able to talk about drinking without wanting to be engaged in it, deep inside. I'm finally secure enough in my identity as a nondrinker to be able to look objectively at my experiences. I have just started this process. It seems like I'm rather late—two years and I haven't made much progress in all that time. But the way I look at it, at least the process has started. With the birth of my daughter six months ago I became responsible for a brand new life. Today, my desire to take care of my family gives me a whole new appreciation for the sober life.

HOLDING MY BREATH

As a senior in college, Andy looks back on significant relationships with his friends and finds that they have helped him learn to be more comfortable with who he is. When he gives up his childhood love of theater and turns to sports in middle school, he assumes a masculine identity that remains important to him, even as he becomes more convinced of his homosexuality. In college, through friendships and romantic relationships, Andy learns to accept all aspects of who he is. He also finds that by being himself, he can contribute to change and the growth of others.

When I woke up that Tuesday morning and jumped down from the top bunk, my legs felt especially sore. The post-season lifting schedule is considerably more grueling than in-season. Lacrosse had gone on for four months. Once the season ended, we started lifting at full blast: front squats, back squats, single leg squats, off-bench squats, cleans, pulls, jerks. As I landed on the ground, six feet down from my bed, my quadriceps felt the impact.

I showered, shaved, brushed my teeth, and put my contacts in like any normal morning. Except I went over the conversation I was about to have so many times in the shower that my fingers turned prune-like after half an hour and that made it more difficult to hold my contacts. My fingers were almost insensitive to the touch of the small plastic objects, and it took me a few extra minutes before I finally got them in my eyes and the fuzzy world became visible. Back in my room, I paced back and forth, repeating words and phrases in my head. None of them sounded right. So I cleaned up the common room as one of my roommates remained sleeping in the bedroom. I straightened up all of the papers on the desk. I put all of the clothes from the chair away in the closet. I put my books on the shelf. None of these mindless actions could take my brain away from the task at hand.

I had worried for the last five years of my life how I would ever tell my parents that I was gay. But when I finally got the words out of my mouth with my mother sitting three feet away from me, my breathing finally slowed down. It didn't matter what came of it—whether she came over and kissed me or got right back in her car and drove home. She did neither. In my imagination, she was supposed to break into tears and tremble and hold my hand and say, "I love you." In my mind we were going to sit together and cry out our feelings and emotions. My mother seemed to have neither at the moment. She simply sat on that couch and told me that she and my father would always love me no matter what.

I showed her a picture of my boyfriend, Adam, and she smiled. She told me that she was just glad I would not have to do this alone, and then she strayed from the topic of homosexuality. I was ready to talk. This was the morning I had chosen to open up to my mother, to tell her the secret burden I had been carrying for too long, and here she was, essentially telling me that it was silly for me to have kept the secret. Why did I think it would be so upsetting to her? Why did I choose to let this eat me up inside when there was nothing to fear on the outside? She acted as if this was any other day of my life.

We went out to lunch, and then I took her to meet Adam. In my mother's attempt to avoid any awkwardness, she gave him a big hug (a welcome to the family kind of thing) and blabbered on for a while about nothing of any importance. When she left, I felt changed. I tried to remember my last family phone call, so I could remember it as the last time I would ever have to lie about who I was dating. Adam hugged me and told me how proud of me he was for coming out to my mother. He felt relieved. I didn't. The worst is yet to come, I thought, when my father hears the news.

The next morning, I awoke to read this e-mail in my in-box:

Hi:

I have one million questions for you—and when you are ready to talk, I am ready to listen. Every night, after going to sleep, we wake up in the morning. As a father, husband, parent, educator, and health care professional, I can honestly say that it is my life-long experience that one's sexual preference is not the issue—the central issue is that when you wake up you are excited with what you will be accomplishing during the upcoming day. Your dreams, goals, and enthusiasm for life are what really count. What we want to do with our precious and precarious lives and how we want to share the joy of living with others is really what this is all about. I am writing this note to tell you that I love you, am very proud of you, and look forward to some frank discussion with you when you come home soon.

—Dad x0x0x0x0x

I started to cry. I needed to read the note again to make sure that my brain was not playing tricks on me. There was no way that I had just received that note from my father. For ten years, I had thought about members of the same sex. For five years, I had actually thought about the reality of being gay. For the last three, I had wrestled with my life, staying up all night unable to fall asleep because I was worried about how my parents would react. Adam handed me a tissue. Part of me was shaking and the other part of me was completely at rest.

When I was younger, I used to wish for bad parents. I used to wish that my parents fought, or that they would get divorced, so that when I turned out to be really screwed up, everyone would know whom to blame. I hoped that they would stop loving me, so that I could pretend I was doing this to get back at them. But as I walked up toward class that morning, I knew how glad I was that my wish had not come true. My father had just told me that he loved me and was very proud of me. In class that morning, my friends asked me what was wrong, since my eyes looked red. I told them that I was just tired. It was true. I was tired of hiding my life from the ones who gave me life. I was tired of feeling guilty for something I never had control over, not a single day in my twenty years of existence. I was tired of worrying that nobody would accept me.

A week and a half later, my father took me out for a lobster dinner—my favorite meal—to open me up. As we drove out to the restaurant, I didn't worry about the things I used to worry about. Instead, I worried that my father would not be able to handle all the answers to his questions. How would he reconcile being blind to my sexuality for so long?

He grilled me about everything during our dinner. As we buttered our rolls, he asked me when I first knew that I was gay. "When I was 19 years old," I told him, "because I knew I would never love my current girlfriend. But really, it was when I was 13 years old, because I started to fantasize about the same sex. And I can trace it back to being aroused when I was 6 or 7. But actually, I remember when I was 4 years old, my friend Rod and I would lie on top of each other naked." My father gasped at this last remark. How could I claim to have known that I was gay at 4 years old?

By the time the clam chowders were served, we were well into my high-school experience. He asked what it was like to hide this from everyone and I told him how awful it really was. He sympathized with me, but he found it difficult to match my emotions. His life works scientifically. There is always an explanation and something that we can learn from everything. We talked about the importance of trust and communication. I saw something new in his eyes. Was this man, in his mid-fifties, trying to tear down all the walls I had built and find out who his son really was? Every once in a while, he would pause and look down, unable to understand how he had let me feel so badly about myself, or how he had not been there when his son needed him. I tried to console him, saying, "Dad, I spent my entire adolescence trying to hide this from you. I became a pretty good liar, even to myself. How could you have seen this coming when I did everything I could to paint a different picture for you?"

I was full after that meal. My father was still full of questions. He would never see the world in the same way again. He had to turn his world upside-down in order to understand me and fit my life into it. The whole stigma of homosexuality was now part of his life, whether he liked it or not. In time, he could make adjustments to his world, to allow the current situation to make sense, but he could never go back to the way it was. That world no longer existed. He could never again look at a gay couple and wonder who made them turn out like that. When he heard a fellow doctor make an off-color joke about homosexuality, he had to speak up now, because it was my father's world that the doctor was making fun of.

Growing up I had every advantage that a Jewish kid from the suburbs would want, from private schools to youth sports to sleep-away camps. At the age of 5, I entered kindergarten in a private school where my sister and brother were in the fourth and sixth grades, respectively. In second grade I started attending Hebrew school three times a week, and that didn't stop until seventh grade when I had my Bar Mitzvah.

My early love was theater. By age 6, I was creating my own musicals, writing the scripts and the music, and recruiting friends to perform my plays. In third grade, I joined a theater troupe with my friend Evan; we were the two youngest members of the group made up of mostly fourth, fifth, and sixth graders. When some scouts from the Boston theater district came to watch us rehearse, I was asked to audition for the role of Tiny Tim in *A Christmas Carol*. I was chosen as an understudy for the character and later received roles as a child in two other professional plays. It seemed that my life was set; my goal was to grow up to be a Hollywood or Broadway actor.

Throughout my acting days, my sister and brother often tormented me for being too artistic. I learned to associate arts with something bad, something nobody wanted to be connected with. My sister and brother would throw around the term "gay" without really thinking about sexual orientation. To them it was just an insult, something that little boys are supposed to avoid. They knew that it was more "gay" to write plays than to play sports, so I was surrounded by these ideas at an early age. One afternoon, before an evening performance at a professional play in Boston, my father handed me the new issue of *Time*. The cover read "AIDS and the Arts." The discussion that followed left me horrified. He asked me repeatedly if the men with whom I performed had tried to touch me in strange places. If his intention was to turn me away from the stage, he succeeded— that was the final professional play of my life. I never believed that my father was insinuating anything about me, or that he meant to do me any harm. As a doctor, he spends his life trying to improve health, and as a father, he wants the best for his children. But in trying to protect me, he alienated me. I knew I could no longer feel proud of my accomplishments around him.

Starting the summer after third grade, I traveled up to East Falls, New Hampshire—a town too small for its own post office—for overnight camp: eight weeks of sports, campfires, and cabin fights, culminating in an event called "color war," which I had the misfortune to lose for four straight years. It was at camp where I first developed strong friendships with boys of completely different backgrounds. Each year, we would come back to see each other, one year older, and we would hope to be placed in the same cabin as our buddies.

The first time I can remember being sexually aroused was during the second summer at camp, when I was 10 years old, watching one of my bunkmates change out of his bathing suit. It was my first real erection, and I didn't know what it meant. A few weeks later, another bunkmate was given a *Playboy* from his older brother, and we all sat around a bed and flipped through the pages, noting how hairy some of the girls were and rating their breasts. When a buddy asked if I was getting hard looking at the girls, I told him I didn't know. I asked him if he was hard, and he said of course, that he always got hard looking at naked girls. I noted this, and also thought about my first erection earlier that summer. How funny that mine came from an undressing buddy while his came from a silly magazine.

My camp had a big teepee right in front of the main lodge, and the director said that on special occasions a few campers could have the privilege of sleeping in the teepee for a night. So during my third year at camp, five of us decided to drag our sleeping bags down to the lodge and spend a night under the stars. We didn't anticipate the rain soaking us, nor did we plan the events of that night. I can't remember how it started, but I do remember another boy and I coupling off into one sleeping bag. Two others boys followed along, both in the same bag. The fifth boy put his head inside his sleeping bag and pulled the string tight so that he could not see what was going on.

We decided to pretend that we were boy and girl, acting like lovers, since we were 11 and did not know exactly how everything worked. We had our pants on during the entire scene, but our shirts were off and our hands were exploring each other's bodies. It felt so great to me, but I didn't know if I was supposed to enjoy it or not. My hand went up and down his back and I felt every bone and every bump from his shoulder blades down to his buttocks. One of the boys in the other two-man sleeping bag said that he was getting hard and asked if that made him gay. The other boy in his bag proclaimed that it meant nothing, that obviously we were all imitating having sex with women and that getting hard was just a consequence of this role-playing. We were just perfectly regular guys using each other to feel what older guys get to feel all the time.

When we woke up the next morning, we vowed not to mention what had happened the night before. We said we'd forget what happened, but I couldn't. I developed feelings for the other boy who shared my sleeping bag with me, and I think he felt the same way. We spent a lot of time together, but we never repeated what we had done in the teepee. Maybe we were in denial, or maybe we didn't understand our desires, but we were able to maintain a unique friendship without speaking directly about that night. You could argue that this was the first "homosexual" relationship of my life, but at that age we did what we enjoyed doing and didn't think much of it.

The summer after sixth grade my father again took me aside and told me that I was going to play football. He told me that I wanted to be tough, not a sissy, and that playing football would not only teach me to be tough, but it would show people exactly what type of person I was. "If you want to be cool," he told me, "you should play football and quit all of the acting business. You don't want to be a sissy, do you?"

When he told me not to be a sissy, we both knew what he was trying to say: acting would make me gay while football would be the answer to everyone's prayers. My older siblings had been calling me gay for years for all of the singing and acting I did, and here my dad was telling me that I could forget all of that and start a new identity in middle school as a football player. There was a part of me that hated my dad for telling me to give up something that I loved so much. To assume that he could change me by changing my after-school interests was naïve of him, but, at the same time, I understood that he loved me and wanted what was best for me. In his eyes, I would benefit from my peers approving of me.

My athletic career took off from there. We had been a sports family for as long as I could remember. I loved sports and they came naturally to me. I guess sports were just overshadowed by what seemed like my more natural talent: acting. I left the stage behind almost cold turkey and dove right into the athletic world.

I became best friends with Austin in eighth grade, my second year in middle school and my second year of football. Austin had a thin build, brown hair, and a boyish face, and was almost a foot taller than me. We bonded during the seventh grade football season. That first year I was clueless on the field and almost never got into the game. I didn't even know all of the rules. But during the summer after seventh grade, Austin and I went to football camp and I learned how to be a receiver and a running back. By eighth grade I led the middle school team in touchdowns. Austin and I became inseparable for the next few years. For a 13-year-old who recognizes his interests in other boys, the ideal relationship is with your best friend. I figured we could be best friends, and in private we could be boyfriends. Nobody would question us since we spent so much time together anyway. What I didn't know was that he never shared this fantasy with me.

While on a vacation to the Caribbean with my family, Austin and I were playing tackle football in the pool. As the contact increased, so did my arousal level. As I pulled him down in the water, I made sure to brush by his waist and let him know of my interest. Later, when we were back in our room watching television, I decided to continue our little game. Without saying a word to each other, I brought Austin to climax. He could argue that he was imagining a female with him and that I was the only thing he had to get him off. But the truth is that we had taken part in homosexual activity without speaking. Incidents like this occurred on more than one occasion, but he never initiated any of them. Perhaps to him it was just messing around with a friend. We never once talked about the few incidents, but I thought it was all understood. I, the initiator, wanted to continue that part of our relationship; he didn't want to talk about it.

By early junior year in high school, Austin and his girlfriend started sleeping together and I knew that I had lost him for good. He pressured me to find a girl of my own and sleep with her, but I wasn't interested. The guy I fell for let me down; he switched over to the straight side and tried to drag me over with him. I couldn't change though. I was gay. While I may have been unable to say it out loud, I knew it then for sure.

I came to college with the intention of fitting in, being like everyone else, and graduating without attracting too much attention. I didn't envision life beyond college because, for me, there was no imaginable life. What gay role models did I have? My uncle and his boyfriend of twenty years? My family had made fun of them and their lifestyle since I was a baby. My understanding of grown-up gay men was that they were unhappy and disliked. This was hardly how I wanted to spend my life, so I blocked adulthood out of my mind. I imagined life until graduation and after that I figured I would disappear. I would go and live the life I wanted without worrying about how I would be judged. Thinking back, it's funny to even consider disappearing into obscurity. I have never been one to sit in the background and let others steal the show. That is not me.

As soon as I got to college, I met three of my future lacrosse teammates. We spent the first few weeks of school together while the rest of the class ran through orientation meetings and scavenger hunts and carnivals. I always knew that my teammates respected me for my abilities on the field, but I was worried about portraying the part of a heterosexual college athlete off the field. One night, early in our first term, a few of my teammates and I ended up in the dining hall on our way from one fraternity to another. When the first cute blonde girl walked by our table, each of my teammates followed her closely with their eyes. Did they notice that I forgot to pay particular attention to the blonde girl? Perhaps they were too distracted to see.

Driving to the fields one afternoon during fall practices a senior turned right to me and said, "Hey, what's your story? I never hear about you with the ladies. Do you get around?" I hesitated. A few seconds later, I managed a laugh. As I was about to respond with something like, "I'm not quite the player that you are," my roommate and best friend Chris jumped in and saved me. "He holds his own." And just like that, it was done. All it took was one sentence, one claim from a reliable source, and my manhood was restored. I didn't have to provide evidence, names and descriptions of each girl I had been with. I didn't even have to say a word. Chris saved me that time. I didn't know how much longer I could keep up the act.

When I later ended up telling Chris the truth, he shrugged his shoulders, smiled and gave me a high-five. That was Chris in a nutshell. He had a way of simplifying everything. Maybe he had really known all along and didn't need to make a big deal of it. Maybe it just didn't matter to him. He confirmed his confidence in me as a friend with a simple high-five. Why did something like this stress me out so much when I had friends who responded by giving me a high-five and a pat on the back?

During my sophomore year, as I was coming out, I roomed with Chris and Shane. Shane, my roommate for most of freshman year, was a fairly good-looking guy with brown hair who came from San Francisco. He was laid back, he liked to party, and we spent a lot of time together. I think Shane trusted me, and he appreciated my ability to make friends. We joked together, listened to music together, and most importantly we enjoyed each other's company. I felt that I had accomplished something important my freshman year, finding a quality friend at college.

While I didn't see Shane as the ideal mate, I certainly saw more than just a good friend. Many times, we would be up late at night studying, and we would end up getting into a wrestling match. If he ever sensed that I had become aroused by the physical contact, he never pulled back. I don't think that Shane was aroused in the same way that I was, but I am sure that he also saw me as more than just a close friend.

During my first three terms at college, I had experienced kissing and other intimate activities with girls on a few occasions, but I always came away from these nights feeling guilt from being unable to enjoy these "normal" activities, fear that the girl would see my lack of desire and tell on me, and a strange pleasure from participating in something that is supposed to bring me joy. At a dance party one night, Shane, seeing me turn down girls who might have been potential hookups, told two female friends that he thought I must be gay. The girls soon told me that my roommate and supposed best friend had been spreading a rumor about me. Completely uncomfortable with this situation, I laughed it off, thinking that my relaxed attitude would show these girls that I was clearly straight.

For three months, Shane and I continued to hang out and eat meals together, and we pledged the same fraternity at the beginning of the winter term. But there was no longer any depth to our relationship. It was clear what had driven us apart; he assumed I was gay and not telling him, while I was offended that he had spread rumors about me. I wrestled with the thought of coming out every day that fall term.

For years, I had considered myself gay, and I hadn't really questioned it in recent memory. But believing something and saying it out loud are two totally different things. When my friend Caitlin was over at my room one afternoon, I leaned toward her and whispered to her through cupped hands, "I'm gay." In saying these two words, it was like I truly became a homosexual. Up until that point, I only thought my homosexuality was something that could come true. But once those words were out of my mouth, I could never take them back. Caitlin shook her head in disbelief and repeated to me numerous times, "That's not a funny joke. I know you are kidding and it isn't funny." I put her hand up against my chest and she felt how fast my heart was beating. It took her twenty minutes of head shaking before she apologized for making this so difficult and not believing me in the first place. Caitlin was the only one I told for quite some time, but eventually I was able to say the words out loud and not feel bad about what I was saying.

My relationship with Shane was still fairly weak, and I felt partially responsible. So one night, instead of going to bed early as was my custom, I decided I would make the effort and appeal to him by staying up and making something of our broken friendship.

"Uhh . . . this is pretty hard to say. I feel like you know what I'm going to say but here goes. All that stuff you said about me, what you thought about me, well, you were right."

"Yeah I know, dude. No worries."

"Ha. Well, it has been pretty difficult for me trying to deal with everything and it didn't help much that you were spreading shit around. I don't know why you would have done that to me." He seemed to understand where I was coming from, and he apologized for the way he had handled it. That night we reestablished a closeness that we hadn't felt since our freshman year, and maybe formed a deeper friendship than ever.

Adam, an older brother in the fraternity I had just joined, e-mailed me one night after a frat event and asked me if I wanted to get something to eat with him.

Adam was about five-foot-ten, with a muscular build and gorgeous blue-green eyes. He was one of the better-looking seniors in school and he was openly gay. After a crazy night of drinking that next weekend, I awoke to read this e-mail in my in-box the next morning:

> Hey, here's the bottom line. I have a bit of a crush on you. I am really drunk tonight and I'm letting it all out. Sorry if this is not what you asked for by joining a fraternity. You seem like such a great guy and I don't want you to be unhappy . . .

Despite some of the drunken rambling, it appeared that he had made the first move. I wrote him back and explained to him that I understood his actions and that I am indeed gay. He asked me to meet up with him that night so we could talk.

I told my roommates that I was going to the library to meet a friend to go over some organic chemistry problems. I met Adam at his car; he suggested that I might feel more relaxed getting away from campus. Something about the comfort in his voice made me forget all about any sexual attraction I had for him. I thought, "Here is this guy who came out to his entire fraternity and even took a guy to his formal. He knows what it is like and he can show me the ropes and help me along." When I looked over at this handsome guy, I saw a big brother, a mentor. He told me about coming out to his family, how difficult that had been for him but how easy they had made it for him. Adam kept trying to get me to speak, to open up, but I preferred to listen.

We drove through back roads on a lightly snowing night, and the car went in and out of lighted areas, in and out of the shadows. I thought, "If my roommates knew I was driving around the dark areas of town with a homosexual, what would they think of me?" We drove by a familiar road that I remembered running once with my teammates in daylight. I thought about my teammates, seeing me now in this car. When other cars drove by, I turned to the side so they couldn't make out my identity.

Just before returning to my dorm, Adam pulled the car over in a shaded area. He started to breathe heavily and he started to babble something like, "Should I do it?" I asked him what was going on, and he just looked over and smiled. He reached his hand across my face. With this soft grip, he pulled my head toward his and we kissed. His heart was beating fast. I could feel his nervousness, but I did not share it. Perhaps I would have been more nervous if I had thought about it. But instead, I was thinking about the past, and how many kisses I had taken part in without feeling anything. The only kisses that I could remember were for show. In this car, I wanted to kiss him more. His lips, slightly chapped from the cold weather, met mine. His beard against my face was a new feeling. It was almost like I could feel his manliness rubbing against my face. My heart didn't start beating fast until he returned me to my dorm, when I thought of two things: how incredible that moment, my first kiss, was, and what I was going to tell my roommates.

After another evening in his car, I told Adam that we would have to choose a warmer spot. Those big winter jackets were ruining the moment. Adam and I agreed to meet in the library up in the stacks, an obscure area only inhabited during exams. Just being here with him was cause for concern, since he was openly gay. Someone who happened to go looking for an East Asian book at this time of night might stumble upon the two of us and piece things together. Sometimes I would close my eyes, clench my fists, and pray that I would not get caught. Other times I wished that somebody would just find me so I could end the whole charade and just bring Adam to my room like everyone else did with their girlfriends.

On Valentine's Day I told Adam that I wanted to spend the night with him more than anything. This was Valentine's Day, the day people spend with their special someone. I put on my khaki pants, a nice collared shirt, and I met Adam for dinner. On my way out the door, a few friends asked if I was going on a date, and I gave them a crazy look as if to say, "Me? Of course not. You guys know that I don't go on dates."

At dinner I told Adam that I wanted to get away from school with him, so that we could share this special night together. Each time I expressed this interest, he countered by reminding me that his room was only a five-minute walk down the path. I knew that. I also knew that he had three apartment-mates who were all in my fraternity. I couldn't bear to think that someone might see me walking into a room and immediately think "gay." Most of the older brothers in my fraternity thought of me first as the lacrosse player. I wanted them to get to know me before making judgments, but I didn't particularly mind the stereotype of the lacrosse player as it associated me with traditional masculine stereotypes. Being thought of as gay, however, evoked just the opposite stereotypes.

Eventually I gave in, willingly, but also feeling as though I was holding my breath under water and praying not to drown. I stood in the doorway at Adam's apartment unsure if I wanted to show my face. I took a deep breath and stepped around the corner. Bob, Adam's roommate and our fraternity brother, smiled and held out his hand to give me a high-five; Bob's girlfriend, Jennifer, said that it was good to see me again. Adam's eyes closed up just a bit as he smiled, one of those "I'm so proud of you and I don't want to forget this moment" type of smiles. Adam and I sat down next to each other on the couch, and I was sure that Bob and Jennifer would be completely conscious of every move that we made. I was wrong though. Holding hands, we watched television like any normal couple on Valentine's Day, and Bob and Jennifer couldn't have cared less about us. Bob was entranced by the show, laughing at every mildly funny joke. Jennifer, as self-conscious as anyone, was probably too worried about how she came off to notice me. As the evening went on, I began to undergo a transformation. I knew I wouldn't be instantly comfortable with this new self, but it was starting to grow on me.

After walking into his room Adam locked the door behind us, and I felt like we were alone, somewhere far off, like nobody could get to us now. He gave me a huge hug, as was his ritual, but this time our shirts were off and our chests met for the first time. He had a little bit of hair, but his chest was muscular, and you could feel the divisions of his abdominals. When we got into bed, everything felt so natural. It was one of those small college beds, wide enough for only one, so he slept on his back, and I slept on his chest. I turned my head to the side so that his shoulder became my pillow, and I lay down to sleep with my boyfriend, like lovers do on Valentine's Day.

We fell in love over the long, dark, cold winter at school. It happened on nights like our joy ride in the fogged up car, or when we waltzed across the frozen pond at two in the morning one night in February, or as we sat inside with hot chocolate as the wind howled down the street towards the river. I looked at him and saw a beautiful human being. Beyond his looks, he was an incredible person who thought of others before himself. He spent his afternoons with underprivileged children in the area and wanted to teach in the Bronx public schools after graduation. Besides all of this, he always showed a great deal of faith in me. I saw him as a role model as well as a boyfriend, and I saw no reason to break up in June. We said "I love you" to each other after we got back from a two-week spring break period without each other, and we never stopped saying it. Soon we would say the words so often that it began to feel like a greeting. Adam was my first love, and for this reason, I will always vividly remember moments spent with him.

We decided that as long as we cared about each other this much and weren't hurting anybody, we should stay together after his graduation. I was off from school in the fall term, and being away from school was a much different experience than being a student. I went to work each morning, came home each afternoon, went to the gym, ate dinner, watched a little television and went to bed to get some rest for work the next day. Every night before bed, Adam and I would talk on the phone and tell each other about how our days had gone. On weekends we would visit each other, and this became our motivation to get through the week.

All of this changed when I was back at school for winter term and Adam was still away. I no longer had a set schedule, and I wasn't always free at any point in the evening to call Adam. He got upset because he was used to stability, part of which was hearing my voice before he went to sleep. When he told me that he thought about me all day and couldn't wait to talk to me, I would have to be honest and tell him that he hadn't crossed my mind all day and that I couldn't really talk more than a few minutes.

Winter term was pledge term and one of the new pledges happened to be a boy on whom I had had my eye for over a year. Keith lived on my hall that year and something about him—maybe it was the way he looked at me—made me think that he could be gay as well. We had developed a friendship, and when he pledged my fraternity we got even closer. Many nights we drank together, and I always had a good time. Sometimes I would go home and start fantasizing about Keith, and I wouldn't stop to catch myself just because I was with Adam. I let the fantasies go because in my mind, they were just fantasies—there was no chance that they would come true. I was with Adam.

By March Adam and I both knew it wasn't working. He had emotional needs: someone to talk to on the phone, someone to visit him on weekends, someone to listen to him and care for him. I had little space for someone else in my life, and I resented Adam for making me feel guilty. While we both felt our relationship had deteriorated, we had separate solutions. He wanted us to find a way to make it work, while I found no need to do so. Something in my mind had changed, some critical connection, some brain synapse completely reversed. I felt like he was a lost soul, someone who had fallen into a mild depression with his job and life in a big city and that I could not be the savior that he wanted or needed. I needed to take care of myself.

I had cut off emotionally from the relationship long before, and by Friday, less than a week after the breakup, I again saw Adam as a friend, a role model. I made a point to go drinking with Keith at the fraternity that night, and when the night was over, I took him back to my room. I had assumed that it would take some convincing, but it didn't. As we walked home from the fraternity, we were in constant physical contact. We elbowed and pushed each other as we walked past the library and up a slight hill to get to the other side of campus where we both lived, and it seemed like our hands were touching so closely that we could have been holding hands. When we reached the point where the paths diverged to his room or mine, I continued on the path to my dorm.

"Where are you going?" he asked.

"To my room. Come." He nodded with a slight smile and followed me to my room. As I unlocked the door and we sat down on my futon a few inches from each other, I realized that I had no prior evidence to suggest that Keith was in fact a homosexual. I had gone on gut instinct up until this point, choosing, unlike Adam, not to e-mail him with my feelings. When I leaned over to kiss him, making the first move as the older, more experienced guy, I recognized a somewhat confused but overjoyed look in his eyes. He had never before kissed a guy, and he had never even imagined this scenario happening in college. His blue hat sat atop his head at a slight angle, and I positioned myself in front of him. He closed his eyes, perhaps not wanting to see what was really happening, and I could feel his breath. It was heavy, and his heart was beating fast, just as Adam's had when he had tried to kiss me the first time. I was not nervous, though, just elated. I had this boy in my room, this boy on whom I had had a crush since I first saw him more than a year and a half before.

Keith has a youthful, boyish look. He swims competitively, and his upper body is strong. Hair covers his upper chest. When one of us lies down on top of the other, Keith is a few inches shorter than me. That night, when I took his lacrosse cap off of his head, I took comfort in the fact that I was in my room alone with the kind of guy who wears a lacrosse cap, the type of guy who nobody would ever imagine to be in my room. Keith doesn't fulfill any of the gay stereotypes. He is the type to take me to a sports bar where people would wonder if we are just buddies or if we are on a date, an aspect of mystery or ambiguity that I enjoy. He has an air of masculinity about him, and this is part of what attracts me to him. We can sit around and push each other and watch sports together. We are best friends, and yet we are so much more than that. This is what I had idealized since I was in seventh grade.

I have learned so much about myself, about the world, and about relationships from my two boyfriends in college. Adam was gay, everyone knew, and he wasn't ashamed. He told me that being gay was a blessing because he had the chance to change people's minds, and that he joined a fraternity because he wanted to teach tolerance to the Greek system. Keith, on the other hand, joined a fraternity because he wanted to meet new people, get closer with the members of his pledge class, and have a good time while at college. His reasons were much more like mine. We both like the party scene, the brother bonding activities, and the tight friendships that we have made.

I have always been a fairly public and social member of my fraternity, and when I came out, nothing changed. My brothers respected me for who I was, and we never had any problems. I never meant to change anyone's mind, as Adam did, but just my presence and my confidence as one of the guys changed the way people acted in a positive way. For instance, when our social chair tells us about our parties, he tells us to "feel free to invite all significant others to the pre-party," a subtle change from saying, "bring a girlfriend," something he said he did for me. Dating one of my fraternity brothers has been a touchy subject for some, but they were never vocal about it. Most of the guys were fine with it.

Being gay is a reality for me, something that was probably determined by the time I came out of my mother's womb. I haven't openly questioned why it happened to me in many years. At certain times, being gay has made me privileged. I have had the chance to affect many more people as an openly gay athlete or member of a fraternity than I would have otherwise. Being an athlete has always given me some sort of crutch in order to feel comfortable and secure with myself. Athletics are often associated with masculinity, and I have always used this conception to forge my identity. Perhaps I am a homosexual, but nobody perceives me as weak or feminine.

Coming into my senior year, I knew the younger members of the gay community at school would look up to me, and I thought that I should take a more active role in that community. I am now an officer in the Gay Straight Alliance, where we meet once a week and discuss important gay issues on the campus and beyond. It is a great chance to get to know guys a few years below me who are going through a lot of the same experiences I did. Now I see freshmen who have already come out to their friends and who contemplate joining a fraternity as an openly gay pledge, something I never imagined. At our weekly meetings, we often look at the state of gay rights in the country today. I have never been extremely interested in politics, but the Massachusetts Supreme Court ruling in 2003 inspired me, and I am not about to give up the right to equal marriage. Half a century ago, people said that interracial marriages were wrong and unnatural. Even though the courts saw this as discriminatory, it took another ten years for the country to recognize legal interracial marriages. Now that the courts have found discrimination in our current laws, how much longer must we wait while our country again holds back equal rights to its citizens?

As I look back at my college career, I am glad that I have figured things out in time to really enjoy myself. My original intention to leave college without making much noise, without impacting people or leaving my mark, failed, and I am extremely happy about that. Through college, I met a few people who convinced me to do my own thing, and I know that I benefited from this advice. Now when I get the chance to talk to younger guys, guys who still have important decisions to make in their college years, I tell them to be themselves, do what matters to them, and their friends will be there. I hope they listen to me, and I hope their time in college is as rewarding as mine has been.

For many years I worried about how I was going to come out to family. Now my mother, father, sister, and brother are the most supportive people in my life. My parents continue to love me; my mother brags about my accomplishments to her friends and my father keeps pictures from my athletic career in his office. This past winter, Keith came with me on a family ski trip, joining my sister and her boyfriend, and my brother and his wife. Both of my siblings are older than me, both are in serious relationships, and, for a few years, I had felt a distance between us. Part of me wanted to show them that my relationship is no different; that our relationship can last as long as theirs. On that ski trip, it was clear that the distance no longer remained. We treat each other like we always have, only now we respect each other as adults.

In the end, I have learned that all romantic relationships are made up of the same components. There is intimacy. There is passion. There is love. Adam and I had all three of these. Keith and I are lucky because we are also best friends. Our relationship is not different from any other college relationship. We go on dates, go to dance parties together, go to formal occasions together, and we wake up in the morning after spending the night together. After college, we would like to share a life, a family. It might be a little more difficult to have children, but we will have them and they will be loved as much as any children on this earth. For the rest of my life, I know that I will encounter people who do not understand me. I also know that I will continue to affect others, because I can change people's minds simply by being honest and by being true to myself.

COLOR-BLIND

*The daughter of an African American father and white Austrian mother, this
college senior was blissfully unaware of racial identity questions during
childhood. As she entered college, however, she began to realize that there was
a powerful racial subtext to her relationships with white men. Realizing for
the first time that some white men desire her because of her color and some
exclude her for the same reason she began to question many aspects of what it
means to be biracial in American society. Likewise, she experienced the
condemnation of black students at college for her interracial dating. Caught
in the middle, and now believing her parents' "color-blind" upbringing of her
to have been naïve and unhelpful, Christine engages in a painful process of
questioning her basic assumptions about race and identity.*

My parents talk little about their interracial marriage and the difficulties they have
encountered as a couple. My father grew up in Alabama, my mother in a small
town in Austria. My father never shared with me his mother and sister's disapproval of his marriage to my mother. I am only aware of this because on one or two
occasions, my mother had made a reference to their hostility toward her and me
during the first two years we were in the United States. After being told of my father's intention of marrying my mother, my grandmother strongly opposed it and
refused to welcome "white trash" into her family. And for a long time, I was not
welcome in her home either, because I was the child of such a sinful marriage.
Once, at about age 2, when I was visiting my father's stepsister, my grandmother
allowed me into her home, though she still rejected my mother, her "white"
daughter-in-law.

My memory of the visit escapes me, but according to my mother, all of the
grandchildren were visiting my grandmother at the time. A cheerful and bubbly
child, I had arrived at her house in good spirits, but when my mother returned, I
was extremely quiet and sad. My mother says that my grandmother had given
gifts to all of her visiting grandchildren except for me—the granddaughter of a
condemned marriage. That was the last time I visited my grandmother until I was

much older. I visited her in a retirement home when she had Alzheimer's disease several months before she passed away. Despite my grandmother's inexcusable actions, I never hated her, nor did either of my parents ever speak negatively about her. My parents attributed her dislike for their marriage to her age and the cultural attitudes of the South.

My paternal grandfather, however, adored my mother. Though I was not extremely close to him, I did see more of him than I did my grandmother from whom he was divorced. He visited us occasionally while I was growing up and my family had once gone to see him in Alabama when I was 16 years old. During our short visit to the South, my family noticed that people stared at us a little longer, both because we were strangers in the segregated town and we were an interracial family. Despite the stares and scrutiny we experienced we dismissed the stares as the stupidity of the South. We did comment on the silliness of it all, but we did not discuss the social implications or the challenges we as children of a biracial marriage might experience as we got older.

Race was not an awkward topic for my family to discuss; we were comfortable with being members of an interracial family. It just did not make sense to dislike someone based on skin color. As difficult as it is to comprehend I never looked at my parents as a black father and a white mother; they were simply my parents. I grew up "color-blind." I knew that they were black and white respectively, but I did not understand what that meant. I was unaware of the difficulties both the black and white communities could have with an interracial couple. I had not yet been personally touched by the hostilities and disapproval of the outside world.

My mother's family was not thrilled about my parents' marriage either, but for different reasons. They did not want their daughter to move to the United States. As a result of the distance and language barrier, I was not close to my mother's parents. Despite their disapproval, my parents were married. I know that my parents had gone through a difficult period during the beginning of their relationship as a result of family members and strangers disagreeing with their choice to marry each other, but my parents were able to weather the difficult times and, overall, they have had a successful marriage.

The eldest of three, I am a child of this Austrian and African American union. My sister is three years younger, and my brother is five years younger. My parents married in Austria while my father was in the service. Soon after I was born, we returned to the United States. Four states and two children later, my family settled in a small, predominantly white community near Portland, Oregon, when I was in the second grade. My father had left the army and had taken a job in law enforcement, and my mother began a career in teaching. For the most part, my community was not ethnically diverse. There were very few African Americans in my public schools as I was growing up, and I was not good friends with any. Overall, my closest friends were white.

Before people knew me or my family in my new town, I sometimes had to answer questions about adoption and why my mother was white. I vividly remember in the second grade, a friend asking me if my mother was my real mom. Even after answering yes, it was still unclear to her how it could be that I had dark skin and my mother had light skin. I had to explain to her that my mother was white and that my father was black. Sometimes classmates would look at my mother with her white skin and blonde hair, then look at me with my black hair and dark brown skin, and in a somewhat surprised and confused voice ask, "That's your mom?" Occasionally, children (and adults) would ask me where my mother was as she stood next to me. Someone once asked me, "If your father had been white and your mother black, would you also be white?" I never took offense at the questions; I simply answered and tried to explain, though there were times when I wished I didn't have to. The one offensive comment I remember, which I did not think of as offensive at the time, came from a friend in high school. She had previously lived in San Diego and one day said to me, "You don't act like the black people I knew in San Diego." It did not occur to me to respond back, "Well, you don't act like the white people I knew in Boston."

My first discussion about race and ethnicity took place during an intense program the summer before my senior year in high school. In the midst of the emotional and mental stimuli during the program's week of "racism and oppression," I was forced to ask myself questions about my background and beliefs. The issue of race hit close to home when Greg, a student in the program and a child of a biracial marriage, shared his personal struggles of growing up in Portland, Oregon, and the difficulty he sometimes faced as being neither black nor white. As he spoke about his background, Greg prompted questions I had never been faced with before. I found myself partly relating to some of his frustrations and not relating to others. For the first time, I wanted to examine my experience as a biracial child. However, in spite of my interest, I was hesitant and did not seize the moment. The social implications of being a biracial child was a new topic for me. I was confused and uncertain about my feelings. For the most part, I had always had a good sense of who I was, but that afternoon as I listened to Greg speak, I wondered. I was 17 years old and I asked myself why my identity was now being questioned. Planning to leave home for college after my senior year in high school, I could not afford to *not* know who I was. I sat there in silence. That summer, the door on race had been opened, but I soon returned to my placidly comfortable home. It would not be until I entered college that the conversation would begin again, and I would be forced to explore the issues surrounding my biracial identity.

The issue of race was never really discussed in my home. Sometimes, we discussed it on a political level, referring to others, but it was never seriously discussed on a personal level in reference to my family. Only once, when I was in the tenth or eleventh grade, did my mother raise the topic seriously. After she had watched a news program on biracial families the night before, she asked us at dinner if we ever had problems being children of a mixed marriage. We all answered no, and we moved on to another topic. I believe my parents had thought it better to wait until we brought up the issue of race, but after seeing the TV show, my mom thought perhaps she better finally raise the topic herself. Since none of us said we had any difficulty, she left it alone. I honestly do not believe that either of my parents were aware of the special challenges we were to face when we got older.

Overall, I was well liked and successful in school; I was ranked fifteenth in my high-school class. I was an athlete on the state track and gymnastics teams, and as the junior-class president, I was very active in student government. I was also president of our honor society, was homecoming princess, and was voted "most likely to succeed" my senior year. I spent most of my time with a small group of close friends, but I also had other friends from many different cliques: the jocks, the stoners, the brains, and so on. Although I was well liked, I never dated nor even kissed anyone in high school. In fact, when I was homecoming princess, I had to ask a male friend from out of town to accompany me to the dance. Though I was delighted and surprised to be given the title, I was also embarrassed and confused about not having a date.

While in high school, I never considered the possible effect race could have had on my relationships with boys. I guess I didn't consider skin color to be an issue because there were two interracial couples in my school, and my sister had also dated a white guy. I also wasn't really interested in dating, so I didn't give it much thought. The few times I did think about it, like most girls, I was more insecure and self-conscious about my body weight and appearance than my racial identity. However, I did not know what was in store for me after leaving my hometown.

The door of racial consciousness that had been opened a little the summer before my senior year was opened wide when I entered college. Before I left for college, my parents did not warn me of the difficulty I would encounter as a result of my ethnic identity. Whether because they themselves did not know what I would encounter, or did not know how to broach the topic, or were trying to protect me, I cannot say. Perhaps as a white person, my mother could not relate, and therefore could not know what I would experience. As a black child of the South, perhaps my father found the issue of race too painful to discuss. I do not know. In any event, the two extremes of their respective colors meant they would not be able to understand my experience as a mixture of them both.

During the first week of freshman fall, I met Vanessa and Shawna, who were to become two of my closest friends. It would be the first time in my life that I was to be good friends with anyone African American. I do not remember our first conversation about race, but I clearly remember debating and even arguing about the implications of being an African American in the United States. We argued about "imposed definition"—the way outsiders perceive each person—and "self-definition"—the way one perceives oneself. I argued that since I was only half black, I could not align myself with one race or the other and, more importantly, that race was not significant. I frequently got the response that we live in a racist society that will never be color-blind. In shock and frustration, friends tried to tell me of the historical backdrop still affecting many blacks today. However, I did not care about ancestors from years ago. In my mind, my background was limited to knowing that my mother was born in Austria and my father in the United States. It was that simple. Even though it struck me as very interesting that so many African American students at my college thought their roots were very important and felt it crucial to strive to obtain more facts, I lacked the desire to do the same.

I believe this attitude was linked to my parents' lack of encouragement during my earlier years to discover my heritage, though now they are very encouraging. My black friends seemed to have parents who strongly encouraged them to explore their past.

I was frequently told by friends and acquaintances that society will always label me as a black woman regardless of my mixed background. Sometimes mistaking my desire to claim my European background as wishing to identify with the dominant culture, people questioned my allegiance to the black community. In response, I argued that by identifying myself solely as black I was denying a part of me. In addition, I found it unfair that blacks were given the right to claim their mixed ethnic-racial heritage, whether it be Cuban-African-American or Haitian-African-American, but as an Austrian-African-American I was challenged. My friends tried to reassure me that they were not trying to deny my Austrian heritage. They questioned why I didn't know more about my black ancestors. Sometimes I felt I had to recognize only my African American heritage in order to avoid being accused of succumbing to the dominant culture's pressures and beliefs. Regardless of others' definitions and explanations, I could never quite comprehend the importance of defining oneself by race or ethnicity. As a product of a family that did not stress race, it seemed odd to me for such emphasis to be placed upon one's racial background. I was criticized as being too idealistic for stressing the primary importance of regarding people as human rather than as members of a racial group.

Another point of tension was the role of ethnic affinity houses on campus. Confused and uncertain about the intent and purpose of these organizations, I often debated with Vanessa and Shawna about the purpose of these groups. Though I now understand the need for the African American organization and other affinity houses, at the time I could not comprehend the need for such groups. Why was it that a WASP-only organization would be considered racist, yet the college African American organization was not? I felt that these organizations negatively accentuated the differences between races and further secluded themselves from the rest of the college community. It was explained to me that the college African American organization was needed for some students because the college campus was not a diverse environment and the organization helped minority students adjust. In my opinion, the opposite was true. There were many people of color at my college, and I found the campus to be diverse.

The African American organization was a very uncomfortable place for me. I did not understand the slang being used, nor the hairstyles and products members referred to, or in some instances, even the food they were discussing. Needless to say, I was not active in the African American organization. The only organization presentation that I attended was on the topic of interracial relationships, or "Jungle Fever." The guest speaker was an actor in the movie Jungle Fever, directed by Spike Lee. He shared his positive experience of having dated a white woman, but his sincerity and love for her was challenged by some members of the audience. Theories on why this successful black man was dating a white woman ranged from his insecurities and self-hatred as a black man to his desire to have the "great prize" or "trophy" at his side. Although not everyone spoke negatively about interracial relationships, I left saddened, angry, and frustrated. I was upset with one audience member in particular. He criticized the black male who marries a white woman, concluding that such a man possesses many insecurities, and that a "true black man" marries his "strong black queen." This statement was made after I shared my experience as a child of an interracial marriage. I couldn't help but feel that his comment was directed at me.

Even at the time of the Rodney King incident when, ironically, I was enrolled in my first black history course, I was not active in "race politics" at my school. I remember gazing out of the classroom window and watching the protests and speeches on the quad, as my history professor spoke of the injustices and struggles of the past. I did not participate in any of the protests and marches; I was still determining my new identity as a minority and what it all meant. My sister, on the other hand, was very involved in the forums and speeches at her conservative college. Like many of the minority students at my school, she felt frustrated with her student body's general lack of concern and understanding of the sensitive issues surrounding the Rodney King case. She told me about her frustrations in trying to educate others on race, while also concentrating on her studies. She felt it should not be her job to enlighten the rest of the campus and that she might be happier at a historically black college. My sister came to feel so strongly about this that she left school to take time off. She is currently applying to schools and hopes to find a more intellectual campus with a strong black student body.

I cannot explain why my sister was able to find and cultivate a stronger tie to the black community than I did. During college, she and I discussed the issue of race several times, and though we have similar opinions and viewpoints, we inevitably end up arguing and abruptly ending our discussion in frustration. I tell her I do not understand how she can feel a connection with the black slaves and experience their suffering any more than I can understand how young Jewish people relate to the pain and suffering of their ancestors in the Holocaust. I can sympathize as a human being, but I can't understand how skin color can create a stronger link and greater understanding of others' suffering. I also do not understand her new belief that, except for our mother, she no longer has anything in common with white people. Our conversations usually end with her accusing me of being influenced by the dominant white forces. Ironically, of the three children in my family, she is the lightest skinned, yet she is the most "militant" in advancing the "black cause." I think her new attitudes are the result of her experience at her small conservative college and the influence of her African American boyfriend and other black friends.

My brother is a junior in high school and is coming to terms with his biracial identity two years earlier than I did. In general, we share some of the same experiences and feelings, though he is more enlightened than I ever was during my early stages of discovery. He has been confronted with race issues and has discussed the implications with my parents. At his predominantly white, well-to-do prep school, he has been challenged by a few of the black students. They question his allegiance to the black community and, on occasion, remind him of his skin color. In spite of our similar experiences, unlike me, my brother has become involved in his school's African American club. Always struggling to keep a foot in both communities, he sometimes finds the fight exhausting.

My most upsetting brush with racial conflict occurred one Friday night in a fraternity basement. I was hanging out and having a good time with a friend who happened to be a white male, when I noticed a black male across the room giving me disapproving looks. Uncertain as to what would warrant such stares, I ignored him and continued talking and laughing with my friend. Eventually the stranger approached me as I went to the bar to get a drink. Taking the liberty to judge my behavior, he informed me that it was wrong for a black woman to date a white man, that we need to stick together and keep the race strong; we cannot dilute it by mixing with other races. With his light brown skin, he looked like a product of a biracial marriage himself. Overcome with complete disbelief, I stood there numb. I was first overcome with shock and anger, which was followed by sadness, and then I was angry again. No one had ever told me personally that interracial relationships were wrong, and I had never been condemned for associating with white males. I was outraged at the stranger. First of all, the male to whom I was talking was just a friend, and second, race should not dictate with whom I will be intimate. Furthermore, I felt he was unfairly judging me and my family.

My friend took me outside to calm me down. He tried to comfort me, but neither he nor anyone could understand the anger and frustration I felt. I left the fraternity alone; I needed to reflect on what had just happened. After calming down, I thought about my parents' marriage and thought about the hardships they must have endured to make their marriage a success. I also wondered if they ever conceived of the hardships their children were to experience as products of their marriage. A few days later, I saw the same guy on campus, and he apologized. I later learned that he came from a very wealthy family and attended a predominantly white prep school. I also found out that his sister was to marry a white man in a few weeks.

Despite that very upsetting incident, I did subsequently have a five-month romantic relationship with a nonblack male at school. His name was John and he was Jewish American. During the time we were together, I never felt judged by the college community nor did I question the community's feelings on interracial dating. That is, not until I saw a fellow student's documentary film on interracial dating on my campus. I went to see the film with one of John's best friends and a friend of mine. After seeing the film, I was disappointed that John had missed it. I believed that the film would have prompted us to discuss our interracial relationship on a personal level that we had not done before. Now I wanted to know how his friends and fraternity brothers felt about him dating someone of a different race. Was he ever confronted by others with the issue of dating a black woman? Before the film, I would have definitely said no, but after the shocking testimonies in the film, I wasn't so sure. Although I ultimately knew that dating across color lines was not a concern for him and that what other people thought did not dictate whom he would date, I was still curious to know if, as an individual in an interracial relationship, he ever felt judged by others.

John and I talked about race early on in our relationship. I was aware from the very beginning that he wanted to marry someone Jewish. On one of the first nights we went out, we talked into the early hours of the morning about his desire to marry someone Jewish. However, our discussion was not on a personal level; it had been a philosophical-sociological discussion, and we did not examine our potential interracial relationship. He tried to explain and justify to me his conscious choice to marry someone within his own cultural group. As someone who was struggling with self-definition and imposed definition and having never felt any strong feelings for one race or another, I found it difficult to understand why and how at the age of 21 he could eliminate all women of races and cultures other than his own as potential partners in marriage. Although John himself had a strong sense of his Jewish culture and had strong ties with his background, his parents were certainly a powerful influence in his decision. I wondered if they were aware that their son was dating a black woman and what their reaction would be. I never asked him because I didn't want to put him in the awkward position of having to defend his parents. Also, I did not want him to get the idea that because I was interested in his parents' potential opinion of me, that I was therefore thinking about marrying him.

The following summer I spoke with a black woman who had a strong desire to marry an African American, and for the first time I had an understanding of why someone would prefer to marry within their own race and cultural group. She said that she would not rule out marrying someone of another race or background but believed that there were many things she experienced as a result of her race which could not be explained to someone who had not experienced it. Her potential husband would have to belong to the same group in order to understand this important aspect of her life.

I had many questions about race and relationships, and the documentary only provoked more. John was my first real boyfriend, and we had been dating for four months. I wanted to share with him my uncertainties about our dating. I feared being viewed as a mere "college toy" since, in his eyes, as an African American woman, I was not marriage material. I wondered why he believed he could only marry a Jewish woman, yet he dated women from other ethnic groups. His previous girlfriend was white. Though I was not in any way interested in marriage, after the film and the discussions I had with others about the issue of interracial dating, I was curious about the role I played for him. I never believed that John would date someone based strictly on skin color, and I never thought that he had an ulterior motive for dating me, but after the film I learned that some people are fascinated with skin color and consider it all a game, while others consider crossing racial lines a sin.

I had always found someone attractive based on their looks and personality and I never thought about getting involved with someone based on their skin color. After seeing the film and having a number of discussions about interracial dating, I realized that some people actually do think that way. All the faces in the documentary were familiar; they were faces I had seen in the library, the student center, dining halls, and at parties. I was surprised at the number of people, both black and white, who were opposed to interracial dating, and I was disturbed by the film's story of a failed relationship largely due to the external pressures of disapproving outsiders. With it already so difficult to find that special someone, why did some people feel adamantly opposed to interracial couples?

In the film, there were two white students who admitted to having "jungle fever." A woman spoke of the black male anatomy and said she had once begun dating a black man based solely on the old myth that black men were better endowed sexually. A white male spoke of his attraction for black women because, according to him, they were better in bed. I sat there disgusted. I could not believe my ears as I listened to their ridiculous claims. I was particularly disgusted with that same white male who, the term before, had told a friend of mine that he found me attractive. I felt disgusting and dirty as I sat in the auditorium and listened to him openly express his racist feelings and desires for black women. What I once thought to be a compliment was nothing more than attraction for my skin color, a false association with great sex. I sat there quiet. I did not want anyone to know that I had been an object of those feelings, that I had once evoked such sick thoughts. I knew I wasn't to blame for his offensive sexual lust, but I could not help feeling dirty and ashamed. This is the guy who had smiled and waved to me crossing the quad on the way to classes. The same guy who was so nice to me in the library, cafe, and in the gym. I could not believe my ears. I kept asking myself if he was acting or were these his true feelings. I had believed him to be a nice and sincere guy. I had guessed that the reason he was extremely nice to me was that he liked me, but I would have never imagined it was because of my skin color. As he continued to talk about how black women are great in bed, he made me feel like an animal. I asked myself how many other guys honestly believe in the myth. I never once considered that someone might be interested in me because they believed it would be "fun" to date a black woman. Was this guy's attitude the exception?

The documentary left me with a lot of unanswered questions. Following the film, I had an interesting conversation with a black student who was one of John's best friends. He desperately tried to describe his frustrations as one of only two black males in a predominantly white fraternity. He described feeling as if white women only wanted to be his friend. He attributed his lack of girlfriends to two things: Few black women came to hang out in his fraternity, and nonblack women were not interested in him since he was a black man. He asked, "You belong to a predominantly white sorority, don't you sometimes feel the same way?"

"It's not a white sorority. My house is ethnically mixed. There are women of many different backgrounds," I said.

"Whatever," he replied. "There are only what, three black women in your house?"

"To tell you the truth," I said, "I never thought about my skin color being an attraction or a turn-off for males. I understand the getting-a-date-for-housefunction-blues, but I never attributed the difficulty to the color of my skin."

My thoughts on the issue continued to spin, particularly about the reasons and implications of crossing race lines. Why was it that I never blamed my skin color for not having a date, yet my friend did? Perhaps my European features "saved" me. The next week, after doing a lot of self-questioning and exploring, I brought the topic up at dinner with a group of black female friends: "Do you think some men are attracted to black women on the sole basis that the woman is black?" I asked. The question was greeted with a simultaneous "Yes!" I was surprised that without any hesitation or moment of discussion they all agreed. One woman stated, "I was told by a friend in a historically black Greek house that he has heard about a mainstream fraternity on campus that actually has a contest to see who can sleep with a woman of each ethnic/racial group. Each race is ranked, and depending upon the woman's background, the guy gains points. It's something like, if the woman is Korean, the guy gets 10 points, Puerto Rican 20 points, and so on. I don't know all the details, but that's what I heard," she said.

"Do you honestly believe that?" I asked in disbelief.

"Yes. It's definitely not something in which the entire house participates, but it's definitely believable. It's just a question of which house." I didn't know how to react. I was just shocked by the thought. I could feel chills down my spine and I was disturbed by the rumor.

It was nauseating to think that someone could become involved with someone else because of skin color and, worse yet, to win a contest. The male was considered the victor of a stupid and disgusting contest; the woman a mere victim. Was it possible that guys at school, supposedly intelligent males, would do such a thing? I called a friend, who is also a minority, and told her of the rumor. She didn't seem at all surprised.

"Do you think that story is true? Do you think there have been guys who have been attracted to me because of my skin color?" I asked.

"Yeah," she replied. "Not all guys, but I am sure that there have been some who liked you because of your skin. Not to say that no one has ever liked you for you, or that you are not attractive, but your combination of dark skin color and traces of European features are a combination of the forbidden and the embraced. Mike liked you for your skin color, and Billy once told me that it was obvious to him that you were not all black. He said he could tell by your nose, cheek bones and hair." I didn't understand her point.

"And what are you saying?" I asked her.

"Well, in Billy's case, I got the sense that your European features assured him that you are not black; therefore, it is okay for him to like you. And as for the guy in the film, your black skin appealed to him, as it does to others who have 'jungle fever.' In both cases, race is an issue—in a negative sense."

For a very brief moment after that discussion, I thought about questioning the motives of all guys interested in me. I could never, however, bring myself to confront any of them with this serious question. I eventually abandoned my shaky belief that race affected my relations with males because it was difficult for me to believe or comprehend that anyone would date someone from a different race or ethnic group out of curiosity or because they thought it would be fun. It just seemed so ridiculous to me. It was not until recently that I began to contemplate seriously the role race has played in my interpersonal relationships.

John had gone to Israel during the summer before our senior year, and during his stay, his ties to his Jewish culture were strengthened. It was a day after returning for our senior year of college that we broke up. I wasn't devastated by the split. During the summer, I had also been thinking about breaking it off; I wanted to be able to spend as much time as possible with friends before graduating. John stumbled through the words when he broke up with me. He mentioned how spending time in Israel really confused him, his parents were pressuring him, he just needed to work through the garbage, and he thought it best if we broke up. Later, when I asked him to please better explain what happened, he simply said that he didn't want to be tied down and didn't want to be in a relationship. Nine weeks later, he started dating someone else. She was Jewish.

Although my experience as a biracial child has at times been difficult, I do not disparage interracial relationships. As a result of my parents' marriage, I believe I hold a unique perspective on the world. I have realized that my skin color may be an attraction to some men and a turn-off to others. I need to confront this issue and ask the next person I become serious about whether I am being ruled-out or ruled-in because of my skin color. I sometimes feel that as a biracial woman I have one more doubt to add to the list of insecurities most women experience when dating. "Does he have 'jungle fever' and like me because I am black? Or does he consider it a sin to mix the races and dislike me because I am black?"

I am still exploring and defining who I am. During my senior year in college, my younger sister wrote me a letter encouraging me not to worry about the future and "life after college." She wrote, "Gather your strength and confidence from our ancestors." With the letter, she included a short family tree. It was then that I discovered my great-grandparents were Native American on my paternal grandmother's side and that my great-grandfather on my father's side was West Indian. It came as a surprise to learn I have even more "mixed blood" than I realized, but so, too, do many black Americans.

In retrospect, it is difficult for me to say whether I would have liked for my parents to broach the topic of race while I was growing up. I sometimes wish that they had talked about the implications of being biracial. Other times, I am very thankful for the journey of self-discovery. I have come to terms with what it means for me to be a biracial child in this country and I am at peace with my self-definition. But I also realize that there is a continuous struggle between self-definition and the external perceptions and assumptions of others. People continue to make judgments and assumptions about my actions based on my skin color. It is usually very subtle, and I find it difficult to address. Recently, a colleague of mine at work told me she knew of a very attractive black man whom I should meet. After her comment, I questioned if she would have given the same offer to a white colleague. Did she assume that I would only date black men? Did she think I should only date black men? Would she have said to a white woman, "I know an attractive white man whom you should meet?"

I also have to cope with many of the same injustices from the white community as all minorities do. As a child of a black-white union, I carry a part of my white mother with me wherever I go, so it is sometimes difficult to feel aligned with the black cause when it requires taking sides between the white and black communities. I have come to define myself as neither black nor white, but as a union of the two. I am still exploring the definitions and implications of the terms black, brown, African American, mixed, mulatto, and so on. I am definitely more enlightened than I was when I began this journey of self-discovery and definition, but I have much more to learn and sort out. I've begun to research my background and have contacted my oldest living relative on my father's side to find out more about my heritage. My grandmother on my mother's side is also helping put the pieces together. I want to be able to give my children the gift of the past. I realize now that my family does not just consist of my parents and siblings. Regardless of the questions in my own mind and those of others regarding my biracial identity, I know who I am and I am proud.

PART III

CHALLENGES

THEORETICAL OVERVIEW

Within the field of adolescent research there exists a debate over whether adolescence is typically a period of storm and stress, of alienation and separation, or a more harmonious evolution in which positive feelings about self and family are extended into the larger realms of peers and society. Each of these perspectives has merit and accounts for the different individual circumstances and coping styles of a complex period of human development. One point of agreement in this debate is that adolescence is a period of radical transformation of the physical and psychological self. Even under the best of circumstances, adolescents travel an exquisitely poignant journey through difficult developmental terrain. Finding one's way would be challenge enough, but when the ground is continually shifting with the ongoing physical, emotional, and cognitive growth of this period, the journey becomes full-time work for most adolescents. When the ordinary stresses of adolescence are overlaid with extraordinary additional stresses, there emerge important risk factors for healthy development. The cases in this section explore both the dangers and strategies for coping with these challenges.

Our notion of "challenges" implies obstacles or special difficulties that must be negotiated in addition to all the more "typical" preoccupations and developmental tasks of adolescence. Challenges are important both because of what they tell us about adolescent coping strategies in general, and because many adolescents face such circumstances at some point. If we add up all the adolescents who must deal with challenges such as physical disabilities; serious illness; divorce; the death of a parent, sibling, or close friend; physical or sexual abuse; mental illness, and so on, we can see that significant challenges, whether acute or chronic, represent, if not the norm, at least a sizable subsample of all adolescents. An autobiographical exploration of challenges also provides the reader a window into resilience. It allows us to learn which coping strategies and character traits appear to be most protective and even promotive of adolescent mental health.

Each of the five cases included in this section represents a distinct challenge to healthy psychological growth at multiple developmental periods: (1) a severe stutter and serious sexual abuse in early childhood, (2) the emotional crisis surrounding an abortion in adolescence, (3) a journey from war refugee to immigrant to the United States and gradual acculturation, (4) the problems presented by untreated attention deficit/hyperactivity disorder (ADHD) and of conflicts with a parent with serious substance abuse, and (5) the special obstacles faced along the adolescent journey posed by a significant physical disability. Taken as a whole, these cases highlight both what is unique and universal, at least for Western culture; unique, in terms of specialized issues these problems raise for adolescent development; universal, in that the cases highlight the way in which the tasks of adolescence remain relatively constant even in the face of powerfully destabilizing events and extraordinary stessors. The overlay of preexisting emotional, social, or physical problems to the already daunting tasks of adolescence can further complicate the transition to adulthood. At the same time, and more hopefully, the evolving ability throughout adolescence to engage in abstract, analytical thought in combination with increasing emotional and physical autonomy and separation can make it possible for the adolescent to overcome some of the more debilitating psychological effects of these issues.

Self-understanding is one of the more important aspects of emerging adolescent abilities for overcoming serious challenges. Prior to adolescence, childhood is characterized by the embeddedness of the child in his or her family and the profound tendency, whether for better or worse, to identify with important persons and norms within the family. The increasing importance of the peer world and the simultaneously evolving capacity to see parents as less powerful and more fallible are conducive to a loosening and diversification of earlier identifications. This evolving capacity for perspective can facilitate healing through important substitute relationships such as teachers, mentors, peers, families of friends, and others (Noam, Powers, Kilkenny, & Beedy, 1990). Such healing may be necessary when families have not been sufficiently nurturing, protective, or enhancing of self-esteem. While these relationships may also be important at earlier periods, the adolescent can increasingly see her *self* through the eyes of these important others. This fresh perspective allows the adolescent to take a more autonomous approach to creating a self of her own choosing. There has long been recognition that this emergent ability to gain self-knowledge and perspective through interaction with others—this "looking glass self" (Cooley, 1902; G. H. Mead, 1934)—helps explain why positive relationships can have such a restorative effect on the damage of earlier events. This "mirroring" becomes especially salient in peer and romantic relationships during this time (Sullivan, 1953; Erikson, 1968) as the adolescent learns to take a perspective on herself by means of gradually modifying the self she sees reflected in the eyes of peers.

Self-understanding has been shown to be an important "protective factor" (Beardslee, 1989) in ameliorating the risk to healthy psychological development from serious life stressors. Ideally, self-understanding should lead to action that transforms one's adaptation to circumstances or changes the circumstances themselves. It is only when insight leads to new and better means of coping with life's challenges that we can say the individual is rising to the challenge. Indeed, insight without action can reflect a profound sense of hopelessness. The cases presented here all reveal the adolescent biographers reacting to significant stress by first developing insight and then taking steps to make things better.

An important emerging field within developmental psychology is devoted to studying individuals who are resilient or seemingly invulnerable to serious risks and stresses that have been shown to affect negatively the mental health and long-term adjustment of many children. This relatively new field represents a significant historic shift from studying almost exclusively those individuals who succumb to developmental risks to studying those who are equally exposed but who overcome the risk and remain healthy. Among the factors shown to place children at risk are serious mental illness of a parent, physical or sexual abuse, serious marital discord, poverty, emotionally unsupportive relationships with parents, foster home placement, and parental alcoholism (Rutter, 1975, 1979; Werner, 1989). While different studies find differing degrees of relative risk for each of these and other factors, it is found that, when only a single risk factor was present, the probability that a child would suffer from a psychiatric disorder was no greater than for a child in a family without any of these risk factors. However, two risk factors produced a fourfold increase in the chances of a psychiatric disorder in the child; four risk factors produced a tenfold increase in risk. It would seem that most children can cope with a certain amount of stress stemming from these risks, but when overloaded with multiple stressors, they become exponentially more likely to succumb. Many children and adolescents, however, do not succumb even under such stress. Therein lies a hopeful avenue for understanding how some children are protected, or protect themselves, against the vicissitudes of serious stress. We might speculate that, whatever these protective coping mechanisms are, they appear to promote good mental health in general and could therefore be helpful even in low-risk individuals.

Three of the most important protective factors to emerge from research are: (1) personality features, such as self-esteem, (2) family cohesion and lack of discord, and (3) external support systems that encourage and reinforce the child's efforts to cope (Garmezy, 1985; Masten & Garmezy, 1985). Protective factors are not fixed attributes; they are subject to development or reduction over time within the same individual, and those that may aid in coping at one time may not work at another. Thus these factors should be seen as dynamic; the resilient individual is one who can adapt his or her coping strategies to changing situations. In this sense, protective factors should not be seen as fixed traits of the individual or circumstance, but rather as interpersonal and interactive. This is what Rutter (1987) refers to as protective *mechanisms* or *processes* that the individual may apply or modify as needed.

The cases in Part Three reveal a variety of risks and developmental vulnerabilities, as well as a number of protective coping mechanisms. These mechanisms are employed to secure important emotional needs, and with the dramatic emotional development during adolescence these needs themselves undergo transformation.

In the case of a sexually abused adolescent, "The Simple Beauty of a Conversation," a severe stutter during childhood and adolescence (that may or may not have been related to his abuse) devastated his self-esteem and his relationship with his parents. This devastation had a profoundly negative impact on his social relations. But the functional needs and possibilities of adolescence propelled him into new relationships—warm mentors at work and an accepting and affirming girlfriend—which gave him belated self-confidence to overcome the more debilitating effects of his stutter and abuse. In this sense, the functional tasks of adolescence became for this young man more than merely something to be achieved on the road to adulthood; they became a crucial opportunity for redressing the developmental damage incurred in his childhood. Each phase of life, therefore, not only provides extra obstacles for adolescents with special challenges, but also represents a fresh chance to redirect the inexorable movement that phase will require. His ability to seek and utilize the support and encouragement of adult mentors, as well as his self-understanding, are the protective mechanisms that may account for his resilience against the vulnerabilities from his abuse and speech problem. These mechanisms and the developmental task of romantic intimacy that emerges in adolescence combine in a powerful protective partnership.

Case 17 represents a long-term challenge, whereas Case 19, concerning adolescent abortion, "Proud of the Strength I Had," involves an acute crisis that results in an extended period of depression, anxiety, and guilt feelings. The resulting effects on this autobiographer's self-esteem, attitude toward sexuality, and capacity for intimacy represent risks to her healthy transition to adulthood. A variety of studies find that many women who undergo abortions experience periods of depression, regret, and guilt (Cvejic, Lipper, Kinch, & Benjamin, 1977; Ford, Castelnuovo-Tedesco, & Long, 1971; Smith, 1973) but that these feelings are typically mild and abate in the short term without negatively affecting general functioning. Other studies have found that the primary response to abortion is relief (Adler, 1975; Ewing & Rouse, 1973; Monosour & Stewart, 1973), and that in the case of adolescent abortion in particular it "is neither psychologically harmful nor in other ways damaging to the patient" (Olson, 1980, p. 440). And while another study showed that some women who underwent an abortion suffered from depression, prior mental health status was a stronger predictor of mental health after pregnancy than abortion or delivery (Russo & Zierk, 1992; Gilchrist, Hanaford, Frank, & Kay, 1995). A longitudinal follow-up study of young women who had abortions found that pregnancy termination was not directly related to an increase in clinically significant depression (Schmiege & Russo, 2005).

In comparison with adult women, adolescent females are found to have somewhat more negative emotional responses to abortion, though not severely worse (Adler, 1975; Bracken, Hachamovitch, & Grossman, 1974; Margolis, Davidson, Hanson, Loos, & Mikelson, 1971; Payne, Kravitz, Notman, & Anderson, 1976). This seems to reflect the experience of our autobiographer, who describes somewhat more lasting negative feelings, perhaps because as a middle adolescent at the time, she was unable to fully anticipate her sense of loss and to prepare for it psychologically as older adolescents appear better able to do (Hatcher, 1976). The sense of betrayal and isolation was intense—her former boyfriend offered no support other than to pay for the abortion, and she felt unable to tell her parents or even her twin sister. She describes how this crisis led to her participation in a college support group for other students who had terminated pregnancies. Emotional catharsis and gradual understanding of her feelings led to active participation in reproductive rights events and close friendships with other women who shared the same experience. The integration of self-understanding and action is central to her eventual success in managing this stress and recovering from her depressed feelings. This emerging insight also brought into focus her family's inability to communicate emotionally and her determination to redress this constriction of her own emotional openness. When her younger sister thought she might be pregnant, our author took this opportunity to soothe her own feelings of isolation and abandonment by providing the type of support to her sister that she wishes she had. Thus the opportunity to reflect on the linkage between how she became pregnant—"not being able to talk about sex and contraception" with her boyfriend—and her family's emotional silence—"I grew up in a family that stuffed their feelings and never talked about anything, including sex"—led to an important self-understanding about the ways she wanted to change. This crisis illuminated an underlying and ongoing challenge to her happiness: her family's dysfunctional emotional communication.

The developmental vulnerability of an unwanted pregnancy is itself reflective of the adolescent tasks of balancing intimacy, identity, and sexuality. In this case, we can witness the painful beginnings of learning how to develop and employ protective mechanisms—sharing intimate feelings with trusted friends, providing the type of support to others she now knows she needs, searching for an ideology that gives meaning and purpose to her experience, and actively identifying with other women who assert their feelings. Her moves in this direction are tentative, but she seems to have a solid understanding of the cause of much of her unhappiness and the means of redressing it. Similar to the lessons of the other cases, the challenge to her emotional development is met by interaction of protective mechanisms and developmental tasks.

In Case 20, "Seeking the Best of Both Worlds," the adolescent tasks related to separation and individuation become especially poignant in the context of an immigrant family having fled a war-ravaged Vietnam. The traumatic experience of emigrating under such circumstance can understandably have profound effects on both the individual and the nature of family relationships. The author describes feeling both great loyalty and respect for his mother's heroic role in rescuing the family from an impossible situation, and feeling shame and contempt for her unwillingness to allow him to adapt to the U.S. culture to which she had exposed him. He wants acceptance and permission from his mother to live in both worlds—the western world to which she brought him and the traditional world of his family. Even though he is willing to accept the dichotomy of worlds and to live according to the rules of family when at home and of society when outside, his mother seems unwilling to make any such accommodation for herself and thinks he should not either. The result is that he chooses to segment his self into "dutiful but resentful" son at home, and "Americanized" adolescent in school and the larger world. He must resort to constant lying and other subterfuge to keep his mother from knowing his other self. This stress of a double life and the alienation from his mother leaves him emotionally isolated and increasingly depressed.

In addition to all the normal preoccupations of adolescence, and beyond the typical parent–child conflicts of the period, this author demonstrates how hard it can be for immigrant adolescents to integrate the best of both cultures if their family demands exclusive loyalty to the native culture. His strategy of alternating his behavior to whatever culture he finds himself in is often effective for immigrant adolescents (LaFromboise, Coleman, & Gerton, 1993) and is even associated with positive mental health (Rogler, Cortes, & Malgady, 1991). In this case, however, we can also see the tremendous emotional stress and developmental risk this form of adaptation can cause. At the same time, the case also illustrates how his increasing competence and validation in the larger culture gradually creates a new and respected role in his family as the intercultural go-between. By the time he writes his autobiography in college, he describes ways in which he has been able to influence his mother in rearing his two younger siblings so as to lessen some of the pain and conflict he experienced.

Finally, in his follow-up essay written nine years later, he describes how his two younger siblings have not fared as well as he and his older sister, both of whom are now physicians. Indeed his younger brother and sister, suffering from the effects of long-term emotional and physical abuse at the hands of his mother, are depressed and suicidal. He has now been granted legal custody of his younger sister whom he is raising with his wife. Although he has now completed medical school and married, his mother's harmful parenting still preoccupies him as he tries to nurture his younger siblings and thereby undo some of the damage their upbringing has wrought. His updated story raises interesting questions about differential resilience in a single family and how individuals can react to similar stressors in different ways.

The title of Case 16, "Bad," reveals how the author felt about herself from a young age. She describes constant behavior problems and poor academic performance throughout elementary school. In turn, these problems led to serious conflict with her mother, which further exacerbated her low self-esteem and feelings of shame, hopelessness, and guilt. It was not until eighth grade that she was finally diagnosed with ADHD, but even then neither medication nor environmental accommodations in school or home were prescribed. By mid-adolescence the result of her untreated ADHD was depression and increasingly self-destructive behavior including serious substance abuse.

ADHD is a disorder of both childhood and adulthood characterized by impulsive behavior, inattention, poor organizational skills, and often oppositional and disruptive behavior. It occurs in 3–6 percent of the school age population. Our author is ambivalent about whether her diagnosis was taken seriously enough for treatment to be provided. On one hand she wishes she had received help: "I now regret so much the way my parents and I let my diagnosis be pushed under the carpet. If I had had some help I could have accomplished so much more. . . ." On the other hand, she states that she is afraid of the medications typically used to treat ADHD because of bad experiences she had abusing them as recreational drugs. Yet her case is a classic example of the tragedy of undiagnosed and untreated ADHD. While girls represent only about 10–15 percent of diagnosed cases, studies show the prevalence of ADHD in school age females to be approximately 33 percent in community-based population studies (Gaub & Carlson, 1997). There are many reasons for this underdiagnosis including the tendency for girls to have the inattentive subtype of ADHD rather than the more obvious hyperactive form. Similarly, boys with ADHD are more likely to exhibit serious behavior problems including aggression and delinquency and therefore are referred for treatment by parents and school officials (Gershon, 2002).

One of the reasons parents often give for choosing not to allow medication to be administered to their child with ADHD is the fear that it will increase the likelihood that their child will grow up to use illegal drugs. There is, however, a substantial body of research that shows that the opposite is true: children with untreated ADHD are significantly *more* likely to abuse drugs than those who take prescribed medication for the disorder (Biederman, Wilens, Mick, Spencer, & Faraone, 1999). It is important to note that our author feels that her Outward Bound experience transformed her, and she went on to have a successful college career without medication or other treatment. Similarly, we should note her emphatic embrace of her ADHD as a gift—an intense way of feeling and being that gives her certain advantages and a competitive edge. And while one should understand ADHD in the context of the whole person and not simply as a disorder or disability, it is also true that for many persons undiagnosed and untreated ADHD poses major challenges to successful performance in school, work, and relationships. This case highlights both the serious negative effects of ADHD while also providing a very hopeful outcome over the course of adolescence.

Case 18, "Forever an Awkward Adolescent," illustrates how physical disabilities can also pose additional challenges along the adolescent pathway. The physically challenged autobiographer describes how he used to experience closeness with his father by allowing him to do virtually everything for him, including helping him dress each morning up until high school. He states that as adolescence and his desire for independence emerged, better late than never, he began to insist that his father restrain "his legendary penchant for interfering." His need for independence, however, didn't obliterate his desire for closeness with his father; it caused him to redirect it along more age-appropriate lines, like shared ideas and interests. We can see how the developmental tasks of adolescence, here for greater autonomy, have similar transformative effects on parent-child relations for a severely disabled adolescent as they do for others. The difference is that it is adapted to those particular circumstances, and in the case of a physically disabled adolescent, the importance of the struggle for autonomy has special salience regarding how much independence they will be able to achieve as an adult. For another adolescent, the same autonomy task might lead to a demand for greater privacy or a right to choose his or her own clothes but with less long-lasting implications.

In addition to the press of developmental tasks, the autobiographer's coping is enhanced by the remarkable self-understanding he demonstrates in his attempts at adaptation. He repeatedly stresses his own responsibility for his adjustment and happiness, and the need to find some means of "fitting in" with his able-bodied peers lest they give up trying to relate to him and leave him to his "'default' pigeonhole . . . of a short, oddly postured disabled kid." And he writes repeatedly of having to create "a persona I could live with" by mirroring himself in the eyes of his peers. This search for identity by means of acceptance and validation by his peers is another important task of adolescence. Thus he demonstrates the interaction of developmental tasks and protective factors, identity formation and self-understanding respectively, which together serve to compensate for the risks of isolation and dependence his physical disabilities represent.

"Forever an Awkward Adolescent" was originally published in the first two editions of this book. We brought it back in the fifth edition because the author had written a retrospective update, "Thirteen Years Later." Writing in his mid-thirties from the perspective of a successful executive in a disabilities advocacy organization, he reflects on his original perspective as a college student on what his future might hold. He writes about what has held true and consistent in his life, and what new challenges and opportunities for growth he has faced and anticipates in his future.

The five cases in Part III reveal much about the opportunities of adolescence for growing stronger through challenge. Unfortunately, not all such challenges are met so successfully. These autobiographers do, however, represent the fortunate fact that most adolescents who face such circumstances do somehow find a path to productive lives. The following cases tell stories of how such challenges can be met, and though the life stories could not be more different, their pathways to overcoming have much in common.

BAD

In this essay,* Gretchen, a 21-year-old white woman, tells the story of her eventual recovery from the psychological injury done to her by others' misunderstandings of her attention deficit/hyperactivity disorder (ADHD). Within her family, Gretchen was labeled a problem child: poorly organized, prone to school failure, and apt to become distracted. Perhaps as a result of her parents' marital difficulties—which destabilized the family generally—Gretchen was afforded little room for error, and as her problems persisted, she was subjected to escalating emotional and physical abuse by her mother. Finally, during her senior year of high school, Gretchen dropped out and ran away to live in the city with her boyfriend. After months in a drug rehabilitation center and a stint in an outdoor therapy program, she chose to return to high school.

Writing as a college sophomore, Gretchen challenges the conventional belief that ADHD is nothing but a problem, a syndrome to be cured, a disease to be eradicated. Instead, based on her own experience, Gretchen believes that ADHD can be a source of joy and life energy, a part of a person's cherished uniqueness. Accordingly, Gretchen advises her readers to adopt a more curious and open stance toward ADHD, warning that failure to do so can result in the misjudgment and abuse of persons like herself.

I woke to the sound of my mother's footsteps hammering down the stairs to the kitchen. Through sleepy eyes, I looked out at the glorious fall foliage, the bright sunshine warming my face as I sat up and stretched my small body, thinking, "It's finally Saturday!" I loved Saturdays in the fall; it was soccer season, and Saturday was the one day of the week I spent with my dad. As part of our Saturday ritual, Dad would always bring doughnuts for me and my sister, one chocolate and one honey-dipped. The smells of coffee, doughnuts, and the newspaper surrounded him when he came to pick us up for my soccer game. I loved the way Dad looked on weekends, his hair messy, his face unshaven and salty from his early morning jog. Handing me the doughnut bag, Dad asked if I had my gear ready, and I realized I didn't know where my uniform, cleats, or shin guards were, though I did know where to look.

I darted upstairs to examine the heap of things on my bedroom floor. I first looked under the bed, where I found one shin guard and one cleat behind my Scrabble box. Beginning to feel frustrated, I scurried around my room, finding only two dirty soccer socks in my doll clothes drawer and a pair of soccer shorts from last year's uniform. Wanting to appear organized, I threw on the mismatched pieces of my uniform, just in time to hear my father's call up the stairs, "Ready, Gretchen?" As I ran down the stairs, I was something to behold wearing my wrinkled shirt, still dirty from my last game, a pair of shorts that were too small, and my dirty soccer socks, carrying one cleat, and one shin guard that had a doll hat stuck to the Velcro strap. I squirmed as my father examined me, his thick, dark eyebrows raised, his eyes squinting skeptically. I spotted my sister's gear stacked neatly in the corner; dropping mine, I scooped hers up and followed Dad out the front door, feeling somewhat relieved by the cool morning air. My very organized father followed with a shopping bag full of cookies and punch for the team; it was his turn to bring the postgame refreshments, and I thanked God for letting me remind him of that yesterday, and not on the way to the field.

We sat in silence as we drove to the field, but I was happy just to be with Dad. I loved watching his strong hands shift the car, which smelled just like his office: a mix of leather, paper, coffee, and new carpet. I liked to feel part of my father's world, and this for me, this time alone, was a bonding experience. I would often pretend I was one of his clients and that we were on our way to a meeting. I'd also pretend that the air of seriousness that surrounded my father was comfortable.

Before the game, I huddled with my team, shivering because I had forgotten my sweatshirt. When my coach shouted, "Get out there girls, let's hustle," I stared blankly, wondering why she hadn't put me in the lineup. Then I heard my dad yelling from the sidelines, "Weren't you listening? GO! Get out there, you're playing defense, pay attention! GO!" I ran onto the field, with my too-small shorts riding up my behind. My mind drifted as I watched my teammates dominate the game at the other end of the field, and I started mentally going over the moves I had learned in gymnastics that week. I started to do a cartwheel, and as my legs kicked over, I saw the ball heading straight toward me. My coach screamed from the sideline, "Gretchen, for Christ's sake, this isn't GYMNASTICS, it's SOCCER! Why are you doing flips in the middle of the game? PAY ATTENTION!" I glanced at the laughing parents standing on the sidelines, saw my father's embarrassed look of disgust. My coach took me out at halftime, and I sat with my back to my father for the rest of the game, hating myself for being so stupid, wondering why I could never be as organized as everyone else. The car ride home was silent. I was filled with shame and devastated that my day with Dad had been ruined. I was not, after all, his client, but merely his unreliable child whom he couldn't understand.

"I would hear my name being screamed from the front of the class."

When I think back on my years as a young student, I can laugh at some of my behaviors in class. I was constantly told to sit down, to stop talking; if the teacher gave instructions, I was always one step behind everyone; if we were supposed to hang up our coats, I would be easily distracted by something else. I was constantly yelled at for being disruptive, and I remember feeling very guilty, but, also confused: I did not mean to disrupt my class, and I often didn't even realize I was doing anything wrong. I realize now that I was not a child with a discipline problem, but a child with ADHD.

But, at that time, nobody knew what my real problem was, and at school embarrassing things would happen to me daily. I was constantly in trouble for taking too long when I went to the bathroom or to sharpen my pencil. I would look out the window and totally forget I was in class. Then I would hear my name being screamed from the front of the room. The thing was, I could not control my behavior. I felt I was not in control of my own mind and body. My frustrated teachers and my parents always wanted to know why I was not paying attention or why I was acting up in class, but I would only tell them, "I don't know, I just did." Often I couldn't even remember what I was in trouble for! But no one ever believed me, and soon I was pegged as a liar—a label that followed me for a long time. Every teacher at my school knew me because I was always in trouble. I was regularly kicked out of class, which bruised me emotionally because I could not explain my behavior. I felt like a really bad kid.

"There are days when I can actually feel my ADHD taking over my mind and body."

ADHD is not merely a part of me or an influence in my life. It is me. It is the main force that controls me mentally, physically, and socially; I cannot separate it from myself or keep it under control. It is hard for me to explain what it feels like to be driven by an inner force that is so powerful and primordial. There are days when I can actually feel ADHD taking over my mind and body. It's kind of like being on a ride at the fair that goes 'round and 'round in circles as it jolts up and down and side to side, and everything is a huge blur of lights, smells, and noises, and you try really hard to single out your friends down on the ground watching you, but you can't focus because it's spinning so fast. That is how hard ADHD can hit. Imagine that happening when you are in class trying to listen, or when you are trying to do your homework. In class, I often have the feeling that I am sitting in the middle of a drain, and I sit there at my desk, spinning furiously, trying to stop the motion. When the force erupts, my anxiety starts to take over, and I have to fight the urge to scream with frustration. My body reacts to this rush, and I have to move. There is nothing that can bring me back to the moment, and the only thing that helps me to relax is space and open air. An escape! This is an extremely complicated psychological state to have to describe when someone asks, "What's the matter?" or "Why can't you just sit still?" I feel that someone would think I was psychotic if I tried to describe the feeling.

The strangest thing about this state is that, though I know what I am supposed to be doing, I have absolutely no control. I can have a huge list of things I know I have to do, or else pay severe consequences, but I still will not do them.

There is a force stronger than my own will controlling me. For example, if I have an important assignment to complete for school the next day, I'll go for a run or clean my room, all the time thinking, "I'm not doing my assignments." Then I might read the paper or go out with my friends, still conscious that I have this assignment, but still not doing it. I want to, but I really can't stop not doing it, can't stop doing something else. This also happens in class: I get the urge to do something else, like go for a hike, and I go. It does not matter what else I should be doing—I have to go. I'm driven.

"How come no one ever saw the fear in me?"

As a child, the hardest part of the day was the bus ride home. I always had a bag full of notes from my teachers, and I knew the school had already called my mother to tell her I had them. I would get off the bus scared to death and very sad. I would contemplate running away, or wonder whether things would be better if I were dead. I would close the front door very quietly, knowing what I would get when my mom knew I was home. I always felt like I had worms in my stomach, and would sometimes vomit from the anxiety. I'd develop a migraine, which my mother would say I was faking because I knew I was in trouble. I often felt like I was spinning out of control, and my parents would make me spin even harder, until finally I would just shut down and cry myself to sleep, feeling worthless and scared. I always felt very misunderstood.

My mother had a mean and violent temper when I was a kid. I know now that she was unhappily married and felt neglected by my father, and she would take out her anger on me and my sister. But as a child I just thought that this was how my mother was. I always got it worse than my sister—I added more stress because of school. When my mother got mad, she screamed so violently that I did not recognize her. She also hit. Instead of sitting and discussing why I was having trouble in school, she would usually beat me. This made me fearful; I started to lie to my teachers and hide my bad reports from my mother because it was my only defense from the abuse.

The first time I was caught forging my parents' names to a progress report was in the third grade, when I was 8 years old. The consequences of lying were always worse than the bad report, but I could not stop. I had to protect myself somehow; nobody else understood what it was like for me. I felt that the only way for me to avoid punishment was to lie, and though I was often caught and punished, for some reason it didn't stop me. It became a habit, and I found myself lying even in situations where I did not have to. I never got in trouble at school for problems like fighting, but I was very dishonest, which gave me a bad reputation. My parents and my teachers overlooked my learning problems and focused on my behavior.

How come nobody ever saw the fear in me? Why did I have to be so deceitful so young? This overwhelming fear started very young, and stayed with me until recently, like a terrible weight I carried inside. I was a nervous child, and the stress caused migraine headaches and a nervous stomach. Stress can do many things to people, especially children, which I feel is one of the largest factors behind my failure in school.

As I got older, things only got worse. I was evaluated several times at my school, which showed only that I had deficiencies in copying from the board, work completion, math, and spelling. I was always off the charts on my vocabulary and comprehension abilities. They always told me that my testing scores were way above average and that I was capable of the work, but that I was careless and lazy.

I was often told that I didn't have my priorities in order, which was why I was doing so poorly in school. When I was in seventh grade, my parents decided to put me in private school, hoping that it would solve my problems. This may have been a good idea, but, in fact, it only brought on a new wave of problems. The private school had parent advisory slips—commonly known as PA slips—that would be sent home if you were disruptive in class, did not do homework, or if you were basically not doing well in a class. I probably hold the record at Cabot Academy for the most PA slips! As I explained, bringing home PA slips was not an option for me because I was so scared of my mother. So, once again I forged and lied daily. I would hand the forged slips to my teachers, but they usually found out my mother had not seen them and would then tell me I was caught. For the rest of the day, I would conjure up possible escapes, imagining myself living on the streets or in the woods, lonely and afraid. But I always went home. I would get home, where I would be verbally tormented by my mother. I would try to explain that I didn't know why these things were happening and that I was as confused as she was, but all she could say was, "You're lying," or "You're a lazy, stupid, selfish child." I was called an "insensitive brat," a "lazy, fat ass," and I often heard my mother say, "I could fucking kill you!" As she screamed at me, she would twist my arm or smack me or push me, then send me to my room, saying, "I don't want to see your face for the rest of the night." I would wish that she could understand that acting that way was only hurting me and killing my self-esteem. I wanted her to realize that I was not doing these things because I was a bad person. I wanted her to realize that my problems in school were caused by something that I didn't understand. Instead, my mother only added to my problems.

Several incidents will never be erased from my memory. I hope that sharing one will help explain why I stayed in this pattern of lying, why I was just too scared to stop. I was in bed one night when I heard the phone ring. I thought it could be one of my teachers telling my parents that I had failed a math test. I heard my mother say, "Thank you very much for calling and letting me know." I knew I was right. I heard my mother scream from her bedroom and come flying down the hallway to my bedroom. The door burst open, and standing in the light of the hallway was my mother. She stormed into the room with a belt in her hand and started to whip me where I was lying in my bed. She was screaming cruel things at me and whacking whacking whacking me with the belt. Finally, my sister ran into my room and pulled my mother off me. It was total chaos. My sister and I were screaming and crying, and my mother was totally flipping out. I was confused and embarrassed that my sister had seen this. I know she felt bad for me, but I also know that she was angry at me for causing this. I put a chair in front of my door and huddled under my blanket, crying and getting sick to my stomach until, finally, I fell asleep. All this because I failed a math test. By the time my father got home from work, the house was silent and we were sleeping.

"I don't ever remember my parents getting along well."

It is amazing to me how much my family influenced how I see myself and shaped who I am. I will start with my parents. I believe that my parents' marriage was doomed to fail from the beginning. They were married at 25, and within two years they had my sister Meredith and me. My father started a job at an accounting firm in Boston, where he has worked for the last twenty-one years. My mother stayed at home for the first few years to take care of me and my sister. The main reason my parents are no longer together is that my father is married to his job; it's the reason they started fighting. My father worked twelve to fourteen hours every day of the week. My mother thought it was unfair that she was left home all day with two babies to take care of and that she was totally alone all the time. When my father did come home, my sister and I were usually asleep; we never spent time with him. I believe that my mother felt neglected, and that she felt bad that my sister and I never saw my dad either. My mother could not handle my father's work schedule, and she became very depressed and angry, and my parents fought regularly over the fact that my father was never home. I think my mother was so angry that she couldn't tell my father that the problem was that she really missed him and wanted to have a better marriage, so she would yell and scream and push him away even further. Eventually, their arguments became violent, and my mother would hit my father. The first time I witnessed this was horrific. It is hard to see your parents acting so irrationally. I was scared my parents would end up killing each other.

Looking back, I understand my mother's frustrations. I know she needed much more affection and communication than she was getting from my father. I know she tried to make their marriage work in many ways. She became an excellent cook and homemaker. She kept herself looking great, always beautifully dressed, and in great physical shape. She was envied by her friends for being so domestic and desirable. Only my father never recognized her efforts, never complimented her or gave her more time. That is why my mother became a very angry person.

My mother's temper became the thing that scared me the most. She would hit me and my sister when she became angry, often enraged over little things like spills or messes around the house. My mother treated every situation with violence. My father never really knew what was happening, and there was no one to help us. My mother's erratic behavior was confusing: after she hit me, she would give me a big hug and a kiss and tell me she loved me, but it never made me feel better. I wanted her to feel bad for what she had done, not kiss and make up. I often felt I was living in the middle of total chaos, but was too small and powerless to stop it.

"The doctor told them I had ADHD."

When I was in eighth grade, my parents decided to take me to see a specialist. I had been evaluated many times throughout the years, but I was still not improving. My parents were desperate to get some help for my problems. I remember the ride to the hospital: it was no big deal for me, since I had become accustomed to being taken to psychologists and doctors. As I went through yet another series of testing—the ink blots, the puzzles, the building blocks—I wondered how these simple games would tell these people anything about me. At the end of the testing, my parents and I met with a doctor, who told them that I had ADHD. He said the drug Ritalin was the latest treatment and told my parents how it was used. I had never heard of ADHD, and at the time it did not mean much to me. I just figured, "Well, that's one more thing we can add to the list, so can we go home now?" That was the extent of my diagnosis; we never got any information about ADHD and we never talked about it again. My parents never thought to seek any advice about my condition, and, for me, it was just another name of another syndrome that was not going to change who I was. It didn't really bother me that we never talked about it because the doctor didn't seem to think it was a big deal. By the end of that school year, I was kicked out of private school and went back to public school still without any mention of my ADHD.

I now regret so much the way my parents and I let my diagnosis be pushed under the carpet. If I had had some help, I could have accomplished so much more and been spared the humiliation I felt when I was expelled from school. The guilt was even worse; I was so tired of disappointing my parents. I knew I was doing poorly in school, but I never expected to be kicked out. I think this was a turning point for me in many ways. I think this is when my parents finally gave up on me and when I gave up on myself. I was tired of not being understood and of being hurt so much that eventually I stopped caring about myself. I became so afraid of failure and admonishment that I was unable to take a risk or try really hard for things. I became scared of conflict or even the possibility of conflict. I couldn't trust anything I believed, and I became a sponge for other people's opinions. I never told anyone my feelings because I was so embarrassed about myself all the time.

Yet all of this did lead to something positive: I became a listener! The one area of my life that gained something from my bad experiences was my ability to be a good friend. I have had the same friends for many years, some since the first grade. I always put a lot into my friendships. All my friends would come to me with their problems because I was a good listener. I wanted to make sure these people felt that their problems were significant and that they were being understood. I never wanted anyone to have their feelings misunderstood as I did. I would change plans for my friends, even if it meant missing the biggest events; I would never desert a friend. I never let myself be in a clique and made it a point to try never to hurt anyone's feelings. I stuck up for kids who were being picked on and felt good about helping people. I was so well liked that I never had to worry about being picked on like I was at home or by my teachers. I was never a victim. Many teenagers have a hard time socially because kids can be really mean, but I never experienced that. This was great for me, but it also became a problem. I became so involved with everyone else's lives that I totally ignored how I was really feeling. Helping other people did make me feel better, but it was not enough.

During my sophomore year in high school, I became involved with Rob, a boy I had known throughout my school years. Rob gravitated to me because he had a lot of emotional difficulties. In elementary school, he had cancer for seven years, but cancer was the least of his problems. When Rob was diagnosed with bladder cancer, his father took off, and Rob never heard from him again. After later bouts with lung cancer and a tumor on his spine, Rob went into full remission when he was 12. A week later, his mother announced that she had cervical cancer and that it was too far gone to help. She had never told anyone because she wanted Rob to be taken care of first. She died when Rob was a freshman in high school, and he blamed himself. This kid had major problems, and he became my new project.

I went out with Rob for five years, devoting myself mainly to his problems. I believe he'd be dead by now if not for me, but it sure didn't get me anywhere. He was a drug user, and I got into heavy drugs with him—acid, pills, coke. For two years straight, that was all we did. It was great: I was "helping" Rob, and I was too fucked up to feel my own pain. Rob hated school as much as I did, so we stopped going after a while, and if I did go, I was high. My parents separated the year I met Rob, so they were dealing with their own problems. My mother was such a wreck throughout her divorce that it was easy for me to get away with things.

But midway through my senior year when my mother had an emotional breakdown, I totally lost it. She wanted me to affirm her and comfort her, but I was so angry at her for what she had put me through that she made me sick. I could not even feel bad for her, and I let her suffer. My dad and sister were gone, so I was left alone with my irrational mother. And I just lost it. I quit school and ran away from home. I got an apartment with Rob and two of his friends in a part of the city surrounded by crack houses. This was the worst possible environment, but I did not care. I felt like I was losing my mind and just had to get out of my house. I have never been so depressed in my life; I totally hit rock bottom. I was still seeing my therapist through all this, and one day I showed up for a therapy appointment to find my dad waiting there with two guys in white coats. My father forced me to take a drug test, after which I was locked up in rehab for a few months.

"Those three months in Minnesota were a period of rebirth."

When I got out of rehab, I had a hard time motivating myself to do anything. The whole world felt dead to me. My relationship with my parents was not great, and my self-esteem was at the lowest place it had ever been. I couldn't pretend I was happy; I couldn't even smile. I was able to put a lot of effort into figuring out what I needed to do to be happy again, and the one thing I was sure of was that I needed to get away from my family, my friends, and my hometown. I needed to see myself in another setting, to cut myself off from the rest of my world and totally concentrate on myself. My father suggested that I try an Outward Bound course for the summer, and I instantly agreed with him. I knew a little about the philosophy behind Outward Bound, but I didn't know what to expect from my trip. I think the main reason I agreed to do the trip was because the distance and seclusion sounded so right.

I spent three months in the woods of northern Minnesota backpacking, kayaking, and canoeing. There is something so amazing about living without a clock or a schedule hanging over your head. Getting away from the noise, hustle, and stress of life, I was able to reflect and think. I found a calming silence in nature that soothed my mind and gave it the time to expand without unnecessary chatter and noise.

My Outward Bound course was the most significant experience I have had, the best choice I have made in my life. The changes I experienced during my trip were so strong and unbinding that I could feel them as they were occurring. I had moments of great clarity that allowed me to separate myself from the cloud I had been living in for years and to free myself from insignificant worries and fears that I had been holding on to my whole life. I think this was the first time I recognized myself as an individual person, rather than as a mere part in the lives of all the people I knew and all that I experienced. Before, I had absolutely no sense of who I was; I viewed myself according to what other people told me I was. Outward Bound gave me the personal freedom to explore inwardly and form an identity for myself. This freedom was the crucial aspect of my experience. I was in a group of seven strangers who did not have a clue about my past, and this was the first time that I could be the person I knew I was. I did not fear that these people would analyze my behaviors like my family did. I had lost the faith of all the people who were close to me and was used to getting few words of encouragement.

Those three months in Minnesota were a period of rebirth. I shed about nineteen years of unwanted skin that was trapping my spirit. With every step I took, I sweated out the toxins in my body and mind. Every day, I struggled and cried, and I released and released all the pain inside me. For the first time my nerves settled, and the sick feeling I had in my body left. My stomach felt empty and happy without the butterflies that had lived in there for years. I smiled and I laughed out loud, and I was happy!

Equally important to my rebirth was that I gained a lot of insight into my family. I had had so much anger at them for so long that I could not distinguish the good in them. I know that I had an inner demon eating away at my spirit, and my family was that demon. In time, I was able to conquer the burdens they had placed on me and recognize my own faults and the ways I had contributed to the deterioration of my family. I had put so much emphasis on defending myself that I hadn't seen my role in the problem. I went home from my trip feeling settled and open to them. The trip also gave me time to decide what I wanted in the future, and I decided to go back to high school to get my diploma.

There is a part of me that would never want to change the fact that I have ADHD. I believe that this condition can be positive in many ways for the person who has it. The main setback for most people with ADHD, especially children, is that they are misunderstood. If I had been taught to believe that ADHD was a learning difference rather than a learning disability, I feel I would have had a more positive view of myself while growing up. ADHD has caused me problems as far as learning goes, but not because I cannot learn. I just do not learn the same way other people do. But then, everyone learns differently, not only people with ADHD. ADHD becomes a learning disability when teachers try to put many different kids together in one room and expect them all to learn the same way. I feel that a lot of the problem for children with ADHD lies within the education system. Most schools have a set curriculum and routine method of teaching, but it is ridiculous to believe that all children will be stimulated by the same things. The problem is that not all classroom settings incorporate a multimodal form of teaching. There are simple strategies that can be incorporated into the classroom that can greatly help all students learn more effectively according to methods that work best for them.

Many specialists believe that medication is the most effective treatment for students with ADHD. This is something that I am very afraid of. I have experimented with a few of the drugs that are prescribed, like Ritalin and Dexedrine. When under the influence of these medications, I am a completely different person. I lose all my energy and emotions. It is like the driving force behind who I am is sucked out of my body leaving me feeling like a hollow shell. My ADHD is the source of my energy, and it is vital for me to have that. I feel that my personality would not be what it is if I did not have ADHD. There are so many positive aspects of ADHD. For example, I can do many things at one time successfully. My mind is always in motion and always looking for something to do. My main goal is to be able to control my ADHD in certain settings, and to use my ADHD as an advantage, rather than taking drugs to suppress all my creative energy.

Although most people look at ADHD as a negative condition, I disagree. I believe that if you were to ask anyone that has a friend with ADHD, they would say that all of these crazy symptoms are what they love about that person. ADHD makes a person an individual unlike anyone else. I know that at times my erratic behavior and spontaneity aggravates my friends and family, but those are the qualities that make them laugh and appreciate me. The problem is that most of the literature about ADHD is written by people who do not have ADHD. They generalize ADHD and say that the symptoms are concrete. This is extremely offensive to me. I understand my symptoms, and I know how my ADHD affects me, but it's all personal. My situation can be totally different from another person with ADHD.

I am happy that I have the opportunity to write about my experiences. They are me, and they are real. I hope this essay will help some people see the importance of dealing with learning disabilities so that they or their child will get the help they need. I also hope people can learn from my story so that they will deal with this issue differently from the way my family did. I want people to understand that ADHD should not be labeled a disability, that it only becomes a disability when it is not understood and when people fail to see the benefits and the positive aspects of it. I believe that my ADHD caused people to look down on me and tell me that there was something wrong with me. I had hundreds of tests for that reason alone; everyone wanted to know what was wrong with me rather than just seeing the energy and passion that I had for so many things. My teachers and parents overlooked all the areas in my life where I was succeeding and instead concentrated on my faults. If I had learned earlier how to turn my ADHD into an advantage, I would have had a better outlook on life and I would have had more respect for myself as a person. It has taken me a long time to be able to see the good in me. Because of all the people telling me there was something wrong with me, I was unable to recognize any part of myself as positive and "normal." All I wanted was for people to listen to me and to really see me, not what the doctors were seeing.

THE SIMPLE BEAUTY OF A CONVERSATION

This author's shocking discovery of his speech impediment in first grade leads him to feel insecure and self-conscious regardless of academic and social accomplishments. Ray's "identity as a stutterer" makes him give up in school, because it is "easier not to attempt something than to fail at it." He plagiarizes and cheats his way through high school without being caught, as much a rebellion against his parents as a way of getting by. His religious faith, a close friendship, and his work in the library help him through some of the most difficult years, providing support and contributing to a growing sense of himself as a valued person. Ray experiences a setback when, early in college, his girlfriend is raped, an experience that causes memories of his own early sexual abuse to surface for the first time. He feels like a stronger person now, "standing on his own two feet." His stutter reappears only occasionally, reminding him of the difficulties each of us has in our lives.

As I started high school many teachers and friends held high hopes for me, but by the end of my senior year there was a question as to whether I was going to graduate or repeat the year. My academic problems did not all stem directly from my learning problems. The most accurate description would be to say that I was burned out. I desperately wanted someone to recognize that I was having problems and to offer help. That never happened and I continually failed at all attempts to get myself on track. It became easier not to attempt something than to fail at it. I could see no future for myself. I never even tried to think about what I wanted to do after graduation. I couldn't handle the present, so trying to plan my future was an impossibility.

I got by the best that I could. High school was very painful and difficult for me, and as a way of protecting myself I pretended that I didn't care about the school or my classes. If I had let myself feel that high school could be a very positive experience for me if I was successful, then the pain would have just been worse. I did very little homework, cheated on almost every test, plagiarized all my critical papers, and skipped school as often as I could get away with it.

I need to go back to my early childhood to explain all the problems I had with school. At the age of 5, I went through kindergarten. I enjoyed it and as far as I knew I was just like all the other kids. However, I found out that while all my other friends were going on to first grade, I was going to go to another kindergarten class. No one ever explained to me why I was repeating kindergarten. When I got to the new class I was with a bunch of other kids who were pretty normal. For one hour a day, however, I was taken aside with a special teacher who came to the class just to work with me. I didn't mind because I remember thinking she was pretty. She would show pictures and ask me to tell her what I saw. For example she would show me a picture of a dog and I would say, "dog."

"No, that's not right. Try it again," she would often say.

I had no idea what I was doing wrong. The picture was very obviously a picture of a dog and as far as I knew I was saying the word "dog." This would happen with pictures of trees, cats, farm animals, and many other simple items. I would tell her what it was and she would say, "No, try again." She never told me what I was doing wrong.

The other kids in class must have picked up on what was going on because pretty soon they all started calling me names like "retard" and "moron." I didn't understand this either. I went home crying to my mother one day and asked her why I was being called these names. I can remember the most pained expression I have ever seen come to her face and she said simply, "Because they're not very nice children."

I made it through that year in pretty good shape, all things considered. In first grade the same teacher came to see me every day again. We would go to a small office in the basement and do the same things we did in kindergarten. I know it was unintentional, but one day she did one of the most cruel things I have ever experienced. I went to see her that day and we went through the same routine. This time, however, she had a tape recorder. She recorded the answers I gave to the pictures. Then she rewound and played the tape back to me. I'm not even sure how to describe my reaction to the tape. I was about 6 and a half years old and like every other little kid I wasn't all that self-conscious or worried about the differences between myself and other kids. But that tape crushed me. The voice I heard was absolutely unintelligible. The voice was stuttering terribly and all the pronunciation was completely off. I couldn't even recognize what it was saying. The voice didn't even sound human. I was sure that I had said "dog" but when the tape got to the point where the word should have come, something completely foreign, not even resembling "dog," came out. I started crying and screaming, "That isn't me! You put another tape in there! That isn't me!" She couldn't calm me down.

I guess everybody assumed I was aware of my speech problems because they were so severe. At the very least I must have been aware of my stutter. But I wasn't aware of it at all. As I've said, no one, my parents included, had ever talked to me about it before.

That tape had an immediate effect on me. I became very withdrawn and would hardly talk to anybody. I particularly avoided talking to my parents, both because I didn't want them to hear me speak the way I did and also because I felt betrayed; I wanted to hurt them with my silence. That might sound like a lot for a 6-year-old but it is very true. Everything that had happened—staying back in kindergarten, the special teacher, all the kids making fun of me—became clear to me and I became very bitter toward my parents for having never talked with me about it. I really hated them. Over the next ten or eleven years I spent much of my time finding little ways that I could hurt them and get back at them for the way they had failed me.

My relationship with school didn't fare much better. Soon after the tape was played to me, the special teacher told me that she was transferring and that we wouldn't be working together anymore. I have no idea if the tape incident had anything to do with her decision, but I am sure now that it did play a part in my parents' decision not to get any more help for me. They couldn't deal with the pain, and I think they felt that the best thing to do was to ignore my problems and hope they would disappear with age. So I no longer went to any special classes. In the regular classes I did everything I could to keep from having to speak in front of the class. I didn't want the other kids to hear how I talked. Through the rest of grade school every teacher I had just about killed himself or herself trying to get me to apply myself more. They all felt I had great potential if I would be more outgoing. I resisted all these efforts. While my pronunciation improved somewhat, my stutter had not improved at all by the time I entered junior high.

It is very difficult to discern how much my stutter affected my image of myself and how much it affected others' image of me. Trying to look back objectively, I would say that for the most part it had its greatest influence on my own self-image. When I was growing up it sometimes seemed that everybody was laughing at me and pointing me out, when in reality probably only a few did so. There are some events that make me realize now that my friends and classmates must have held me in fairly high regard. In the fourth grade I was elected class president. In sixth I was given awards for sportsmanship, leadership, and math ability. In the seventh grade I was chosen as the "Most Intelligent" out of a class of about 150. Still, these did very little to raise my self-esteem, so sensitive was I about my stutter. The effect of these positive reinforcements was minimized to the extreme by my self-consciousness. The only identity I had for myself was as a stutterer. None of my other accomplishments came close to having the effect on me that the fear of stuttering and speaking incorrectly in front of others did. I felt that no one else knew who I really was because I had become so proficient at hiding my speech problems. I saw myself as hiding who I really was from others. To some extent this was true.

In junior high my self-esteem reached its lowest point. My outlook on everything was dictated by my view of myself. I built a reputation at school for being able to get away with cheating, skipping classes, forgery, and other things like that. During lunch at school a lot of kids would come to me looking for help. I'd make a cheat sheet, sell an essay, or do whatever the occasion called for. This was my first niche in junior high and freshman year. It was fun at first because it was novel and it got me a lot of attention. Sometimes it was more innocent and sometimes it was of a much more serious nature. For example, I went through the honors English sequence in high school and plagiarized almost every critical essay I was assigned to write. Some other students were caught doing this but I never was. I learned how to choose obscure, yet valid, sources and how to change things around just enough so that there was very little chance of getting caught. I cheated on almost every test I took and spent a minimal amount of time on homework.

I was shy with girls and doing things like this created opportunities to talk with them. This was very important. I've been attracted to girls as long as I can remember. My first kiss was in kindergarten—the second year that is. I was embarrassed afterward and I was afraid the girl would start telling the other kids that I had kissed her, so a couple of days later I went back to her house and beat her up, which sounds worse than it was. I had my first opportunity to have sex when I was in the sixth grade. The girl was in the eighth grade and I'm pretty sure she was drunk. We were behind some bushes in the church playground across from my house. She came over to me and took off all her clothes. She kept saying, "Come on over and lay me." I had never done more than kiss a girl at that point and I didn't know what "lay me" meant. I went over to her and she stuck her hand down my pants. I ejaculated as soon as she touched me. She laughed at me and said she wanted me to do that again but this time while I was "porking" her. I didn't know what that meant either. To be honest, I had no idea what to do at all. We fooled around for a while but we didn't actually have sex because I didn't know what to do. She kept laughing at me the whole time. I put my clothes back on and left her lying in the bushes. Immediately after this experience and for the next few days, I felt awful. I was cold and shivering all the time and I couldn't stand to have anyone closer than a few feet away from me. I didn't understand why I felt this way but then I didn't understand anything to do with sex at that time.

I went through puberty at an early age. By the end of the sixth grade I had had a couple of wet dreams and I was masturbating often. The incident with the first girl made me curious about and interested in girls. A friend and I used to climb trees in our backyards together. It started a few years earlier as an innocent childhood pastime and we just kept on doing it. One late afternoon during the summer after sixth grade, we were sitting up in the tree talking quietly when we saw a light go on in my neighbor's house. It was the bedroom of a girl who was about a year older than we were and who was my sister's friend. My friend said to me half jokingly, "Wouldn't it be awesome if she changed and didn't pull her shade down?" I agreed, of course, but we really didn't expect anything. But then she did change into her bathrobe without pulling down the shade. We sat for a while without saying anything. I think we were both embarrassed to talk or to move because we both had erections and didn't want the other to know.

One day later in the summer the girl we spied on, Jean, stopped by to see if my sister was around. I was home alone that day and told her so. She came in for a while anyway and we started talking. I got an erection and since I was wearing my bathing suit it wasn't long before she noticed, although I tried to hide it as best

I could. At first I was embarrassed, but pretty soon we started talking dirty. We kept daring each other to say dirtier and dirtier things and to shift our clothes around to reveal more. Eventually we went into the shower and I lost my virginity. I think it was her first time also, but I'm not sure.

The time in the shower felt pretty good to me but I don't think Jean enjoyed it very much. She looked like she felt very guilty. Nevertheless she started coming over often when I was alone. We fooled around and tried a lot of things. She must have known more than I did because I really didn't understand how girls got pregnant, but after the first time in the shower she never let me penetrate again. Instead we did other things. At the time we did it I liked it, but I always felt dirty after she had left. Every time we fooled around she would ask for a few of my father's beers to take back home (he never kept track of them). One day she came over with a *Penthouse* and read some of the letters to me. She said she would try those things if I could get her a full bottle of wine. My father had one and I gave it to her. I had heard about prostitutes in church and what it meant if you got into that stuff. I started thinking that what we were doing was almost the same thing. I had a terribly guilty conscience, but every time she came over the same thing would happen.

There was something more than just a guilty conscience though. I couldn't bear having people being physically close to me. If I ever was in a crowd, such as in a mall, I would get lightheaded and have dizzy spells. I also hated to have anyone stand behind me. If I was in any line I would stand a little off to one side to prevent people from being directly behind me. I thought that maybe these feelings had something to do with what Jean and I were doing but I didn't understand them.

When school started again, Jean stopped coming over. We never talked about what we had done again and I think both of us really wanted to forget it. I have never bragged about these experiences to anyone. There are just too many painful feelings and too much confusion connected with it for me to be able to talk about it lightly. As a Catholic I felt what I did was morally wrong, and then there were all those other feelings which I couldn't figure out. In college I told the first girl I slept with that I was a virgin. She said she was, too (and she was probably telling the truth), and that it made it more special because it was the first time for both of us. I've only slept with one other girl since, and I told her that my only experience was with the other college girl. Right now I just don't feel comfortable letting anyone know about what happened.

After the summer with Jean I entered junior high school. That's when most kids start dating, but I became very shy with girls. I knew what sex was like but I had a lot of trouble talking to girls. Each day I was becoming more and more self-conscious about my stutter; I felt that no girl would ever go on a date with a guy who talked like I did. As a result I didn't have any dates in junior high or high school, although I did begin to talk to girls more. I had other problems then as well. I've mentioned what my academics were like. My grades were respectable but they were not earned honestly. My parents and I were moving further apart. About the only time we ever talked was when we were fighting.

As a result of my problems with my family and in school, I needed to find a place I could find some solace and security. Actually, I found three areas: religion, friends, and work. I was raised in a fairly strict Catholic manner. My mother took me to church every Sunday and we fasted before and after mass. I went to classes preparing me for all the sacraments and attended service on every holy day. Sometimes the tedium and monotony of these rites would get to me but overall I have always been a religious person. Often prayer and hope for the future has been the only outlet I have had when times have been really bad. I have never had a serious question about my belief in God and the scriptures, and for most of my life I have prayed every day. While my religion is and always has been an important part of my life, I have often questioned the attitudes of the Catholic Church itself. Nevertheless, I do have strong faith and I try to follow as best I can the teachings of forgiveness, forbearance, and humility. I take pride in my faith.

When I was a sophomore in high school, a priest in my parish, a person whom I really admired, came to me and tried to convince me to enter the priesthood. I actually considered this for a time. In the end I decided against it. But that is not the significance of that incident. This was the first time that someone I really admired let me know he saw some value in me. He was seeing good in me that I couldn't see myself. It had a profound effect on me. I didn't turn myself around in a day because of it, but I did have my first thoughts of where I was going and the person I was as opposed to the person I was capable of being. These were brief, very scattered thoughts, but the seed had been planted. It was the encouragement of other people like him that helped me learn that many people saw me in a better light than I saw myself. I had very little self-respect so I had to get it from others, most of whom have been very religious. At least they are religious in my estimation of how the religious should be; they practice their faith and they show their belief in how they treat other people rather than by preaching to them. And they are secure enough in their faith that they can accept faiths that differ from their own. I have a lot of respect and admiration for these people. I learned from them that a strong belief in the self often goes hand in hand with a strong belief in a set of principles and precepts.

The Catholic Church requires public worship and professing of faith, but I was always very private about it. In that sense I made a poor Catholic. In fact, along with most of my friends, I denied holding any beliefs. I made jokes about the church and about older adults who were very religious. It's also true that I outwardly denied my faith because my mother was Catholic and worship was an integral part of her life. I didn't want to be anything like my parents, and it was a form of rebellion. But, still, inside I found it a source of comfort and hope. As I grew older I started understanding the readings at mass more and saw that they could be applied to my life. I often looked at myself as a modern-day Job. I suffered through trials and hardships as a test of my faith. Not only my faith in God but also my faith in myself and my ability to keep hope alive in my breast and work for something better. I had occasional thoughts of suicide, and three times I made concrete plans to go through with it, but there was always something inside that wouldn't let me give up on myself. Religion helped add to my sense of identity, but that still wasn't enough. There was only so much I could get through my private contemplations and beliefs; I needed experience on a more social level.

This leads to the other two areas—friends and work. I had enough friends that I didn't feel like an outcast, but I had only one really close friend, the one who was my peeping-Tom partner. The two of us had met when we were 5 and have been best friends ever since. The strength of our friendship cannot be overstated. We never pressured each other into doing anything (like trying drugs) and we could share our secrets and problems. My friend, Bill, had a much better relationship with his family than I did, so I adopted his family as my own in a way. I didn't look up to or respect my parents, but I did his. Their opinions had more weight with me than my own parents' opinions. I don't mean to imply that my mother and father were failures as parents, but I held hard feelings against them and looked to Bill's parents for guidance.

Bill and I did everything together. We liked the same shows and music and hung out together all the time. In fact, it wasn't uncommon for teachers and other kids to get the two of us mixed up. There was a great amount of security in that relationship for me. I felt that Bill accepted me for who I was; he was the only person who I wasn't afraid to stutter in front of. Bill and I were (and still are) blood brothers. When we were very young, probably 7 or 8, we slit our thumbs with a knife and rubbed our bleeding fingers together. I assume that isn't done much today. We took everything from swimming lessons to guitar lessons together.

Our parents all worked and much of the time we were left to ourselves. During the summer we spent most of every day unsupervised. Some of our activities were questionable. For example, there was the summer that a moose was spotted in our town. A moose had not been seen in our town for over a hundred years so the news stirred up some fear along with the curiosity and fascination. Only a handful of people had seen the animal, and it was assumed that it had just moved on out of town. One afternoon Bill and I came up with a brainstorm. Our local paper had carried a picture of the tracks left by the moose so we cut that out. Next we got some wood and cut out models that resembled the prints. We tied the models to the bottom of our sneakers and walked in the backyard. Sure enough, we left tracks in dirt that were very similar to those in the picture. The next few nights we snuck out of our houses and went to the swampier areas of town. We put the moose feet on the bottom of our sneakers and walked in the mud of several backyards. A couple of days later we read in the paper that the moose was back and, the paper said, it was possible now that there was more than one. The police had been placed on alert. Aside from our terror of being found out by the police, we loved the whole episode. We had fooled the adults again.

The two of us did everything together and continually made future plans. In the long run this may have come close to hurting me; I relied too much on Bill's friendship and didn't try to be more outgoing and build my confidence. On the other hand, if I hadn't had Bill and the security of our friendship, I never would have learned how to function well socially.

The summer before high school I got a job at the town library, and I was excited about starting work. I had spent a lot of time at the library (it was very close to my house) and I knew several of the librarians. My immediate boss, Mrs. Johnson, turned out to be one of the most special people I have ever met. She was kind, friendly, intelligent, always quick to praise but also ready to point out mistakes in a constructive way, and an all-around lovely person. She could discern everybody's personality. She must have known that I needed a place where I could feel I belonged because she soon gave me many important responsibilities that were within my capabilities. This helped my confidence tremendously. I felt everyone there wanted to see me succeed, and when I made mistakes they treated them as very minor in comparison to all the other things I had done right. It wasn't long before I was working very hard at my job. I would do everything they wanted done—and more if I could find other little jobs. If they needed someone at an awkward time on short notice, I always volunteered. At first it was simply that I wanted Mrs. Johnson and the others to keep giving me praise and that their good opinion was very important to me. Eventually, though, I began to realize that to do a task with integrity and diligence was important and was its own reward. Before working at the library I had never felt what it was like to accomplish something that I had spent much time and effort doing. There was great satisfaction in it. It was a long time before I applied this to schoolwork, but that would come.

I worked at the library for about six years. It's hard to summarize all I learned and all the feelings connected with the library and the staff, but there are a few key points. First is the dedication of the staff. Many of the full-time employees held a master's degree in Library Arts and yet were making under $22,000 a year. They unfailingly did their best to work for the community in what was often a shamefully thankless capacity. I admired their dedication. I felt I wanted to emulate that, and often now when I feel I'm unfairly overloaded with work and responsibilities I think of those people and remember that I should appreciate what I have going for me. The other staff—the part-timers, custodians, and such—were the same. They all did their jobs well and created an enjoyable atmosphere for everyone. Sometimes I wondered how so many good people could be concentrated in one small place. Maybe I'm a naïve optimist but I came to the conclusion that it was the atmosphere, the congenial and supportive feelings around us all, that was responsible for it. Most people have it in them to be their best but the circumstances surrounding them are not as favorable. And where did this atmosphere come from? I think it came from Mrs. Johnson and a couple of others there who were much like her. They were very supportive, generous, and kind to everyone, and so everyone else began to emulate and encourage this attitude. I don't know how well I have succeeded, but I have tried to hold this attitude and to project it to those I come into contact with. I've learned that how you treat people can really make a difference. Sometimes a kind word from the right person at a certain time can make all the difference in the world.

Another aspect of the library that was very important to me were the patrons, whose questions and requests for help had a great influence on me. I felt I held a certain power. If I knew the answer to a question, then I could solve a person's problem. Perhaps if a person was particularly nasty I could purposely misdirect that person (I never did that but I was aware that I held the power). It really built my confidence. I was given certain responsibilities and I was living up to them. This was something I couldn't find in school.

After a couple of years of working at the library, I noticed that many people recognized me outside of the library. For a very shy person this really fed my ego. One of my favorite memories happened right in the library. A mother brought her little girl to check out some children's books. The girl was no more than 3 and a half years old. She could walk and talk only a little bit. Her mother sat her on the counter as I checked out her books. I was talking to the girl like I usually did with little children; I asked if she enjoyed reading or if her mother read her stories at night. When I was done checking out the books and the mother was taking her off the counter she smiled and said, "He's a nice man, isn't he, Mommy?" Her mother agreed. I felt about ten feet tall the rest of the day. I knew from my experience at the library that I wanted to work in some capacity with people.

The problem was always that I couldn't seem to apply myself to anything outside of working at the library. I matured a great deal while working there, but I needed to extend that to other areas. I continued cheating on tests and papers throughout all of high school, but after freshman year I stopped advertising it. I quit helping my friends cheat and bragging about my crooked accomplishments. I wanted to become a more serious student, but I wasn't secure enough in my abilities to give up cheating. I felt I needed to cheat to get good grades. It was also partly force of habit; I was accustomed to cheating—not studying—and that was hard to break. I was still very withdrawn in class and did not participate. I avoided all high school social events. Overall, high school did not have a great effect on me because I put so little into it. What I did outside of class was of greater consequence.

When I wasn't working and my friend Bill wasn't around, I spent most of my time by myself feeling very lonely. Only those who have experienced extended periods of loneliness know what it can do to you. Fortunately, I had enough interests to occupy some of my time. For example, I was very interested in astronomy, and early in July there is a meteor shower that appears every year. One summer I decided to get up in the middle of the night to watch it. I had never seen a meteor shower before and I was not expecting it to be anything too spectacular. I got up around one in the morning and went outside the house. It took a while before I could discover the section of the sky in which it was taking place, but when I first saw it, I was frozen in place. Every few seconds a bright streak would shoot across the sky and disappear. Each one couldn't have lasted more than a second, but the power they seemed to display left me awestruck. They sped over the sky so quickly that they were hard to follow and I got dizzy from turning my head so quickly.

Then I decided I wanted to enjoy this more. I went inside and made a couple of sandwiches and got a drink. On leaving the house I caught a glimpse of my father's old pipe. It was a big, awkward thing but it seemed to match the moment perfectly. I had never smoked before—I had never even considered it—but I grabbed some tobacco and some matches and went outside with my little package. When I got outside I wasn't satisfied with my view. My house is on a hill but the house next to mine was taller and was blocking my line of sight. Nothing was going to get in my way of enjoying this show so I decided to climb up my neighbor's roof. I had scaled the side of their house several times before a few years earlier (to peek in their windows) but I had never been on the roof. The house had a fairly sturdy drain pipe so I tied my things in a bundle around my waist and climbed up to the roof. It was an old house with a lot of nooks and crannies in it so I found a good comfortable spot which couldn't be seen from the ground and sat down to rest. Lighting up the pipe took a few tries, and when I did light it at first I felt sick from the smoke. After a while I got used to it and started on the sandwiches. There was no moon that night and the sky was very dark. I looked upward and watched the lights streak from one side to the other.

I was all alone. I could see no one and no one could see me. The darkness of the sky was very soft and deep and the warm yellow streaks painting a path across the backdrop every few seconds were both magnificent and calming. My troubles were all below me and the show I was watching seemed to put everything into its right place. This was so much larger than anything else I had ever seen. How many trillions of miles and billions of years had these meteors travelled only so I could watch them burn out in flame? Everything else seemed insignificant. There were no happy families, no unhappy families. No good students and no bad students. There were no words locked inside my head refusing to come out right. All of us were little and of no importance to what I was witnessing. A quote from Dickens floated over me and didn't seem as harsh as when I first read it: "The universe makes a rather indifferent parent." I stayed on the roof for a couple of hours and for that time all was right in the world. Unfortunately, that was only a passing moment—no matter how good it made me feel, it didn't help me deal with everyday life.

After barely graduating from high school, Bill and I went together to a community college. It was something of a joke academically; my high school classes were more difficult. In spite of skipping a lot of classes we ended up with As and Bs and decided to transfer to a technical college. A couple of weeks into the semester I realized engineering was not for me and decided to transfer again in order to become an English major and live at school. It meant separating from Bill the next fall, but I felt it was time for me to try going out on my own.

That summer I met a girl named Ellen and soon started dating. Everything seemed perfect—almost too good to be true. We understood each other's feelings and problems and were able to give support to each other. For example, one day we were talking and I stuttered a little bit. She asked me directly about my stutter. No one had ever done that before. People had avoided mentioning it because they thought it would embarrass me. That attitude carries the implication that there is something wrong with having a stutter. Ellen asked me about it very straightforwardly. I realized that she accepted it as simply a part of me—just like my hair is brown and my eyes are blue. It had a great influence on me and I felt myself falling for Ellen. I took her to her prom and we saw a lot of each other during the summer.

So much happened that summer that it's hard, even in my own mind, to organize it all. Most was due to Ellen's influence and the nature of our relationship together. She was the first girl I ever developed an intimate and supportive relationship with. We shared our secret hopes and dreams and could rely on each other if we wanted to talk over problems we were experiencing in our lives. We each knew that we could depend on the other. We took things very slowly as far as a physical relationship went. When I think back to the time we shared, I think my favorite memories were when we went to the park and had a picnic. We would lie on the grass, sometimes I would lay my head on her lap, and talk or just sit quietly. There was something very special about being able to spend quiet time with someone as close to my heart as she was. All the days we spent together seemed to be sunny, happy, and fulfilling. I'm probably romanticizing our time together, but that is the quality of my memories of Ellen. Being able to build a relationship like that, particularly since Ellen and I were so well matched, resulted in my maturing a great deal.

I can't give a surefire explanation for it, but my stutter was decreasing markedly. By the end of the summer, stuttering had become a rare incident whereas before it had been the norm. Perhaps it was because I was at the age when men finally stop growing. My metabolism may have changed slightly. Maybe it was because I was maturing mentally and emotionally. By the end of the summer I was almost speaking normally. I am determined never to forget, however, what it was like having a problem such as that and what it was like to have people judge me and put me down for something over which I had no control. I'm very fortunate to have experienced that and to have had it corrected for whatever reason. I work with the mentally handicapped now, and it's always surprising to see how far they can go beyond what is expected of them. I've learned never to place restrictions on the abilities of other people, and more important, on my own abilities.

Ellen was going to a school about 1,500 miles away. We could have made a commitment at the end of the summer, but we both thought that we should go off to school with full freedom and then see how we felt. It was difficult because we were both very much in love by that point. It was a good decision though, and we promised to keep in touch. Without Ellen's support, I don't think I would have had the confidence to leave my home and all my established friends and go off to an unfamiliar environment. She was never even aware of that. It was one of the ways she helped me without knowing it.

We left for school and, as promised, we kept in touch. I wrote her every day, and she called me often. After three weeks we found it very hard to be apart. We kept on saying how much we missed each other. Toward the end of September, Ellen said that she was coming home in a couple of weekends. She wanted to get together and spend a day with me. I'm pretty sure we were both ready to make a commitment—we were going to become engaged, so to speak. Ellen hinted that she felt ready to begin a sexual relationship. We started talking on the phone more often, and Ellen began thinking about transferring to a school in my area so we could see more of each other. I was on top of the world.

Friday night around 11:00, about a week before Ellen was to come home, I was in my room studying when I heard the phone ring. It was Ellen and she sounded upset. She said she had been assaulted that afternoon and described what happened. When she had finished, I said, "Ellen, you keep saying that you were assaulted but I think it's important that you admit outright that you've been raped."

It was a painful phone call for both of us. We talked for an hour or so; I said I knew a place I could call to get some information and I would call right back. I called a rape crisis hotline and found out all the medical, legal, and physical aspects I could. I called Ellen back and we decided to fly her up here, take her to a hospital, and see what she wanted to do as far as pressing charges. She felt she couldn't tell her parents what happened, so I had to help her on my own. I did what I could for her, but I don't know how much help I was. I was very upset. It was an extremely difficult weekend. She went back to her school in a couple of days, which was probably the hardest thing of all. I wanted to keep her with me and protect her. But she had more courage than I did and went back to finish the semester.

I was in a bad state after she left. I didn't eat for a total of six days and when I did start eating, it was only in little bits. I couldn't sleep, and when I did I was having terrible nightmares. I would dream of people chasing me and then setting me on fire; people surrounded me and hacked at me with knives. The nightmares were bad, but I wondered why they were always about me. Ellen was never in any of these dreams. I felt very selfish, like I didn't really care about her. This brought on a tremendous feeling of guilt.

Soon the dreams started to change and seemed to reflect something that had actually happened. I couldn't put my finger on it, but each time I woke up I seemed to be close to recalling something I hadn't thought of in years. Bits and pieces started coming together, and it just got worse and worse. I began calling back memories in my waking hours. For over thirteen years my mind had withheld these incidents and blocked them from coming forward. However, now with Ellen's experience, it all came back. I remembered being a small child and a man I knew brought me into a bedroom. I remembered him laying me on my stomach and his hot breath on the back of my neck and the pain as he pushed down on me. It happened more than once; he did things that I didn't understand then but I understand now. I can't say how many times he did this because they are all blurred together. The experiences had been locked in my memory for years—I had never recalled or spoken about them to anyone before. I must have been afraid at the time to tell anybody, including my parents, what was going on.

By the end of the semester, I was a mess. I was in a crisis situation and my grades were horrible. I did pull through it, but the next semester I decided to get counseling. I started understanding a lot of things. I understood now why I hated crowds and having people stand behind me. I understood why the experience with sex brought up so many confusing emotions. What I have never learned to understand is why some people will use other people weaker than themselves to satisfy their own selfish wants. I still know the man who did the things to me and it really seems he doesn't remember it at all. Maybe he does and is suffering with a terrible conscience, but I don't think so. I have been watching him since to find out if he has been doing it to any other child. I don't think he has. If I find out that he is, I'm not exactly sure what I would do. Most likely I will kill him if I think I can get away with it. I don't have violent feelings toward most people, but if someone like him keeps hurting innocent people in that way, I don't think he should live. I want people who do things like that to know that they are in a lot of danger.

The relationship between Ellen and me was never the same. We stopped dating. She wasn't able to continue a physical relationship with me, or start one with anyone else at that time. It wasn't a complete loss because we developed a very strong and supportive friendship. I eventually told her what had happened to me as a child, and we helped each other in many ways. Our friendship became something very important to each of us, and we have both benefited from it. I learned from her what love and generosity in the face of pain really is. Since then we have both gone on to date successfully and are both happy and contented people. We both had something horrible done to us, but neither of us is guilty of ever hurting another person.

I have found a role for myself. It was very painful growing up, but through the pain and all my mistakes I have learned a lot. I do very well in school, and I'm working my way toward studying counseling psychology in graduate school. I earn As and a few Bs now, and I'm finally the student that I've always wanted to be. In fact, I'm more successful in college than anyone else in my family. I'm not spiteful and bitter and don't rub it in my family's face, but I do like the feeling (and the place in the family) it gives me. I find that even now I tend not to participate in class discussions as much as I could, but that is more from old habits than from shyness. I date girls, but I haven't dated steadily since Ellen. I guess I'm guilty of comparing every girl to her and the quality of the relationship we had. A friend who is studying for her doctorate in psychology and knows my history with Ellen would like to see me get into counseling men who physically and sexually abuse women. I can't consider that right now because I still have very violent feelings toward these people and I know that is wrong. Maybe sometime in the future I'll be able to think about it.

Some days I go through mood swings. In the morning I can be the most cheerful optimist and yet come back in the evening seeing red with rage. However, it has been a long time since I've experienced any sort of depression, and I think that is the important thing. I simply write off my mood swings to my Irish temperament. Besides, these mood swings are so minor compared to my former depths of depression that I can joke about them.

Recently I became very ill and spent several days in the hospital confined to a bed and connected to an IV tube. For the next several weeks I was very weak. During this time my speech regressed terribly. It made me realize that my problems had not gone away, but rather I had learned to compensate for them. When I was weak and fatigued I didn't have the concentration necessary to maintain my methods of compensation. I was at first upset and felt once again that I was very different from others. Soon, however, I came to the conclusion that it was a good thing. It would come back every once in a while to make certain that I didn't forget where I came from and how far I've come. I would be reminded from time to time that we all have our strengths and our weaknesses and it is important to accept both from all people. I would be reminded of the simple beauty of a conversation.

Altogether, I have been very fortunate in my life. Some terrible things have happened to me, but then I have also been lucky enough to come into contact with many wonderful people. These people have shown me what it means to be a caring and responsible person. They've allowed me to make all my mistakes without placing any judgments on me. I have learned from them that the way you treat other people really can make a difference for the better. Treat everyone with the dignity and respect they deserve and it will always come back to you. Stand by others when they're in need because when you're in need you'll find you have a lot more friends than you thought you had. But most of all, learn to stand on your own two feet. If you can't help yourself, there is little that others can do for you. Everyone is going to experience pain and hardship at some point in their life, and that is when we learn the depth of both our own strength and of our relationships with others. If we have planted strong roots, we should be able to withstand much of what comes our way. At the library, there was a saying on the bulletin board which I have always liked: *Be optimistic even when you feel desperate.*

FOREVER AN AWKWARD ADOLESCENT

This is the story of a young man born with serious physical disabilities. David describes the tension between his parents over how high their expectations for his autonomy should be. His father's "legendary penchant for interfering" results in his doing everything for him, whereas his mother, having "less patience with incompetence," expects him to learn to do for himself. College becomes a new opportunity for forming close female friendships and for academic achievements, but these are tainted by doubts over whether he is held to the same standards as his peers. And he asks, "What is to become of my sexuality?" and envisions "a 35-year-old with the sexuality of a 14-year-old, and the prospect does not please me." As he plans to begin graduate school for a career in media, he will not accept society's narrow expectation that he should practice his profession as a representative of the disabled because he says "I do not think of myself as a disabled person."

My first clear memory is from nursery school. When I was 3 years old my parents sent me to a small nursery school for three or four hours about twice a week. It was in the basement of a local church, and I distinctly remember being carried down a long corridor past beautifully colored stained-glass windows. Someone was carrying me and pointed out the colored shapes that were on the opposite wall as the sun shone through the windows.

I should note that at this point I had not yet learned to walk. I still think of it as "learning" to walk, but this is not quite accurate. Because I was born with physical disabilities, the first three to five years of my life were interspersed with multiple operations, where the doctors tried to stretch my hamstrings surgically. After each of these operations I was put in a plaster cast—at one point, both legs up to the waist. It was all in an effort to unclub my feet so that I might someday be able to walk. Everyone was very excited when I finally did, spontaneously, while waiting with my father in a doctor's waiting room. My parents and all their good friends were in tears, I guess, because the professionals had been about evenly divided on whether I'd ever walk at all. I don't remember this important occasion, however, which is one of my peculiar tricks of memory—I never seem to understand the full implications of various "remarkable" events in my life.

I don't have a lot of clear early memories of my parents. I always took them for granted, at least until I began to figure out ways that I might lose them. Like when I began to realize that their marriage wasn't that great. They really should have divorced twenty-five years ago. Except then, they wouldn't have had me! Even so, they are very unsuited to each other, and their arguments and periodic leavings and returnings were a bit of a cloud in my childhood.

I am sometimes embarrassed and worried about how little their sour relationship has seemed to affect me. I have had moments of tears and fear during particularly bad patches but, by and large, I have never had those self-blaming feelings that everyone says kids have when their parents have problems. I think it is a testament to my parents that despite their trials, life at our house always had a sense of security and permanence. I don't know if they did it on purpose; more likely it was their conservative view of how one conducted one's life that did it. Breakfast was always there. Dinner was always at 6:30. Everything was predictable. At the time, I came to envy my friends' younger, more adventurous parents (they went to movies—we never did), but now I think that it was better for me to have parents who took refuge in routine. I never really worried that I wouldn't be taken care of, that I wouldn't be loved.

I entered adolescence (and eighth grade) at about the time we made a cross-country move. Thinking back on that period, I am certain that the move was good for me. For one thing, my best friend had moved away the year before, at a time when our relationship was becoming difficult. We first became friends, at age 5, because we shared a disdain for the crowd. We weren't joiners. For me, this trait was determined by my disabilities; I had had to learn how to entertain myself. The fun I had was sedentary: matchbox cars, model planes, books about WWII fliers, and TV—which spent a great deal of time catering to the imaginations of would-be fighter pilots and space travelers. My friend also liked these things, but more by choice. After a while, we reinforced our reclusive tendencies, and as we grew older we grew farther and farther apart from our peers who were either getting into sports or getting into trouble.

Predictably, as puberty struck, my friend and I began to reevaluate (separately) where we stood. I suspect that my friend began to see that others his age were having a lot of physical fun, horsing around in ways that seemed impossible, or at least improbable, for me. Suddenly going over to each other's houses to play with Legos no longer sufficed to sustain our friendship. I, too, began to identify with other peers, people who also stood out, but who seemed to have made the transition from Legos to a kind of makeshift intellectualism. When a group of us began reading *The Lord of the Rings,* my best friend did not join in. Soon after this, he moved away.

For my family, the move across country was very traumatic, though they tried to act as though it was an adventure. My main concern was whether I would be able to survive in the new public school I would be entering. Having spent all my grade school years at an "experimental education" school on a college campus in my hometown, I was not used to a structured school environment. The realm of real schools was a mysterious and sinister one in the lore of this "campus school," and I'm afraid I bought into the horror stories of academic rigor and regimentation, which passed for information on public schools among my 12-year-old school-mates. I think that entering middle school in the new town, far from any familiar people or places, was the best way for me to get into regular schooling; kind of like being thrown into a pool as a way of learning to swim. As it turned out, it was all right. I gained confidence in my academic abilities by having my intelligence con-firmed for the first time by grades. The teachers there were every bit as human as in my other school, and the kids were far more numerous, so I could hide in anonymity. At least, that is what I thought. Actually, because of my disabilities I was almost instantly known, or known of, by everyone in the school. I was also treated with uniform kindness and curiosity from the first day, but even then I wondered, as I do now, how much of that kindness was actually pity for me be-cause of my disability.

Since I have been physically disabled all of my life, I have managed to cope with the purely practical problems arising from this with a minimum of fuss on my part; I felt no loss, because I had no feelings of "normality" to compare with. One of my physical problems is that I am short, about four feet, two inches tall. Until I began growing whiskers on my face and driving a car, I was constantly mistaken by strangers as being a little kid. It's a hell of a pain for a 16-year-old boy to be handed a kiddie's menu every time he enters a restaurant. It is even worse when mere coherent speech is greeted with awe. If explaining to the old lady in church that I am taking five classes in high school provokes an assumption that I must be terribly smart, how am I supposed to know whether I really am or if everyone is just impressed that I don't drool on myself? I have high standards for myself, per-haps not as high as many straight-A college students, but I am always impressed when I witness, say, good writing and intelligent conversation in others and I as-pire to such standards of intelligence. During my teen years it was a constant nag-ging irritation that everyone around me had what I felt were extremely low expectations. I never knew where I stood.

Almost everybody treats me well, whether or not they really know me. In fact, I gained a reputation among some of my high school peers for being really smart, even though plenty of students within my range of ability (such as those with whom I went through an Honors English program) had better grades and study habits than I did. After awhile, I began to realize that people were predis-posed to treating disabled people with extra kindness. Perhaps, I thought, my "smart kid" reputation, which I considered to be disproportionate to my actual abilities, was part of this extra kindness. Supporting this notion was my observa-tion that many people who had known me for a long time, even some members of my extended family, tended to express admiration for my accomplishments with an enthusiasm far beyond what I considered to be appropriate. I was able to gauge this by comparing my parents' response with that of my brother and certain close friends, all of whom had gotten used to the fact that, indeed, I had learned to walk and talk and go to school like any normal kid, and hence, responded in a more subdued fashion to what were, after all, fairly minor accomplishments on my part.

My desire to do well academically did not, oddly enough, compel me to become an especially studious student. My parents never really put the pressure on me to get straight As, and when I came home with report cards that were mixed As and Bs, they seemed to feel these were fairly wonderful. Either they were too old to understand grade inflation, or they were falling into the same trap I already explained—being glad that I was still alive and walking and apparently intelligent. I tend to think that it was a little of both, which means that I have been guilty, on occasion, of taking advantage of the very tendency which I despise. I have often allowed myself to rest easy in others' low expectations. This is something that I continue to fight in myself. Still, it was terribly important to me that I never got less than a B. I constructed a sort of artificial line of performance, below which I told myself my parents would be disappointed. For some reason, I was never too concerned about what my teachers or my friends thought of my grades; I looked solely to my parents for approval on that score.

If, as I surmised, peoples' expressed admiration of me was exaggerated by the issue of my disabilities, then how could I be sure exactly how much of that praise and admiration had been earned and how much was phony or misplaced? Naturally, as I moved through adolescence, I cared more and more about where I stood in the grand scheme of things. Since the whole business of looks and sex appeal was entirely outside my league, my only arenas for competition and comparison were in academics and in "being likable." I tended to look to everyone I met for approval and conversation was my weapon. At first, I was just naturally inclined to have an odd sense of humor, and to express both this humor and my interest in history and politics in conversations with adults and with as many interested friends as I could find. After awhile, though, around my senior year in high school, I began to sense that being able to carry on a conversation about a wide range of topics was not just fun but an asset, too.

I have long thought that one of the real handicaps of having congenital disabilities is that one often grows up isolated from all the trivial things that adolescents banter about: music, girls, cars, clothes, films, TV, and magazines—the whole range of popular culture is a special language that the adult world too easily dismisses as unimportant. But for the teenager cut off from this language, relating to peers who are already leery of him or her because of a disability is doubly difficult. The goodwill most people have to "give it a try" with the disabled teen may be there at the beginning, but unless the teen is able to "run with the ball" and "fit in" at least by speaking the same language as his or her peers, the goodwill quickly turns to embarrassment, and then the disabled teen will be ignored. If it were up to me, people who counsel disabled kids and their parents would stress the importance, often denigrated in "normal" kids, of "fitting in."

In retrospect, I think that a lot of what I was doing in high school was constructing a character, a persona, I could live with. Most adolescents do this, but for me, it was doubly important because the character I had, my "default" pigeonhole in the eyes of others, was that of a short, oddly postured, disabled kid. I wasn't sure at the time, and I'm still not positive, just what kind of persona I want to have. This has made constructing myself an ad hoc process. For the most part, however, I think I have been able to impress others enough with images other than disability. When I get scared, though, when I think about it too much, I wonder if it's all my imagination. Does everybody still think of me as a disability, and not as a person? I don't know. I'll never really know for sure, because I am always suspicious of others' response to me. I guess that I function from day to day on a veneer of faith; I survive with happiness and pride by assuming that other people see me as I see myself.

My parents are two people whose reactions to me I have trusted. From my mother I get a cartload of political convictions, or perhaps prejudices, because at times I think that her convictions are as much prejudice as they are considered opinions. I count among the greatest gifts of my college years the ability to critique and analyze my own political and social beliefs. By and large, I inherit from Mom a respect for what good can be done by government, along with a profound and unquenchable skepticism which prevents me from ever being satisfied with what government or any other authority is doing. I realize, because I have seen it in my mother, that this is a frustrating way to approach the world. Always having to "bitch, bitch, bitch," not because it's right or good or a citizen's responsibility but because I can't contain myself, is a burden—especially in a society that frowns upon excess in expressing one's views.

Having lived for the most part away from my mother for four years, I have found that I still care deeply about what she thinks of my actions. I don't think I could ever pursue a career, for instance, that violated her standards of morality. This cancels out a lot of possibilities, but fortunately, I have no desire to become a stockbroker. Nevertheless, as I pursue graduate studies in mass media and popular culture, I find myself wondering about how she would feel about my being an advertising copywriter, or a television producer or network reporter. I tend to think that as long as I stay true to my own standards, I will not run afoul of hers, but sometimes I am not sure, and that worries me.

One of the peculiar dynamics of my relations with my parents has been growing up in an atmosphere thick with a history of Dad's legendary penchant for interfering. When I was much younger this didn't bother me, because I sought the security he provided. He was always the provider, the caretaker. In fact, he even helped dress me in the mornings right up till I entered high school. He was always looking for ways to make my life easier. Of course, the problem with this is that it retarded the development of my self-sufficiency. Mom was dead set against this. It wasn't that Mom was uncaring, it is just that she had less patience with incompetence.

In the long run, she was right; it was more help to me to force me into doing things myself than to smooth out any remotely rough areas of day-to-day life. As I got older, Mom became increasingly adamant that Dad was now an abnormally doting parent. She felt that perhaps it was more selfishness on his part—his need to feel needed and in charge—than a true concern for my welfare, which kept him so involved in my physical challenges. Eventually, she began to suggest to me that I ought to resent his "interference" as much as she did. In a way, this was good, because it finally caused me to increase and jealously guard my self-sufficiency. At first for Mom's benefit, but eventually for my own, I began to oppose my father's instinctive moves toward helping me dress, get in and out of cars, put on jackets, and so on. He knew that it all was for the best, and I no longer saw him as my guardian for life. Instead, I began to see him as a friend, a father, and sometimes a pain!

Our relationship has since changed for the better. We now have more arguments than we used to, but they are adult-type arguments. And on the whole, we share a mutual interest in each other's lives. I am sure that he harbors more than a little "controlling interest" in my life, but if he does, he at least is honest enough to admit it, and often interrupts himself midsentence, chuckling at his own tendency to criticize and worry the joy out of new adventures.

Other people, too, have influenced me in less vital, but no less enduring ways. I think that I first got a taste of the joys of discussing politics from the high school librarian. He was a balding, middle-aged man with a bit of a paunch, and a wonderfully dry sense of humor. A fan of George McGovern, he introduced me to the blessings of "Norwegian charisma" while we both watched Walter Mondale stumble through the 1984 campaign. I would come in after lunch and wander over to his office, where we would swap political stories we had heard or read about.

Here was a man, as well educated and articulate as my parents, and with similar political stripes, who actually enjoyed watching the "march of folly" that politics provides. It was a liberation for me. There were very few of my peers with whom I could talk about politics, either because they didn't care or because my views were hopelessly out of sync with theirs. For two years, then, I was able to spend at least an hour of every day just yakking away about anything that popped into my head. In fact, from testing my wings with him, I was finally able to spar with my parents on political topics.

I suspect that this kind of jabbering contributed as much as anything else to my interest in editorial journalism. When I approached the journalism advisor about taking the journalism class (thereby becoming a member of the paper staff), I remember that I had a goal in mind of writing a column. My work in his English class impressed him, so he helped me convince the editor that I should have my own column. In retrospect, I am sure that part of his admiration of me was that damnable tendency I mentioned earlier—to see any accomplishments by a disabled person as a miracle—but I guess I didn't really mind it that much if, in the end, I received recognition purely on my own merits.

I am sure that is one reason why I loved writing that column and the one I wrote for four years in college. In college, I began my column before very many people knew who I was. Consequently, when I got favorable comments from strangers, it was all the more special to me. For the first time in my life, I could be sure that I had earned every bit of the praise I got. I am a person who has never been short of expressions of approval from others, but anonymous praise is like gold to me. This is why I look forward to continue writing of this nature and then hopefully, as a career.

There is one incident from my adolescence that has had perhaps the greatest impact on my outlook. During the long drive from the West Coast to what would be my college in the East, I became seriously ill. At this point, the most severe aspect of my disability stemmed from the effects of severe scoliosis on my lung functions. As I grew, my spine curved even more; the more it curved, the more it applied pressure on my lungs. Hence, my breathing capacity was getting progressively smaller. While a spinal fusion operation at age 10 prevented this from becoming fatal, as it turned out, the procedure left enough room for worsening to make it nearly so.

Knowing that the high altitude we would have to endure on the drive east would make me uncomfortable, my doctors prescribed an oxygen tank that I could use whenever I got too tired by the lack of oxygen. Unfortunately, this did not solve the physical problem of actual breathing, and the result was a potentially deadly spiral; the more oxygen I breathed in, the less my brain was induced to stimulate breathing—the less I breathed, the less I was able to expel carbon dioxide. By the time I had reached my destination I was unable to sleep, because I would stop breathing and wake up.

At one point, I was told that I would never recover fully from this malady—as, in fact, I have not—and that I had about five years to live. The only alternative was to surgically install a permanent tracheostomy so that, in addition to using extra oxygen at night, I could have the help of a respirator in breathing. We waited a few weeks in the vain hope that somehow I would spontaneously pull out of this hole, and during this time I continued to prepare for my first day of classes which was less than two weeks away.

Most of the people around me, my mother and father in particular, saw my entering college as a fantasy. After all, I did look pretty bad, and I could barely cross a room on foot, much less walk to class. Only my older brother seemed to think that they were all overreacting. For all of my life he had lived with the constant and recurrent threat that I would die, that I would never walk, that I could never do thus and such. Every time I had taken a turn for the worse he had been told that "you'd better come and see him, it could be the last time." Every time I had "proved them wrong," as he put it to me. While he was particularly worried with this incident, he still felt that as long as I was certain I would start college on time, there was hope.

To hear him tell it, I am some kind of brave hero for having kept my faith in my ability to recover. From my point of view, it wasn't bravery or faith. I never really realized how serious my condition was. All along, my mind refused to accept the gravity of the situation. Instead, I whiled away these "sick" hours thinking about how I'd decorate my dorm room, and what classes I would take. Finally, it got bad enough that it was decided to do the tracheostomy. Within a week I was going to my first class. To me it seemed natural. It was what I'd planned all along. I was feeling much better, the oxygen with the respirator at night left me quite healthy during the day, and I was doing what I wanted to do.

In a number of ways, this incident is typical of my outlook as I have grown up. First, it shows how I have generally dealt with adversity: I ignore it. I refuse to accept it. I do not think of myself as a disabled person. While this has helped me thus far, it may not continue to do so. Out there in the nonacademic "real" world, disabled people, like any minority group, have to organize and vocally assert their rights. I have always shied away from doing this. For one thing, my relatively privileged family background has to a large extent smoothed my path. I have not had to advocate strongly for myself because money and my father's position as a doctor have advocated for me. Besides that, though, I simply do not want to be labeled. I take no particular "pride" in being disabled, even though I have as much reason to do so as any disabled person. It all comes back to that nagging problem— how can I earn praise and self-esteem without having my disability in the equation?

But as I inch toward a career, perhaps in journalism, certainly in some kind of media, I am finding that I will have to fight society's tendency to view me primarily in terms of my disability. In my chosen field, there is a tendency to pigeonhole people. Blacks report on race issues. Women report on feminism. I don't really want to be a writer or producer of columns or programs about disability. I understand that people see me as a useful tool—articulate, intelligent, and poised disabled people are hard to come by because so many of them have social disabilities that come with their physical problems. Some would say that it is my duty to serve society in the most natural way possible to me, to become an advocate for disabled people. While I accept the logic and morality of this, I simply don't want that!

In addition to calling my attention to this desire in me to be seen in my own terms, my near-death episode also made me more aware than I had ever been before of how important my relationship with my brother is. He was 14 when I was born, and I am pretty sure that he got short shrift because of the all-consuming problems of my infancy. Although he may harbor some resentment toward me, he also has a devotion to me that I always find surprising. Most importantly, he has supported and challenged me consistently throughout my life—from the time he set out to teach me to get up after falling down, to the times he questioned my opinions and forced me to take steps toward independence and maturity that I was unwilling to take. While others let me grow up somewhat spoiled and lazy, he insisted that there was no reason why I couldn't do dishes or cook dinners. During my years at college, the longest time I have ever lived near him, my brother has had a major role in helping me grow up.

By far the richest time in my life has been my four years in college. The intellectual benefits have been enormous, not so much in the amount of stuff I have learned, but in the atmosphere. My college and I were peculiar matches. Traditionally a very athletic campus, it nevertheless fits my personality in that its students have tended to opt for a kind of athleticism that emphasizes the enjoyment of the sport over outright achievement. I, too, get most of my enjoyment out of activities that have no intrinsic value, no tabulation of results.

Socially, college would have been a waste for me had it not been for my fraternity. It is a cliché that fraternity members learn as well as party in the frat, but it really is true in my case. Of course, mine was an atypical one; for fifteen years coeducational, it has for an even longer time been a contradiction, a fraternity for nonjoiners. Because some of the members had the courage to invite me to rush in the spring of my freshman year, I was able to live for two full years in a house with eighteen men and women who considered themselves a true family. We cooked together, studied together, and fought with each other over how to take care of our family and the structure that housed it. Because I lived with these people, they had plenty of time to get to know me.

Far from shutting me up in a closed community, my fraternity experience gave me the confidence to branch out and become better acquainted with others on campus. When people met me, I was identified with my newspaper column and with my fraternity. Thus, I was more than just a disabled student; I had other identities to start me off. I used them as a launching pad from which to make other people understand who I was in a deeper way.

Before writing this meditation on my adolescence, I was asked, among other things, "What makes you want to get up in the morning?" I think that my first answer would be "whatever it is I have to do on that particular day." This illustrates an important tendency of mine. All my life I have done what's been put in front of me to do. Kids go to school, so I went to school. After that, in my family, you go to college, so I went to college. After college, you either get a job or continue your education, so I will attend graduate school. I pay my bills. I do my reading. I grade papers. I cope. I get along. At the same time, however, I am motivated by a need for approval from others.

Some aspects of adolescence are harder to cope with than others. I often wonder what is to become of my sexuality—I cannot envision (except in erotic dreams) a time when a woman would find me attractive enough to spark a long-term love relationship. I have read of other people far more disabled than I am who have found both love and sex with compatible, willing partners. Yet, a paraplegic is, if immobile, still normal in appearance. I am not. I am short, my back curves severely, and because of my rapid metabolism and restricted abdominal cavity, I am skinny to the point of being emaciated. I have had many female friends, but what could possibly provoke them to see me and be sexually attracted to me?

I have tried on two occasions to move closer to two different female friends. In both cases, this consisted of my acting as comforter and patient listener in time of crisis or stress. On both occasions, they appreciated it and the friendships deepened. But in both cases, I suspect, they had no idea that I had any other motive than a friend's concern. And in each instance, I felt like a beast, because I knew that I had ulterior motives. I know something of the dangers of a male/female relationship based on the weak and emotionally distressed woman and the strong "I'll take care of you" man, and I have no desire to become a "co-dependent"— with or without sex.

I look at the future of my sexuality and I see a 35-year-old with the sexuality of a 14-year-old. In this area, I am likely to be forever an awkward adolescent—and the prospect does not please me. At the same time, I hope that the sense of humor, the curiosity, and the weightlessness of carefree adolescence can be preserved, to some extent. I look around me and see many people in both journalism and cultural studies who seem to have retained these characteristics. Perhaps I can, too. I hope, finally, that I do not ever really grow up.

In sum, I have come a long way. Because of me and those who have supported me, I have accomplished many things and done a lot of growing up. I am still an adolescent, though. Only an adolescent has the audacity to hope for what I hope for, which is—everything.

DAVID: THIRTEEN YEARS LATER

Everyone likes to think of themselves as unique. Nobody likes to admit that they are subject to "textbook" psychology, the courses of their lives determined by recognized trends and phases. Reading what I wrote thirteen years ago, I am struck by how typical I was and how predictable the changes in my life—and lack of changes—since then have been. My disabilities and life history may make me seem different to others, but I know just how common my life experiences have been. This doesn't bother me; in a way, it's even comforting.

In some ways, thirteen years ago, I was at the tale end of adolescence. I had graduated from college and was halfway through graduate school. I had lived on my own for almost five years. I had distinct interests and a good idea of where my talent lay, and had a coherent worldview. I knew (or thought I knew) who I was, what kind of person I was.

Looking back I realize that I was actually in the deep end of adolescence, and that I'm only now really leaving that period behind me. I was still very dependent on my parents, not physically, but emotionally and philosophically. I had little "real world" work experience, and no real leadership experience. I had no sexual experience at all, at least none that involved other people. I had no strong, deep relationships with anyone, platonic or otherwise. I was like what has been called a "functional alcoholic," a person with a definite drinking problem, but one that doesn't interfere with most everyday life activities.

Yet I was a mess. Parts of me were fully developed, but others woefully underdeveloped. I didn't realize it, in fact, because my deficits didn't prevent me from living a seemingly normal life. I was happy and was either unaware of my problems, or, because they hadn't caused anything bad to happen, figured they weren't anything to worry about. Remember my tendency to ignore my medical problems, and therefore be able to survive them? I think that the same held true for my emotional and developmental problems: I felt okay. People seemed to think I was okay, so, I thought, "if it ain't broke, don't fix it."

Before I get into these deeper, more troubling matters, I need to make a list of the ways I have changed in thirteen years:

1. Thirteen years ago, I thought of myself as a politically radical, or at least a lefty dissenter. Today I am still left of center, but in other ways I am quite conservative, and think maybe I always have been. Growing up during the Reagan administration, I assumed that authority was always wrong, possibly corrupt, definitely stupid. I figured that I'd carry this attitude through all of my life, like my parents, who were never satisfied no matter who was running the country. During the Clinton administration, however, I discovered how restful it could be to sit back and be comfortable with the group in charge. I still enjoyed analyzing and sometimes disagreeing with the finer points of policy, but I quickly got used to feeling that, basically, people in government at all levels were good, smart people who thought mostly like I did about things. If they did stupid things or advocated policies I didn't like, the difference was more like that between Catholics and Episcopalians than between Hindus and Muslims. Lively debate was still possible, but I felt that those in authority and I were heading in the same direction. It was during this time, too, that I began to feel that a lot of what was wrong in the world was due to faulty systems, not faulty people. That's an idea that has played a major part in my professional life, but more about that later.

2. Thirteen years ago, I had rarely, if ever, experienced open hostility or competition from my peers. An Ivy League education is supposed to be "competitive." In my experience it was difficult, but not competitive in the personal sense. Nobody wanted me to fail so that they could prosper. Also, if people disliked me, they kept it to themselves for the most part. I don't know whether this was because my disability made them feel that it would be inappropriate to oppose me, or because I hadn't yet tried any activities that brought me into real conflict with people. The result is that I was totally unprepared emotionally for open interpersonal conflict. Also, I lacked even the most basic skills for competition and conflict—skills that most 8-year-olds acquire after their first few Little League games. I've come some distance since then, but I still avoid conflict, even when it is necessary, and several times I have missed the signs of serious interpersonal conflict until it was too late.

3. My parents separated, my father found another love in his life, and my mother died of cancer. These events had their impact, but that impact has been gradual. Even my mother's illness and death had less impact on me as they occurred than her absence has had in the six years since. I have missed her support and guidance greatly. At the same time, I have been able to make my own way in my hometown in a way that I couldn't have if she were still here. I feel bad saying so, but I know that my mother would understand. She was always the one who wanted more than anyone for me to be my own person. Meanwhile, my relationship with my father has improved in some ways and deteriorated in others. We now relate to each other as adults, and Dad has expressed pride in my accomplishments.

4. After graduate school, I settled in my hometown. I did so because there was a job available there, but my mother, who lived there, and the attractiveness of familiar territory also led me there. I still live there, and probably will for some years to come. While I often think about an alternative career, I have no strong desires to leave my home just for the sake of starting over in a new town.

5. The most significant change in me over the past thirteen years has been the complete turnaround in my attitude toward my disability and toward working in the disability services field. The job offered to me in 1991 was a position at a new nonprofit organization in my hometown, an organization serving people with disabilities, that was governed and staffed primarily by people with disabilities. I had never heard before of such an organization. Philosophically, it rejected most of the negatives I had come to associate with disabilities: pity, charity, narrow group self-interest, paternalism, and segregation. Instead, this organization was a practical service and advocacy offshoot of the disability rights movement—another thing I knew nothing about even though I had lived with a disability all of my life. I started off doing publicity work for the organization, which wasn't so far from what I thought my career path in writing and media would be. I figured I would spend a year or two gaining work experience, while attempting to do some writing for our local newspaper. I never did write for the paper, not counting letters to the editor and editorials on behalf of the organization for which I worked. One reason was that I didn't have the energy and motivation to pursue journalism while holding down a full-time job. The other reason was that, in the disability rights movement, I found an approach to disability that fits my personality and a mission I am uniquely qualified to serve.

The disability rights movement fits my personality in that it approaches individuals' problems by seeing systemic problems that are at their root. My organization not only helps individuals with disabilities deal with their specific concerns, we also identify ways in which the structures, policies, and practices of ordinary society make life more difficult for people with disabilities. For instance, we typically help an individual with disabilities deal with architectural barriers in a workplace, but we also work to remove such barriers wherever we find them. The disability rights movement has its roots in 1960s activism and political engagement. In other words, it views disability in the same way I view pretty much everything.

Most important, we work in this field not because we feel sorry for people with disabilities, but because we *are* people with disabilities, and because it is just. Previously, I avoided association with any kind of "disability community" because the only ways I'd seen such associations was in the context of charity, and that disgusted me. It also prevented me from truly seeing how my disability gives me a kinship and solidarity with others who have a disability. In a way, I denied myself an important source of support and pride. By working within the field as I do, I have reclaimed my membership in an exciting and vibrant community, rather than joined a sad and depressing begging crew.

The most important qualification for working in the disability rights movement is having a disability. I also bring a superior education and an analytical mind to the movement. I find that I am able to conceptualize disability issues in the abstract, while also emotionally connecting with them. There are many who can do one or the other, but relatively few who can do both. This transforms my choice to work in the field from a mere preference or convenience into a sort of mission. It also led to my taking on local leadership in the movement. I am now the executive director of the organization I joined in 1991.

One thing that hasn't changed in me is my wish to do something with my life that is both personally satisfying and useful. Finding and joining the disability rights movement has been the single most positive development in my life over the last thirteen years.

Although I would have learned more about my strengths and weaknesses no matter what I'd done after graduate school, the fact is that the work I have chosen has brought both my strengths and weaknesses into much sharper focus. I have already mentioned the strengths I have discovered. However, the weaknesses I have discovered may be more important in the long run.

In my original reflection, I wrote about not being sure where I stood in other people's eyes because I felt that they might be taking my disability into account when assessing my personality or performance. I implied that I didn't want or like unearned praise and admiration. I have since discovered that, even though I don't agree with it intellectually, I have become used to people "cutting me some slack," most likely because of my disability. I believe this caused me to be too dependent on being liked, which has led to some of the more serious problems I have had in my working life.

When the executive director's position opened up, I applied for it. As I've said, I was probably the logical choice, based on my resume, life experience, and ability to understand disability issues. However, in retrospect, I see that I was really not prepared for leadership and supervision. I had no previous experience of either and understood them only in the simplest terms. There were one or two people in the organization who, I think, knew this better than I did, and once I became director they made it known in subtle ways that they didn't have much confidence in my abilities. Of course, this was a shock to me. It was the first time I had ever experienced real opposition—not to an idea or opinion, but to my actual abilities and personality. A vicious circle developed in which I was afraid to confront this opposition, which confirmed my weakness and encouraged bad behavior on the part of employees, which I failed to deal with because of my fear of being disliked and creating conflict, and on and on.

Finally, after several years of alternating bad times and good times, I have begun to get a handle on leadership. The biggest hurdle was finding out that if someone doesn't like me or is angry with me, the world doesn't end. My life doesn't collapse. At one point, I even discovered that two of my employees were complaining to the Board of Directors about my "inconsistency." I can't blame them, because, as I've said, I tended to let people get away with things I shouldn't have. This meant that less contentious employees often got better treatment than hard workers. Unfortunately, it took staff plotting and Board intervention to get me to face up to this and other related problems.

Gradually, though, I have changed the way I do my work and the way I relate to people, including those at work. I am more willing to confront people when needed. I procrastinate less. I have learned how to accommodate individuals' needs and strengths, while also holding them to a fair standard of performance.

The best thing about this experience, however, is that it has made me stronger. I always understood the idea that adversity makes you stronger, but never really believed it to be true. I had survived a lot of physical and medical adversity, and didn't see myself as being especially strong. Now that I have experienced the much more difficult forms of adversity found in the workplace and between people, I realize what adversity really is—and that I can survive it. As I said before, the world didn't end just because I screwed up, and this has given me the confidence I need to change myself in ways that will actually improve my performance. So I guess you could say that I had to fail in order to learn how to succeed.

With all of this going on, it's a good thing that I am usually able to put it all aside and enjoy my free time at home.

I still don't feel completely comfortable saying that I like to watch television, but it happens to be true. I don't apologize for it, but I'm certainly aware of the image it presents: a lonely guy letting his mind rot by watching the "idiot box" every night. For me, though, television is not a passive medium. I've always "read" TV. That is, I process it the way serious readers read books. Maybe a better comparison would be to say that I watch TV the way Roger Ebert watches movies. Even the worst shows say something and I'm interested in what TV shows say. It is both a relaxation and intellectual exercise.

Music is one of the few things that instantly reaches me emotionally. It is also one of the areas of my life where I don't mind saying I'm still an adolescent. If anything, I prefer today's music to the music I grew up with. My tastes are fairly broad. I like any genre of music if it is performed with passion and animated with ideas. The ideas don't have to be intellectually sophisticated or even admirable, but if I feel that something genuine is being communicated, then the quality of the musicianship or the sophistication of the composition isn't important to me. Music may be the only form of expression that I enjoy on a completely gut level.

My other spare time obsession is my website and weblog or "blog." I taught myself some of the basics of website design and, using blog software, created my own site on the Internet, which I add to several times a week. The blog has turned into the diary I always told myself I should keep, but never did. It's almost three years old now, and looking through the archives I'm amazed at how much I have written in small, unconnected nuggets, peppered with Web links to news stories, books, music, and other strange things I'm thinking or reading about. I don't get very personal with the blog, which probably makes it less interesting. I guess it's an indication that I am still too shy to share much of my inner self with the world, even though I'm pretty sure only a handful of people ever visit my site. Still, it's fun, and it will be easy to switch to more personal observations and thoughts if I ever resolve to do so.

I often spend hours working to make a single page on my site look the way I want it, but have to force myself to do the more difficult tasks. I know the professional work I do is more important than playing with my website. It helps real people live better lives. It improves my community. It's something I can do that most other people can't. My current work also has the advantage of being the status quo: As difficult as the road ahead may be, at least it's a familiar road. In addition, the idea of doing something for a living that I do for pleasure is very attractive to me.

Lately I've been thinking about picking up my old idea of writing for the local paper. Since I like to watch TV and to write short pieces (as in my blog), I'd like to try to write a television review column. One of the benefits of living in a small city is that it may not be that difficult to achieve. I wouldn't do it for the money or recognition, but as a way to find out if I can combine my two greatest pleasures into something like a job. I like what I'm doing now, but part of me is restless to try something new, something different, something less safe.

I wish I could say that I've solved all of the "intimacy" issues hinted at and referred to directly in my original essay. While I don't feel that I am still an "awkward adolescent," in regard to sexuality and deep interpersonal relationships, I haven't made much progress. Sometimes I feel that I missed out on a window of opportunity—a time when other life concerns were relatively minor, and allowed space to pursue relationships. As a professional, and a single adult among adults with families and careers, I find few opportunities to explore relationships I should have explored when I was younger. I just don't have the time, and neither do most of my peers. Add to that the same old barriers, most of them in my mind, having to do with my disabilities, and I find myself still alone.

For the moment, I'm at peace with that. I have good friends—some of them co-workers, others people I have met through other associations, and still others people I have maintained contact with since college. There are people I can share my ideas and feelings with. It's of little importance to me that I'm not married, that I don't have kids. I miss the intimacy and strong devotion that these bring to my peers. However, I also know peers who, like me, have built their lives of other elements. In fact, I have lived as I do for so long now that I find it hard to imagine any other kind of life. That in itself may be the greatest barrier to forming deeper relationships. Cut through all the noble-sounding words, and it all boils down to what sounds like a sitcom cliché: I'm "afraid of commitment." Whatever. I'm certainly not going to go on some great self-conscious quest for love, connection, commitment. I can't think of any endeavor so dismal and boring. Either another cycle of my life will come about when new opportunities arise, or it won't. I'm keeping my eyes and ears open, but I'm not "holding my breath" for it, as the saying goes.

I'm finally finishing up this adolescence thing. It was delayed. Thirteen years ago, I was just beginning it when I thought I was finishing it. There are still more things to learn, more experiences I haven't had. It's possible that parts of me will always be 19 or 20 years old. I think I can live with that, and happily. On the other hand, I thought thirteen years ago that I knew what my life was going to be like, and have since been surprised in many ways. Thirteen years from now, will I be satisfied with my life? I don't know. But I'm pretty sure that whatever happens, I'll be a better person then than now, just as I think I am a better person now than I was thirteen years ago.

PROUD OF THE STRENGTH I HAD

This writer describes her experience of teenage pregnancy and how she copes with its effects on her emotional and social development. Without the support of her former boyfriend or the knowledge of her parents, Connie decides alone to have an out-of-state abortion soon after her high school graduation. She shares her struggle to find meaning in her actions and to redefine her own identity. In college, Connie finds support from a campus women's group that helps her make sense of her experience and understand herself better. She begins to examine her family life and the impact of those relationships on her feelings about men and the coping styles she has developed. Connie also comes to acknowledge her own strength and courage in dealing with this extremely difficult adolescent experience.

It was a week or so after high school graduation. The air was musty and the cement floor was cold. I played nervously with the phone cord and traced its path to the door with my eyes. The garage was the safest place, but I prayed that no one could hear me. It's funny how you suddenly believe in God when you think something bad might happen.

The woman on the other end of the line finally found my records. "Let's see," she said, "Oh yes, your test came out positive!" She sounded excited. I wasn't. I almost dropped the phone. My stomach felt like lead. I couldn't believe her.

"Are you sure?" I barely managed to utter. "Yes, isn't that what you wanted to hear?" Was she stupid? She had to look up my name for the results, didn't she know I was only 17?

"No," I said. She gave me the name of some abortion clinics and I hung up the phone.

On August 18th I had an abortion. In September I left for college. My grades were never affected; in fact, I got a 4.0 my first semester. Studying kept me from thinking too much. Six months after my abortion I saw a sign for a support group for women who had had abortions. I knew that I needed to go. Shaking, I called the number, and they told me where and when it would be.

In this group I began to let out some of the feelings that I had kept bottled up for months. Listening to the other women taught me that I was not alone, although many told stories and expressed feelings that were different from my own. Sometimes I left the group aching with the pain I felt from reclaiming all those feelings I'd pushed to the back of my mind. Other times I was amazed at how well I connected with these women, how much I learned from them, and how much I looked forward to this meeting every week. In the journal I kept, things came out on paper that I never could have said aloud.

MARCH

My boyfriend and I had just broken up when I found out. He wouldn't even speak to me so that I could tell him, but eventually I cornered him. He didn't care, and he didn't want to help. All he could say was, "Jesus Christ, are you sure?" I reminded him that it was his problem too, and he said he would give me the money, but he wouldn't go with me. He assumed, as I did, that I would have an abortion. My Mom would hate me for it. She had always condemned abortion, saying that it was killing a baby. Maybe it is; maybe I did.

After a few phone calls I found out that you have to be 18 to get an abortion in my state without parental consent. I was just four months too young. Eventually I made an appointment with a clinic in a nearby state. The woman I spoke to was very supportive, but I had to figure out how I would get there. A week went by before I asked a friend to take me. Then a few more weeks of wishing I could tell someone and trying to hide the hurt and tears. I guess I did a good job, because no one noticed. The worst part was when I saw my half-brother, an adorable 3-month-old. I couldn't hold him or look at him without thinking that I might as well be killing him.

APRIL

I live constantly in two worlds. One is where I can talk or write about it and show my real emotion—when I'm alone and cry, when I'm with the few friends who know, or when I'm with the support group, the only people who really understand. The other world is all the other times. Then I have to pretend that I am okay. I have to conceal my feelings. If someone reminds me, I can't share the hurt inside. Nor can I when some guy makes a joke or comment about a girl who had an abortion, when Amy eats a peanut butter and banana sandwich and Jean asks if she's pregnant, or when everyone giggles at the jokes, even me, but they don't know what's going on in my head. The pain is when there is an editorial in the paper about abortion and Mary says, "My friend at home had one—I'll never forgive her. She could have given it up for adoption; I was adopted." If only she knew. The pain is when I walk by a poster advocating reproductive rights that someone has scribbled "Fetus-Bashers" on in red magic marker. I want to scream at the person who did it, but they aren't there. I want to rip the poster down, but I don't. I want to tell the person I'm walking with how upset I am, but she won't understand.

MAY

Mom,

I know you'd hate me if you knew. To you it's disgusting, it's killing. I'll never be able to tell you. Maybe I'm hurting myself or our relationship by not telling you. I would have liked your support. I needed your help, but I couldn't tell you, and I still can't. I never wanted to hurt you.

Sometimes I wish you had guessed somehow. But you would have wanted me to have the baby; you wouldn't have let me make my own decision. Maybe it was a bad thing to do, maybe it wasn't the "right" thing to do. But I don't want a baby, and I don't want to give birth to one only to give it away. I wanted to go to school and learn and have fun, not be trapped in my own body for nine months. I didn't want to be stared at by mothers who warn their teenager at their side: "She can't be more than 16; I hope you never do a stupid thing like that!" I didn't want my sisters to be ashamed of me. I didn't want my friends and teachers to think I was a bad person. Because as we all know, girls who have sex are bad, and girls who get pregnant are stupid.

When I read these journals over again, I remember feeling so isolated and scared that everyone would hate me if they knew. When I did start telling people, I felt terrified of what they might think or say. But the more people I told the less it hurt to retell and the more confident I felt that I was right. The decision I made was a good one, and it was mine to make. I felt proud of the strength that I had to make it through this crisis on my own and stick to what I really wanted to do.

Experiencing for myself the inaccessibility of abortion for teenagers and going to the support group both pushed me to explore feminism and identify with it. I joined a pro-choice group on campus, went to protests against Operation Rescue, and wrote an article for a women's newspaper. I told my closest friends and even some not so close. My experience with abortion was becoming an integrated part of my life. But I also felt disillusioned by "the feminist movement." The political group I joined talked about "rights," and I didn't feel comfortable talking about my abortion, or talking at all, for that matter. It was hard for me to talk about abortion without including my own experiences. But I continued going because I had to make sure that abortion didn't become illegal, or in my case, more illegal. Being involved politically made me feel like maybe I could make a difference.

The pro-choice group organized rides to Boston for the protest against Operation Rescue, which was trying to close down clinics there. I rode down the night before with Sarah, another woman in the group, and we stayed at my dad's house. I don't remember when exactly I met her, or if we knew before that ride that we'd both had abortions, but for two and a half hours we talked about our experiences. It was amazing how close I felt to her; she made me feel even stronger. We found that we both felt alienated from the political group, and we talked about it a lot. She told me that she was in the support group that I had been in the semester before. I realized how much I missed talking about my abortion with women who understood.

It was an emotional weekend and maybe one of the best ones in my life. Talking with Sarah and being with her at the protest made it seem that much more important to me. I felt so good and real and so passionately involved. This was something I believed in like I never believed in something before. It was an incredible feeling facing, inches away from me, the people who believed I was a murderer and wanted to take away my right to control my own body.

After the protest I saw little of Sarah outside the pro-choice meetings until a later semester. She called and asked if I wanted to help her start a support group, or what we later decided to call a consciousness-raising group, for women who had had abortions. We both missed and needed those discussions. We put signs up and met the people who answered in a café on campus. Soon we were a group of eight, and the first night we met I found myself in tears, realizing how much I still needed to talk about it and how much was still left unresolved. I wanted to piece my life together. Why had all this happened to me? Can I go on hiding it from other people, from my family? At the fourth meeting I decided to tell my whole story. I didn't just talk about my abortion, I talked about my whole life. I was trying to make sense of it all. I began to identify some reasons behind my getting pregnant. One was my family. I told the group; "No one ever talked about anything in my family. My dad left when I was 13 and my mom told us not to tell anyone. My twin sister and I never said a word to each other about it. When my dad told us he was leaving we cried. Actually she cried, I didn't. I went upstairs to my room and closed the door. And that was the end of it, no one ever talked about it again."

The second explanation that I alluded to was my early sexual relationships with men. I described myself during that time as very insecure: "In school I wanted desperately to be liked, and boys actually seemed to like me. When some guy asked me out, I couldn't believe it. I'd say yes. I didn't know what else to say, even if I didn't like him. I dated a few guys and each time one of us got scared off and then avoided each other. Then Rick asked me out." I had difficulty talking about him even with this group of women. I tried to describe him and our relationship. "God, I don't know why I ever went out with him. He was . . . so awful. And we had a nine-month 'relationship.' After the first month I just wanted to break up with him, but I couldn't do it. I didn't want to hurt his feelings and I was afraid of what he'd do. He was always trying to get me to sleep with him. I was only 15. He ended up basically raping me."

Rick said he wanted me to be his girlfriend. There were guys I liked a lot more than him, but no one had asked me out before like that. He was nice and funny and said he loved me. Though I soon found him annoying and pushy, I couldn't break up with him, even after he raped me. I was scared that he might kill himself. I was afraid he might freak out and hurt me. I was attached to him and the attention he gave me. And I didn't even know I had been raped. "I just thought I was a horrible person because I couldn't keep him from touching me. I felt horrible, but I didn't know why. I thought I'd done something wrong. I just cried. I didn't even think of saying anything to anyone; I wouldn't have known what to say. I couldn't believe that I'd just had sex with someone; I couldn't even say the word. My parents never talked about sex either, except my mother's little innuendos about it being bad. So I thought I was the worst person in the world."

I finally broke up with Rick, but I often felt pushed into later sexual experiences as well. I said to the group, "I slept with Chris, too, or he convinced me to sleep with him. That's what it always seemed like. I didn't want to do it, but I would give in. It was always like the guy was trying to convince me and I never really wanted to, but I always would." With Chris, part of me did really want to sleep with him, but I was unsure and I didn't know how to talk about it. I think most of time I didn't want to was because I was afraid of getting pregnant, and I didn't know how to talk about birth control either.

Chris and I broke up when he went to college, partly because he was going away, and partly because I was interested in someone else. I was 16, almost 17, and a senior in high school. Darren was a junior, but I thought he was the greatest. He drank a lot and did some drugs, and I hated both. But for the first time I really felt comfortable sleeping with someone. To Sarah and the other women I said, "Birth control was just never an issue for us." It was the first time I had admitted it, but it wasn't completely true either. It was an issue, but we never talked about it. I didn't ask him about it and he didn't ask me about it. It was really strange because I was terrified that I was going to get pregnant. I always thought about it, worried about it, but I couldn't do anything about it.

Although we didn't use contraception, and we didn't talk about it, I thought about it constantly, and I was scared. I even wrote a paper about teenage pregnancy for a psychology class. I remember working on it, thinking, "This could be you, you have to do something about this." I remember having this feeling that I HAD to talk to him about it, but I couldn't. It seemed easier not to say anything and put it out of my mind, to try to forget about it.

At one point I thought I was pregnant, and I told him. He couldn't believe it and he said something about me being on the Pill. I said, "No, I'm not, where did you get that idea?" But inside I felt relieved that the subject finally came up. He said that he just figured that I must have been, since I never seemed worried about it. It seems almost funny now, but it wasn't then. How could he have thought that all this time, when for me it hurt so much to pretend it wasn't a problem?

It turned out that I wasn't pregnant. He was so happy and I was relieved. We talked more after all that, we started using condoms "most of the time," and I worried about it less. Then he started to drink more and got more into drugs, and he wanted to be with his friends and not me. He tried to break up with me, but I took a fit. "You can't leave me, Darren," I cried, "I love you, I can't believe you are doing this to me, you said you loved me!" Finally he gave in and said he still did, but he kept away from me and finally he broke it off completely. I was still hurt, but I knew I didn't like the drinking and our disagreements around it, so I didn't argue this time. Two or three weeks later I worried that I was pregnant again. I tried to call him. He was never home, and his brother once just said, "He doesn't want to talk to you." Finally I got in touch with him and told him. He just said, "Jesus Christ, I can't believe this!"

My mother is totally anti-abortion. I knew if I said anything to her, I would be having a kid. I only told one of my girlfriends; she was the only person I thought I could trust. I did one of those home pregnancy tests; I hid it behind the books in my bookcase because you have to let it sit for a couple hours. I totally freaked out when I looked at it and it came out positive. My friend was more clueless about what to do than I was. I turned to another close friend, this time a guy. I asked him to drive me to the hospital so that I could have a real test done. I didn't tell him why I was going, and he drove me, no questions asked. I was convinced that this test was going to be negative, that the first test was wrong. I was sure of it. The next day the woman on the phone told me it was positive.

Meanwhile I started getting involved with someone else. Todd and I started spending a lot of time together. We weren't going out yet, but we were close. One night I told him about it. He said he'd been through it with a girlfriend, but she turned out not to be pregnant. He said he'd take me for the abortion appointment. I was so relieved. I told my mom and my boss that we were going shopping for the day; Mom even let Todd take her car.

When we got there he just dropped me off, he didn't come in with me. At the time it was exactly what I expected, but now it seems strange that I didn't want him there for support. It didn't even occur to me to ask him to come in with me. I think I felt that it wasn't his responsibility and it was something I wanted to do on my own. I am still in awe of the idea that I went through this all by myself.

I walked in alone with my $250 check from Darren. I was nervous, but I felt better once I was inside. The woman on the phone warned me that there might be picketers, but no one bothered me. Most of the people in the waiting room had someone with them, but it didn't bother me too much at the time. I was so relieved to actually be there. I started to get scared waiting, but I still couldn't believe that I had made it there and that I was going to be okay.

The first thing they did was counseling, or at least that's what they called it. It's just when they describe the procedure in detail. I went into this room with the counselor and a 30-year-old woman who was there for the same reason but seemed totally relaxed. The counselor started to explain to the two of us exactly what happens with the doctor and the instruments.

Suddenly I was terrified and I started to cry. I couldn't help it. I was scared of how much it would hurt, of what it would be like. The counselor and the other woman were like, "Oh my goodness, what's wrong?" as if there was no reason whatsoever for me to be the least bit upset.

What bothers me about the whole thing is that no one ever talked about it, I mean really talked about it. They were all robots, just doing their job, describing the procedure, taking blood, giving out pills, acting like it was no big deal. It seems like it wouldn't have been so scary if we could have talked about it more. If someone only said, "I've been through it, too. It's okay to be scared, but you will be okay."

Someone sent me to get changed and directed me to the next waiting room. I was there for two hours in my gown. Or maybe it was just an hour, or only twenty minutes, but it seemed like forever. There were around five other women there, and a woman came in to call a name once in a while. The chairs were arranged in a circle around the room. We sat there facing each other and no one said anything. Everyone seemed scared except the older woman who flipped through a magazine and made comments here and there. But the person who really stuck out in my mind was a girl who looked no older than 13. I felt so terrible for her—she looked so scared. I just wanted to reach out to her, and tell her everything was going to be okay.

Finally they called my name and I followed a woman to another room. Another woman was there to talk to me and to hold my hand during the abortion if I wanted to. The doctor said, "So you are going to college in the fall? So what's your major?" I couldn't believe he was asking me about college; I could barely answer, I was so terrified. But I guess it was better than him not saying anything at all. It was so painful. I remember screaming and crying, literally. Afterward I wondered if anyone heard me. They said it would hurt some, but this was the most painful thing I had ever felt. It hurts to think about it.

Afterward I went into a room with other women who were recovering, lying down with blankets and eating slices of oranges and crackers. After about fifteen minutes I felt a lot better, so they said I could leave even though you're supposed to stay for longer afterward. I started to get cramps after about fifteen minutes driving home. We stopped and bought some pain reliever but it kept getting worse. They said that cramps were normal, so I didn't really worry about it. I didn't realize how bad it was until the next day when I got up and got ready for work. I was still bleeding heavily. I knew I should call the clinic. According to the information sheet they gave me I should have called them if this happened. I thought about it, but I knew they'd want me to see a doctor. I don't know if I was more scared that something was wrong with me or that my mother would find out. For three days I was in agony and then finally it stopped.

My experience with abortion and the support groups I've involved myself in have allowed me to experience a great level of intimacy with other women that I never felt before. But it also seemed to pull me away from my family. It was something I couldn't go talk to any of them about, something I hid from them. I hate that they can't really understand a part of me. The people I'm closest to don't know my deepest secret, my deepest hurts, and the greatest motivation for some of my interests. Sometimes I feel guilty about not sharing it with them. I'm afraid that one of my sisters may have to go through the same thing one day and she wouldn't tell me either. She would have to deal with the same silence I did. But last year I realized that I hadn't hidden everything from them. One day my 17-year-old sister called me at school. She was scared that she was pregnant and didn't know what to do. Even though she didn't know I'd had an abortion, she knew how I felt about it. She said, "I can't have it. School and field hockey, I just couldn't." I told her it was okay and she didn't have to do anything she didn't want to do. I told her where she could go for a test and that she could call me anytime she wanted. If she was pregnant, I told her, "I'd know what to do, it's all right." I was scared for her, but I was happy that I could be there for her. It made me feel good that she wouldn't have to go through it alone.

I know I will never tell my mother, and that's okay now, but sometimes it still makes me sad. We are still very close, though. I'm probably closer to her than any of my sisters. We talk a lot about boyfriends (both of ours), school, jobs, and my dad. I know she's not the best listener in the world, but I like to be there for her. Sometime she really surprises me and gives me good advice, but she has trouble just listening. One of my greatest fears is that she will find out and it will ruin the relationship we have. I think she'd hate me for a while, and she'd feel guilty, too. I'm sure her love for me would overcome it, but I just don't want to put her or myself through it.

I want to tell my twin sister. It is absolutely bizarre to me that she doesn't know this about me. Although we fight and still compete, we've shared a lot more since we've been at school and I feel pretty close to her. I told her about being raped and we talked about that often. But I can't seem to tell her about my abortion. I want to. I'm not afraid of what she will think of me anymore because I've had one, but I'm afraid of what she will think of me for not telling her. I'm afraid that she will really freak out. That she wouldn't believe me anymore or she'd hate me for not telling her. I'm afraid of totally shocking her.

Recently my mom said to me while looking at an old picture of the four of us kids, "You were always so happy as kids, laughing all the time, having fun." I had a really weird feeling when she said it. I never remember being happy as a kid. Scared of my own shadow might be a better description. I couldn't bear to tell her that; I just nodded and smiled.

I remember all of us kids fighting a lot. I remember my mom yelling a lot. I don't remember my dad being home much. I remember him coming home at 1:00 in the morning. I remember them yelling a lot on weekends. We bought a sailboat, but it was mostly just another place to fight. I remember a teacher who I loved in seventh grade. We wrote in journals in her class. Once I wrote about one of our boat trips, only I left out the bad parts, the fighting. When I got the journal back she wrote, "Sounds wonderful!" I felt like she liked me and what I wrote, but I also felt horrified. I had a sick feeling in my stomach, like I knew it wasn't true; it wasn't wonderful.

In the autobiography I wrote my senior year in high school I identified my dad leaving as one of the two events that had the greatest effect on me (the other was being a twin). The hurt was fresher then, and I was angry and jealous. Those feelings certainly haven't gone away, they just aren't so strong. Then it seemed I wanted so badly to believe that my family was perfect before the day he destroyed it all and left. Now I tend to think of the bad times, all of the fights, and I can't remember the good stuff. Now I see that something was very wrong with my family before he left. No one communicated, but everyone fought. I guess my dad just wasn't happy, and he spent less time at home and more at work, and then my mom became unhappy. Or maybe it was the other way around. I don't know how it really happened or whose fault it really was.

To me then it was all my dad's fault; he did everything that hurt me. But sometimes I think my mother's reactions, as well as our own, made things worse for us. No one in the house talked about it, except my mom, who was an emotional wreck. She'd try to pry information out of us after we'd been to my dad's. She told us, begged us, to ask him to come home and to tell him that we loved him. She said he'd come if we did. We couldn't tell him how much it was hurting us; we just went to see him and tried to be "good." But mom telling me this made me feel even more like it was all our fault. She also told us not to tell our friends; she didn't want anyone to know. Until we moved two years later, I told my friends he was on a business trip when they came over.

I don't blame my mother for any of these things, even though they hurt me. I feel thankful that she survived and didn't just give up. As for my dad, I try to see him as much as I can. We can have fun together, but I feel like he can't ever be there for me emotionally. It still makes me sad. For the most part, I'm not bitter anymore. But he still tries to get away with giving my mother as little money as possible and he pays almost nothing toward our college bills. Though they've been divorced for years, the hurt still seems to drag on. Mom still makes comments about his wife and kid. I understand her hurt, but I'm still caught in the middle.

I have tried here to explain my inability to deal appropriately with sexual relationships as being the result of my not having been able to talk about sex and contraception. The feelings from the beginnings of my adolescent sexuality were of being scared, not having control, and not having a choice. I now know that this is related to having grown up in a family that stuffed their feelings and never talked about anything, including sex. My family always avoided subjects that were upsetting, embarrassing, or controversial. So when it came to talking about contraception with my boyfriend, I had no basis to deal with it and felt it was beyond my control. My way of coping with the inevitable crisis of a pregnancy was not to practice contraception, but to put it out of my mind. That was easy; I had practiced that all my life.

SEEKING THE BEST
OF BOTH WORLDS

*This is the story of a harrowing emigration from Vietnam to the United
States as part of the "boat people" crisis after the war. The author describes
his struggle to be both a good son to his very traditional mother and to find a
means to belong and succeed in the culture to which his family fled. As he
enters adolescence, he begins to feel that his mother's many troubles and
unbending ways are harming both him and his siblings. When he discovers
that his stepfather is abusing his younger brother and that his mother will
not intercede, he experiences a turmoil of shame, guilt, and powerlessness.
His mother's insistence on traditional child rearing forces him to live a
double life as an increasingly "Americanized" teenager on the outside while
playing the role of dutiful son at home in spite of numbing sadness and
overwhelming rage toward his mother. Eventually, it is his success in the
world outside his family that allows him to gain his mother's respect and
thereby influence how she raises his younger siblings.*

Con không biết mạ đã trở qua bao nhiêu là nỗi khổ để đem con qua nước Mỹ nay—You
don't know how much I went through to bring you to this country," my mother
said in a soft voice as she lay staring at the ceiling. A continuous stream of tears
flowed from the outer corner of her eye down into her pillow. At times like this, I
would sit next to my mother on our torn carpet while she recounted the tragedies
that had happened to her in her previous life of misery, the life she left behind in
Vietnam. My older sister Chau, on the other hand, could never stand to listen to
our mother's repetitions. She would usually brush her teeth and go to bed or go to
our other bedroom, close the door, and delve into the imaginary world of her romance novels. I remember praying at the start of the episodes that I wouldn't end
up crying myself (because my mother instilled in me her belief that *"nam nhi đại
trượng phu đổ máu không rơi lệ*—real heroes never show tears even if they are bleeding to death") as these painful stories entered my mind. However, no gods or

spirits answered my prayers, and after each occurrence I would feel low and unmanly because I had let tears fall even though I wasn't bleeding to death.

"*Dạ mạ*—Yes, Mom (respectfully)," I said. In Vietnamese a child must always acknowledge his or her parent with a polite "*Dạ*" (pronounced "ya"). It matters not that the parent did not ask the child a question; any less respectful response could very well lead to a beating! I learned this lesson soon after I learned how to talk (being polite was much better than being hit).

"When I was your age living in my village, I never had a full meal to eat," my mother continued. "Most days we would only be given one small bowl of rice and a dab of fish paste for flavor. I wasn't as lucky as you are today. I could never eat meat every day like you can." As far as I can remember, my mother would, without exception, start her stories by establishing that her youth was utterly miserable compared to my life of luxury. To this day I still am not sure whether by stating this she merely wanted me to feel grateful that I had enough food to eat or whether she was actually pitying herself as she realized the vast contrast between her childhood and mine.

"I was cruelly beaten daily by your grandmother and often for no good reason. She had fourteen children, but I was the only one who ever got punished. I don't know why. She'd beat me if I didn't fetch enough firewood for cooking. Or if I didn't cut up enough food to feed the pigs. Or if I stopped fanning her during those scorching summer days because my hands felt like jello." As my mother went on, at this point in her talk I would have a difficult time understanding her because her nose was plugged up from crying so much. Sometimes I tried to pay closer attention so that I could catch everything she said; other times I would not bother since I more or less knew by heart all that she wanted to say.

"The worst period in my life was after I married your father. I had just given birth to your sister when your father disappeared without a trace. I tracked him down finally in Hanoi. I found that he was living with his first wife, a woman that he never told me about. I was more than shocked that the man I loved and trusted lied to me."

After hearing my mother describe my father's deceit, I simultaneously felt resentment, sympathy, guilt, vengefulness, incredible sadness, and, oddly, joy. I resented and even hated my father for ruining my mother's life. The anger I felt inside was so overwhelming that I would often tremble while gasping for air. Sometimes I sat there and wished that he were standing right in front of me so that I could pick him up by the throat and slam him against the wall as hard as I could. I'd scream at him, "You damn asshole! How could you treat your wife like that? Don't you have a conscience? Is this the model that you want your children to follow? I am ashamed to be your son! But don't worry, I won't turn out to be like you, you piece of shit!" At the same time, I felt sympathy for the incredible pain that my mother must have endured since that episode. She did not do anything wrong; her only mistake was falling in love with a lying womanizer. Yet mixed with my negative emotions was a slight ripple of joy. I felt happy to see that my mother was courageous enough to take her children and leave him behind in his poverty-stricken home. I was shamelessly content that he still has to live in filth with his first wife while our family, although poor compared to others in America, has enough to eat everyday.

Throughout my early childhood, occurrences like the one above were commonplace. Almost anything could provoke my mother into telling those stories: seeing happy couples walking together in the park, seeing my sister and me not doing our chores, watching television shows that depicted any aspect of Vietnam, and especially having her children do badly in school (i.e., not getting straight As). Those nights I would cry myself to sleep thinking of how much I should hate my father and how much I should love and respect my mother. I racked my brains wondering how my father could have consciously treated my mother with such inhumanity. "How could he? How could he?" I hollered silently to myself over and over. "There must be some reason for what he did. My mother must be leaving a lot of details out. I should not listen only to her side of the story." I convinced myself that I could not make final judgments about him until I heard what he had to say. Thus, for years I wondered what his story was.

My first memories are of escaping Vietnam and landing in Hong Kong on the way to our final destination, America. I only remember random scenes of our journey; the rest of what happened my mother has filled in through our conversations over the years. Thus, I have a fairly detailed knowledge of what happened in those few days that drastically altered our lives.

In the spring of 1981, my mother, then fairly wealthy thanks to a prospering business, decided that she wanted to give her two children educational opportunities that her country could not offer. I was only 4 years old and my sister just 6 when one ordinary night my mother told us to say good-bye forever to our homeland. . . .

A blinding flash of light snatched me from my restful sleep. Five seconds later the inevitable boom of thunder crashed on our little boat and sent everyone into a state of panic. When I peered out at the darkness, I saw rushing at us some of the largest waves I'd ever seen.

"*Mạ, con sợ qúa*—Mommy, I'm so scared," I cried. However, the raindrops on my face camouflaged my tears, and the roaring thunder drowned my attempts to communicate with my mother. I finally caught her attention by pulling on her sleeve as hard as I could.

"*Con đừng sợ nhe*—Don't be afraid, son," my mother comforted, "It's just a little storm. It'll be over real soon." She covered us with a plastic bag, and we huddled so close that I could feel her heart pounding against my cheek.

"*Chị Hong, Chị Hong*—Sister Hong, Sister Hong," my uncle Oanh approached us from out of nowhere and said in a disconcerting tone, "There's too much weight on this end of the boat. We need more people to move to the bow. If we don't do it fast, the waves'll flip us right over."

"What do you want us to do?" my mother answered calmly.

"You put Phuoc on your back and I'll put Chau on mine. Then we'll slowly walk up there."

"Okay, okay," my mother approved. I did not realize what was happening. All I knew was that I wanted to cling to my mother for dear life. "Phuoc," she spoke directly into my ear because at any other distance the thunder would drown out her voice, "We're moving to the front of the boat. I'm gonna give you a piggy-back ride, so you grab on as tight as you can, okay?"

"*Dạ*," I acknowledged and quickly climbed onto her back while the storm blanketed my body with what felt like a thousand pebbles every second. Without thinking, I immediately locked my arms around my mother's neck and grabbed each of my wrists with the opposite hand. Just as instinctively, I wrapped my legs around her waist and also bolted them in place. As we began inching toward our destination just a few meters away, my awareness of the surroundings increased tenfold compared to when I was sitting with my mother. I saw every wave as it crashed on the boat's side, I anticipated the direction of impending thunder, and I felt the blowing raindrops on my skin as if they were needles piercing all parts of my body. Another acute awareness was of my body's position in space. Because I did not budge, it seemed as though I became an extension of my mother's body. When she lifted her left foot to take another step, I felt the entire left half of my frame move accordingly.

"*Gần tới rồi con à*—We're almost there, son," my mother said, "Don't worry." When I looked up, I saw the bow just a few steps away. However, I did not feel as though I could breathe a sigh of relief because a few steps is still a few steps. I kept my tight lock around my mother's neck and waist. It turned out that this choice saved my life, because just then a huge wave slammed into the side of our boat with such force that it threw her off her feet and sent us plunging into the freezing water of the South China Sea. I do not recall feeling scared. When I was under water, instinct made me hold onto my mother as tightly as I could, shut my eyes to avoid the stinging seawater, and close my mouth so that no saltwater entered my system. I do not know why I didn't panic. I just didn't. Fortunately, the two of us avoided staying in the water long enough for hypothermia to set in. My uncle, who was following closely behind us with my sister, dived in after us when he saw us fall.

Following our dramatic rescue, the heavens blessed us with sunshine and peaceful waters. The gods also bestowed another miracle on us. Several days after our departure, just when we had almost depleted all of our food supply, we came across a cargo ship headed in the same direction we wished to go: Hong Kong. A year later in April 1982, my mother realized her dreams of raising us in a land where more opportunities and fewer obstacles lay before us. What my mother did not realize was that she herself would become the major obstacle in her children's future.

Throughout my early adolescence, I wished I had a better, more understanding mother. To this day I still believe that most of my "growing pains" could have been alleviated or missed entirely if my mother had also experienced these same "pains" when she was an adolescent. She did not know how best to assist me through my tough times, because she had no understanding of the cultural and social pressures facing teens growing up in America. She was often insensitive and apathetic when I came to her with an adolescent issue such as schoolmates making fun of me.

Puberty started rather simply for me in the sixth grade; there was no big event that announced its arrival. I remember exactly when I knew that I had entered this period of change. One evening while I was showering, I noticed that I had started growing pubic hair. At first I felt confused. "What's this stuff?" I asked myself. Thinking that it was just dirt or something, I tried rubbing it off. After a few unsuccessful attempts, I realized, "Oh, yeah, this is what my sex education class last year taught us. I'm supposed to start this business at my age. Don't worry about it. It's just puberty." I thought about telling my mother to make sure it *was* just puberty, but after some thought I decided against the idea because these topics were not spoken of in our household. Subjects such as sex, love, human genitalia, and rape were taboo in my family because they were supposedly "impure" things to talk about. We were not to adulterate our minds and hearts by bringing them up in conversation. Consequently, many issues that "normal" families in America talk about were never brought up in our household. This lack of discussion forced me to learn about them from other sources, such as television.

At first I did not think that puberty was going to be the time of tremendous psychological change that the sex education videos at school had depicted. I felt like the same little kid I was before, going to class in the morning, coming home to do homework and watch television in the afternoon, talking to my mother before going to bed, and then repeating this same monotonous routine. The only other difference was that my voice started cracking when I spoke, but that did not bother me because I understood that was a natural part of human development.

Although I was only aware of my physical changes, I was also changing mentally. I remember my sudden self-consciousness, low self-esteem, new found interest in girls, and awareness of my lack of peer relationships, all of which started in junior high. Now when I look back, it seems that my experience was nothing out of the ordinary for children of that age. Yet my life then had an additional *extra*ordinary factor. The conditions under which I interacted with others my own age were, culturally, American conditions, while at home I confronted a Vietnamese cultural environment. On the one hand, my mother did not understand American culture and disapproved of the American beliefs (such as gender and racial equality, free speech in the family, etc.) that I had adopted. On the other hand, the children at school who were not Vietnamese did not accept the culturally Vietnamese side of me, probably because they saw it as strange and not "normal." (Back then it was a dream of mine just to be normal like everyone else.) I shall illustrate my point with a few examples.

Before the sixth grade, I never thought about how physically different I looked. I knew that I was Vietnamese, but I never felt that I was an outsider in school because of my skin color. When I began adolescence, however, I became acutely aware of my bodily characteristics. In grade school I was your stereotypical skinny, short, brainy Asian kid with a bowl haircut. When kids made fun of me by calling me "chink" or "nerd," I usually never paid any attention to them. This was true until the day I received a disciplinary referral and was sent home. During music class, a Caucasian classmate of mine, Eugene, was getting upset because Mr. Marmastein told him he was out of tune. The entire class giggled as Eugene squeaked the words to "Yankee Doodle Went to Town." I, being a wiseguy, said loudly, "No more, Eugene, please!" With a frustrated look, Eugene quickly turned to me and yelped, "Shut up, you damn *chink*!" The old me would have just laughed it off without giving it a second thought, but that day a rush of anger swept through me, and I wanted to beat him up right there on the spot. The only thing that restrained me from doing so was my music teacher. I did not want to disrespect him by disrupting the class; I decided to wait till later. When recess time came and we were all let out to the grass field to play kickball, I only had one thing on my mind. As soon as I caught sight of Eugene, I ran over and tackled him onto the ground with all the might that my eighty pound body could conjure up. We wrestled around on the grass throwing blind punches at each other until the recess supervisor pulled us apart and gave us both referrals. The principal sent me home because I was the one who started the fight. Eugene's words somehow triggered a highly reactive area inside me, an area that told me that I was not the same as everyone else, and this made me feel inferior. At the same time, though, the fight made me proud and confident because this time, unlike previous times, I had stood up for myself when others thought I would be weak and passive. However, my raised spirits received a powerful blow from my mother's reaction.

"What? You got in a fight because he said you were Asian? *Sau con ngu qúa vậy*—Why are you so stupid, son?" my mother said, as if she didn't believe that "chink" was a derogatory word. Maybe if I told her again, she would understand.

"But, Mom. That word is racist! He wasn't just saying that I was *Asian*," I repeated, "He had a different meaning."

"Who cares what he meant," she replied. "It's just a word. Those white people are all racist anyway. Next time he says that to you, just ignore him." Ignore him? *What*? How could I do that when Eugene insulted me? And how could my mother say that *all* Caucasians are racist? Didn't the fact that she uttered those words brand *her* a racist? "And they're bigger than you, you know. I don't want you to get hurt again. We're smaller than they are, so we just have to act our size. So next time he makes fun of you, just turn your head and laugh." I did not know how else to persuade her. My mother did not seem to understand that in America, equality is cherished and prejudice is not tolerated. Wasn't that why she decided to risk her life and the lives of her children to come here in the first place? My mother's words directly conflicted with what my teachers had taught me in school all these years. How could I reconcile this? I could not believe what she said nor do as she ordered, because the morals I had acquired in school were too strong. This incident posed yet another problem for me—when should I listen to my mother and when should I not? In the past, she had always taught me how to be a good person, including the dos and don'ts of life and the difference between right and wrong. It was simple—Mother was always right no matter what. Thus, I always listened and took her words to heart. Now that I recognized a flaw in her beliefs, I did not know what to do or who to go to.

Another example of my mother's lack of empathy was how she laughed at me when I told her that other kids made fun of my name. For as long as I can remember, almost everyone I met has mispronounced my name at least twice before getting it right. It was such an embarrassing scene whenever I met anyone new that it made me wish I did not have to meet new people at all. The worst part of it was the name-calling I endured all my life. Through elementary school and beyond high school, my name was the subject of a laundry list of teasings. It may be difficult for others to understand how my name can be so damaging to me psychologically. However, it was not as if I had a name like "Jaime," which everyone pronounced "Himee." People can easily turn my name into vulgar words if they want to (and I believed that everyone around me wanted to). Here are a few of those hurtful teasings: "Fok," "Foo-ok," "Pook," "Fuck," "Phuoc you!," "What the Phuoc!," "MotherPhuocer." In my high school junior yearbook there is a picture of me playing volleyball (I was on the team). Underneath it the subheading reads, "Phuoc 'U' Nguyen spikes one!" Those kids did not realize that every time they poked fun at me I wanted to crawl into a cave and not come out until everyone was mature enough to accept my name.

The only person who understood my agony was my sister because she too has an uncommon name, but hers had less potential to be the butt of everyone's jokes than mine. On occasion when she and I went somewhere together, we would temporarily change our names to make the experience a lot more pleasant for ourselves. For instance, when I was a sophomore in high school and Chau was a junior, she wanted me to accompany her to a meeting of students interested in applying to college. She was sure that no one we knew would be there, so we decided to become "normal" for the evening. When the hosts asked us to write our names on those "Hello, my name is . . ." stickers, we picked random "American" names. As it turned out, we both found it easier to meet people when we weren't feeling self-conscious.

Whenever I told my mother about people making fun of my name, she would usually laugh and say, "Fuck? Ha, ha . . . isn't that a bad word? Ha, ha . . . That's kinda funny." At times like those I thought my mother was the most insensitive and uncaring person in the world. How could she sit there and laugh at her son when he had just told her that everyone in school was already laughing at him? Did she think that it would make me feel better if she laughed as well? Of course I did not voice those questions. Thinking about it now, I believe that my mother's concept of emotional pain was completely different from mine. The physical pain and agony she endured for most of her life in Vietnam was probably ten times more intolerable than mine. That's probably why she couldn't understand the emotional pain I felt when kids made fun of me.

My mother also hindered my healthy adolescent development by refusing to let me associate with girls. I recall one incident in junior high when a seventh-grade girl wrote me a letter. Minh, a Vietnamese girl who played in the orchestra with me, sent me the first "I like you" letter I ever received; in it she expressed her admiration for me because I was smart and musically talented. Frankly, I did not have the slightest inkling what to think of the situation. No one had ever taught me how to initiate intimate relationships. The guy friends I had at school were all uncool "nerds" like myself who did not have any experience with girls either. I did not even consider asking them for help. I never had an older male role model to turn to with questions; the only older men I was in contact with were my uncles, and they were unlikely candidates because they did not grow up in America.

Asking for my mother's advice about girls would be tantamount to suicide. She always forbade my sister and me to date or see any members of the opposite sex until we were college graduates. One may think that she was just joking—no parent can be that strict, right?—but believe me, she wasn't. She strictly enforced her commands with severe actions. For instance, one day after school when I was waiting for my mother, one of my female acquaintances came up to chat with me. We were talking about how Mrs. Sloboda's world history test was too difficult. But when my mother drove up and saw us standing there together, she thought the subject of our conversation was something less than innocent. She immediately rolled down her window and screamed at the girl, "*Ây, đồ con quỷ sứ kia, mày làm chi với con tao rứa*—Hey, demon, what are you doing with my son?" My friend asked me whether my mother was yelling at her; I told her that she was just telling me to get in the car (this was one of the perks of having a mom who does not speak English). When I stepped into the car, my mother started chastising me for talking to the girl. She did not listen to my explanation and warned me that if she ever saw that scene again, I'd end up in an orphanage. That was the last time I stood next to girls after school.

There I was holding my first love letter in my hand, but I had absolutely no idea what to do with it. I did not understand my role as the male figure: Was I supposed to ask her out first or wait until she made the first move? Should I talk to her just as a friend or try to flirt with her? My mind was filled with confusion at the time. The only places I could think of to turn to for direction were Hong Kong mini-soap operas. These translated productions were usually set in ancient China, where a gentleman was one who followed the Confucian code of conduct and women were innocent and supportive. Honestly, I learned more about relationships from watching those shows than from any other source. They taught me that real men were brave, polite, chivalrous, confident, and independent, while women were caring, sensitive, nurturing, and passive. Of course I am much wiser now, but back then I embraced these ideals. However, even though I knew from those movies how I *should* have acted toward Minh—who I thought was pretty and intelligent—I did not put that knowledge into practice. Instead of initiating any type of conversation, I tried to avoid her. Whenever she walked up to me to talk, I would turn around and walk the other way. Finally, after realizing that I seemed repulsed by her, Minh gave up on me and started seeing someone else. Later on I felt like such an idiot for letting her go. "Why didn't I go for it?" I asked myself repeatedly. "Am I not a guy? She liked me! She really did, and I just let her go." I thought that I did not possess the qualities that a "real" man had, those qualities that the Hong Kong mini-soap operas presented to me. It was not until my last years in high school that I realized what "manly" qualities actually were. It was also then that my self-esteem gradually rose to a level where I was confident enough to look people in the face when I was talking to them. These changes came slowly and originated from an incident that was a milestone in my life. This incident served as the beginning of my long and successful struggle to break free from my mother's emotional influence.

The changes took place shortly after my mother allowed her ex-husband, my stepfather, back into our family. A few months following his return, I learned with horror what kind of man he really was. My half-brother Tai, a vibrant 4-year-old, told me that his father liked to pinch and bite him just for fun; he also liked to fondle Tai's genitals for prolonged stretches of time.

Something like this was not easy to accept or deal with, especially for a 14-year-old. I trembled at the realization that this beast of a man, this perverse monster, sexually abused his own son, my innocent brother. And all of this occurred right beneath our unwitting noses for weeks on end. "This cannot continue," I resolved. "I *will* not allow him to hurt my brother any longer!" Never in my life had I been more sure of what the right thing to do was. Although I knew that this could potentially hurt everyone else in my family, particularly my mother, I did not falter for a moment. I was willing to destroy my mother's happiness to protect Tai.

My method of expressing my frustration was to slam doors. Every time I saw my stepfather touching Tai's genitals, I would walk to my room and slam the door behind me. Our home only had two bedrooms, so Tai's father definitely heard and understood my signal. He understood all right, but he did not change, and the abuse persisted. However, my stubborn-headedness kept me from giving up. I wanted to reach a standoff, a sudden-death situation. That day came about two weeks after my initial resolution to fight. Thoughts of me being courageous or honorable never entered my mind; everything I did was by gut instinct.

It was a windy Saturday afternoon, and everyone was at home except for Chau, who was at work. My mother and stepfather were talking in their room while Tai and I played *Civilization* on my computer. All of a sudden Tai's father summoned him to their room. The inevitable happened, and again a rush of rage crashed into my body. I breathed hard as my heartbeat shot up like a bottle rocket. Shoving my chair behind me, I stepped out into the living room and looked into their room as I walked by. The scene did not differ from the ones I had witnessed over the past few weeks. After standing in the living room for a moment, I went to my room taking loud, heavy steps along the way and, upon reaching my destination, slammed my door with as much force as I could conjure up. I did it! My mother had to say *something*. I wanted to confront him that very moment; I wished that deep inside me there was a courage that would manifest itself now by giving Tai's father the hardest punch on the jaw. I waited for them to come in.

"Phuoc, what the hell are you doing!" my mother screamed as she raced over to my room and gave me a slap on the left side of my cheek. I still vividly remember the physical and emotional pain I felt the instant her hand landed on my face. "He's his father, and he can do whatever he wants with him. It's not like he's killing him or anything, he's just playing. And besides, it's none of your business! Now if you don't want to live here anymore, then I can always put you into an orphanage!" I knew then that my mother cared more about her own selfish needs than about the welfare of her younger son. My respect for her started fading behind a curtain of disappointment. What could I do? Everyone around me could not see what I saw, and after trying fruitlessly to expose the truth to them, this was what I received. Fear and alarm overwhelmed me at that moment, and I did not, could not, fight any longer. I had already drained myself of all the fortitude I possessed, and no matter how deep I searched, my well of courage was dry. At that time, fear—the emotion I detested most and the emotion I constantly encountered—took control of my mind. I didn't want to end up in an orphanage, a ward of the state. I didn't want her to put me in a foster home. No. No. I couldn't let that happen. "It was the wind, Mom," I responded innocently. "The wind slammed the door." And that was that. I was tired. I didn't want to feel any more emotions. I just wanted to lie in bed and pretend that none of it had happened.

I had never been more disappointed with my mother in my life; the time she ignored my pleas for new shoes, the time she made fun of my name, could not begin to compare with this. I wished she was not my mother. I wished that I had never been born into this backward family.

Two months later my mother kicked her ex-husband out. Apparently, he emptied her bank account with his gambling habits. While he had been staying with us, he constantly took her money to play cards at the local casino. Eventually my mother had no money left to pay the bills. This time his leaving was for good, she said. His departure left me with a feeling of relief for my brother because it released him from constant victimization. Yet I knew that what he went through might leave lasting psychological effects.

The problems between my mother and myself did not spontaneously disappear when my stepfather left. I remember not feeling anything at all for her; it was as if my stepfather had taken with him all of my emotions about my mother and left only a void. I did not speak with her for half a year following his separation from us. I constantly asked myself how my mother, whom I regarded so highly— a woman who had risked and sacrificed everything for the sake of her children— could ignore the obvious abuse of her child by her husband. This inner questioning led to my emotional isolation from her. Withdrawing from my mother's world allowed me to step back and reevaluate from a different perspective my perceptions of her and myself. With the help of this new vantage point, I painted a new picture of myself and my relationship with my mother.

"*Thưa mạ con đi học*—(Respectfully) Mother, I am going to school." "*Thưa mạ con đi học về*—(Respectfully) Mother, I am home from school." These eleven words, which tradition forced me to utter every day, were the only words I remember saying to my mother during those silent six months. How did I do it? What did I feel? What did I use to replace my relationship with my mother?

My first few weeks of silence I attribute to hatred. I loathed being in my mother's presence. When we were together in the same room, I never looked at her face or even positioned my body toward hers. At the dinner table, I swallowed my food without tasting it as fast as I could to shorten the torture of sitting near her. When we had company over and she asked me to come out and greet them, I stayed only long enough for them to see my fake smile before returning to my room. I did not think she deserved to be a mother, thus I did not treat her like one. I regarded her like a distant relative—with respect, but with no warmth or emotion. At night when my mother slept with Tai in her arms, so much anger welled up inside me that one time I released my rage by biting on a pillow with all my strength. "How could she go on like nothing happened?" I asked myself. "How could she not feel guilty?" Those nights I stayed up until two or three in the morning feeling sorry for my brother, furious at my mother, and disappointed in myself. I did not talk to anyone about my problems. Chau had isolated herself from the rest of our family, so she and I did not communicate, and I did not feel close enough to any of my friends at school to share with them my inner emotions. I also felt too ashamed to tell anyone about the unhappy circumstances in my family. Consequently, I existed for weeks like a walking balloon full of negative emotions just waiting to burst when I could no longer contain them. But I did not burst. I needed to appear strong, stolid (like the heroes in the Hong Kong movies). I needed to show my mother and myself that I did not depend on her for my emotions. The way I subdued these feelings is similar to what happens when a chemist immerses a helium-filled balloon into a vat of liquid nitrogen. Like the helium in the balloon, my emotions underwent a condensation into a colder, less active state.

For the remaining months of my silence, hatred and anger no longer played a large role in my reluctance to communicate with my mother. I figured, "Why should I torture myself with all these bad feelings? They don't do any good. I can't go on living so miserably." Convinced that emotions only hurt rather than benefited me, I gradually suppressed them. Soon I replaced those gut-wrenching feelings of guilt, sadness, and animosity with apathy and insensitivity. I no longer felt uncomfortable sitting next to my mother, because I had no feelings for her. Although I still remembered the events that occurred several weeks prior, it ceased to cause pain and anguish. My indifference made it easier for me to sleep at night, increased my ability to concentrate in school, and lifted the midnight clouds that hovered over me. In retrospect, I can understand the attraction of this defense mechanism; it was an easy escape from emotional pain and dependence on my mother. The side effect of my remedy, however, was that I lost the ability to feel other types of emotions as well, such as sympathy, sadness, and joy. I felt like a machine. When I watched inspirational movies, I did not have warm, fuzzy sensations. When I was elected president of the sophomore class, my only reaction was, "Good, this'll look good on my college applications." When my friend Vu made a full recovery after undergoing chemotherapy for lymphatic cancer, I never felt ecstatic, just relieved for him. Now I realize the price of indifference, and I have been trying hard to gain back—with little success—my ability to feel deep emotions.

In the months following my isolation from my mother, I found numerous ways to convince myself that she had absolutely no influence on me and that I had completely and irreversibly broken away from her. I guess this was the rebellious stage of my adolescence. However, I did not rebel in the typical demonstrative fashion, like screaming "I hate you" to my mom or getting drunk. Instead, I rebelled in a passive way so that only *I* knew I rebelled, while everyone, including her, still thought I was the perfect son. One of my defiance strategies was to achieve top grades in my classes without putting in any effort. I cheated in almost every subject. After school, when my mother asked me if I had any homework, I always replied, "No, Mom, I'm already done." She never asked me to show her my completed work because she could not read a word of it. I also started lying a lot to my mother. One time I told her that my friends and I went to the library to study, but actually we drove to San Francisco and spent the day playing volleyball on the beach. I cannot count all the times that I lied to her and she never found out the truth. I felt much satisfaction knowing that I had some control over her; it raised my self-confidence and esteem and felt like sweet revenge for her dominance over me when I was younger. I simply wanted to believe that my mother had no part in my success in both academics and life. Yet I allowed her to continue assuming that I was the model son and that without her I would have been nothing.

I figured she deserved at least that much because of the sacrifices she made in bringing me to America and raising me in a strange land.

What did I use to replace my mother's absence from my life? Certainly not other relationships! I found it difficult to make close friendships in high school for several reasons: my school environment, my inability to share feelings (mostly because I had no emotions), and the fact that I thought close friends were unessential for my well-being. The school I attended had the lowest SAT score averages in the country. Fifty percent of the student body was black, while about 90 percent of the faculty was white; the remaining students consisted mainly of Hispanics and Asians, with a few token white students. Almost everyone came from poor households; I once read an article about our school that revealed that over 70 percent of the students' families depended on welfare as their sole source of income. I witnessed gang fights almost every week, mostly between black gangs—the Bloods versus the Crips. But sometimes I also saw some action from the smaller Asian gangs like the Oriental Boyz. The extraordinarily high incidence of violence and drug abuse in my school forced the government to establish a gun- and drug-free zone around the school and the nearby housing complexes. Fortunately, I participated in the school's magnet program, called the Academy of Math, Science, and Engineering, that better prepared me for college. I limited the group of friends I hung out with mainly to other Vietnamese students from the Academy, and I stayed away from most of the black students because I was afraid of being associated with any of the gangs. My friends and I had lunch together, copied homework from one another, and joined the same clubs. However, outside of school we did not go out on a regular basis or call each other to have heart-to-heart conversations. Even when my friends did call me, we never discussed my family problems or feelings, probably because I didn't want to admit that I had any troubles at home. I also never developed strong companionships in high school because I did not feel that I needed them to make me content. I felt satisfied that I had friends to turn to when I wanted to copy homework from someone; other than that I had no burning desire to have best friends.

Relationships with girls also did not fill the void left by my mother's absence. In my high school years, a number of girls wrote me love letters, asked me out to proms, or tried to get to know me, but not once did I take the initiative to pursue a relationship with any of them. Sure, I went to their proms, but I only did it because I did not want to turn them down. It wasn't that I didn't find women attractive or that I didn't want a steady relationship; rather, I think that the combination of my mother's strict rules and a lack of male role models contributed to my nonaggressive behavior. As I stated before, my mother adamantly forbade me to have girlfriends, and although I wanted to establish my independence from her, I still needed to abide by her rules because I was living under her roof. The other reason I wasn't able to tell girls that I liked them was because I didn't know how. No one ever taught me the correct procedures for getting to know women, and what I saw on TV seemed too straightforward for my tastes. My closest male friend in high school, Vu, never had any experience with girls either. Thus, even if I wanted to go out with someone, I did not know how to approach her and ask.

I do not believe anything replaced my relationship with my mother. Her dominant presence simply disappeared as a result of my ability to suppress my emotions. How she felt no longer dictated how I felt. When she cried, I no longer cried; when she laughed, I no longer laughed with her; and when she told her disturbing childhood stories, they no longer affected me emotionally. It may seem heartless, but that was how I felt. I did not need anyone to take her place; what I *did* need, however, was to fill up the free time I had now that I wasn't spending it with my mother. I kept myself busy in high school by joining numerous clubs, volunteering at nursing homes and hospitals, playing on the tennis team, participating in math and science competitions, working, attending Vietnamese school on the weekends, and enrolling in night courses at the closest community college. I occupied my days with so many activities that on a typical day, I would not return home until eight or nine in the evening, and by that time my mother would be in bed.

In other ways, I came to understand my mother at a deeper level. In junior year I had a history class in which we learned about ancient China; we discussed Confucius's philosophy and how his ideals still permeate East Asian culture. One of the most important aspects of Confucian theory is its emphasis on role-playing in the family and in society. I remember writing a report on Confucian influence on contemporary Vietnamese society and realizing that my family performed the parts that he outlined centuries ago. Observing my family as a source for my essay, I learned that Confucius dictated our use of verbal and physical affection.

To this day I cannot say "I love you" to my mother, older sister, or younger brother. The only person whom I *do* verbally acknowledge my love for is Carol, my 4-year-old half-sister. It may seem strange, but Carol is also the only one that I hug, kiss, or show any other form of affection to. The same is true for my mother, Chau, and Tai—from an outsider's perspective it may seem as though all of us love only Carol. I also hear Chau verbalizing her love for Vinh, her fiancé, and it seems perfectly natural. What would be completely *unnatural* and unprecedented is if she said "I love you" to me, my mother, or my brother.

During elementary school my mother nurtured and cared for me as if I had just learned how to walk. One of the ways she made me state that I loved her was by asking, "Phuoc, where do you put your love for me?" My rehearsed answer was, "Mom, I put my love for you on my head!" (She considers the head the most important part of the body, so putting my love there meant that it was the most important love.) We kissed and hugged one another all the time and without reservation. By the time I started junior high school, however, we suddenly yet intuitively stopped being physically affectionate. Even though I missed my mother's touch, especially when I witnessed her affection for Carol, I knew that its cessation was appropriate for my age. Thinking back, the start of my adolescence and newfound need to break away from the nest, particularly when kids at school filled my head with the notion that kissing your mom was "sissy" and "gay," influenced the shift in our relationship. A change in my mother's attitude also contributed; she no longer asked me where I put my love for her. Instead, she asked Tai, who was 2 at the time, this question, which I thought she had reserved just for me. It was as if the game had age limits, and I had already passed them. My mother now expected me to show my love for her by obeying her and bringing home the As. Accordingly, she showed her love by feeding and clothing me.

"*Con không cha như nhà không nóc*—Children without a father are like houses without rooftops." My mother never failed to remind me of this Vietnamese proverb whenever she wanted to show off how she had disproved the old saying. She was correct in her claim, because we never grew up with a father, yet our house definitely has a "rooftop." My mother played the roles of breadwinner and caring mother at the same time. She disciplined us while bandaging our wounds, taught us how to ride a bike and then cleaned our scrapes and bruises, encouraged us to succeed in the real world while wishing we would never leave her side. In December of my last year before entering college, I unwittingly replaced my mother as the rooftop and the foundation of my home.

The news jumped at me out of the blue. "I'm going to Vietnam next month to visit Grandpa and Grandma," was all my mother said. "I'll leave some money for you while I'm gone. I'll be there for a month." She never discussed with me the possibility that I did not want to take care of 1-year-old Carol and 8-year-old Tai for an entire month, especially December, when I had so many things to do in my senior year. She never taught me how to cook dinner, potty train Carol, comfort her when she cried, and keep the house clean all in one day. Yet I never raised a single objection to her vacation plans. The only thing I recall telling her while we said good-bye at the airport was, "Have a safe trip, Mom. Don't let anyone con you over there, okay? Let me know when you want me to pick you up." For the next thirty-one days I enrolled in a crash course in parenting in which the teacher and student were one—me.

The most difficult part of the day came after Tai got home from school. During those few hours before bedtime, I ran around my two-bedroom home like a madman in nerve-racking attempts to prevent my hyperactive sister from hurting herself while also trying to complete multiple tasks. Within a two-hour stretch, I made dinner, did the laundry, mopped the floors, took out the garbage, changed Carol's diaper when I forgot to remind her about the mini-toilet, helped Tai with his fractions and long division, answered phone calls from friends seeking advice on how to fill out college applications, and played with Carol to keep her from wrecking the floors I had just mopped!

Every night I longed for nine o'clock to come around so that I could put the two children to sleep and actually attend to my own affairs. This was the time during my senior year when the college application deadlines loomed. In addition to completing seven or eight college applications, I worked on finishing nearly a dozen scholarship applications, all of which kept me up late every night. Luckily, I did not have trouble finding a topic for my personal essays; it was easy to write about my experiences performing the duties of a parent and how much I learned from them. This topic proved productive; the following spring I was accepted to a prestigious college and also won a full scholarship to the school of my choice.

Looking back on that month, I recognize now the richness of my experience and just how much it contributed to me as a person. During that time I learned what qualities an ideal man and woman should possess. My firsthand knowledge replaced my archaic notions of men as chivalrous protectors of passive, caring women. Another new concept I developed was that there weren't any obvious differences between the required traits of a man and a woman. I no longer divided the genders and designated specific attributes each should acquire. It was as if I took my culture's gender role assignments and synthesized them into one person, and that was who I became. Whether it was hugging Carol to sleep when she cried in the middle of the night, explaining fractions to Tai, cooking, cleaning, or fixing the door handle, I did not feel as though I switched roles when I performed them. I never thought to myself, "No, I can't do this because I'm a man. That's not what I'm supposed to do. But, since Mom's not here, I *have* to do the woman's work." Those thoughts didn't cross my mind. What I did think, however, was, "Of course I'll do this. I'll do it because I love my sister and brother. No other reason."

Ever since my sister went away to college, my role and responsibility in my family has changed dramatically. I have much more say in household affairs than before. Now whenever I am at home I take care of all the bills and paperwork that my mother has accumulated over the months while I was in college. If there is a decision to be made, I usually make it and then tell my mother why I did so. I think she finally realized that I was old enough to make the right choices for our family. Along with my added responsibility, the weight of my word has increased markedly since high school. Again, I think my mother takes my opinion more seriously because I am old enough now to play the role of an influential person in our family. Knowing that what I say has a more profound influence on her than ever before, I have not wasted an opportunity to help my little brother and sister. Whenever I have a chance, I persuade her to change her ways toward Tai and little Carol so that they can have a smoother childhood than I did. By this I mean that I encourage her to allow them to make friends within and outside of the Vietnamese ethnicity, let Tai talk to girls his age because he can benefit from them and vice versa, and most importantly discipline them with words instead of whips. I believe my words have not gone unheard, especially those dealing with punishment, because since I started college I cannot recall ever hearing about her spanking Tai or Carol.

My years in college have allowed me to develop a new, more equal relationship with my mother. I think the time I spent at school three thousand miles away has made us both appreciate and respect one another (although she would never admit that she respects or appreciates me). She now sees me as an independent individual, and I see her as both a mother and a friend. I know that she takes much pride in seeing me succeed in my academic life, but even though I want to make her proud of me and hope that she gains the proper admiration she deserves from those in Vietnam, I do not base my goals and aspirations on pleasing her. If in the process of attaining my goals I also make her happy, then I will have lived up to both my American and Vietnamese ideals—doing things for myself and doing things to show respect for my parents. I praise my mother when I see the improvements in the way she is raising Tai and Carol compared to her raising of Chau and me. I think she knows that she cannot apply every aspect of Vietnamese culture to children she is raising in America. When I go home for vacations, I still function as the man in the house, the person who takes care of the bills, fixes door-knobs, and attends the parent–teacher conferences. At the same time, I am also the only male figure for my brother, which puts pressure on me to be the best role model I can. I play these roles willingly and with satisfaction.

As for my search for the culture that suits me best, I have come to the decision that neither Vietnamese nor American culture alone can fulfill my needs. Thus, I chose to pick out the best aspects of each culture and synthesize them into one. For instance, while I believe in the American ideal that every person is equal, I also disapprove of children not treating their elders with respect and proper manners. I do not consider myself Americanized or Vietnamized; rather, I'm enjoying the best of both worlds.

What are the issues that I am still struggling with? As I enter my senior year, I'm still trying to inflate the emotional balloon that I've suppressed for so long. Recently, my girlfriend Jennifer has been helping me recover my ability to feel strong emotions again. Last month she and I cried together, something I haven't done since my sophomore year in high school! However, I find it much more difficult to bring back the emotions than to tuck them away, and so far I haven't made much progress.

From the academic success my sister and I have earned, it may seem that our family is living out the American dream. We escaped from a war-scarred country that offered us few opportunities and arrived in a land we knew nothing about. My mother worked hard all her life to provide her children with a home that was conducive to learning. She created such an atmosphere by using the whip, along with guilt-provoking stories to encourage us to learn. Now that two of her children are excelling in their respective postsecondary institutions, my mother feels that she has done an admirable job of raising us. However, her feelings of pride come at a high cost to the relationships in our family. Maybe she did not know any other way to raise us than by using her native culture's means. She did not realize that most families who bring up successful children do not use the switch as their tool of support. I believe that practicing Confucian ideals in the family will lead to decreased communication and ultimately to feelings of isolation similar to those that Chau and I felt and are still experiencing. Fortunately, after seeing her family structure crumble because of her, my mother realized that her rearing methods needed improvement. She knows now that her children will inevitably become "Americanized" to some degree. Accordingly, she now allows Tai and Carol more freedom; hopefully, they will also live up to her ideals. I can sense that the relationships in my family are becoming more intimate. We all can hug and kiss each other now, and I am optimistic that in the near future my mother and I will be able to say "I love you" to one another.

PHUOC: NINE YEARS LATER

"Plea hep me. I don spea Englit very mut," uttered my mother softly into the microphone shortly after the middle-aged judge took her seat. "Okay Ms. Nguyen, the court will appoint a Vietnamese interpreter for you." With that, she thanked the judge and sat down to focus on the stack of documents she brought with her to contest the change in legal guardianship of her youngest daughter.

Mom wore a simple, body length, white business suit, decorated herself with make-up, gold, and jade, and styled her hair to highlight the tuft of gray that had appeared almost overnight. I stood not more than ten feet to her right, with my wife, Erin, standing on one side of me while the attorney representing Carol, now 13 years old, on my left. We had been sitting in that probate and family courtroom for over an hour, yet neither my mother nor I had spoken to, or even looked at, one another. This scene took place seven months ago when we attended the final hearing that ultimately led the judge to grant Erin and me legal custody of my sister, Carol. This was also the last time I saw my mother.

When the editors of this book asked me to write a follow-up to "Seeking the Best of Both Worlds" they didn't realize that in these past months I have been facing the most challenging crises and transitions in my life. The portrait of me as an adolescent in my earlier essay will now be abruptly replaced by a portrait of me as a parent. I have also switched from being the filial child to the disavowed son who has broken his mother's heart and taken away all that she had been living for. If I had written this essay one year ago instead of now, the circumstances would have been drastically different. A year ago, I would have reported that our family was relatively intact, despite still working through years of deeply embedded emotional scars. A year ago I was nearing the end of medical school, having just completed a year of clinical rotations and graduated with a master's in public health from UC Berkeley. A year ago we were ecstatic to learn of the birth of our new baby niece, Kayla, my older sister, Chau's, first child. A year ago I was seeing my younger brother Tai regularly even though he was far away in college at UCLA. And a year ago, my younger sister, Carol, was finishing seventh grade, was living just ten minutes away from Erin and me, and was becoming a teenager. In the span of just several months, the entire landscape of our family has been fundamentally and irreversibly altered. Yet, one element would have stayed unchanged: the consequences of my mother's abuse reverberate powerfully still in each of her children.

At the end of "Seeking the Best of Both Worlds," I described my newfound influence in the way my mother raised her two younger children, Tai and Carol. She no longer physically abused them; she gave them more freedom to make friends and did not expect perfect grades from either of them. I was proud of my mother for making these positive changes so that Tai and Carol could have more "normal" upbringings. Unfortunately, I learned not soon after that mom had replaced physical abuse with even more devastating forms of punishment: emotional and psychological abuse. That Tai and Carol proved more susceptible to these methods of mistreatment further compounded their distress, which manifested itself in broken family and social relationships, decreased academic performances, and even thoughts of suicide. This final consequence of my mother's words and actions compelled Erin and me to take the decisive step to protect Carol's health and well-being.

Shortly after writing "Seeking the Best of Both Worlds" I requested a year-long leave of absence from college to study acupuncture and language in Beijing, China. Having declared a double major in biochemistry and Chinese, and not knowing whether I would pursue advanced studies or place myself in the market after graduation, I jumped at the chance to delay that decision while combining both my interests. This year of complete independence was instrumental in my decision to pursue a career in medicine and international public health, with a focus on health in China. Learning a traditional modality of healing and theory of disease broadened by a more culturally based scope of knowledge continues to serve me well today as I treat patients from varied ethnic and cultural backgrounds. The personal and academic growth I gained in China was well worth the price of not graduating with my original college classmates.

Despite times of loneliness at the start of my year in Beijing, I quickly made new Chinese friends and plugged myself into the small, but welcoming Vietnamese expatriate community. The group of Vietnamese friends I made consisted of international graduate students from Ho Chi Minh City, and several families from Europe, Australia, and the United States. They were the first ethnic Vietnamese families I had met since leaving California to start college. Indeed, they were the first Vietnamese families I had known that were not my close or distant relatives. My interactions with them over the course of the year provided a starkly different, and decidedly preferable, model of family dynamics compared to what I grew up knowing and resenting. Not unlike the struggles of my own family, my new friends were also refugees at one point, also spent years in camps in neighboring Southeast Asian host nations, also encountered discrimination and xenophobia after settling in our respective industrialized nations, and also somehow were able to succeed against the odds. Yet, unlike my mother in my own childhood experiences, these parents did not beat or emotionally abuse their children, nor did they teach their children to embrace only Vietnamese culture. I remember one family that I still keep in touch with, the Phans, who came to Beijing from Paris because Mr. Phan was promoted to a managerial position in a French firm that operated in China. The Phans had a 5-year-old son, Bathy, whom they treated with respect, as though his feelings and concerns were every bit as valid as their own.

They didn't slap him when he interrupted conversations among the adults; neither did they laugh, shame, and criticize him for his shortcomings. They made sure that he learned about and appreciated his heritage by only speaking Vietnamese in the household, exposing him to other Vietnamese children, and taking him on yearly trips to Saigon. At the same time, both parents were able to speak Chinese and emphasized to Bathy the importance of learning Chinese culture and language.

At first, I thought the Phans were a rare example of a "functional" immigrant Vietnamese family, to be admired only, and not to be expected. However, I soon met two other Vietnamese families in Beijing with similar backgrounds and child-rearing philosophies. In one family the father was Caucasian, yet he went out of his way to master Vietnamese so that his children would learn to embrace their mother's heritage. These model families, having *found* the best of both worlds, left a dramatic impact on the way I saw myself raising a family.

My year in Beijing also gave me new insights into romantic relationships with women. By the time I wrote "Seeking the Best of Both Worlds," I had already come a long way since my naïve idealization of the masculine role that I garnered from watching Hong Kong soap operas in high school. I had dated several women, and even had a year-long, serious relationship. Yet, it wasn't until I observed the model of healthy romantic relationships embodied in the Vietnamese couples I've just described, that I realized what it means to have a long-term romance based on mutual respect and dependence. Since leaving China, these insights were reflected in two subsequent relationships, the latter of which continues and grows to this day.

On the eve of my return to the United States and my planned application to medical school, I called my mother for the first time in months. She sounded frantic, saying that Tai had stolen money from her to feed his "hoodlum" friends at school and that she was ready to go insane because of him. She recounted how she even tried to call the police to have 12-year-old Tai taken away and put into an orphanage before he became "*b_i__i*," the dust of life, and brought even more shame to the family. I asked to speak to Tai, and as soon as he picked up the phone, I could hear the torrent of tears rushing down his face. As we spoke I readily recognized the similarities between what he was suffering and the difficulties I had at the start of my own adolescence. I shared in his desire to be a "normal" teenager with typical teenage problems. I decided then that I would postpone my graduation by yet another year to be close to home and to try to give my little brother a fighting chance at a "normal" adolescence.

Coming home I found a brother who was withdrawn, depressed, emotional, and mortally afraid of his mother's verbal violence against him. He related to me how much he hated to be yelled at by our mother, and how this had escalated during my time abroad. My efforts at persuading mom to stop this emotional abuse were met only by Tai's rebukes. "You don't know what it's like after you tell her off," he protested, "after you leave she yells at me even more! You can easily go back to your apartment, but I have to stay here and listen to her yelling all the time. And she doesn't stop for days! She tells me how much pain she's in because of me and asks herself why I'm not getting good grades. She even says that she should've aborted me in Kansas when my dad found out she was pregnant. She calls me stupid all the time, and says I'll never be as good as you or Chi Chau. She blames everything on me!" My feeling of powerlessness then was similar to my helplessness at stopping Tai's father from molesting him years earlier. Besides entertaining the idea of calling Child Protective Services, I was at a loss for options at that point.

For the next year I lived only half an hour from my family, initially working two full-time jobs to pay off debt that I accumulated while in China, then enrolling at UC Davis to occupy my time with Japanese, Spanish, biology, and philosophy courses. I spent time with Tai and Carol weekly. I strategically picked times when mom was at work so as to give them a break from her. We dined out, watched movies, bowled, skated, fed ducks at the park, camped, and enjoyed activities of "normal" families. I even went as far as taking Tai on a two-week trip to Beijing during his winter vacation. This time together provided safe environments for Tai to voice his frustrations and fears about mom to someone who had lived through a similar situation. I shared with him some coping mechanisms to help him avoid mom's abuse as much as possible. By the time I prepared to return to college and finish my senior year, I felt relatively reassured that Tai was better off than when I had arrived a year earlier. However, it took little time at all for mom to unravel Tai's sense of self-worth and the gains he had made.

In his subsequent high-school years, Tai continued to be inhibited and introverted, but he always made sure he did enough to stay on mom's good side to avoid verbal punishment. Even during his senior year in high school, he would hug and kiss mom before and after school, gestures that I had rejected soon after I distanced myself from her emotionally in high school. Tai never had the good fortune of severing his emotional ties with and dependency on mom, however, and because of this, I believe he still suffers from these psychological wounds today.

Tai is now in his third year at a competitive university in California, where he is performing well academically, and maintains many good friends. My older sister Chau, now a practicing physician in the Midwest, and I have been concerned over Tai's years-long struggle with clinical depression. We've urged him to see a therapist, and have gone so far as to send him samples of an antidepressant. To our disappointment, however, and likely to his detriment, Tai decided to suffer through this illness alone. In the past several months Tai's mental health has consumed the attention and time of our entire family. One evening a few months ago, Tai confided in Erin over the telephone of his intentions to end his life, saying that he wanted to tell her good-bye. Stunned by this news she had no choice but to let me know and also involve our older sister. After driving through the night from our home and arriving at his apartment in the early hours of the morning, he sat with us in our car for an hour, but was unmoved by our offers of alternatives. He even scolded us for coming down to see him, saying that it made things even worse for him. That morning we anxiously called the police to have him committed, as we did not know when he would carry out his plan. We were afraid that our visit would ironically hasten his decision. The scene of a half dozen police officers surrounding his apartment, blocking all exits by car or on foot, came straight out of a Hollywood action movie. Since then, Tai has been hospitalized twice for suicidal ideation. He reluctantly started taking antidepressants and antipsychotics, just to appease his psychiatrists, but he never had any intention of continuing his medication on a long-term basis. The only intervention he willingly accepted and actually appreciated was a PhD therapist who had experience with immigrant adolescent experiences, specifically those from Vietnam. In addition, he has made it clear that he needs time separated from his older siblings, and even Erin, whom he sees as those who betrayed him by committing him against his will. I don't know how long this voluntary isolation will last, but we have all honored his wishes, despite our deep sadness.

Looking back on this crisis, I remember mentally cursing my mother for what she had caused. I imagined how much more positive life for Tai would have been if he had been born into a different family, and lamented the fact that he couldn't break away from her emotional stranglehold. I criticized myself for not acting on my earlier impulses to call child protective services so that Tai could have a better chance at life, even if foster care were the only other option. I vowed that I would not let the same thing happen to Carol, my younger sister.

Our other major crisis in the past months, which has dramatically changed the course of our lives, has been over Carol's health and future. When Tai graduated from high school and left home for college, Erin and I encouraged my mom to move down to Palo Alto, where Carol could receive a better education and be closer to me, as I was at Stanford Medical School. The junior high school in which Carol was preparing to enroll was known as a particularly "ghetto" school filled with future gang members, high-school dropouts, and teenage mothers. Only after considerable discussion, and our offers to do all of the relocation work, did mom relent to uprooting her home of eighteen years to start afresh. As the only child left living with mom, Carol bore the brunt of mom's frustrations about her new environment, about not having enough Vietnamese people around, and of course mom's unceasing criticisms of Carol's weight, poor grades, poor manners, laziness, impoliteness, and more. In the last year, since Carol turned 13, she often would spend weekends with Erin and me, to "get away from mom for a while." We would console her and dry her tears while doing our best to undo the damage that mom had inflicted on Carol's senses of self-esteem, self-worth, and self-image.

At the beginning of her eighth grade year, Erin and I arranged for Carol to see her school counselor so that she would have another source of support. I remember Erin calling me during my clinical rotation in the neonatal intensive care unit to say that Carol's counselor had forbade her from going back home to mom's, that Carol was to stay with us for the time being, and that Child Protective Services had been called to investigate. This was the start of many weeks of anguish for Erin and me. Although we knew that Carol was still dealing with emotional abuse from mom, we did not recognize the extent of her suffering. Carol disclosed to her counselor that she occasionally had thoughts of hurting herself at times because of the guilt ingrained into her daily by her mother. These thoughts were deemed serious enough to warrant Carol's hospitalization in an adolescent psychiatric ward. At this point there was no doubt in my mind as to what I needed to do; Erin and I subsequently filed for legal custody, or guardianship, of Carol.

My final conversation with my mother occurred several weeks before the court hearing, while Carol was still hospitalized. She called me one evening, and speaking through her tears, asked me why I was out to destroy her family. She said that she gave everything to us, did nothing for herself, and even loved her daughter-in-law even though she isn't Vietnamese. She added that whatever I did, I should not spread word of this to the Vietnamese community as it would bring her too much loss of face. I could not comprehend how my mother could have uttered those sentences. With my sister suffering alone in a hospital bed, my brother still damaged seemingly beyond repair, that moment was a tipping point for me. I unleashed my fury at her like never before.

"If you were such a great mother, if you had no faults, then tell me, just tell me, why are three of your children seeing psychiatrists!" I screamed, not letting her interrupt me, "Why *is* it that two of your children were hospitalized for being suicidal? Why? Tell me, why?! Because you are *NOT* a great mother. Let me tell you right now, if any of my siblings dies because of you, my hate for you will be unending!" I can only imagine the shock my mother felt as these words landed on her ears, for I even surprised myself.

Her only response was, "I don't know what's wrong with them. I didn't do anything wrong. I just tried to love my kids and now you're trying to take them from me!" The last thing I said to her before hanging up was, "There's nothing more to say then. Let's just see how the judge decides what's right."

Carol's permanent entry into our home has cast Erin and me into the roles of parents of a teenager. The last eight months have brought countless challenges, from ordinary teenage needs like braces, school dances, tenuous friendships, Myspace.com, and classroom stressors, to the *extra*-ordinary trials like antidepressants and psychiatry visits, uncontrollable bouts of guilt and crying, and Carol's nightmares about her mom coming after her. We have no illusions that the healing process will be fast, and expect that therapy will continue for years to come. Carol has already amazed us with her resilience. Since ending her relationship with mom, she has blossomed into a more extroverted, social teenager, and her grades have shown further improvement. Along the way, Carol was blessed with caring teachers and counselors who have played important roles during this transition.

I sometimes ask myself what mom could do to reconcile with her children. At the very least she must acknowledge and show heartfelt remorse for the role she played in the psychological trauma of her children. I doubt that day will come. For the past half year, she has not made any attempts to visit Carol, despite having the option to see Carol with our supervision. It would seem that she has made the ultimate sacrifice of losing her teenage daughter in the name of saving face. Currently, the only remaining child who is on speaking terms with our mother is Tai. Rooted in feelings of guilt and sympathy, he now reluctantly plays the role of the "good son." However, this communication with mom has taken a toll on him, as his roommate has recounted to me that Tai has been more moody since he started talking to mom again. Recently he has also been the only link between mom and the rest of the siblings. I don't believe that Tai's role as liaison has any positive impact on Carol, who still feels guilty for not wanting to see or speak with mom.

To this day when I meet new people and tell them of how my family fled to the United States as part of the "boat people" in the early 1980s, they invariably comment on how brave and selfless my mother must have been to risk everything for her children. In response, I always say, "Yes, she most certainly was." My mother had a decades-long goal of one day moving back to Vietnam to bask in the glory of her "good works," returning to find admiration and respect among her family and peers in Hue. She often told me of her dream to build a four-story house, adorned with portraits of her successful children. "My two oldest ones are doctors," she would point out to guests. The house would be big enough to offer individual rooms for each of her four children and their families. Obviously, these dreams have been crushed literally overnight. She now has no "face" to return. How can she explain that her children, who outwardly are so successful in American society, do not talk to her, do not revere her, would not visit her in Vietnam?

At the end of "Seeking the Best of Both Worlds" I described my effort to regain the ability to feel deep emotions, which I intentionally buried during my psychological "break" with mom in high school. Certainly my loving wife of three years has helped me move forward in this regard. In addition, I found that the process of treating gravely ill patients in intensive care units has had a therapeutic effect on releasing my dormant ability to feel deep sadness. On the other hand, I have a disconcerting ability to transition to new environments without much hesitance. For example, just last week, as my wife and I were preparing to move from California to the East Coast to start my residency, Erin asked me, "I just don't get it. How come Carol and I are both torn apart and crying over moving to Boston, and yet you seem to have no problem with leaving after living here for five years?" I guess at this point I am still a "work in progress."

In the past, I readily attributed many of my mom's failures to her intractable adherence to cultural values that were maladapted to the environment in which she raised her children. I explained her severe physical abuse of me and Chau as common and accepted child-raising tools among uneducated villagers in Vietnam. I rationalized the reasons for her privileging males over females as deeply seated Confucian teachings that survive to this day in most of East and Southeast Asia. I even succumbed to her reasoning for why we should respect her and obey her to the end ("Even the eighty-year-old emperor has to kowtow to his one-hundred-year-old mother"). Only in the past few years, after considerable thought, have I come to the conclusion that mom's culture and upbringing cannot account for all the harm she has brought to us. Recently, Erin triggered a lengthy discussion by asking, "If you could imagine taking your mother and placing her, the way she is, back to her village in Vietnam, would she fit in? Would her treatment of you and your siblings be considered normal?" Armed now with experience treating patients with numerous psychiatric and psychological pathologies, my sister Chau and I strongly suspect that mom indeed has hidden a personality disorder under the guise of traditional values. Sadly, despite a court order mandating psychological therapy as a condition of visitation rights, mom stubbornly has decided that "face" is more important.

Nine years have passed since I wrote "Seeking the Best of Both Worlds." During these years I was blessed with opportunities to study, volunteer, and work in many developing countries. Now that I am able to speak the languages and negotiate the traditions of many peoples, I feel uniquely suited for an eventual career caring for underserved populations in developing countries and partnering with local communities to implement public health interventions. Erin has encouraged me, and even joined me, in my pursuit of health care equity and justice for those who are marginalized and displaced. Like the husband I befriended in Beijing who learned Vietnamese so that his children will embrace their mother's cultural roots, Erin also sees us raising our children in a bilingual household. After residency, we hope to spend some time in Vietnam, where I can practice medicine and public health, and where Erin can master the language and follow her own career ambitions in child advocacy.

CONTRIBUTORS

Andrew Garrod is Professor of Education and Director of Teacher Education at Dartmouth College, where he teaches courses in adolescence, moral development, and contemporary issues in U.S. education. His recent publications include two co-authored articles, "Forgiveness After Genocide?: Perspectives from Bosnian Youth" and "Culture, Ethnic Conflict, and Moral Orientation in Bosnian Children"; and the co-edited books, *Souls Looking Back: Life Stories of Growing Up Black* and *Learning Disabilities and Life Stories.* In 1991 he was awarded Dartmouth College's Distinguished Teaching Award.

* * *

Robert Kilkenny is Clinical Associate in the School of Social Work at Simmons College. He is co-editor of *Souls Looking Back: Life Stories of Growing Up Black* (with Andrew Garrod, Janie Ward, and Tracy Robinson). With Andrew Garrod and Christine Gomez he is completing a manuscript for an edited anthology on growing up Latino. He is the founder and Executive Director of the Alliance for Inclusion and Prevention, a public–private partnership providing mental health and special education services to at-risk students in the Boston Public Schools.

* * *

Sally Powers is Professor and Head of the Clinical Division in the Department of Psychology, and Director of the Center for Research on Families at the University of Massachusetts, Amherst. She teaches a course in adolescent psychopathology and her research focuses on interpersonal, cognitive, and psychological factors that contribute to the development of adolescent depression and anxiety.

* * *

Lisa Smulyan is Professor and Chair of the Department of Educational Studies at Swarthmore College, Swarthmore, Pennsylvania, where she teaches courses in educational foundations, adolescence, gender and education, and comparative education. Her publications include *Balancing Acts: Women Principals at Work; Collaborative Action Research: A Developmental Process;* and several articles. Her research focuses on classroom-based research with teachers, life/case history as a basis for understanding school practice, and investigations into the role of gender in teachers' and administrators' work experience.

BIBLIOGRAPHY

Adams R., & Laursen, B. (2001). "The organization and dynamics of adolescent conflict with parents and friends." *Journal of Marriage and the Family* 63:97–101.

Adelson, J., & Douvan, E. (1975). "Adolescent friendships." In J. Conger, P. Mussen, & J. Kagan, *Basic and Contemporary Issues in Developmental Psychology,* 277–90. New York: Harper and Row.

Adler, N. (1975). "Emotional responses of women following therapeutic abortion." *American Journal of Orthopsychiatry* 45:446–56.

Allen, J., & Land, D. (1999). "Attachment in adolescence." In J. Cassidy & P. R. Shaver (eds.), *Handbook of Attachment: Theory, Research, and Clinical Applications,* 319–35. New York: Guilford Press.

Allen, J. P., Hauser, S. T., Bell, K. L., & O'Conner, T. G. (1994). "Longitudinal assessment of autonomy and relatedness in adolescent-family interactions as predicators of adolescent ego development and self-esteem." *Child Development* 65:179–94.

Ames, N., & Miller, E. (1994). *Changing Middle Schools: How to Make Schools Work for Young Adolescents.* San Francisco: Jossey-Bass.

Aristotle. (1941). *Rhetorica.* New York: Random House.

Arnett, J. (2004). *Emerging Adulthood: The Winding Road from the Late Teens through the Twenties.* New York: Oxford University Press.

———. (1987). "Development perspectives on adolescent risk-taking in contemporary America." In C. E. Irwin (ed.), *Adolescent Social Behavior and Health,* 93–125. San Francisco: Jossey-Bass.

Baumrind, D. (1989). "Rearing competent children." In W. Damon (ed.), *Child Development Today and Tomorrow.* San Francisco: Jossey-Bass.

———. (1989). "The role of self understanding in resilient individuals: The development of a perspective." *American Journal of Orthopsychiatry* 59(2):266–78.

Belsky J., Steinberg L., & Draper P. (1991). "Childhood experience, interpersonal development and reproductive strategy: An evolutionary theory of socialization." *Child Development* 62:647–70.

Benedict, R. (1950). *Patterns of Culture.* New York: New American Library.

Biederman, J., Wilens, T., Mick, E., Spencer, T., & Faraone, S. V. (1999). "Pharmacotherapy of attention-deficit/hyperactivity disorder reduces risk for substance use disorder." *Pediatrics,* 104(20): 104–20.

Blos, P. (1962). *On Adolescence: A Psychoanalytic Interpretation.* New York: Free Press.

———. (1972). "The child analyst looks at the young adolescent." In K. Kagan and R. Coles (eds.), *Twelve to Sixteen: Early Adolescence.* New York: W. W. Norton.

Blos, P. (1979). *The Adolescent Passage.* New York: International Universities Press.

Bracken, M., Hachamovitch, M., & Grossman, A. (1974). "The decision to abort and psychological sequelae." *Journal of Nervous and Mental Disorders* 15:155–61.

Brown, B. B. (2004). "Adolescents' relationships with peers." In R. M. Lerner & L. Steinberg (eds.), *Handbook of Adolescent Psychology.* Hoboken, NJ: John Wiley & Sons, I 363–94.

Carter, P. (2006). "Intersecting identities: 'Acting white,' gender, and academic achievement." In E. Horvat & C. O'Connor (eds.), *Beyond Acting White: Reframing the Debate on Black Student Achievement.* Lanham, MD: Rowman and Littlefield.

Chodorow, N. (1989). *Feminism and Psychoanalysis*. New Haven, CT: Yale University Press.

Chu, J. (2004). "A relational perspective on boys' identity development." In N. Way & J. Chu (eds.), *Adolescent Boys*, 78–106. New York: NYU Press.

Clark, R. (1983). *Family Life and School Achievement: Why Poor Black Children Succeed or Fail*. Chicago: University of Chicago Press.

Collins, W. A. (1995). "Relationships and development: Family adaptation to individual change." In S. Shulman (ed.), *Close Relationships and Socioemotional Development*, 128–54. New York: Ablex.

Collins, W. A., & Laursen, B. (2004). "Parent-adolescent relationship and influences." In R. M. Lerner & L. Steinberg (eds.), *Handbook of Adolescent Psychology*, 331–36. Hoboken, NJ: John Wiley & Sons.

Collins, W. A., & Repinski, D. J. (2001). "Parents and adolescents as transformers of relationships: Dyadic adaptations to developmental change." In J. R. M. Gerris (ed.), *Dynamics of Parenting: International Perspectives on Nature and Sources of Parenting*, 429–43. Leuven, Netherlands: Garant.

Collins, W. A., & Russell, G. (1991). "Mother-child and father-child relationships in middle childhood and adolescence: A developmental analysis." *Developmental Review* 11:99–136.

Connell, R. W. (2000). *The Men and the Boys*. Berkeley: University of California Press.

Connolly, J., Furman, W., & Konarski, R. (2000). "The role of peers in the emergence of heterosexual romantic relationships in adolescence." *Child Development* 71:1395–1408.

Cooley, C. H. (1902). *Human Nature and the Social Order*. New York: Scribners.

Cooper, C. R. (1994). "Cultural perspectives on continuity and change in adolescents' relationships." In R. Montemayor & G. R. Adams, *Personal Relationships during Adolescence*, 78–100. Thousand Oaks, CA: Sage.

Côté, J., & Levine, C. (1987). "A formulation of Erikson's theory of ego identity formation." *Developmental Review* 7:273–325.

Cross, W. (1991). *Shades of Black: Diversity in African-American Identity*. Philadelphia: Temple University Press.

Csikszentmihalyi, M., & Larson, R. (1984). *Being Adolescent*. New York: Basic Books.

Cvejic, H., Lipper, I., Kinch, R. A., & Benjamin, P. (1977). "Follow-up of 50 adolescent girls two years after abortion." *Canadian Medical Association Journal* 116:44–46.

Darwin, C. (1936). *The Origin of the Species by Means of Natural Selection*. New York: Modern Library.

Eder, D. (1985). "The cycle of popularity: Interpersonal relations among female adolescence." *Sociology of Education* 58:154–65.

Elder, G. (1980). "Adolescence in historical perspective." In J. Adelson (ed.), *Handbook of Adolescent Psychology*, 3–46. New York: John Wiley and Sons.

Erikson, E. H. (1959). "Identity and the life cycle." *Psychological Issues* 1:1–171.

———. (1964). *Insight and Responsibility*. New York: W. W. Norton.

———. (1966). *The Challenge of Youth*. New York: Anchor Paperback.

———. (1968). *Identity: Youth and Crisis*. New York: Norton.

———. (1975). *Life History and the Historical Moment*. New York: W. W. Norton.

———. (1980). *Identity and the Life Cycle: A Reissue*. New York: W. W. Norton.

Ewing, J. A., & Rouse, B. A. (1973). "Therapeutic abortion and a prior psychiatric history." *American Journal of Psychiatry* 130:37–40.

Feiring, C. (1999). "Other-sex friendship networks and the development of romantic relationships in adolescence." *Journal of Youth and Adolescence* 28:495–512.

Feldman, S., & Elliott, G. (1990). *At the Threshold: The Developing Adolescent.* Cambridge, MA: Harvard University Press.

Ferguson, A. (2000). *Bad Boys: Public Schools in the Making of Black Masculinity.* Ann Arbor: University of Michigan Press.

Finkelhor, D. (1984). *Child Sexual Abuse: New Theory and Research.* New York: Free Press.

Flores-Gonzáles, N. (2002). *School Kids, Street Kids: Identity Development in Latino Students.* New York: Teachers College Press.

Ford, C., Castelnuovo-Tedesco, P., & Long, K. (1971). "Abortion: Is it a therapeutic procedure in psychiatry?" *Journal of the American Medical Association* 218:1173.

Fordham, S. (1988). "Racelessness as a factor in Black students' school success: Pragmatic strategy or pyrrhic victory?" *Harvard Educational Review* 58(1):54–84.

Freud, A. (1946). *The Ego and Mechanisms of Defense.* (C. Baines, trans.). New York: International Universities Press.

———. (1958). "Adolescence." In *Psychoanalytic Study of the Child.* New York: International Universities Press.

Freud, S. (1953). *Three Essays on Sexuality.* London: Hogarth Press.

———. (1962). "The transformations of puberty." In *Three Essays on the Theory of Sexuality,* 73–74, 85–96. New York: Basic Books.

Furman, W. (1999). "Friends and lovers: The role of peer relationships in adolescent romantic relationships." In W. A. Collins & B. Laursen (eds.), *Relationships as Developmental Contexts* (vol. 30), 89–103. Mahwah, NJ: Erlbaum.

Furman, W., Simon, V. A., Schaffer, L., & Bouchey, H. A. (2002). "Adolescents' working models and styles for relationships with parents, friends, and romantic partners." *Child Development* 73:241–55.

Galliher, R. V., Rostosky, S. S., Welsh, D. P., and Kawaguchi, M. C. (1999). "Power and psychological well-being in late adolescent romantic relationships." *Sex Roles* 40(9): 689–710.

Garmezy, N. (1985). "Stress-resistant children: The search for protective factors." In J. E. Stevenson (ed.), *Recent Research in Developmental Psychopathology.* Oxford: Pergamon Press.

Gaub, M., & Carlson, C. L. (1997). Gender differences in ADHD: A meta-analysis and critical review. *Journal of the American Academy of Child and Adolescent Psychiatry* 36:1036–45.

Gershon, J. (2002). "A meta-analytic review of gender differences in ADHD." *Journal of Attention Disorders* 5:143–54.

Gibbs, J. T. (1984). "Black adolescents and youth: An endangered species." *American Journal of Orthopsychiatry* 54(1):6–23.

Gilchrist, A. C., Hanaford, P. C., Frank, P., & Kay, C. R. (1995). Termination of pregnancy and psychiatric morbidity. *British Journal of Psychology* 167:243–48.

Gilligan, C. (1982). *In a Different Voice.* Cambridge, MA: Harvard University Press.

Gilligan, C., Lyons, N., & Hanmer, T. (eds.). (1989). *Making Connections: The Relational Worlds of Adolescent Girls at Emma Willard School.* Troy, NY: Emma Willard School.

Goethals, G. W., & Klos, D. S. (1976). *Experiencing Youth: First Person Accounts.* Boston: Little Brown.

Gold, M., & Yanof, D. (1985). "Mothers, daughters and girlfriends." *Journal of Personality and Social Psychology* 49:654–89.

Gonzales, N., & Cauce, A. M. (1995). "Ethnic identity and multicultural competence: Dilemmas and challenges for minority youth." In W. D. Hawley & A. W. Jackson (eds.), *Toward a Common Destiny,* 131–62. San Francisco, CA: Jossey-Bass.

Gray, M., & Steinberg, L. (1999). "Unpacking authoritative parenting: Reassessing a multi-dimensional construct." *Journal of Marriage and the Family* 61:574–87.

Grello, C. M., Welsh, D. P., Harper, M. S., & Dickson, J. W. (2003). "Dating and sexual relationship trajectories and adolescent functioning. *Adolescent & Family Health* 3(3):103–12.

Grotevant, H. D. (1998). "Adolescent development in family contexts." In W. Damon & N. Eisenberg (eds.), *Handbook of Child Psychology (vol. 3): Social, Emotional, and Personality Development*, 1097–1150. New York: Wiley.

Grotevant, H. D., & Cooper, C. R. (1986). "Individuation in family relationships." *Human Development* 29:82–100.

Hall, G. S. (1904). *Adolescence: Its Psychology and Its Relations to Physiology, Anthropology, Sociology, Sex, Crime, Religion, and Education*. New York: Appleton-Century-Crofts.

Hartup, W. W. and Laursen, B. (1991). "Relationships as developmental contexts." In R. Cohen & A. W. Siegel (eds.), *Context and Development*, 253–80. Hillsdale, NJ: Erlbaum.

Hatcher, S. (1976). "Understanding adolescent pregnancy and abortion." *Primary Care* 3:407–25.

Hauser, S. T., Houlihan, J., Powers, S. I., Jacobson, A. M., Noam, G., Weiss-Perry, B., & Follansbee, D. (1987). "Interaction sequences in families of psychiatrically hospitalized and non-patient adolescents." *Psychiatry* 50:308–19.

Hauser, S., Powers, S., & Noam, G. (1991). *Adolescents and Their Families: Paths of Ego Development*. New York: Free Press.

Hauser, S. T., Powers, S. I., Noam, G., Jacobson, A. M., Weiss, B., & Follansbee, D. (1984). "Familial contexts of adolescent ego development." *Child Development* 55:195–213.

Havighurst, R. J., Bosman, P. H., Liddle, G., Mathews, C. V., & Pierce, J. V. (1962). *Growing Up in River City*. New York: Wiley.

Heath, S. B. (1995). "Race, ethnicity and the defiance of categories." In W. Hawley & A. Jackson (eds.), *Toward a Common Destiny*, 39–70. San Francisco, CA: Jossey Bass.

Hemmings, A. (2006). Shifting images of blackness: coming of age as black students in urban and suburban high schools. In E. Horvat & C. O'Connor (eds.), *Beyond Acting White: Reframing the Debate on Black Student Achievement*. Lanham, MD: Rowman and Littlefield.

Hetherington, E. M., & Stanley-Hagan, M. (2002). "Parenting in divorced and remarried families." In M. H. Bornstein (ed.), *Handbook of Parenting* (vol. 3), 287–315. Mahwah, NJ: Erlbaum.

Hill, J. P. (1987). "Research on adolescents and their families: Past and prospect." In C. E. Irwin (ed.), *Adolescent Social Behavior and Health*, 13–31. San Francisco: Jossey-Bass.

Hollingshead, A. B. (1949). *Elmstown's Youth*. New York: Wiley.

Jackson, J. S., McCullough, W. R., & Gurin, G. (1981). "Group identity development within black families." In H. McAdoo (ed.), *Black Families*, 252–63. Beverly Hills, CA: Sage.

Jordan, D. (1971). "Parental antecedents and personality characteristics of ego identity statuses." Unpublished doctoral dissertation. State University of New York at Buffalo.

Kimmel, M. (1994). "Masculinity as homophobia." In H. Brod & M. Kaufman (eds.), *Theorizing Masculinities*, 119–41. Thousand Oaks, CA: Sage Publications.

Kohlberg, L. (1969). "Stage and sequence: The cognitive-developmental approach to socialization." In D. A. Goslin (ed.), *Handbook of Socialization Theory and Research*, 347–480. Skokie, IL: Rand-McNally.

Kohlberg, L., & Gilligan, C. (1972). "The adolescent as philosopher: The discovery of the self in a postconventional world." In J. Kagan & R. Coles (eds.), *Twelve to Sixteen: Early Adolescence*. New York: Norton.

LaFromboise, T., Coleman, H., & Gerton, J. (1993). "Psychology impact of biculturalism: Evidence and theory." *Psychology Bulletin* 114(3):395–412.

Laursen, B., Coy, K. C., & Collins, W. A. (1998). "Reconsidering changes in parent-child conflict across adolescence: a meta-analysis." *Child Development* 69:817–32.

Leadbeater, B., & Way, N. (1996). *Urban Girls: Resisting Stereotypes, Creating Identities.* New York: NYU Press.

Lee, S. (1996). *Unraveling the "Model Minority" Stereotype: Listening to Asian American Youth.* New York: Teachers College Press.

Lesko, N. (2001). *Act Your Age!: A Cultural Construction of Adolescence.* New York: Routledge/Falmer.

Lewin, K. (1939). "Field theory and experiment in social psychology: Concepts and methods." *The American Journal of Sociology* 44:868–97.

Manaster, G. J. (1989). *Adolescent Development: A Psychological Interpretation.* Itasca, IL: F. E. Peacock.

Marcia, J. (1966). "Development and validation of ego—identity status." *Journal of Personality and Social Psychology* 3:551–58.

———. (1967). "Ego identity status: Relationship to change in self-esteem." *Journal of Personality* 35:118–33.

———. (1980). "Identity in adolescence." In J. Adelson (ed.), *Handbook of Adolescent Psychology.* New York: Wiley.

Margolis, A. J., Davidson, L. A., Hanson, D. H., Loos, S. A., & Mikelson, C. A. (1971). "Therapeutic abortion: Follow-up study." *American Journal of Obstetrical Gynecology* 110:243–49.

Martin, J. R. (1981). "Sophie and Emile: A case study of sex bias in the history of educational thought." *Harvard Educational Review* 51(3):357–72.

Martin, K. (1996). *Puberty, Sexuality and the Self: Girls and Boys at Adolescence.* New York: Routledge.

Masten, A. S., & Garmezy, N. (1985). "Risk, vulnerability and protective factors in developmental psychopathology." In B. B. Lahey & A. E. Kazdin (eds.), *Advances in Clinical Child Psychology* (vol. 8). New York: Plenum.

McLaughlin, M., & Heath, S. (eds.). (1993). *Inner City Youth: Beyond Ethnicity and Gender.* New York: Teachers College Press.

Mead, G. H. (1934). *Mind, Self and Society.* Chicago: University of Chicago Press.

Mead, M. (1958). "Adolescence in primitive and modern society." In E. Maccoby, T. Newcomb & E. Hartley (eds.), *Readings in Social Psychology.* New York: Norton.

Mickelson, R., & Velasco, A. (2006). "Bring it on! Diverse responses to 'acting white' among academically able Black adolescents." In E. Horvat & C. O'Connor (eds.), *Beyond Acting White: Reframing the Debate on Black Student Achievement.* Lanham, MD: Rowman and Littlefield.

Miller, A. (1983). *The Drama of the Gifted Child.* New York: Basic Books.

Miller, J. B. (1976). *Toward a New Psychology of Women.* Boston: Beacon Press.

———. (1991). "The Development of Women's Sense of Self." In J. V. Jordan, A. G. Kaplan, J. Baker Miller, I. P. Stiver, & J. L. Surrey (eds.), *Women's Growth in Connection,* 11–26. New York: Guilford Press.

Modell, J., & Goodman, M. (1990). "Historical perspectives." In S. S. Feldman and G. R. Elliott (eds.), *At the Threshold,* 93–122. Cambridge, MA: Harvard University Press.

Monosour, K., & Stewart, B. (1973). "Abortion and sexual behavior in college women." *American Journal of Orthopsychiatry* 43:803–14.

Montemayor, R. (1983). "Parents and adolescents in conflict: All families some of the time and some families most of the time." *Journal of Early Adolescence* 3:83–103.

Moran, J. (2000). *Teaching Sex: The Shaping of Adolescence in the 20th Century.* Cambridge, MA: Harvard University Press.

Mosley, D. T., Follingshead, D. R., Harley, H., & Heckel, R. V. (1981). "Psychological factors that predict reaction to abortion." *Journal of Clinical Psychology* 37:276–79.

Muuss, R. (1996). *Theories of Adolescence,* 6th ed. New York: McGraw-Hill.

Noam, G., Powers, S., Kilkenny, R., & Beedy, J. (1990). "The interpersonal self in life-span developmental perspective: Theory, measurement and longitudinal case analysis." In M. Perlmutter, D. L. Featherman, & R. M. Learner (eds.), *Life-span Development and Behavior* (vol. 10). Hillsdale, NJ: Lawrence Erlbaum Associates.

Olson, L. (1980). "Social and psychological correlates of pregnancy resolution among adolescent women: A review." *American Journal of Orthopsychiatry* 50:432–45.

Parker, J. G., & Gottman, J. M. (1989). "Social and emotional development in a relational context: Friendship interaction from early childhood to adolescence." In T. J. Berndt & G. W. Ladd (eds.), *Peer Relations in Child Development.* New York: Wiley.

Payne, E. C., Kravitz, A. R., Notman, M. T., & Anderson, J. V. (1976). "Outcome following therapeutic abortion." *Archives of General Psychiatry* 33:725–33.

Piaget, J. (1972). "Intellectual evolution from adolescence to adulthood." *Human Development* 15:1–12.

Plato. (1921). *Republic.* Oxford: Clarendon Press.

Ponterotto, J., & Pederson, P. (1993). *Preventing Prejudice: A Guide for Counselors and Educators.* Newbury Park, CA: Sage.

Powers, S. I. (1988). "Moral judgment in the family." *Journal of Moral Education* 17:209–19.

Powers, S. I., Hauser, S. T., Schwartz, J., Noam, G., & Jacobson, A. M. (1983). "Adolescent ego development and family interaction: A structural-developmental perspective." In H. D. Grotevant, & C. R. Cooper (eds.), *Adolescent Development within the Family.* San Francisco: Jossey-Bass.

Pritchett, V. S. (1971). *Midnight Oil.* London: Chatto and Windus Ltd.

Rogler, L. H., Cortes, D. E., & Malgady, R. G. (1991). "Acculturation and mental health status among Hispanics: Convergence and new directions for research." *American Psychologist* 46:585–97.

Root, M. (1999). "Multiracial Asians: Models of ethnic identity." In R. Torres, L. Mirón, & J. Inda (eds.), *Race Identity and Citizenship,* 158–68. Malden, MA: Blackwell Publishers.

Russo, N. F., & Zierk, K. (1992). "Abortion, childbearing, and women's well-being." *Professional Psychology Research and Practice* 23: 269–80.

Rutter, M. (1975). "Attainment and adjustment in two geographical areas. I: The prevalence of psychiatric disorder." *British Journal of Psychiatry* 126:493–509.

———. (1979). "Protective factors in children's responses to stress and disadvantage." In M. W. Kent & J. Rolf (eds.), *Primary Prevention of Psychopathology: III: Social Competence in Children.* Hanover, NH: University Press of New England.

———. (1987). "Psychosocial resilience and protective mechanisms." *American Journal of Orthopsychiatry* 57(3):316–31.

Rutter, M., Graham, P., Chadwick, O., & Yule, W. (1976). "Adolescent turmoil: Fact or fiction?" *Journal of Child Psychology and Psychiatry* 17:35–56.

Santrock, J. W. (1990). *Adolescence,* 4th ed. Dubuque, IA: William C. Brown.

Savin-Williams, R. (2005). *The New Gay Teenager.* Cambridge, MA: Harvard University Press.

Savin-Williams, R., & Berndt, T. (1990). "Friendship and peer relations." In S. Feldman & G. Elliott (eds.), *At the Threshold,* 277–307. Cambridge, MA: Harvard University Press.

Schmiege, S., & Russo, N. F. (2005). 'Depression and unwanted first pregnancy: longitudinal cohort study.' *British Medical Journal* 331:1303.

Sears, J. (1996). "Black-Gay or Gay-Black? Choosing identities and identifying choices." In G. Unks, (ed.), *The Gay Teen*. New York: Routledge, 135–57.

Smetana, J. (1988). "Adolescents' and parents' conceptions of parental authority." *Child Development* 59:321–35.

Selman, R. (1979). "A structural-developmental model of social cognition: Implications for intervention research." In Mosher, R. L. (ed.), *Adolescents' Development and Education*, 123–32. Berkeley, CA: McCutchan.

———. (1980). *The Growth of Interpersonal Understanding*. New York: Academic Press.

Sisson, L., Hersen, M., & Van Hasselt, V. (1987). "Historical perspectives." In V. Van Hasselt & M. Hersen (eds.), *Handbook of Adolescent Psychology*, 3–10. New York: Pergamon Press.

Slaughter, D. (1972). "Becoming an African-American woman." *School Review* 299–318.

Smetana, J. (1989). "Adolescents' and parents' reasoning about actual family conflict." *Child Development* 60:1052–67.

———. (1996). "Adolescent-parent conflict: Implications for adaptive and maladaptive development." In D. Cicchetti & S. L. Toth (eds.), *Adolescence: Opportunities and Challenges* (vol. 7), 1–46. Rochester, NY: University of Rochester.

Smith, E. M. (1973). "A follow-up study of women who request abortion." *American Journal of Orthopsychiatry* 43:574–85.

Spracklen, K., Andrews, D., Patterson, G. & Dishion, G. (1996). Deviancy training in male adolescent friendships. *Behavior Theory* 27(3): 373–91.

Steinberg, L. (2001). "We know some things: Adolescent-parent relationships in retrospect and prospect." *Journal of Research on Adolescence* 11:1–19.

Steinberg, L., & Silk, J. S. (2002). "Parenting adolescents." In M. H. Bornstein (ed.), *Handbook of Parenting* (vol. 1), 103–34. Mahwah, NJ: Erlbaum.

Stern, L. (1989). "Conceptions of separation and connection in female adolescents." In C. Gilligan, N. Lyons, & T. Hanmer (eds.), *Making Connections*, 73–87. New York: Emma Willard School.

Strouse, D. L. (1999). "Adolescent crowd orientations: A social and temporal analysis." In J. A. McLellan & M. J. B. Pugh (eds.), *The Role of Peer Groups in Adolescent Social Identity: Exploring the Importance of Stability and Change*, 37–54. San Francisco: Jossey-Bass.

Sullivan, H. S. (1953). *The Interpersonal Theory of Psychiatry*. New York: W. W. Norton.

Surrey, J. (1984). "The self-in-relation." In *Work in Progress*. Wellesley, MA: Stone Center for Developmental Services and Studies.

Taylor, J. (1996). "Cultural stories: Latina and Portuguese daughters and mothers." In B. Leadbetter & N. Way (eds.), *Urban Girls*, 117–31. New York: NYU Press.

Troiden, R. (1998). "A model of homosexual identity formation." In P. M. Nardi & B. E. Schneider (eds.), *Social Perspectives in Lesbian and Gay Studies: A Reader*, 261–79. London, New York: Routledge.

Tyson, K. (2006). "Shifting images of blackness: Coming of age as Black students in urban and suburban high schools." In E. Horvat & C. O'Connor (eds.), *Beyond Acting White: Reframing the Debate on Black Student Achievement*. Lanham, MD: Rowman and Littlefield.

Walkerdine, V., Lucey, H., & Melody, J. (2001). *Growing Up Girl*. New York: NYU Press.

Ward, J. (1989). "Racial identity formation and transformation." In C. Gilligan, N. Lyons, & T. Hanmer (eds.), *Making Connections: The Relational Worlds of Adolescent Girls at Emma Willard School*. Troy, NY: Emma Willard School.

Ward, J. (1996). "Raising resisters: The role of truth telling in the psychological development of African American girls." In B. Leadbetter & N. Way (eds.), *Urban Girls*, 85–99. New York: NYU Press.

Waters, M. (1996). "The intersection of gender, race, and ethnicity in identity development of Caribbean American teens." In B. Leadbeater & N. Way (eds.), *Urban Girls*, 65–81. New York: NYU Press.

Way, N., & Chu, J. (eds.). (2004). *Adolescent Boys*. New York: NYU Press.

Welsh, D. P., Galliher, R. V., Kawaguchi, M. C., & Rostosky, S. S. (1999). "Discrepancies in adolescent romantic couples' and observers' perceptions of couple interaction and their relationship to depressive symptoms." *Journal of Youth and Adolescence* 28(6):645–66.

Welsh, D. P., Grello, C. M., & Harper, M. S. (2003). "When love hurts: Depression and adolescent romantic relationships." In P. Florsheim (ed.), *Adolescent Romantic Relations and Sexual Behavior: Theory, Research, and Practical Implications*, 185–211. Mahwah, NJ: Lawrence Erlbaum Associates.

Werner, E. (1989). "High-risk children in young adulthood: A longitudinal study from birth to 32 years. *American Journal of Orthopsychiatry* 59(1):72–81.

Wilson, A. (1996). "How we find ourselves: Identity development and two-spirit people." *Harvard Educational Review* 66(2):303–17.

Williams, T. K. (1996). "Race as a process: Reassessing the 'What are you?' encounters of biracial individuals. In M. Root (ed.), *The Multiracial Experience*, 191–210. Thousand Oaks, CA: Sage.